DREAMS, AND SONGS TO SING

Dreams, and songs to sing
A New History of Celtic

TOM CAMPBELL
AND PAT WOODS

MAINSTREAM
PUBLISHING

EDINBURGH AND LONDON

First published in 1996 by
MAINSTREAM PUBLISHING COMPANY (EDINBURGH) LTD
7 Albany Street
Edinburgh EH1 3UG

ISBN 1 85158 848 5

A catalogue record for this book is available from the British Library

Typeset in Garamond
Printed and bound in Great Britain by Butler & Tanner Ltd

For James Woods and Pauline,
and for the Lisbon Lions Celtic Supporters Club
and Edinburgh No.1 Celtic Supporters Club

Contents

Acknowledgements

Our appreciation is due to the following (some now dead) who allowed themselves to be interviewed, and who answered our questions so frankly: Sir Matt Busby, Jim Craig, Pat Crerand, Brian Dempsey, Sean Fallon, James Farrell, Willie Fernie, Tom Grant, Sir Robert Kelly, Matt Lynch, Fergus McCann, Malcolm MacDonald, Jimmy McGrory, Peter McLean, Billy McNeill, John McPhail, Joe Mercer, Neil Mochan, Bobby Murdoch, Len Murray, Davie Provan, Jock Stein and Desmond White.

Our thanks are also due to the following journalists and commentators who gave us encouragement, advice and assistance: Bob Crampsey, Cyril Horne (*The Herald*), Hugh Keevins (Radio Clyde and *The Scotsman*), Archie Macpherson (Radio Clyde), Kevin McCarra (*The Times*), Gerry McNee (Scottish Television), John Motson, Ian Paul (*The Herald*), John Quinn (*Evening Times*), Ken Robertson (*Scottish Sunday Express*) and Andrew Smith (*The Celtic View*).

The following contributed valuable material as well as encouragement and help: Seaton Airlie, Ronnie Campbell, Frank Glencross, Frank McAlinden, Eugene MacBride, Bill Murray, Jack Murray, David Potter and Eric Shannon.

The following institutions and individuals helped greatly in answering our enquiries: Bibliothèque Nationale, Paris and Versailles; British Library; Newspaper Library (Colindale, London); Mitchell Library, Glasgow; Brother Patrick Sheils, Marist Order (Wolverhampton); Kathleen McHugh, St Vincent de Paul Society (Glasgow); Ulrich Matheja, *Kicker* magazine, Germany; and Sligo County Library, Republic of Ireland. And lastly to Judy Diamond of Mainstream Publishing for her patience, understanding and professionalism as our editor.

In the Beginning

The 1887 Scottish Cup final, played in Glasgow between Dumbarton and Hibernian on 12 February, attracted much more interest than usual in the West of Scotland. Dumbarton, 'the Sons of the Rock', may have been the 'home' side but Hibernian's support was increased vastly by throngs of sporting members of the local Irish community, as predicted by the *Edinburgh Evening News*. 'The Glasgow Irishmen are preparing to give the Hibs a grand reception, and possibly the followers of the team in the East, should their favourites be on the winning side, will not be much behind them.'

From their inception in 1875 as a recreational venture for the Catholic Young Men's Society attached to St Patrick's in the city's Cowgate, Edinburgh Hibernian had been a focus of much interest for the Irish and Catholic population of all Scotland. Canon Edward Hannan, an Irish-born cleric, was prominent in Hibernian's founding and the club was run as a strictly Catholic organisation in its earliest days. As a consequence, his club faced problems at the start. For example, it was refused admission to the Edinburgh Association, and had its original entry fee returned by the SFA because 'the Association was founded for Scotchmen'. Hibernian persevered, and were eventually accepted – although most reluctantly – by the football authorities.

Hibs' progress from Hampden Park back to Edinburgh after a historic 2–1 victory turned into a triumphal procession, starting with the final whistle: 'The Hibernian players had to undergo a considerable amount of good-natured but somewhat rough congratulations before they reached the pavilion. Hundreds waited outside the gates for the players, and on their appearance they were loudly applauded.' (*Edinburgh Evening News*. 14 February 1887)

The players and officials were further delayed in returning to the capital because the Edinburgh party was transported after the match to St Mary's Hall in the Calton district, a few miles from Hampden. There, in Glasgow's East End, crowds of admirers – locals who had identified for years with the most successful of the 'Irish' clubs in Scottish football – fêted the victors and celebrated with them.

Presiding over the gathering was John Conway, a much-loved doctor and a highly active member of the Catholic community. Conway, the son of a prosperous East End grocer, was a brilliant student when at Glasgow University and a member of the Royal College of Surgeons, but chose to work in that impoverished area despite his glittering qualifications. His welcoming speech underlined the significance of Hibernian's achievement for their compatriots, seeing in the football club's determination to win on the field a political example to be followed in order to ensure that 'the goal of every Irishman's ambition – the legislative independence of his country – would soon be attained'.

John McFadden, the Hibs secretary, overwhelmed by the reception and flushed with the joys of victory, accepted the congratulations. In his speech, frequently interrupted by cheers, he all but dedicated Hibernian's triumph to 'every Irish Catholic in Scotland'. Perhaps carried away by the warmth of the reception at a gathering which broke up to the strains of 'God Save Ireland', the nationalist anthem of the day, McFadden dropped a broad hint to the more football-minded people present just before he left. He suggested that they could form a similar club in Glasgow for the Catholics of the West of Scotland. Perhaps it was a casual remark, perhaps a challenge to his Glasgow hosts . . .

The celebrations for Hibernian did not end there, as the *Edinburgh Evening News* reports: 'The special train from Queen Street to Edinburgh conveying the team, their friends and others was timed to leave the station at 8.20 and, a few minutes before that, large numbers made their way there to bid goodbye to the players. On the arrival of the team they were greeted with deafening cheers – the platform being now densely crowded – while a flute band did its part in the rejoicing.' (14 February 1887)

Among the crowd in the packed St Mary's Hall was Brother Walfrid, the headmaster of St Andrew's School in the city centre and the Brother Superior of the Marist teaching order in the Glasgow district. Beside him was his assistant, Brother Dorotheus, the headmaster of St Mary's School in the Calton. Also present was John Glass, 'the silent but hardworking member' of a local builder's firm which he ran in partnership with his brother Peter. Dr Conway, John Glass and Brother Walfrid were in the habit of meeting regularly to discuss ways and means of helping the less-fortunate members of the Irish Catholic community.

Many in the early waves of Irish immigrants who poured into Clydeside – the poorest by cattle boat – had found employment with the expansion of the Scottish textile mills; in 1840 Professor Cowan of Glasgow University estimated that Irish Catholics made up a quarter of the city's population and constituted 80 per cent of the workers in the local cotton mills. The 'incomers' (from an agrarian economy in Ireland which left them ill-prepared for a more industrialised society) formed a pool of largely unskilled and widely despised labour. The Irish provided much of the muscle for the sudden growth of industrialisation in Scotland; they would be the labourers for the building of railways and docks, the diggers of canals, the hewers of coal, and the sweated, exploited labour in textile mills and factories.

Less skilled, the Irish inevitably were among the first casualties of the failure of the City of Glasgow Bank in 1878. A catastrophic slump in trade followed, causing widespread unemployment and economic distress. In the East End of Glasgow, work at the Parkhead Forge steelworks was halted as well as at other local ironworks. Hundreds of workmen, many the heads of families, were thrown out of work while those who remained 'hardly earned a bare subsistence doing the odd job'.

In those days no safety-net existed for the unemployed from public funds. With state intervention unknown, Brother Walfrid was raising money not only to help run his schools but to provide boots, clothing and food to the most needy children. Hunger remained a constant factor in the lives of the poorest in the slums of Glasgow, the most densely packed city in Europe. Walfrid, born Andrew Kerins of farming stock in Ballymote, County Sligo, Ireland, and reared during 'the Hungry '40s' in one of the counties most affected by the Great Famine, was haunted by that enduring folk memory. Brother Walfrid,* a household name in a part of Glasgow where Catholics venerated the clergy for their devotion and self-sacrifice, could see the consequences of the degrading poverty at first hand. Since his earliest days as a teacher in St Mary's, and throughout his 12 years as headmaster at Sacred Heart School in Bridgeton, he had been all too aware of the chronic absenteeism forced upon the children by hunger and the

---

* Brother Walfrid took his religious name from the practice of the Marist Order in assigning a novice a 'saintly' name which signified the cutting of all ties with 'life in the world'. 'Walfrid' is the Anglicised version of Galfrido della Gherardesca, a prosperous citizen of Pisa in the eighth century who had a wife and six children. He felt a calling to enter the religious life, which he did under monastic discipline. He later founded a monastery and became its abbot. He was canonised as St Walfrid.

lack of warm clothing. He could despair at the pathetic rags worn by his pupils, and at the bare feet even in winter; he could take alarm at the noticeable increase in Protestant soup kitchens and fret about their potentially proselytising effect on the younger members of his flock – or he could do something about it.

A sketch of Walfrid – in the form of a staged dialogue between Irish immigrant Catholics reminiscing about Sacred Heart parish – makes the Marist Brother's motives clear: 'An' 'twas afeerd Bro. Walfrid was that some av his little wans wud be snared away, an' get a thract [tract] for kitchen wid eviry plate av soup, the same as they used to do in Ireland long ago.' (*Glasgow Observer.* 24 November 1900)

In 1884 he had enlisted the aid of the conference (or branch) members of the St Vincent de Paul Society attached to the Sacred Heart mission in Bridgeton to open a little shop in Savoy Street. The establishment (close to Brother Walfrid's school in Old Dalmarnock Road) provided 'penny dinners' to 'keep the life' in his poverty-stricken pupils. The St Vincent de Paul Society, introduced into the Archdiocese of Glasgow in 1848 was (and remains) a truly remarkable organisation; within its first half-century the members had made nearly one million visits to the homes of the Catholic poor in the course of charitable work. The zeal and energy of such activists – doubtless inspired also by the Marists' enthusiasm – ensured that the children were provided with a warm and nourishing meal for their penny. In Walfrid's own words: 'Should parents prefer, they could send the bread and the children could get a large bowl of broth or soup for a halfpenny, and those who were not able to pay got a substantial meal free. This has been a very great blessing for the poor children.' (*Glasgow Observer.* 16 March 1895)

Within a short time Brother Dorotheus introduced a similar scheme at St Mary's Boys School, and soon found himself providing a thousand dinners a week from a disused blacksmith's shop at the end of the schoolyard. The scale of hardship, however, was such that both Marists realised that other avenues had to be explored.

The most fruitful prospect, Walfrid believed, would be the exploitation of the passion for football which was being exhibited among the working class in all the large cities such as Glasgow. Thus, a series of football matches staged for charity was arranged, largely through Walfrid's efforts. Tom Maley, a noted Celtic player and committee man, writing about his own life in football for a series in the *Weekly Mail and Record* in 1916, eulogised Walfrid's 'wonderful organising power' and 'the lovable nature' of a man who 'had only to knock, and it was opened'.

Expanding on the cleric's sphere of influence, Maley makes it very clear that Walfrid moved wider in Scottish football circles than has been hitherto recognised: 'Clyde, Cowlairs, Northern and Thistle [all Glasgow clubs] always welcomed him and lent ungrudgingly their services. Renton and Hibernian in like manner came at the old man's invite . . .'

It was through such contacts that, for example, St Peter's (Partick), a parish club in the West End of Glasgow, played a side representing Edinburgh Hibernian in September 1886 before a gathering of a thousand paying spectators at Glengarry Park in Bridgeton with the proceeds going to St Mary's Poor Children's Dinner Table. Glengarry Park had been named after a part of Bridgeton settled by Catholic Highlanders who had come to Glasgow in search of work in the expanding cotton industry at the end of the eighteenth century. It was also the home pitch of Columba, a juvenile football team formed by Brother Walfrid primarily to keep those boys out of mischief after they had left his school. Football, to Walfrid, was another means of reinforcing community identity, particularly the religious dimension: '. . . as he [Walfrid] sed, 'twas the most dangersome time for the young fellos, jest afther they had left school, an' begun t' mix up wid Protestand boys in the places where they wor workin'.' (*Glasgow Observer.* 24 November 1900)

In April 1887, two months after listening to John McFadden's invocation in St Mary's Hall, Brother Walfrid was given even greater encouragement when he arranged another charity match in aid of the Poor Children's Dinner Table at Sacred Heart School. At Barrowfield Park, also in Bridgeton, a crowd of 4,000 turned up to see Clyde play Dundee Harp.

A month later, he must have been overwhelmed by the size of the crowd that watched the famous Renton, holders of the Glasgow Charity Cup, take on Hibernian, the holders of the Scottish Cup, at the same venue. The clubs were competing for the East End Charity Cup, a one-off trophy for the match played in aid of the Poor Children's Dinner Tables of both St Mary's and Sacred Heart School. An estimated 12,000 spectators were present and, according to the *Glasgow Observer* (the principal newspaper of the Irish Catholic community), 'The amount of money received was considerable'.

The match ended in a draw and was replayed in August with Renton winning comfortably. At the 'social' held in Sacred Heart Boys' School after one of those matches it occurred to several in the Catholic community in Glasgow who had increasingly seen football as a source of funds for charity that it would be 'a great thing to get up a club of our own'. (*Glasgow Observer.* 8 December 1900)

By the early autumn of 1887 Brother Walfrid was becoming convinced that the teeming Irish and Catholic population of the 'football-daft' city of Glasgow would prove fertile soil for such an enterprise. If Edinburgh could operate a successful Catholic club, Glasgow, with its greater population, could surely do so. After discharging the necessary expenses in running it, the club could channel all the remaining money towards supplying the East End conferences of the St Vincent de Paul Society with the funds to maintain the Dinner Tables in the missions of St Mary's, Sacred Heart and St Michael's.

The idea was taken up enthusiastically by the three local parishes of St Mary's, St Andrew's and St Alphonsus's. The highly energetic representatives of St Mary's (the 'mother' parish) took the lead in bringing the project to fruition. That parish ran a particularly flourishing branch of the League of the Cross, the Catholic temperance organisation, whose members included John Glass, John H. McLaughlin and James McKay. These enthusiasts had exhibited considerable enterprise in raising funds to build a parish hall to hold such meetings and stage events. The building of such a hall marked a major undertaking and accomplishment for a Catholic parish in the 1880s.

The centenary history of St Mary's in 1942 commented on the vigour and determination that those members would soon transfer to the formation of Celtic: 'It was difficult to restrain the enthusiasm of the younger members, and to keep them within the bounds of prudence.' No wonder then that Celtic FC marked the celebration of the centenary with a gift of one hundred guineas as a token of the club's 'filial regard'.

Thus, a meeting to formally constitute Celtic FC was held in St Mary's Hall on East Rose Street on 6 November 1887, a Sunday afternoon, and was chaired by John Glass. A highly visible and active member in the local community, participating in such bodies as the Catholic Union, the Irish Foresters and the Home Government Branch of the United Irish League, John Glass would justify Brother Walfrid's confidence in him. Handpicked by Walfrid, he was the man with the energy and commitment to make a business and administrative success of the club that the Marist envisioned and originated.

Later, one journalist would nominate Walfrid as 'the father of the Celtic', while another asserted that 'he did more to start the club and set it on its feet than any other man'. But Tom Maley, who was there from the start alongside him, paid the finest tribute of all: 'Through the organising genius, the wonderful persuasive powers, and the personality of Brother Walfrid the Celtic club was established. His men carried out his every wish and idea. They knew and trusted their leader, and in the knowledge that he, like them, wanted the club for the most laudable objects – charity, and as a recreation for his loved East Enders – they persevered.' (*Weekly Mail and Record*: 15 July 1916)

'The good ship Celtic', as one of the earliest helmsmen described the club later, was about to set sail.

ONE

Reaching for the Top

1887–92

Celtic, as the new club was called in accordance with Brother Walfrid's wishes, became identified quickly by the sporting newspapers as an Irish club, although some historians have detected in the choice of name an attempt to link Ireland (the native land) and Scotland (the adopted country). The *Scottish Referee*, however, would describe Celtic as 'the shamrock representatives', while a rival paper (*Scottish Sport*) headlined a match report of a later Celtic v Queen's Park encounter as 'Scot v Celt'. The latter newspaper described Queen's Park as 'the premier club in Scotland' and Celtic as 'the best combination of Irishmen that has ever been raised in Scotland, knitted together by an unquenchable desire to do honour to the Emerald Isle, from which they spring'. (20 November 1888)

Clearly the term 'Celt' or 'Celtic' appears to have carried more Irish than Scottish overtones then; Willie Maley, Tom's brother and a man who played for Celtic and later managed the club, was wont to describe Celtic as 'the great Glasgow Irish club' rather than a Scottish one. Two Celtics who played in Glasgow in the juvenile or junior rank during the 1880s (prior to *the* Celtic) appear to have had Irish Catholic connections. A team called Celts featured in the 1884 football coverage of the Irish immigrant newspaper *The Exile* as a club based in the Partick area, while the *Scottish Athletic Journal* of 2 August 1887 reported a meeting at which the office-bearers of Celtic FC, a team from the north side of Glasgow, were elected. In obvious tribute to Edinburgh Hibernian's accomplishments, that juvenile club had voted in John McFadden (Hibernian's secretary) as their honorary president. Unfortunately, this Celtic had only a short-lived career, and they disappeared from view around November that year, having failed to turn up for a fixture against Lonsdale Swifts at Possilpark.

The demise of that particular Celtic coincided roughly with the inception of *the* Celtic at an emotionally charged meeting in St Mary's Hall on 6 November 1887. Intriguingly, Brother Walfrid may have known of the travails of the juvenile or junior club of that name through his extensive contacts in the world of football in Glasgow. R.M. Connell, a journalist who worked for the *Scottish Umpire* at the time, would recall that it was Walfrid who dropped in at his office in Jamaica Street to inform him personally of the existence of the city's newest senior club. Perhaps 'Celtic' had struck Walfrid's fancy when pondering the choice of name, and it is worth noting that the Scottish Junior Football Annual of 1887–88 lists Columba (the juvenile club founded by Brother Walfrid); the name appearing immediately above it in the publication is the short-lived Celtic. Coincidence? Perhaps . . .

Whatever the reason for Walfrid's choice of name, prosaic or otherwise, the arrival of the fledgling club on the Scottish football scene was rightly greeted with some scepticism about its prospects of survival – given the track record of its compatriots. In our research we came across 40 Irish Catholic clubs which existed as junior or juvenile outfits in Scotland prior to the advent of Celtic, but only Hibernian of Edinburgh and Dundee Harp managed to attain any prominence at the senior level. Limited resources proved the primary factor in their conspicuous lack of impact in Scottish football, and most of these clubs confined themselves to playing against similarly disadvantaged sides. These pre-Celtic football clubs were social and recreational in nature, and the hospitality after the match often culminated in the singing of 'God Save Ireland'.

One official from Mossend Emmet complained in October 1884 to *The Exile* that bigotry in the Scottish press had impeded the progress of clubs such as his by ignoring their fixtures. This particular club represented the work-hungry immigrant Irish who had flocked to that part of Lanarkshire after iron ore and coal had been discovered there in the 1830s. Celtic's advent, however, *was* noted in the *Scottish Umpire*: 'We learn that the efforts which have lately been made to organise in Glasgow a first-class Catholic football club have been successfully consummated by the formation of the "Glasgow Celtic Football and Athletic Club" under influential auspices. They have secured a six-acre ground in the east end which they mean to put in fine order. We wish the "Celts" all success.' (29 November 1887)

Tom Maley recounted a brief outline of Celtic's origins in the *Glasgow Observer* in April 1910, stating that 'stalwarts of Faith and Nationality . . .

the backbone of the lay life of Glasgow, Catholic and National' were represented in the first list of subscribers. Maley recalled later – in another series, for the *Weekly Mail and Record* in 1916 – that several contributors voiced their doubts as to the durability of the new club but many parted with their money, more out of personal regard and esteem for those promoting the club than anything else.

Some may have been following the example of His Grace the Archbishop, Charles Eyre, whose name headed the subscription list. The Archbishop was noted for his constant and active interest in the welfare of the children of the diocese, and he must have had little hesitation when he observed that the first rule in Celtic's constitution was laid down as 'the maintaining of a fund for providing dinners to poor children in the three East End parishes of Glasgow'.

Celtic's entirely different *raison d'être* was revealed in their preparations for football. On 13 November 1887, only one week after the inaugural meeting, the club leased a ground, bounded on the west side by Janefield Cemetery and on the east by Dalmarnock Street (now Springfield Road), in the Parkhead district of Glasgow. To judge by a map of that time, the site appeared to encompass roughly the recent southern extension of Barr's soft drinks operation.

The new club had decided on a revolutionary approach. Until then, the evolution of clubs had followed a pattern. Young men, sharing a common occupation or seeking relief from a desk-bound job, started to gather for kick-about games. Only when the idea of playing on a regular basis and forming a football team seemed acceptable did the concept of a club take root among the players – as was the case with 'occupational clubs' such as Telegraphists and John Elder, the latter from the shipbuilding yards of the same name. And only after considerable doubt and tribulations would the members start to think about the prospect of acquiring their own ground. For example, it had taken Queen's Park six years to move into the first Hampden Park, and Rangers three years before leaving Glasgow Green for quarters in Burnbank in the city's West End after having flirted with the idea of settling in the Shawfield district, close to the future Celtic Park.

Modern observers, when viewing the trappings of wealth at today's Ibrox Stadium, might find it hard to credit Rangers' humble beginnings in 1872 on the public park that is Glasgow Green: sharing a pitch with another side called Eastern, changing behind adjoining shrubbery and holding a whip-round among players to buy a match ball. Sir David Mason, Glasgow's Lord Provost, when opening the impressive new grandstand at Ibrox Park in 1929, recalled that, on the Fleshers' Haugh section of the Green, Rangers had 'just enough space to play on and nobody paid the slightest attention to them'. Before settling at Ibrox, Rangers had been a nomadic club; at the time of Celtic's formation, in fact, they were just emerging from yet another financial crisis, one which had necessitated a £30 loan from the president, George Goudie, in order to keep going.

Celtic's vision was dramatically different. The immediate purpose of the club was to raise money for Catholic charities. Therefore, there could be no gradual improvement, no evolution into acceptance. Celtic had to be successful financially, and on the pitch, from the very start. The club could not afford to enjoy an infancy and a childhood.

Two things had to be done immediately: the club had to find a home, and had to sign up players with popular appeal.

Within a week of Celtic being constituted, the club had leased half a dozen acres of ground off the Gallowgate in Parkhead, and before six months were up, a largely voluntary workforce had helped to build Celtic's first stadium, a construction which matched the highest standards of the day. The field was level and grassy, 110 yards long by 66 wide; the pavilion, located under an open-air stand, contained a referee's room, an office and trainer's quarters in addition to spartan dressing-rooms with washing and toilet facilities for both teams. A rough earthen mound around a narrow track provided the most basic of terracings, but the more athletic of the spectators would enjoy the best view from the wall of the adjacent Janefield Cemetery.

The rapid rate of progress was most impressive, but not entirely unexpected, to judge by the *Scottish Umpire's* account of the first general monthly meeting, held in St Mary's Hall on 19 January 1888. Before a large and enthusiastic turn-out of patrons and members, Dr Conway, the honorary president, announced that 'the committee expect to put a first-class team on the field in the coming season', and, in only one of several committee reports delivered on the various aspects of establishing a new club, Mr Brien, convener of the Park Committee, reported that 'the pitch is finished, the paling well nigh up, and the grand stand – capable of accommodating from 800 to 1,000 – would be begun in the course of the ensuing week'.

The professional outlook and tremendous drive which made all this progress possible reflected the resourcefulness and expertise of the early committee. The new club could call upon a wealth of advice from its members, reflecting every aspect of a business: legal, clerical, commercial, technical and practical. John Glass, the president, was a working joiner; Joseph Shaughnessy and Michael Cairns were lawyers; John H. McLaughlin was employed as a clerk in a Bridgeton leather firm; and John O'Hara, the club's secretary, had started off as a shoemaker but an aptitude for organisation had seen him become secretary of the Operative Shoemakers' Society; Joseph M. Nelis and Hugh Darroch, the honorary treasurer, were both pawnbrokers – an essential business in impoverished districts such as Calton and Bridgeton. The crucial practical knowledge of the arcane world of football was provided by only two men, the Maley brothers, Willie and Tom, who served as both players and advisers.

The club's landlord had a taste of this committee's mettle before a ball was ever kicked on the first Celtic Park. The factor responsible had leased the ground to the club without informing the landlord of the purpose of the lease; the latter was dismayed at the changes being made on his property, and he threatened legal action. As one journalist recalled: 'The ground was barricaded with railway sleepers, and a second-hand wire rope, or "tow", from a Lanarkshire pit brought to enclose the playing portion so that "round the ropes" was literally true in those days. The landlord threatened to interdict; the Celtic barricaded, turfed and terraced all the more. Seeing the bold spirits he had to deal with, he offered to withdraw interdict of the ground if they promised to remove all rubbish, ashes etc at the end of their five years' lease. But not even this would the Celts promise; they had leased the ground to play football, and a football ground they meant to have.' (*Evening Times*: 16 April 1904) The landlord caved in when Celtic made it clear they would carry the case all the way to the Court of Session, and the arrangements for the first match were duly completed.

The committee had arranged the opening fixture for 8 May 1888, an exhibition match between Hibernian (Edinburgh) and Cowlairs (Glasgow), two well-known teams. They were delighted with the gate, and the enthusiasm of the 5,000 spectators who watched the 0–0 draw.

Three weeks later, on 28 May 1888, a Monday evening, Celtic played their first match on their own ground against 'a side of Rangers' before a crowd estimated at 2,000. Celtic's side, apparently an all-Catholic one in line with a short-lived policy stemming from the circumstances of the club's birth, consisted of invited players: Dolan (Drumpellier), Pearson (Carfin Shamrock), McLaughlin (Govan Whitefield), W. Maley (Cathcart), Kelly (Renton), Murray (Cambuslang Hibs), McCallum (Renton), T. Maley (Cathcart), Madden (Dumbarton), Dunbar (Edinburgh Hibs), Gorevin (Govan Whitefield). Celtic took the field in a strip gifted by a Bridgeton sports-outfitters, Penman Bros., consisting of a white shirt with a green collar and a Celtic Cross on the breast.

Celtic won comfortably by 5–2 over a Rangers XI composed largely of their reserve team, known as the Swifts, possibly because the Ibrox club did not wish to risk a dent to prestige by losing to the newcomers while fielding a full-strength side. Whatever, they could not cope with the lively play of

Celtic after Neil McCallum headed the opening goal within a few minutes.

Afterwards, players and representatives of the two clubs adjourned to the nearby St Mary's Hall for the customary 'social', a supper and a concert. A newspaper reported that 'the proceedings were of the happiest character', attributable in part to the numerous toasts offered by hosts and guests alike. This early friendly relationship between clubs fated to become such deadly rivals was illustrated by John H. McLaughlin, a highly active – if somewhat maverick – member of Celtic committees and the first chairman when the club became reconstituted as a limited liability company in 1897; McLaughlin was a talented amateur musician who played the organ for Sunday Mass at St Mary's and also accompanied the Rangers Glee Club and Choir on the piano at smoking concerts for several years.

The younger half of the future Old Firm could take heart from the verdict of the *Scottish Umpire*: 'It would appear as if the newly formed Glasgow club, the Celtic F.C., has a bright future before it. At any rate, if the committee can place the same eleven on the field as opposed the Rangers last Monday evening or an equally strong one, the Celtic will not lack for patronage or support.' (5 June 1888)

Indeed, it did not, and Celtic's success in its first season (1888–89) was no accident. It stemmed from the enthusiasm and the pragmatism of the committee, a group consisting of 20 or so men who had little knowledge of the sport and its ways, but who made up for that deficiency by an instinctive awareness of one basic tenet. They recognised the necessity for Celtic to field a competitive and attractive side from the outset, and they were wise enough to rely on the expertise of the Maley brothers to obtain players suited to that purpose. Early on, these 'knowing' Celts recognised the important principle that the team makes the club.

Celtic's boldness in leasing a ground before a ball was kicked was unprecedented in Scottish football; similarly, the club's pursuit of established players was another indication of their professional approach.

The acquisition of the player who went on to become the most important figure in Celtic's first 50 years hints at divine intervention. In December 1887 three Celtic representatives, John Glass, Pat Welsh and Brother Walfrid, made their way to Cathcart to speak to Tom Maley. They believed he would make a fine capture: an intelligent young man who was training to be a teacher, a noted player with experience at Edinburgh Hibernian, Partick Thistle and Third Lanark . . .

Tom was not at home that night, but the visitors were welcomed by his father, a retired soldier, and Tom's teenage brother Willie. During the course of the evening Willie impressed the visitors more and more as being 'an old head on young shoulders'. Finding out that the youngster played a bit with Third Lanark, although he was more interested in athletics,

Brother Walfrid invited him to accompany his brother to a meeting with the club's founders with the words: 'And why don't you come along too?'

Tom Maley would recall later that the brothers were talked into helping out the new club by the 'blarney' of Brother Walfrid, the sheer persuasiveness of John Glass and 'the soft tones' of Pat Welsh. They knew Pat Welsh best of all as an old friend of the family; their father, a sergeant in the British Army, had allowed Welsh, a Fenian, to escape from Dublin after an abortive rising there in 1867 and to make his way to Glasgow where he had established himself as a tailor. In truth, the Maleys thought privately that Celtic would have a short life and (as Tom put it later) 'go the way of many others started with almost as much enthusiasm'.

It turned out to be the most providential of visits. Along with Tom, Willie Maley answered the call; he joined the club as an acceptable player, and graduated to being a competent match secretary, and a figure who evolved into a strong-minded, highly successful secretary-manager. For over 40 years he was largely in charge of Celtic and (sharing the distinction with Jock Stein) he has to be considered the most influential figure in the club's history.

Initially, though, Tom appeared the better prospect. He had preserved his contacts with Edinburgh Hibernian and he was instrumental in persuading some members of that club to consider joining Celtic. By the start of the 1888–89 season, several players had defected from Hibernian including Michael Dunbar, Paddy Gallagher, John Coleman and Mick McKeown, as well as Jimmy McLaren and Willie Groves who had starred in the 1887 Scottish Cup final against Dumbarton. It was a considerable coup for Celtic, with one newspaper noting that some observers considered these players to be 'the pick of Scotland'.

Celtic officials pointed out that all of them, with the exception of Groves, did have links with the West of Scotland, and claimed that these players had approached them out of anxiety over Hibernian's financial situation – a reasonable claim in view of the crisis that would soon engulf Easter Road. Given the fact that all players in Scotland were deemed amateurs, however, there is an element of irony in the players' concern over Hibs' finances.

Celtic's ruthlessness was a two-fold violation of the code of conduct expected of clubs: the players were 'tapped' in a flagrant breach of SFA rules, and the fact that these were Hibernian players added treachery to the deception. The heroic deeds of the Edinburgh side had inspired the foundation of the Glasgow club; they had given Celtic every encouragement and assistance including, it was said, a financial donation in the earliest days. The loss of innocence came early at the fast-growing club whose ground in Glasgow's East End would come to be known as 'Paradise'.

Resentment lingered for decades, and indeed still persists, over Celtic's breaching of the gentlemen's agreement that neither club should tap nor poach the other's players. It should not be overlooked, however, that footballers in Scotland at that time, as nominal amateurs, were free to play for whichever club they pleased; the only restriction against the players being completely free agents in a particular season lay in turning out for a club in the Scottish Cup, thus becoming 'cup-tied'.

Nevertheless, John McFadden, Hibernian's autocratic secretary – and the man who had spoken at St Mary's Hall – was sufficiently outraged to write an open letter to the *Scottish Umpire* of 7 August 1888; under the pseudonym 'Easter Road', he predicted that the duplicity of the Celtic people concerned would defeat its intended purpose. In asserting that 'Evil deeds never prosper', he seems to have been suffering a lapse of memory; Hibernian's triumph in 1887 owed much to their having 'persuaded' the half-back line of McGhee, McGinn, and McLaren to join them from Lugar Boswell Thistle four years earlier. In the end, any claim McFadden had to the moral high ground was abandoned some six months later when it was discovered that he had absconded to America with a large sum of money belonging to the Catholic Young Men's Society.

One can only wonder how much Brother Walfrid knew of the quagmire into which his own club was now stepping. He surely could not have approved of the actions of the committee, men whom he would normally have regarded as upstanding, practising Catholics.

Feelings against Celtic were running so high that, in October 1888, when they made their first appearance in Edinburgh for a friendly against Hibernian, mounted police had to clear the pitch of angry home supporters who surrounded and threatened the Celtic players during the second half; the match had to be abandoned some ten minutes from the end to help the visitors make an escape.

Significant though the plundering from Hibernian was, the unfortunate affair was not the only crucial development in Celtic's drive to recruit players. From all over the country, men had written to the new club offering their services; Tom Maley could comment wryly that 'Many were the scouts and many were the emissaries who strove for us; talk about the study of names!'

The committee members spent many hours that first winter of 1887–88 in reading those letters, pondering the nuances, and trying to make football decisions in St Mary's Hall (the new club's first headquarters). John Glass, considered by many to be the practical driving force behind Celtic's development, felt that the best way to attract good players would be the acquisition of the country's outstanding player, James

Kelly of Renton, an attacking centre-half and a Scottish international. Celtic delegated several committee men to work on the young man and, after a lengthy courtship, the persuasive John Glass finally convinced Kelly to turn out for the new club, thus winning a tug-of-war with Hibernian for his services. Glass insisted later that Celtic would have 'fizzled out' without the capture of a player of that stature; one alliterative chronicler was to describe the situation as 'No Kelly, no Keltic'.

Celtic's first key acquisition was the finest centre-half in Scotland, an inspiring presence on the field who was described by a contemporary player as 'a fast half-back with superb powers of recovery'. When he ventured upfield, as he did frequently, 'his long drooping shots were very often the means of adding one more goal to the register, the forwards invariably being up in time to "embrace" the custodian before the latter had an opportunity of clearing his charge'.

Perhaps more significantly the new club had indicated it was here to stay — and meant business. Football was a chancy venture then, as witnessed by the number of clubs who came into existence for only a brief period; if Celtic could capture such a player, they had to be taken seriously from the outset. Edinburgh Hibernian might have adjusted to the 'loss' of Kelly but, within a few weeks, they were to be devastated by a mass defection of their players to Parkhead. Significantly, less than a year after Kelly's arrival, the press was speculating about the source of the considerable sum of £650 spent by the player in purchasing a public house; a young joiner like Kelly would be doing well if he earned £2 a week in wages. Obviously, he had been rewarded (illegally) for joining Celtic, who made little secret of their blatant infringements of the strict, amateur tenets of Scottish football.

In fact, just about every club in the country — with one very notable exception — broke the rules as a means of retaining players attracted to England, where professionalism had been legalised in 1885. All the payments to the players had to be concealed from the authorities, though, usually by the widespread practice of keeping false sets of books. The Scottish Football Association's Committee of Enquiry into such abuses throughout 1890–91 catalogued the methods: 'inadequate' checks or records of gate-money, routine destruction or loss of vouchers or admission tickets, 'carelessness' in the making of ledger returns . . .

In October 1890, the SFA called in the books of 45 clubs for scrutiny, and Celtic were a week late in complying with the edict. The club's representative claimed that his house and effects had been placed in quarantine 'owing to an outbreak of some infectious disease in the household' and, as a precaution, the books had been sent first to the Sanitation Department for disinfecting. Needless to say, the books were given a clean bill of health and approved by the SFA . . .

Supporting the belief that the balance-sheets of most clubs were forms of creative accountancy, *Scottish Sport* claimed in October 1892 that as much as two-thirds of the gate at a recent match involving a Glasgow club and an Edinburgh one had been 'set aside', the surplus obviously intended for the payment of amateur players. One official, almost certainly John H. McLaughlin, Celtic's honorary secretary, admitted to the writer of the article that 'the amount disbursed to Celtic players last season in one month was almost equal to the entire sum paid during the first year of the club's existence'.

The only sanctioned form of payment to players was money paid for loss of wages in their regular work when playing football and training for important matches. The system ('broken time', as it was called) was abused widely with the connivance of club treasurers who were chastised by the aforesaid SFA committee for 'failing to check amounts asked by the players which were in excess of their actual loss or outlay'.

This was a risk that even the most modest of clubs were willing to take for the sake of local pride and supremacy: Clackmannan found their players were being targeted by county rivals Alva, who hired a private detective to snoop on the former's players in order to uncover infringements of the SFA's rules. His work completed, the sleuth had to sue Alva to collect his fee of £6 for five days' work; in the end, he had to settle for £3.

Willie Maley, that most ardent of Celtic apologists, had to admit: 'Celtic were reared on breaches of the professional law, but charity covereth a multitude of sins.' The case of Dan Doyle, a favourite with the club's supporters, illustrates the brazen flouting of the law. The 'amateur' Celtic's capture of the famous full-back from Everton in 1891 provoked not only incredulity and outrage in England, but also a temporary boycott of the Scottish club by the Football League for poaching the player. The Merseyside club were so disturbed that they raised a High Court case for breach of contract, but the upshot was that Doyle remained at Parkhead as a Celtic player.

Celtic were established as one of Britain's biggest clubs when once again they provoked anger in the Edinburgh area. Jimmy Blessington, a talented inside-forward with Leith Athletic, was tapped by Celtic in the summer of 1892 despite the close attentions of Leith officials. He was hustled off to Glasgow by train although he was spotted by Leith Athletic's secretary as he was about to board the express for Glasgow. The player was confined to secret lodgings in the city for a few weeks, 'practically a prisoner', as he recounted later. The Leith officials scoured Glasgow in a vain attempt to locate him, while simultaneously filing a complaint with the SFA which stated that Blessington had been taken against his will, a submission backed by evidence from his employer to the effect that the young man's apprenticeship as a blacksmith had been 'abandoned' as a result of his prolonged absence. The intervention of Sandy McMahon, a noted Celtic player who had once played with Blessington at Hibs, proved crucial. McMahon was able to convince a sufficient number of the members of the SFA committee of Blessington's genuine, long-standing desire to play for Celtic. The Glasgow club was cleared of a poaching charge, but a West of Scotland newspaper published its verdict with a cryptic headline: 'Blessington Suspended One Week For Fibbing'. That sentence reflected the committee's suspicions about the player's confused testimony as to the circumstances of his recent move.

Celtic proved equally aggressive in retaining players. Tom Maley positively revelled in recounting how, as a member of the committee, he foiled attempts by two English clubs to acquire the services of Peter Dowds. This defender, a great favourite with the Parkhead crowds in the early 1890s, has been described frequently as one of the best all-round footballers ever to represent the club. Alerted to Everton's scheme to poach the player, Maley and a friend jumped in a cab and managed to overtake the one occupied by Dowds, Dick Molyneux (the secretary of the Merseyside club) and a companion. On the road between Dowds' home in Johnstone and Glasgow, Maley's cab 'bored them, so to speak, into a hedgerow, and then, having compelled them to stop with gloved hands, disposed in pistol-shaped fashion, sternly ordered Peter to get off and get up – off the Everton machine on to the Celtic. This removal effected, we gave Dick and his pal the order to "git" . . . The following day, getting wind of a telegraph from Fred Dewhurst, the Preston North End secretary, to Dowds which asked that the player meet him in a certain Glasgow hotel, Tom Maley himself wired a signed reply: "Peter can't come, I will". This meant, as Maley recalled with a chuckle, that "Fred didn't bother to meet me".' (*Weekly Mail and Record* 3 June 1916)

Celtic's judicious recruitment, when allied with tenacity in holding on to their better players, was to guarantee that the club's first season (1888–89) would be a considerable success. In August 1888 the new club made its competitive début in the Exhibition Cup, a minor tournament staged in Kelvingrove Park to mark Glasgow's current international exhibition. They opened with a meritorious 1–1 draw against Abercorn, a well-known Paisley side, and advanced in the tournament for reasons which still remain mysterious as no mention in print has been found of a replay. They knocked out Dumbarton Athletic 3–1 and Partick Thistle 1–0 before falling 2–0 in the final to a Cowlairs side strengthened by players from other clubs. Willie Maley, unable to see any irony in losing to a side thus reinforced, bristled with indignation at Cowlairs' ploy even years later, and recalled bitterly that 'our Celts were jeered at and insulted in disgraceful fashion'. The reception was so hostile that it hardened the committee's resolve to make their club a real power in the land, and acted as a stimulus to Celtic's development.

In the more important Glasgow Cup, Celtic made splendid progress by thrashing Shettleston 11–2 at Parkhead and Rangers by 6–1. The *Scottish Umpire* went into raptures over the Celtic style after the latter victory: '. . . the Celtic came away with a brilliance which has seldom, if ever, been equalled on Ibrox Park. The dodging and dribbling of the whole forward quintette was a caution, while their shooting was dead on.' (30 October 1888) Their progress in the competition came to a halt against Queen's Park in a tie at Celtic Park which ended – not too surprisingly – in a 2–0 win for the Amateurs.

The Scottish Cup, a tournament destined to become almost synonymous with Celtic, established the club as a genuine force in football by the end of its first season. In September they defeated Shettleston by 5–1, and gained ample revenge on Cowlairs by inflicting an 8–0 humiliation on the visitors at Parkhead. In October a 4–1 victory over Albion Rovers drew accusations of 'rough play' from the Coatbridge side, and early in November Celtic travelled to Edinburgh to eliminate St Bernard's by the same score.

A mere four months into their first season, Celtic found themselves accused of 'unsportsmanlike conduct' after losing 1–0 at home to Clyde in the next round of the competition. Willie Maley, in his role as match secretary, promptly lodged a protest with the SFA; he alleged that the match finished in storm conditions which had rendered the pitch so slushy and heavy as to be virtually unplayable. The contest ended in semi-darkness largely as a result of Clyde's arriving late for the kick-off and because the match was delayed further when three Clyde players were ordered by the referee to remove illegal bars from their boots. Protests were fashionable in that season's Scottish Cup; in a competition which drew a record number of entries (161 clubs), 35 protests were lodged. Celtic's, supported by the testimony of the referee, was one of the nine successful.

For the rematch, the Clyde players turned up at Parkhead stripped for the fray, and refused to enter the pavilion; Celtic crushed their aggrieved neighbours by 9–2. Two away ties followed: a late rally enabled Celtic to scrape through by 2–1 over East Stirlingshire at Merchiston Park, Falkirk, after being behind with only three minutes left to play; but 'the bould, bould Celts' (as a contemporary poem hailed them) fully justified a growing reputation for sparkling football with a splendid 4–1 result against the formidable Dumbarton at Boghead. At that time, semi-finals were not played on neutral territory, and Celtic had to face a real challenge against a club with an impressive record in the competition. The correspondent of *Scottish Sport* arrived late due to a delayed (and packed) special train from Glasgow. He had to squeeze himself into a ground where 'every square inch of space was already annexed by the earlier birds'. The home side, recent winners of the Scottish Cup, were totally outclassed by the fast, skilful combined play that was already becoming Celtic's hallmark. *The Scotsman* noted that 'the beautiful passing of the Celts was a matter of general admiration, whilst their swiftness and general agility were superior to Dumbarton'. The paper added that, after going four up through deadly finishing which included a Willie Groves hat-trick, Celtic began to take the mickey out of a demoralised Dumbarton, passing the ball 'from one to another to the bewilderment of their opponents'. (14 January 1889)

The 'upstarts' were fancied in some quarters to pull off an upset in the final against the stiff opposition of Third Lanark, originally formed as the regimental team of the 3rd Lanarkshire Rifle Volunteers.* As kick-off time approached on 2 February 1889 at (the second) Hampden Park, the weather deteriorated rapidly; persistent snowfalls forced both clubs to entertain second thoughts about playing the match as billed, and a legal document was drawn up on their behalf formally consenting 'to play a friendly game instead of a cup-tie, the ground and weather being unsuitable'. This paper was handed to the referee before the kick-off for him to convey to the SFA later. Nobody in officialdom gave any consideration to the 18,000 spectators who were now to witness – unknowingly – a friendly match although they had paid twice the usual amount for admission and had contributed £920, at the time the largest gate ever taken at a Scottish ground. Third Lanark had little difficulty in winning the now meaningless fixture 3–0. The SFA sanctioned a replay, solely on the testimony of the referee and umpires, thus refusing to acknowledge the clubs' private agreement.

A week later the final was played in earnest at the same venue before a crowd estimated at 16,000. Celtic, handicapped by an early injury to Coleman, found themselves a goal down midway through the first half. The goal itself was a controversial one: the referee, after consulting the umpires, agreed that the ball had crossed Celtic's goal-line, although many believed that Kelly had managed to scrape it clear. (Incidentally, the referee was a Charles Campbell of Queen's Park – a man reared in Galway, fond of singing 'The Wearing of the Green', and who was known to have 'a warm side to the Celts'.) After that bodyblow, Celtic raised their game and Third Lanark struggled against the newcomers on a frost-bound, sanded

* This was the first major final in which Celtic wore the green and white vertical stripes, first used on Hogmanay 1888. This jersey was worn until the introduction of the famous hooped strip in August 1903.

pitch. Celtic's hopes were raised when Neil McCallum equalised in the second half and Thirds had to survive an anxious period as Celtic, spurred on by deafening cheers, attacked furiously. However, the favourites rallied to scrape through in the end by 2–1. Not too surprisingly, no more was heard of Third Lanark's 'protest' about the underfoot conditions for the replay, nor about the reluctance of three of their players to take the pitch to contest a trophy they felt they had already won.

Thus, Celtic's first season ended on a bittersweet note with the major honour in football tantalisingly close, as a 'poet' of the time felt moved to indicate:

> From Parkhead's classic precincts came a wail of discontent,
> The air was filled with sounds of woe, with lamentations rent.
> Right gallantly the Celts did fight; Alas! 'twas all in vain,
> Old Erin's heroes bit the dust – they never smiled again!

Still, the club had made an astonishing impression. In every way it had turned out to be a remarkable season. Off the pitch – to judge by the first balance-sheet, issued in June 1889 – identifiable Catholic charities benefited to the tune of around £330, a huge sum in those days. On the pitch, the club was already attracting plaudits for that refreshingly positive outlook which has earned for Celtic down through the years the reputation of being the most consistently attractive footballing side in Scotland. The emphasis, as one contemporary writer noted, was on 'pure, unadulterated soccer', and from the outset the skill of Celtic's players had so fascinated spectators that it was soon reported that this amateur club was in a position to charge an admission price for practice matches, where enthusiasts could see particular favourites such as Groves and Kelly go through their paces.

After the disappointment in the Scottish Cup there was the consolation of winning the club's first trophy – the North Eastern Cup. This was a competition for clubs in that area of the city, and Celtic picked up the silverware by beating Cowlairs 6–1 in the final.

In the precarious early world of football, survival alone would have been grounds for celebration, but Celtic – the pride and joy of their supporters – established themselves immediately as a top club. The impact that they made on the Scottish scene was truly phenomenal, and cannot be assessed on mere statistics, impressive though they are. Consider the gate for the first match of the 1889 Scottish Cup final, which amounted to takings double those of the previous year; also, Celtic's first appearance in a Glasgow Cup final later that year doubled the previous biggest gate in the competition's history and trebled that for the previous year's final.

More than a century later it is difficult for modern readers to gauge fully the significance of Celtic's arrival on the scene, but only 30 years later, one sportswriter ('Veteran') had no such difficulty: 'The game [football] languished, gradually decayed, and would probably have gone the way of amateur cricket and professional foot-running. The press did its best to stimulate interest in the doings of Dumbarton, Cambuslang, Hibernian and Renton, but to city enthusiasts at least, Queen's Park were the only club, and, when the amateur team failed to hold its own with the pseudo-amateur association football lost all interest for them. It was at this stage the Celtic Club was formed, and football given a new lease of life. The Eastern club brought a new following to the game. Thousands who had never previously given a thought to football rallied to the new club, while thousands hitherto oblivious to the fascination of the game decided, for reasons of their own, to support the club likeliest to oppose the new organisation. Just as opposition is the life of trade, so did the rivalry, healthy or otherwise, between the new club and its challenger breathe new life into football, and thus we find the Celtic in their first Scottish final against 3rd Lanark attracting a record attendance to Hampden.' (*The Bulletin*: 19 May 1917)

Celtic's successful approach was to make a nonsense of the claim made by Tom Vallance, Rangers' president, in October 1887: 'Football professionalism as it is known in England could never exist in Scotland. I do not believe there are two clubs in the country which could afford to pay men a weekly wage of even 25/- [£1.25] or 30/- [£1.50] for playing football.'

The first major boom in Scottish football attendance came in the late 1880s and early 1890s, and owed much to the vision of an early Celtic committee which realised almost immediately the possibilities of professional football. Those men also saw that football could be part of the entertainment industry, as much a part of the fabric of working-class leisure as the Victorian music hall. As one writer quaintly put it: 'To the Celtic directors belongs the credit of initiating the newer reign of large enterprises which have marked the conduct of the game . . . They set themselves out from the first to lick creation in everything pertaining to the game and its appurtenances, and they have kept the interesting competition going ever since.' (*Evening Times*: 4 April 1904)

By the end of the century the annual Celtic Sports, held in the close season, would come to be widely regarded as the finest meeting of its kind in Britain and drew large attendances up to and beyond the First World War. The perennial success was due primarily to Willie Maley, himself an athlete once, and winner of the 100 yards at the Scottish Amateur Championships. He had a talent for organisation and a flair for promotion, regularly persuading noted athletes, Americans and Australians as well as

Scots and Englishmen, to appear and perform at Celtic Park. As early as 1892 the Celtic Sports attracted a crowd of 15,000 – a record for any sports meeting in Scotland.

In their rise to the top Celtic were drawing on a natural constituency, tapping into a reservoir of support which had previously been dispersed among the less flourishing Irish Catholic clubs of central Scotland – the Harps, Hibs and Emmets of the mid-1880s. An estimated 350,000 Irish immigrants had arrived on Clydeside within the first 40 years of the nineteenth century, and that ever-swelling community was desperate to be associated with success in any form, its members taking an extraordinary interest in Celtic and all the club's doings.

The *Scottish Referee* was struck by this devotion in an era of primitive spectating facilities: 'The Celtic are blessed with having a following that simply defy the elements, whose enthusiasm for their club is never lukewarm.' (7 September 1891) Within two years of the club's founding, brake-clubs had been formed by supporters in various Catholic parishes, the first being St Mary's in the Calton, formed in 1889. The brakes were soon transporting their membership to matches in horse-drawn wagonettes holding a couple of dozen people, their course through the streets heralded by boy buglers. They became sufficiently organised to form an association, the United Celtic Brake Clubs, which held annual rallies in addition to negotiating discounts for season tickets. Dan Drake, a veteran Celtic supporter, interviewed for the June 1972 issue of the *Celtic View*, gave some idea of the nature of the new club's attraction. He recalls as a ten-year-old being taken by his father to watch the club's early matches. Previously, his father had been indifferent to football, but Celtic's founding 'gave an interest to the down-trodden Irish community in Glasgow, who were able to identify themselves with the uphill fight of the club'.

The Irish in Glasgow did have a hard life: considered second-class citizens, alienated from their Scots neighbours by nationality, religion, politics and customs, and despised by the native Protestant population for their stereotypical representation as feckless, violent, criminally inclined, ignorant and all too ready to offer themselves as scab-labour in the struggle for survival at times of economic distress. A Dr James Devon, writing of the Calton in which he had lived between 1866 and 1894, underlined the physical and cultural apartheid: 'The Irish were looked upon as an inferior race, hewers of wood and drawers of water, who should be treated with consideration but kept in their place. The less we had to do with them the better. Their religion was not our religion, which was the best, and their customs were different from ours, as was their speech. Doubtless there were good folk among them, but the unruly and turbulent ones showed us what we might become if we did not keep to our own people.' (*Old Glasgow Club Transactions, 1930–31 session*)

Little wonder, then, that the Irish seized upon Celtic as a symbol of hope. Their community pride in the club's success was a sublimation of appalling living and working conditions. On Saturdays – exulting in another victory – they could exact some form of revenge for the rest of the week.

And what heroes awaited the crowds pouring into Celtic Park! Tom Maley, a greyhound of a winger; the captain, James Kelly, at centre-half whose pace and anticipation served to cover for his wing-halves when opposing forwards had given them the slip, and that same speed enabled him to join the Celtic assaults on the other goal; inside-forward Sandy McMahon, nicknamed the Prince of Dribblers, whose height and heading skill made him a threat at every corner-kick, when defenders would stand on his toes in an effort to foil him; the first great Celtic full-back partnership, Jerry Reynolds and Dan Doyle: broad-chested Reynolds, 'the Man with the Iron Head', reputed to be able to head the ball as far as most players could kick it, and Doyle, 'mighty among mighty men', idolised for his sureness and speed in the tackle, and his ability to hoist gigantic punts right into the opponents' penalty area even from his own half, sending Celtic supporters wild with delight and anticipation; and Willie Groves, a dexterous centre-forward, sometimes accused by colleagues of selfishness but blessed with great acceleration and the gift of avoiding robust challenges with neat sidesteps, a performer who entranced spectators with superb ball control and delighted the ladies (admitted free) with his dashing looks.

The followers rolled up in impressive numbers, particularly to witness attractive encounters with top English sides at Celtic Park. Teams such as the famous Preston North End, Bolton Wanderers and Corinthians made appearances in Glasgow in front of appreciative crowds. Until the advent of the Scottish League gave a structure to the season, these contests were not to be missed. But it was the epic struggles in the Scottish Cup, matches fought out in earnest for the country's premier competition, that held the crowds in thrall. Setbacks in Celtic's early seasons only intensified the desire – and resolve – of the club, its players and supporters to win 'the Blue Riband' of Scottish football.

Thus, after three seasons of fruitless striving by their favourites, the supporters waited impatiently for the campaign of 1891–92 to begin. Surely, the most important trophy in the land could not be denied Celtic much longer! Excitement rose as the club retained the Glasgow Cup, another much-coveted trophy in the 1890s, on 12 December by thrashing Clyde 7–1 in the final. At the same time, Celtic would continue their free-scoring ways in the Scottish Cup, averaging four goals per match on the way to the final. The semi-final, against Rangers at Parkhead, was a thriller: Celtic raced into a 4–0 lead before half-time but Rangers rallied amid great excitement to score three goals in the second half; in the closing minutes Celtic sealed a 5–3 win with the final goal of the contest.

The appearance in the Scottish Cup final of Celtic and Queen's Park became the focus of interest and press coverage. It was anticipated that a capacity crowd of 36,000 would congregate for the final at Ibrox on 12 March 1892, and the authorities had hired 150 policemen, a few of them mounted, to control the massive crowd expected. The excitement was not confined to the clubs' followers, to judge from the breathless prose of the *Scottish Sport* correspondent, aptly pen-named 'A Puffer': 'All records broken! Unparalleled scenes! Procession of vehicles of all descriptions miles long! Gates closed at 3 p.m. – an hour before the kick-off! Spectators on trees and surrounding housetops! Thousands gain free admission! £1,800 drawn at the gates and stands! A protest! Crowd breaks in! Mounted police controlling the crowd! Official consultations! Excitement throughout the country! These and many more items furnish elaborate material for a graphic description of the most remarkable event that has ever happened in the history of the Association game.' (15 March 1892)

Despite the formidable police presence, the first invasion of the pitch took place two hours before the kick-off. The *Scottish Referee* complained of 'the numbers entering pell-mell into the field, [who] burst aside the feeble resistance of the police and scampered over the field of play like lunatics let loose . . . the orderly spectators who, hours before, had taken up their stand around the field, annoyed at the invaders, pelted them with loose snow'. (14 March 1892) An estimated 20,000 had been left milling around on the streets outside Ibrox; some 5,000 of them leaped over the barricades after the gates had been closed.

The conditions underfoot remained another matter for concern. Snow had fallen in Glasgow in the days preceding the final, and the pitch was still snowbound on the morning of the match. Fortunately, a thaw had set in and the ground was soft rather than hard. The surface would be greasy and treacherous despite being sanded and cleared of snow. The highly professional Celts had arranged for a cobbler to be present at Ibrox, fully prepared to change at the last minute from the usual studs to bars for better footing.

Queen's Park dominated the early proceedings, as befitted the winners of nine Scottish Cups, before Celtic settled into the game. As early as the 20th minute, farce intruded into the final with another crowd break-in; during the prolonged stoppage the captains consulted Mr Sneddon (the referee and President of the SFA) and his linesmen. The interruptions, and the vagaries of the surface, were reducing the final to a game of chance, and the captains informed the referee they would both be protesting the match.

The game was completed, however, and Celtic's Johnny Campbell scored from close range after 60 minutes. That was the only goal, and most spectators left the ground convinced that Celtic had won the trophy. Normally, the silverware was presented inside the pavilion with the spectators excluded – and, of course, no public-address system existed then to inform the crowd of the 'decision'.

As expected, the joint protest was upheld and the final ordered to be replayed at Ibrox a month later. The price of admission was doubled to 2/- (10p) in an attempt to control the size of crowd without reducing the profits. At any rate, a smaller crowd, estimated at 23,000, turned up for the replay on 9 April to witness Celtic's first triumph in the competition. Queen's Park took advantage of the strong wind in the first half and settled down first; the Blazers profited by that early burst of ascendancy to lead by 1–0 at half-time. Celtic had defended well and James Kelly was outstanding at centre-half. There had been speculation – vigorously denied – that the captain might be dropped because of his recent uncertain form, but he marshalled his defence impressively on this occasion with a much improved performance.

Celtic totally dominated the second half, confirming the grip they had started to take just before the interval. Within six minutes they had equalised, when either Sandy McMahon or Johnny Campbell netted with 'a wonderful overhead shot'. Contemporary match reports varied wildly in the naming of scorers, but no doubt exists that it was Celtic's famed left-wing combination, 'as inseparable as Siamese twins', which turned things around. Shortly afterwards, Campbell added a second, following a delightful piece of combined play with his partner, Sandy McMahon.

Celtic's confidence was growing by the minute, as was the corresponding delirium on the terracing. In 65 minutes the free-running, resourceful McMahon, dribbling past several defenders in an individualistic sortie, sealed the victory with a third goal; certainly, that was the opinion of *Scottish Sport*: 'By the scoring of the third point the crowd began to journey homeward, a very significant indication.' Presumably the Celtic followers stayed to watch Kelly's free-kick from the edge of the penalty area in 75 minutes being deflected past the Queen's Park keeper by Sillars, a member of his own team; in the dying seconds McMahon, considered to be the best header of the ball in the game, made a characteristic leap to complete the rout at 5–1.

The final whistle soon set off fervent celebrations in the Irish community throughout Scotland with bands parading in the vicinity of Calton and Parkhead amid vociferous cheering. One commentator was heard to remark drily at time up that 'the various temperance establishments will be kept busy next week'. Filled to overflowing, one might say.

TWO

A Change in Direction

1890–97

The performance of Celtic's left-wing pair, McMahon and Campbell, who displayed an almost telepathic understanding and skill in the 1892 Scottish Cup final, suggested that the standard of play in Scotland had improved since the inception of the Scottish Football League in 1890. The rigidly amateur Queen's Park, victims of superior teamwork, clinical finishing and all-round sharpness in that 5–1 defeat, had paid the price for choosing to shun the Scottish League, but they would continue to do so for its first decade. Along with Celtic, who had been one of its strongest advocates, the following clubs participated in the League's first season: Abercorn, Cambuslang, Cowlairs, Dumbarton, Hearts, Rangers, Renton, St Mirren, Third Lanark and Vale of Leven. One notable absentee was Hibernian. The Edinburgh club was on the verge of collapse because of a precipitous decline in their playing fortunes and some inept financial management. They were to be forced out of business in May 1891, but fortunately the club was resurrected two years later.

From the club's inception Celtic had been in the forefront of change, advocating reform and progress. John H. McLaughlin of Celtic, the club's principal spokesman, was duly appointed the first secretary of the newly formed Scottish League in 1890. The club's involvement in the politics of the game, including the formation of the Scottish League, stemmed from the high profile (and corresponding clout) gained by its success and drawing power. McLaughlin, a forceful, autocratic personality, was later to become president of that organisation, and then attained the same eminence with the SFA. John McCartney, a historian of the Scottish League, writing in 1930, considered him to be 'the most powerful, progressive and eloquent legislator Scotland ever possessed'.

The League had been introduced because no guaranteed income existed for the bigger clubs. Prior to its introduction, fixture lists could be haphazard to say the least. Up to then, a successful club's schedule might contain an uneven mixture of lucrative friendlies against visiting English teams and unprofitable ones against village sides, competitive matches in local tournaments of varying appeal, and ties in the Scottish Cup. An early exit from the latter competition could be ruinous, effectively bringing the season to an end in terms of public interest. Much depended on the ingenuity of the match secretary in securing attractive fixtures, and Celtic were fortunate in having the indefatigable and efficient Willie Maley in this role. Other clubs were not so lucky, as arrangements for some fixtures were so casual that it was not unknown for visiting teams to turn up late for the advertised kick-off time, or even fail to appear at all.

The advent of the Scottish League was rightly viewed by Queen's Park as a manoeuvre by Celtic (and others) to force the issue of professionalism into the open. The leaders in Scottish football were aware that the game was being undermined by the absence of some two hundred of their best players performing in England. South of the border, where professionalism had been legal since 1885, no subterfuge was necessary to conceal the fact that young men could earn money from kicking a ball. McLaughlin waged a relentless campaign for professionalism in Scotland; at one meeting he fulminated, 'Why not be honest and banish canting humbug by openly declaring for professionalism?' In his ongoing campaign he was not averse to leaking snippets to the press, outlining the most common tricks being used to circumvent the rules. Throughout, Celtic's spokesman was no advocate for players' rights, being more concerned with the benefit to the clubs: 'With veiled professionalism players are masters of the clubs, and can go and debauch themselves without being called to account. Under the new system the clubs will be masters of the players, and the standard of play will rise.'

The introduction of a league competition (in 1890) and the legalisation of professionalism (in 1893) are arguably the two most important measures in the development of football in Scotland. They stand as a monument to the influence and perceptiveness of those running the young Celtic club, quick learners who realised that the sport was outgrowing its middle-class, amateur origins and had an attraction for working-class men either as players or as spectators.

The appeal of the Scottish Cup, particularly when Celtic were involved, was again in evidence in 1893, when another massive crowd for that period (25,000) rolled up for the final at Ibrox to find themselves deceived – if not defrauded – by watching the playing out of another 'friendly' between Celtic and Queen's Park. The pitch had been declared unplayable, a fact which the majority of spectators learned about only later in the newspapers. After the 5–1 triumph of the previous year, Celtic were favourites and confirmed that status by winning the friendly 1–0.

The actual final two weeks later was a different story. Queen's Park started well, Sillars scoring in ten minutes after Cullen had parried a close-in shot; on the half-hour, the same Queen's Park player scored a second, this time one hotly disputed by the Celtic defenders. The uproar arose over whether the ball had passed between the posts! Celtic had wanted the final to be played with goal nets, a recent introduction into Scottish football; Queen's Park objected because their players were not used to them – and the authorities ruled in their favour. No Celtic player (or sympathiser) was convinced that Sillars' shot had been on target. Celtic's goalkeeper, Joe Cullen, queried why the game was allowed to proceed until the 'scorer' badgered the referee into halting it with his cries of 'It's a goal, Mr Harrison, it's a goal!' Strangely, the Queen's Park player was successful in his belated appeal, and the 'goal' was allowed to stand.

Willie Maley, attempting to head the ball clear just prior to this incident, found himself on the receiving end of 'a well-directed boot', and he was forced to leave the field briefly for treatment to his mouth (and the removal of four teeth!). Two goals down at the interval, and with other players limping, Celtic came out fighting for the second half to display the spirit that had already become their trademark in cup competitions. Blessington scored shortly after the restart, and in the last 20 minutes Dan Doyle moved upfield to centre-forward in a desperate, but vain, attempt to get on equal terms. Willie Maley, in a 1936 newspaper series, remembered the match in particular for the efforts of the lion-hearted Doyle: 'He led a forlorn hope with immense courage, and no small skill, against a strong, hard-hitting, relentless opposition. He inspired the rest of us to put up a glorious fight right to the end.'

Celtic's sense of injustice rankled, prompting John H. McLaughlin to move successfully for the general introduction of goal nets into the Scottish game.

Celtic emerged from the season with their first championship (at the third attempt) and retained the Glasgow Charity Cup by thrashing Rangers 5–0 in the final at Celtic Park. This competition had been devised 17 years earlier in order to benefit local charities, and remained a popular feature of football in the city until the early 1960s.

Celtic held on to the championship and the Charity Cup the following season (1893–94), but found Rangers more difficult opposition in the Scottish Cup final; the Ibrox men won 3–1 in the last of their three victories over Celtic in four matches that season, and brought the Scottish Cup to Ibrox for the first time after two decades of striving. They proved to be the more confident and energetic side as the match wore on, Celtic wilting noticeably in the heavy, stamina-sapping conditions which suited their more youthful opponents. The growing appeal of the two Glasgow sides is suggested by the size of crowd which saw (the second) Hampden Park 'overtaxed with an enormous concourse of spectators . . . At the appointed hour of the kick-off every point of vantage was taken up, and it is imputed that 25,000 spectators were present.' (*Glasgow Observer*. 24 February 1894)

This spell of local supremacy by Rangers had a crucial impact in influencing the balance and focus of support in Glasgow. It started when Rangers managed to beat Celtic for the first time in any encounter by winning the Glasgow Cup final in February 1893. Celtic unwittingly tipped the balance further in Rangers' favour by alienating the supporters of the other Glasgow clubs by inflicting humiliations such as a 5–0 thrashing of Third Lanark in the league, and a 7–0 drubbing of Clyde in a friendly. 'Veteran', writing in the sports edition of the *Evening Times* (Glasgow) recalled: 'The winners did not make many friends by these smashing victories. For that matter, they never have had other than lip service outside their own following. What more natural then than for the disgruntled supporters of Third Lanark, Thistle, Clyde and other city clubs to look elsewhere for consolation, and transfer their allegiance to Ibrox, the home of the giant-killers? From now onwards all roads led to Ibrox. Partick Thistle were virtually driven out of Meadowside by the over and under river trek to Ibrox, and other clubs have seen a large section of their following making Ibrox their Mecca on a Saturday afternoon.' (8 August 1931)

Celtic shrugged off this antipathy to defeat Rangers in the finals of the Glasgow Cup and Charity Cup in 1894–95 and to recover the championship in emphatic fashion in 1895–96, a season of high scoring with Celtic's forwards frequently on the rampage: Rangers were victims by 4–2 and 6–2 in the league, and by 6–1 in the Charity Cup, while Third Lanark were thrashed 7–0, only two weeks after the 11–0 demolition of Dundee at Parkhead on 26 October 1895 in the previous league fixture. This result still stands as the club's record score in a competitive match, and was attributed more to Celtic's brilliance than to Dundee's finishing the game with only nine men through injury. Noting that the half-time score was 6–0 for Celtic, one reporter commented wryly that the visitors 'made a better show thus handicapped than with the full eleven'. The very first issue of the *Daily Record* – a newspaper to whom the mass appeal of football would prove indispensable – marvelled at 'the phenomenal performance' of Celtic's forward line in which 'individuality was discarded'. (28 October 1895) Contrarily, the correspondent of the *Glasgow Observer* seemed harder to please, complaining that 'for every goal scored against Dundee, two certain goals were thrown away', although he conceded that the forwards had shaken off 'the tig-toying with which of old they were cursed and set themselves seriously to the task of goal-scoring'. (2 November 1895)

Celtic were chalking up success after success but, as their first decade drew to a close, the club would be racked by internal dissension which was already being mirrored by problems on the field.

In February 1895, the side for an important league match against Heart of Midlothian at Tynecastle had been picked on the train to Edinburgh – and alterations were made on arrival at the ground. Celtic went down 4–0, a defeat which could have been worse but for brilliant goalkeeping by Dan McArthur, an agile and fearless keeper. One close observer was prompted to remark that neither the club officials nor the team appeared to have much interest in the proceedings; for him it confirmed the rumour of 'want of harmony in their ranks'. This indifference proved fatal as Celtic remained hopelessly adrift of Hearts, who marched on to championship glory.

The other Edinburgh side, Hibernian, would feature in an even more sensational development on 28 November 1896 at Parkhead. Three Celtic players (Meehan, Battles and Divers) refused to play unless the reporter from the *Scottish Referee* was barred. Disgruntled at what they felt was unfair recent criticism, they insisted on delivering their ultimatum to John Glass only minutes before the kick-off; Glass and the other Celtic officials refused to back down. Willie Maley, although more or less retired as a player, had to don a Celtic jersey again; the twelfth man, Barney Crossan, was promoted to the side; and Celtic played with a man short until Tom Dunbar, recalled from the reserve side at Hampden Park, entered the field 15 minutes into the second half (according to one account of the 1–1 draw). Dunbar may have been the original 'fan in a jersey', creating consternation and amusement when he took to the field by 'jumping the palings from amongst the spectators on the sixpenny side'.

Retribution was swift and harsh. The club suspended all three players indefinitely and cut their wages, but the ensuing unrest contributed to the club's greatest embarrassment to that date. On 9 January 1897 Celtic faced Arthurlie at Barrhead in the Scottish Cup, but an easy-looking fixture turned into a fiasco as the non-leaguers outfought Celtic by 4–2 on a tight, bumpy, sloping pitch known as 'The Humph'. Local knowledge of the peculiarities of the pitch helped the home side frustrate Celtic's traditional close-passing game.

Willie Maley, the sorest of losers, could describe it even 50 years later as 'the greatest take-down ever experienced by any first-class club'. The three regulars who had gone 'on strike' were absent through a club suspension, others were missing through injury and Dan Doyle, the idol of the support, simply neglected to turn up, embroiled as he was in a wages dispute with the club. Two decades later Tommy 'Ching' Morrison, Celtic's right-winger that day, would describe the state of disarray in the Celtic camp, claiming that the visitors started the match with only seven men, enabling Arthurlie to swarm all over Celtic before Barney Crossan could again be pressed into service in the emergency; Crossan, a forward, had to be fielded at left-back in place of Doyle.

Once more the club's officials were not amused, as their angry reaction suggests: Doyle was fined £5 and a week's wages; Madden and Morrison, two forwards who had performed unsatisfactorily that season, had their wages reduced. By the end of the season, in a determined purge, six players had left Parkhead: Morrison, King, McIlvenny, Meehan, Battles and Divers.

Unquestionably, matters would never have reached that level of disintegration had not a bitter battle been raging backstage for at least five years for control of the club – a clash characterised by those participating and observing as a struggle between idealists and pragmatists. The former wanted to hold the executive to the club's original (and somewhat narrow) remit, while the latter were convinced that the club had to be restructured to be put on a sound business footing. The pragmatists, representative of a section of the Irish community intent on making its mark, could point to the amazing growth in football's popularity in the last three decades. The game, they said, had come a long way since the pioneer days when Queen's Park could not afford to accept an invitation to play at Ayr, only 30 miles from Glasgow. The times were changing, and Celtic, the pragmatists insisted, had to move with them – or stagnate.

Ironically, the immediate success that the original members must have prayed for spelled the end of the idealistic motives for which the club was founded. Consider the popular appeal of the team. On 3 January 1889 almost 20,000 people, a record crowd for a fixture in Scotland, turned up to see the home side thrash the noted English club Corinthians by 6–2; on 7 September in the same year, an estimated 25,000 (reportedly the largest crowd to watch a match in Scotland till then) flooded into Parkhead to watch Celtic take on Queen's Park in the Scottish Cup.

Within a few years of their birth Celtic were raking in sums of money unmatched throughout Britain, their drawing power making them a magnet even outside Scotland. When they visited Birmingham in February 1890 to play Mitchell St George's, they were billed as 'the greatest team on Earth – that fine Glasgow combination, the Celtic!'. Late in 1892 Celtic attracted a record gate for the Potteries when they played Stoke in a friendly, with the proceeds going to aid the Hanley Catholic Church Restoration Fund. A visit to Lancashire to play Ardwick (later Manchester City) for the benefit of local Catholic charities saw 'the crowd burst out into wild and prolonged demonstrations of enthusiasm' during the match which Celtic won 5–0. After the game 'hundreds followed the Celtic brake in its progress through the streets, cheering lustily'. (*Scottish Sport*, 30 December 1892)

The club's growing fame was further enhanced around that time when members of the Football League Committee visited Celtic's new ground, and the Englishman had no hesitation in describing it as 'far and away superior to any field in Great Britain'. This was an indirect tribute to the now-forgotten James McKay, Celtic's treasurer, who had superintended the operations connected with the construction. He had devoted almost 18 months to the project to ensure personally that the stadium was up to the highest possible standards.

The need for a new ground had been prompted by continuing trouble with the landlord and, in 1891, when he attempted to raise the annual rent from £50 to £450, it was time for a move. When the committee made its decision, the only advantage appeared to lie in the fact that it involved a short flitting across Janefield Street. Otherwise, it seemed a foolhardy decision, but 'they went straight and negotiated for a five-year lease of a disused clayhole on the other side of the road, and out of the clayhole they built the famous ground that houses the International today'. (*Evening Times*, 9 April 1904)

The first job was to drain the clayhole of water, and then fill it in by the unloading of some 100,000 cartloads of earth. Much of the labour was free, volunteered by the same Irish community that had adopted Celtic as its symbol of hope and which had worked so hard on the earlier ground. The new stadium had an estimated capacity for 50,000, and when fully developed by the end of the century, it could hold 70,000. It was ready for the start of the 1892–93 season and, for the rest of that decade, it was a splendid ground, ideal for football, athletics and cycling.

The playing surface was level and covered with lush grass; two tracks, one for athletics and the other banked for cycling, surrounded the pitch and provided a secure barrier between the spectators and the players; one grandstand was constructed on the north side, parallel with Janefield Street, and it extended for 320 feet with 15 tiers that provided seating for 3,500 onlookers; the pavilion, a separate two-storey structure, was located

15 feet west of the stand and rose to a height of 30 feet. It contained apartments for the teams, lavatories and hot and cold baths, a club office and a hall with a veranda above the dressing-rooms from which officials and invited guests could view the match and mingle afterwards. The plans called for the erection of another stand to be built on the London Road side of the ground, but work on this could not begin until the soil had settled completely.

So impressive was the conversion that it confirmed John H. McLaughlin's prediction at the May 1892 AGM that 'a desert would become a garden of Eden'. This comment prompted one member to enquire if the players would 'dream of Paradise when flitting on its sward?' This exchange seems the most likely source of the ground's nickname which has survived to the present day.

Paradise it may have seemed, but Willie Maley, a lifetime admirer of Celtic's early leaders, always maintained that they had made a major mistake when developing the site. In a 1955 newspaper interview a few years before his death he stated that Celtic should have purchased all the land right down to London Road, and he pointed out that the school building presently adjacent to the site was not in existence at that time: 'They had the opportunity but didn't see the possibilities. What worried them was the cost of the old-fashioned wooden terracing.' Maley argued (with the considerable advantage of hindsight) that the playing surface could have been laid north and south instead of the present east and west. Thus, there would have been ample room for vast terracings and large stands, he claimed. If his view had prevailed back in 1892, Celtic's long-running problems with the stadium might not have arisen.

The enterprising committee saw the opportunity of profits to be made in renting the facilities. Their bid to host international matches was successful: the four home fixtures between Scotland and England from 1894 to 1900 were staged at Celtic Park, as was that of 1904. For the 1894 match Celtic repaired the roof of the stand (damaged in a winter storm), supplied additional seating, redrained and returfed the playing surface, provided more space and better facilities for the press – and were rewarded with their share of the huge sum of £2,650 drawn from the 46,000 spectators who watched Scotland and England settle for a 2–2 draw. By 1905, it was reckoned, Celtic had spent the then colossal sum of £50,000 in developing, enlarging and refurbishing the ground to cater for international matches.

How ironic, therefore, that the issue of the stadium would become a major factor in altering the direction of the club within its first decade – just as it would be a century later.

The battleground for the soul of the club was the club's AGMs and half-yearly meetings, increasingly forums for contentious motions, inflammatory speeches and highly personal attacks. Votes were contested, recounts demanded; members formed and re-formed into factions as the debate and struggle raged throughout the early and mid-1890s. One observer of the shenanigans recalled the occasion when a member 'took charge' of the ballot box with the result that, 'when the figures were called out, an amazed majority found itself in a decided minority'.

The kernel of the dispute which divided the club was graphically illustrated by a contretemps at the December 1895 half-yearly meeting between Frank Havelin, a gas-works labourer and Celtic member, and John H. McLaughlin, Celtic's vice-president. Havelin was forced to defend himself at Glasgow Sheriff Court in a slander action brought against him by McLaughlin the following month for an allegedly 'false and calumnious statement' made at the meeting. In his defence the labourer claimed that Celtic was being ruptured by a class divide, and asserted that working men had been attracted originally to the club because of its charitable aims and had become enthusiastic supporters. But now, he went on to claim, the club had abandoned its primary purpose 'and what is known as professionalism was introduced by the executive in the system of management dividing the membership into two different camps or parties, one representing the working-class element and the other the better-to-do party'.

The latter group was symbolised by such as McLaughlin, now a Hamilton publican, who had clearly been irritated by Havelin's spirited defence of the club's status quo at a special meeting held in the Celtic Park pavilion in April 1895. That meeting had seen McLaughlin move that the management committee be granted the power, if necessary, to call upon the members to pay such sums as may be their pro rata share of the club's existing liabilities and that any members failing to pay up after receiving the 14 days' notice by registered mail would be deemed to have let their membership lapse'. Havelin immediately moved an amendment, during which he affirmed forcefully that such a rule as McLaughlin proposed would drive out all working-men, 'the backbone of every club'. After a lengthy and lively debate, Havelin's amendment was carried by a large majority.

It came as no surprise, therefore, that McLaughlin's court action, one which claimed the sum of £100 in damages, should be viewed as a tactic to silence opposition through financial intimidation. The amount would have represented almost two years' wages for a labourer such as Havelin. Fortunately for the defendant, the sheriff shared this general opinion and dismissed the claim. He observed tartly that such an action should never have been raised, and awarded the costs to Havelin.

The first public manifestations of the growing tension between the factions had surfaced in the summer of 1889 after 'a hole-and-corner meeting' involving an office-bearer and a few committee men in a pub in Main Street, Bridgeton. The disgruntled members discussed 'the present committee's mismanagement, and the advisability of those present [in the pub] taking charge of the club' and, as an alternative, raising the junior club Benburb, a useful nursery for Celtic, to the senior level as a rival. Nothing specific came from the meeting, and the main hopes of the 'plotters' soon revolved around persuading Edinburgh Hibernian, now in decline, to leave the capital and relocate in Glasgow. Given the history of strained relations between Hibs and Celtic, that would have been a fascinating development – but the talks broke down.

The only viable option was to form a new club; thus, 'Glasgow Hibernian' came into being with a ground in the Oatlands district, a couple of miles from Parkhead. According to *Scottish Sport*, the new club constituted 'an attempt to outrival the Celtic, and the measure of support it is likely to receive from the lieges will depend on the eleven they are able to place on the field'. (9 August 1889) Despite reported pledges of support from players all over the country, Glasgow Hibernian could not deliver, being unable to compete with Celtic or undermine the loyalty that the latter had engendered. It was poorly supported at the turnstiles, and any hopes for improvement on the field were doomed to failure because the goalkeeper (John Tobin, on loan from Edinburgh Hibernian) was an active agent for English clubs and induced several of his new team-mates to move south. The short-lived club played its last match in October 1890, and folded shortly afterwards, heavily in debt. The abrupt termination of the threat posed by a rival club, competing for the same community's affections, was a relief but did little to quell the underlying discontent within Celtic.

The animosities resurfaced at the 1891 AGM, held in the Mechanics' Hall in Bridgeton. Dr John Conway, the honorary president of the club since its beginnings, was deposed; later in the six-hour meeting he suffered another humiliation when he lost in a bid to replace John Glass as president. A man of unimpeachable integrity, Dr Conway – lauded by the St Vincent de Paul Society as a generous contributor and publicly thanked by them for his 'gratuitous [free] attendance to the Poor' – was paying the price for having the temerity to deplore the committee's introduction of paid officials without the sanction of 'the general body of the club', and for seeking to have those appointments annulled. He maintained that there were available 'gentlemen who could and would take over such duties for love of the club, and the object for which it was formed and, so long as such could be got, he would oppose paying anybody'.

No sentiment was extended to that gentleman after his removal from a position of influence. He became, in effect, 'a non-person' in the Soviet sense and, unlike those of lesser committee men, his death in January 1894 went without tribute or notice at the club's next AGM. The *Glasgow Observer* did comment on his work in the larger community, and his contribution to the club: 'It was greatly owing to his exertion that the Celtic Football Club was started, and in acknowledgement of his efforts in that direction the members appointed him honorary president for three years.'

The *Glasgow Observer* itself would become a target for muzzling when it appeared to be running a crusade to shame the club into fulfilling its responsibilities towards the Poor Children's Dinner Table. On 6 October 1894, their football correspondent ('A Celt') suggested that, with the approach of winter, the Table might be assisted by Celtic playing a match on its behalf; the columnist added cryptically that 'less deserving matters have had greater attention given them by the Club Executive'.

A few months later, the correspondent called on the club to donate to the same worthy cause its share of the gate from a Scottish Cup replay against Hibernian since the match constituted 'an unexpected reprieve' – the result, in fact, of a successful protest by Celtic against an ineligible player fielded by Hibs. Predictably, the plea fell on deaf ears, as had a request from the Sacred Heart Conference of the St Vincent de Paul Society two years earlier when they had asked Celtic to play a match for the same purpose. Realising that 'their' club would not oblige, they turned to Clyde and Edinburgh Hibernian, two clubs with an admirable record in turning out for charity. The game was played at Barrowfield Park in April 1893, drawing 'a fair turnout' but not a lucrative one as only £16 5s 3d was drawn at the gate – of which £12 15s 2d went in expenses. The appeal of Celtic would have guaranteed more; in fact, on the same day as the Clyde v Hibernian match, Celtic went to Ibrox to play Rangers in a friendly and pocketed their share of the proceeds of a much larger attendance.

Shortly after such campaigning, the *Glasgow Observer* found that the revenue from Celtic's advertising had been transferred to a rival, the newly formed *Glasgow Examiner*. Coincidentally, the football column of the latter newspaper would be compiled by no less a personage than John H. McLaughlin, that noted flayer of the 'malcontents'.

Insinuation escalated into allegation in the columns of the *Glasgow Observer* after it was disclosed at the 1895 AGM that, out of another large income accruing to 'the biggest-drawing club in Scotland', not one penny had been donated to the Poor Children's Dinner Table for which the club had been instituted. And this was at a time when the St Vincent de Paul Conference of St Mary's parish was under pressure to maintain the level of their charitable work. The demand for free dinners alone had increased from nearly 66,000 in 1894 to over 97,000 in 1896.

'Justitia' of Polmadie (Glasgow) was moved to write to the *Glasgow Observer*, complaining that this neglect, 'while thousands were spent in junketing, trips and wages to more or less incapable players, is simply a blazing scandal'. (22 June 1895) Within the next few weeks accusations of outright corruption had been made on the letters page, with the focus on one particular issue. 'Leaguer' linked 'the question of funds, balance-sheets notwithstanding' to the fact that 'since the foundation of the club fully a dozen members (players and/or officials) have become the proprietors of public houses in Glasgow and Lanarkshire. Whence came the wherewithal for the purchase of these gin-palaces?' (6 July 1895) In the following issue of the newspaper, 'Aqua' reinforced the point that a club originated for charity had turned into 'a gravy train' for certain individuals. Any expertise gained in manipulating and falsifying gate receipts for the purpose of underhand payments to players was not being allowed to rust now that professionalism was legal.

Astonishingly, this matter of 'fiddling' was raised in a semi-public forum, at Celtic's half-yearly meeting in the club pavilion in December 1894. Stephen Henry, a former committee man, had been ousted at an AGM seven months earlier after querying whether those running the club were fully accountable to the membership. This time, he asked a question about a reported 'irregularity in connection with the stand drawings on a certain day not very far back', thought to be a reference to the Scotland v England match in April. An embarrassed John H. McLaughlin admitted that suspicions had been aroused, but he was quick to insist that an internal investigation had found no evidence of wrongdoing.

However, a committee man who had acted as an auditor in the affair, Tim Walls (described as 'ready-witted and keen-tongued'), spoke out: 'In fact, so plain did he speak that a member of the committee informed the chairman [president John Glass] that, if Mr Walls said any more, the matter would not be settled there. Whether Mr [James] Curtis meant in the arena of play or the court of justice he did not further enlighten the hearer. Mr Walls objected to Mr Curtis taking charge of money on the day mentioned, as Mr Curtis had nothing to do with that matter. This matter was then dropped . . .' (*Scottish Referee.*14 December 1894) It no doubt came as a considerable relief to some members of the committee that Mr Walls emigrated to South Africa five months later.

That particular episode must have reinforced the suspicions of those such as 'Aqua' who, in his letter to the *Glasgow Observer* of 13 July 1895, remarked that it was 'to say the least a trifle curious how certain men, players or officials, not in what one could call a flourishing financial condition, suddenly blossom out into publicans'. He obviously had in mind several prominent players, notably James Kelly, Paddy Gallacher, Sandy McMahon, ex-player Mick Dunbar and Dan Doyle.

The issue discomfited the president of the club; at the AGM held a month previously, John Glass refused point-blank to answer a question from the floor about the source of funds for Doyle's pub in Baillieston. Changed days from when the voluble Glass was attempting to recruit the player from England! Doyle had been so amused then at the committee man's eagerness that he chided him: 'Steady on, John! Be careful! Don't put my name over the door until I've got the licence.'

In the spring of 1895 the *Glasgow Observer* published a series of profiles of the Celtic stars, and made a point of referring to the premises of the aforementioned players as having been acquired 'since being connected with the Celtic club'. The newspaper (an advocate of temperance) singled out their team-mates Jimmy Blessington and John Divers as 'League of the Cross men' and among 'the few footballers who really take care of themselves'.

The lure of owning a pub was not confined to players, as our research has identified the committee members who effected a career change at around the same time. John H. McLaughlin entered 'the wine-and-spirit business' when he moved to Hamilton in 1893; John O'Hara had been an East End publican since the early 1890s; and Arthur Murphy, described as 'the champion of labour' when he opposed a limited liability proposal at Celtic's AGM in 1893, was revealed by the *Scottish Referee* in February 1895 as the owner of the Celtic Bar opposite the Camlachie Institute close to Celtic Park, an establishment he had acquired for the princely sum of £1,200.

Such allegations of profiteering, although difficult to prove because of the circumstantial nature of the evidence, could not be treated lightly in the increasingly hostile climate of opinion towards the 'demon drink' prevailing at the time. The trade occupied an anomalous position in the Irish Catholic communities then. Certainly it offered one of the few businesses in which its members could succeed and prosper without a formal education. James Kelly, Celtic's first captain, within a decade of joining the club as an amateur and an apprentice joiner, acquired the tenancies of public houses in Blantyre, Hamilton and Motherwell. The success he enjoyed in running these businesses undoubtedly smoothed his path into public life as a Justice of the Peace, county councillor and School Board trustee.

On the other hand, drink wreaked havoc and devastation in family life, especially among the Irish poor. One historian of that community, John Lynch, writing in 1956, would lament 'the drink' as 'the chief failing of our people'. He was only endorsing the views of many of the Catholic clergy down the years, notably Father Francis Hughes of Bridgeton's Sacred Heart parish who regularly bemoaned in his sermons 'the prevalent poverty in the district, caused in very many cases, both directly and indirectly, by indulging in strong drink'. (*Glasgow Observer*.17 November 1894)

Father Hughes could point to the number of public houses in his poor parish, one on virtually every corner to judge by a contemporary estimate of over one hundred 'low drinking-dens of ill-repute' in the square mile of the adjoining Calton alone. At the time the priest was voicing his concerns the Celtic Football Club was embroiled in controversy over the issue. As early as October 1890, Archbishop Eyre was rumoured to be questioning the judgement of those of his clergy who bestowed their support on a football club which was attracting unwelcome publicity for allegedly bankrolling the unsuccessful application of Willie Groves to the licensing court for a pub in Taylor Street in the Townhead district.

The archbishop did not go so far as to withdraw his patronage, but 'the unholy alliance' with the drink trade at the perceived expense of the club's charitable remit would continue to dog the Celtic executive as it moved inexorably towards the introduction of limited liability. When that became a *fait accompli*, some members of the brake clubs, constitutionally also members of the League of the Cross, wondered if they could continue to support a club whose first board of directors, elected in June 1897, consisted of six 'wine-and-spirit merchants' and a 'builder's merchant' (John Glass). One critic referred to the Board as 'six publicans and one Glass'. As Mr Ward, an angry delegate, told a United Celtic Brake Clubs' meeting in July 1897, it was now a question of 'supporting temperance on the one hand, and brewers and publicans on the other'.

Celtic FC was no longer the sort of club envisioned by Brother Walfrid, whose concept was echoed in a 1949 newspaper interview of a former colleague. Brother Ninian recalled that Celtic players and officials in the early days 'used to go to Mass and Communion before major games, not to pray for victory, but because they were Catholic sportsmen in the truest sense of the word', who realised that the Catholic concept of sportsmanship 'calls for health of soul and mind as well as of body'.

Indeed, Brother Walfrid's influence seems to have been waning before he was transferred to London by his superiors in 1892. Although the cleric held no official position, he was widely regarded as the founder, or originator, of the club and the very embodiment of that ideal. Only after he had departed could the advocates of limited liability – and paid officials – characterise their opponents safely in such terms as 'impertinent meddlers', 'Dinner Table soreheads' and 'soup-kitchen cranks'.

The opposition to the idea of limited liability would be eroded and worn down over a period of four years but, even before he left for London, Brother Walfrid would have ample indication of the fragmentation of his dream. The treasurer's report in May 1892 revealed that contributions to charity had been cut from £545 the previous year to £230, marking a one-third reduction in the donation to the Poor Children's Dinner Table. The 1893 report brought the first official indication of the trend towards reneging on the club's primary charitable obligation. From Celtic's huge income of nearly £6,700, a mere £63 was handed out in donations, and nothing was given to the Poor Children's Dinner Table.

This backtracking on the part of the executive was justified by frequent references to further expenditures on the new stadium. These costs had been the major factor in putting the club in debt to the tune of £2,068, including £1,450 to the Clydesdale Bank – a situation exploited by the proponents of the limited liability scheme at the AGM of 1893.

The idea was first brought forward at a committee meeting by Joseph Shaughnessy, the club's honorary president and a Glasgow lawyer, ironically once praised in a newspaper profile as a pillar of the St Vincent de Paul's Rutherglen conference. At that committee meeting the majority in favour of the scheme was 11 to 4. John H. McLaughlin formally proposed the motion at the AGM in May 1893, and it was seconded by Shaughnessy (who took pains to deny any suggestion that monetary gain was at the root of the proposal). McLaughlin went on to claim that its adoption was necessary to ensure that the burden of debt 'would be taken off the shoulders of the members and would be placed on those who were willing to accept the responsibility'.

In the manner of all lawyers, Shaughnessy played the role of Cassandra, hinting that the bank could demand repayment of the money at any time, while asserting that the reorganising of Celtic into a limited liability company would forestall that. He did not enlighten the sceptics present in the Mechanics' Hall as to why any sensible banking institution should want to foreclose on a concern consistently generating large revenues.

The ensuing furore, with the opponents of the motion claiming that such a move would put the club in the hands of 'a few moneyed speculators', ensured a heated and lengthy debate. The motion – the first of its kind in Scotland – was defeated by the general membership on a count of 86 to 31 'amidst a scene of terrific enthusiasm and prolonged cheering'. Judging by the size of their support, however, the proponents of the scheme had been making significant headway.

One year later the treasurer reported with considerable satisfaction that the club had reduced the existing liabilities to around £1,850, thanks to the largest income (almost £7,000) yet enjoyed by a Scottish club. There was general approval of treasurer James McKay's rather self-satisfied comments on the club's financial soundness, and of his fellow office-bearer James Curtis's assertion that, once these liabilities had been cleared, 'there will not exist an association that will come more to the assistance of the poor and the needy than the Celtic club'.

One member, a P. Gaffney, deflated the balloon of complacency by expressing his indignation that Celtic had reneged for the second successive year on its agreement at inception to pay £5 weekly to the Poor Children's Dinner Tables in the East End parishes of St Mary's, St Michael's and Sacred Heart. The chairman, John Glass, could not deny the drawing-up of this agreement, but he brushed aside the reasonable suggestion that two hundred new members be taken on with a view to handing over their subscriptions immediately to the charity for which the club had been founded. Mr Glass added that when the club was free of debt it would be 'only too willing to do whatever it could to assist the charities mentioned'. But the meeting had few qualms about approving a handsome honorarium of £100 for the treasurer, a chorus of assent rendering a formal vote unnecessary.

In December 1895, at the half-yearly meeting, the membership was called upon to debate and vote on the merits of Celtic becoming a limited liability company. Tom Maley rose to attack this move, objecting to it on the constitutional grounds that an AGM or an extraordinary meeting with advance notice would have been the appropriate forum. He stated that he would not object to any scheme brought forward if he thought it would enable the club 'to carry out the noble purpose for which it was started, namely, charity'.

Unlike his brother Willie, Tom had lost some favour with the committee, probably because he frequently castigated them on their neglect of the Poor Children's Tables. His passion at this meeting was derided by one office-bearer, William McKillop (ironically, a prosperous restaurateur), as 'mere claptrap'. A highly esteemed figure, Tom Maley was a man who contributed personally to charity, and nobody should have questioned his genuine concern for the poor nor his commitment to the Poor Children's Dinner Tables and the St Vincent de Paul Society. In addition, Tom Maley could speak from first-hand experience in commenting on the poverty in Glasgow's East End. A teacher by profession, he had been appointed Superintendent of Slatefield Industrial School designed for the practical education and the welfare of children 'who had been found begging, or destitute, or without a guardian'.

In June 1896 James McKay, the honorary treasurer, could report that Celtic had taken in more than £10,000, a record sum for any British club at the time. He intimated that £1,156 had been spent on alterations and extensions to the ground, and the debt reduced by a further £723. Once more, a request from the St Vincent de Paul Society for a specific donation to the Poor Children's Tables of St Mary's, Sacred Heart and St Michael's was turned down . . . but funds were made available to award the treasurer and the match secretary (Willie Maley) £75 each in honoraria.

At the half-yearly meeting held six months later at the same venue (the Annfield Halls in the Gallowgate), James McKay could report that the club had enjoyed 'a colossal revenue'. He described it as one unprecedented in any comparable period in the club's brief history, adding that the members could congratulate themselves on having carried out further extensive ground improvements and, at the same time, having paid off £1,000 of the £1,400 debt. He concluded by expressing the hope that six months hence, at the next meeting, he would be able to announce that the 'trifling debt' of £400 had been wiped out and that the club had a substantial balance in its account.

These confident assertions rather undermined the case for limited liability, an issue with which the membership was again suddenly confronted only two months later in February 1897. The pretext was the funding of structural changes to the ground in order to comply with the terms of an offer made two years earlier by the Scottish Cyclists Union to hire the stadium.

In the latter part of the nineteenth century the sport of cycling was enjoying a vogue, and Celtic had catered to the craze for such meetings by constructing a banked circuit around the running track. The SCU had offered Celtic £500 to use the stadium and cycling track for three days in July 1897 to hold the World Cycling Championships. With the increased service of tramcars and omnibuses, Celtic Park was only a ten-minute journey from the city centre, a factor which had enhanced the ground's appeal as a venue for international events.

The offer, however, was a conditional one. Celtic would have to make further renovations to the cement track, upgrading the banking and adjusting the circuit in line with the requirements of the organisers. The sub-committee appointed by the club to negotiate further with the SCU revealed that the costs of altering the track to bring it up to international standards would amount to an estimated £900 and, as the SCU had promised only £500, this would mean an increase of £400 in the club's debt.

The circular distributed by Willie Maley which called for a special general meeting of the membership to discuss the matter smacked more of opportunism than of a genuine crisis: 'A number of the committee present [at an 18 February 1897 meeting] objected strongly to any additional expense being incurred, and opinions were expressed that it was now high time – the club being so free of debt – that the liability of the members in future should be limited.'

On the face of it, the membership was scarcely being presented with a dilemma. The club had expanded beyond the expectations of even the most optimistic member. This expansion, made in order to meet the club's original purpose, had been necessary: the morale of a whole community had been lifted by the success of the club; the prestige of staging the World Cycling Championships for the first time in Scotland was appealing; and, at the end, when the debts were cleared off, surely charity would benefit even more?

After a long discussion at the subsequent special general meeting, held at St Mary's Hall on 25 February 1897, a committee was struck to draw up a scheme to be submitted to the membership as a matter of urgency. Ironically, the committee would include Tom Maley, Frank Havelin and M. Hughes, all critics of the executive's failure to live up to the club's original goals. Hughes, for one, had argued at the 1895 half-yearly meeting that the debt being incurred by increased expenditure on ground alterations was being 'kept there for the purpose of forcing the Limited Liability scheme'. The inclusion of these three men was the clearest possible indication that 'the rebels' had bowed to the inevitable.

The scheme prepared was formally adopted a week later, on 4 March 1897, at a well-attended 'follow-up' meeting of the full membership at the same hall, Celtic's birthplace. After a relentless four-year campaign by the executive, the general membership had come to endorse the committee's advocacy of Celtic's becoming a limited liability company. Less than ten years earlier in the same building, charity had been uppermost in everybody's mind; this time, money had talked.

The advocates of the 'Celtic Football and Athletic Company Limited', which came into existence the following month, could soon point to the club's new-found ability to raise additional capital. Thus, Celtic would become the first football club in Scotland to own its ground outright through an outlay of £10,000 to purchase the site of Celtic Park from the landlord in December 1897.

Opponents of the new set-up could feel more than justified in questioning the real motives of its advocates when they noted the distribution of funds in the first year of its operation. An income of £16,267 (a new record amount for Britain) resulted in a 20 per cent dividend for the shareholders and directors — but for charity, nothing. The original impulse was truly dead.

Nevertheless, one suspects that the 'malcontents' became reconciled to the situation in time. Even Brother Walfrid, who had followed the disintegration of his original aims from afar, seems to have come to terms, however reluctantly, with a changed world. He never lost interest in the doings of the club, despite what can only be described as a miserable and cynical betrayal of his ideal. In his only published comment on the matter, and writing more in sorrow than in anger, he recalled that the expenses of the Poor Children's Dinner Table at Sacred Heart had been met 'by subscriptions and collections, sermons etc. until the Celtic F.C. was started, the committee of which gave the good Brothers [of the St Vincent de Paul conference] about thirty-three shillings a week up to a short time since'. (*Glasgow Observer.* 16 March 1895)

One of his Marist successors in Glasgow, Brother Clare (perhaps better known as James E. Handley, the author of an officially sanctioned history of the club published in 1960), was more blunt in a 1968 history of the Marist Order in the British Isles: 'The committee, after a long and bitter struggle against the honest element among the team's supporters, got their way at last and turned the club into a business with themselves as directors and shareholders.'

Brother Walfrid's recognition of the new reality was clear when he met some of his old colleagues for the last time. When Celtic were returning from a continental tour in 1911, he parted from them in London with a farewell remark: 'Well, well. Time has brought changes. Outside ourselves there are few left of the old brigade. It's good to see you all so well, and I feel younger with the meeting. Goodbye, God bless you.'

Tom Maley, by then a journalist, recorded the poignant meeting and Walfrid's words, describing how the cleric, now elderly and spare, slipped away into the anonymity of bustling London leaving Tom, a fellow idealist, to reflect on the unlikely central figure in the foundation of Celtic, the architect-in-chief of 'the greatest and best of athletic and football institutions', but one which had changed irrevocably.

THREE

A Pattern to the World

1897–1916

The first Celtic board of directors undoubtedly got it right on 23 June 1897 – within a week of its election – when they appointed Willie Maley as secretary-manager, a post that was tailor-made for him. Energetic and practical, Maley, not yet 30, was to play an increasingly important part in making Celtic the most renowned football club in Britain. He would be regularly acknowledged in the sporting press as having no equal in getting the best from his players. Typical was this tribute in the *Glasgow Observer*, a Catholic newspaper famed for having an outrageous bias in favour of all things Celtic: 'He is at once a chum and a guide to the young player; he is "Mr Maley" and "Willie" at the same time. He has the happy knack of gaining the confidence and respect of every man on the wage-list, and knows full well how to draw the line between undue familiarity and rigid aloofness. It is this feeling of comradeship between players and manager that has enabled the club to stand where it does and, so long as this spirit remains, success will follow.' (7 June 1913)

'Mr Maley' exuded authority, his imposing build and presence playing a part in his domineering streak. One former player – decades later – remembered him as a sore loser, so upset and grim-faced in defeat that famous Celts, household names, had learned to steer well clear of him afterwards. A demanding personality certainly, but one who lived for the club and strove to ensure that each Celtic player would be inculcated with that same spirit.

No one could question the fact that Maley worked in impressive tandem with a board of directors which proved a happy blend of ex-players (James Kelly and Mick Dunbar), well versed in football matters, and astute businessmen (John McKillop, restaurateur, and James Grant, wine-and-spirit merchant) to lay down the sound management and leadership qualities that would bear such rewards in the first great epoch of the club's history. James Grant, a blunt and straightforward Northern Ireland man, made no secret of his scant knowledge of the playing side of football and left team selection to Kelly, Dunbar and Maley. Grant's contribution to Celtic lay in the fact that, before ill health forced his retirement to Ireland, 'he superintended all these improvements and extensions which have made Celtic Park second only to Hampden after being without a rival until the Amateurs entered the field'. (*Glasgow Observer.* 17 October 1914)

The period between 1897 and 1904 was essentially a transitional one for the team, though it was not without achievement and turbulence. Following the political in-fighting, the dressing-room unrest and trophy-less on-field mediocrity of the previous season, Celtic steadied themselves and managed to secure their fourth league title in 1897–98. It could be considered a triumph for defensive excellence rather than for free-scoring. The team went through the campaign undefeated, winning 15 of their 18 fixtures, but the Parkhead executive still felt a nagging sense of dissatisfaction about the effectiveness of the front line.

Celtic may have finished a comfortable four points clear of the runners-up, Rangers, but they had scored 15 goals fewer. The club's top scorer, George Allan – signed from Liverpool in May 1897 – had netted 14 goals in 17 league matches, but five of them had been scored on Christmas Day 1897 against a hapless Clyde, who eventually finished up in last place. Allan could not settle at Parkhead and rejoined the Merseyside club at the end of the season, feeling that he had been driven out by unfair and vindictive criticism from both management and supporters. Apparently, he was categorised as a misfit, unable to adjust to 'Celtic's studied style of play'.

The club had to wait some years before the centre-forward position would be filled satisfactorily – and would pay heavily for it in the meantime. The championship was won for the next four seasons by Rangers, and then by the most unlikely duo of Hibernian and Third Lanark, both of whom were regarded as 'cup-tie elevens'. That same label could be tagged on to Celtic just as accurately at the turn of the century.

The club's 2–0 victory in the 1899 Scottish Cup final at Hampden Park over Rangers came as a total surprise to most, since the Ibrox men had just completed the unique record of having won every match in their league programme. Just as surprising was the relative ease of the triumph, the defence coping fairly comfortably with Rangers' many raids and then troubling their rivals with counter-attacks. Ten minutes after the interval, the tall Sandy McMahon outjumped his markers to head home a corner-kick for the first goal. The issue was settled in 75 minutes when right-winger Johnny Hodge, prompted by the limping Jack Bell on the other wing, scored from a suspiciously offside position, but Rangers' frantic appeals were ignored by the referee, Mr T. Robertson (Queen's Park).

Celtic retained the trophy the next season, defeating Queen's Park at Ibrox on 14 April 1900 in that club's last national final. Few expected the amateur side, still a non-League club, to give professional opponents, particularly a club who boasted nine fully-fledged internationals, such a good run for their money. In fact, they created a mild sensation by opening the scoring, but by half-time Celtic had asserted themselves to lead by 3–1. The incomparable Sandy McMahon led the charge. At times the ungainly inside-forward deserved to be criticised for over-doing his dribbling to the detriment of the team's effectiveness; his style had borne comparisons to 'the pirouetting of a premier danseuse'. On this occasion, though, he netted Celtic's equaliser by settling for a strong cross-shot which deceived goalkeeper Gourley. A few minutes later, despite being surrounded and jostled by defenders, he headed on Bell's corner for Divers to score easily. Celtic added a third before half-time, but Queen's Park fought back bravely. Celtic's vaunted defence survived various alarms and excursions in that second half, and the favourites ran out winners by 4–3. In Scottish football it marked another victory of the new order over the old.

The twentieth century had dawned with the greatest rivalry in British football emerging and taking shape – that between Celtic and Rangers with its quasi-racial and religious overtones, the 'Irish Catholic' Celtic and the 'Scottish Protestant' Rangers being linked together under the appellation of the Old Firm. The tag suggests both the monopoly of the football honours which they were beginning to enjoy, and the economic strength derived from their pulling power. This rivalry had become even more profitable and had been sharpened by the introduction of the league competition and professionalism.

Their symbiotic relationship was not of the smoothest, as 'A Celt' observed after Celtic's 5–3 victory in an 1894 league match at Parkhead. The columnist bemoaned the virtual disappearance of the socialising, once a feature of the sport and of this particular fixture. He added that he had been informed by Celtic players that 'the language some of the Rangers players used was most disgraceful – "Fenian", "Papist", "Irish" all being hurled with, of course, the most vulgar accompaniments. This is not how it used to be; Rangers and Celts were always pretty friendly, and the change of front seems strange. If players were out of gear, so too were officials. A more grumpy lot it would have been hard to find than the Light Blue officials. They seemed to have a grievance more imaginary than real concerning the gate receipts, which, by the way, amounted to £430.' (*Glasgow Observer.* 29 September 1894)

The decline in the former friendship between the clubs was particularly marked by the competition to rebuild their stadiums in bids to host the most lucrative fixture in the football calendar, the Scotland v England international. The SFA chose Ibrox Park for the 1892 fixture, but preferred Celtic Park for the other four matches held between 1894 and 1904 with one ill-fated exception – and from 1906 onwards chose the new (third) Hampden Park. The mood was one of ill-concealed displeasure down Ibrox way when their new ground, opened in 1899, lost out overwhelmingly in the voting to host the match between Scotland and England for the following year. This prompted 'Man in the Know' to gloat over the Parkhead club's influence in the corridors of power where its 'expert wire-pullers' had been so quick off the mark that 'the club officials who seek to overreach them on such a question as this will have to rise very early'. (17 February 1900)

The fall-out could not be delayed for long, the ill-feeling duly manifesting itself in May 1901 when a Charity Cup tie between the clubs inaugurated the athletic programme of Glasgow's second International Exhibition. Jimmy Quinn, a mere stripling at the time, was fielded at outside-right in the match held at the compact and picturesque Exhibition Ground at Gilmorehill. He would recall vividly the indignities visited on his two famous team-mates, Sandy McMahon and Johnny Campbell: 'When passing through the stand-passage to and from the field they were both spat on – indeed, Sandy was in an awful mess. I never saw anyone in such a rage as Sandy was, and it was with the greatest difficulty he was kept back from attempting to gain redress. Of course, the jeers and slights and carry-ons of the biggest section of the crowd affected the players, and there were a few skirmishes.' (*Scottish Weekly Record.* 18 June 1910)

That unpleasantness clearly influenced Celtic's stance in a row which broke out after the Glasgow Cup final of October 1901, a 2–2 draw at Ibrox Park. The venue had been chosen as the result of a ballot, and Celtic's contention that the replay should take place at Parkhead was overruled by the Glasgow Football Association. The vote marked a significant coup in Rangers' determination to overturn Celtic's supremacy and influence in the council chamber. Rather than agreeing to another match on Rangers' ground, Celtic chose to scratch from the competition in protest.

Celtic lost out again when, after another backroom skirmish, Ibrox was given the nod over Celtic Park for the upcoming 1902 international between Scotland and England. A catastrophe at that match, which caused 25 deaths and more than 500 injuries when the wooden planking on a section of the west terracing gave way, prompted the *Glasgow Observer* correspondent, an apologist for the Parkhead club, to point out that Celtic's 'splendidly equipped ground, which had stood the test of previous record crowds . . . would have safely accommodated Saturday's mammoth muster'.

The sports pages of that newspaper mirrored the disappointment felt by the Parkhead club, whose representatives had already hinted that Rangers had been less than scrupulous and diligent in guaranteeing the stability of the new structure. Conveniently, the newspaper had forgotten to mention the overcrowding at the same fixture at Celtic Park only six years before, congestion which had led to an overspill onto the perimeter of the pitch. At that point, the Celtic officials responded to the anguished cries of the spectators caught in the crush on the terracings by belatedly shutting the admission gates.

After that Ibrox Disaster of 1902, the Scottish Football Association was all but bankrupted, having subscribed its available assets to the Relief Fund inaugurated by Glasgow Corporation. The sum of £30,000 was raised, and the money allowed all claims to be settled without recourse to law. In 1903, to protect itself against such future eventualities, the SFA was incorporated as a limited liability company.

Rangers organised a competition in an attempt to raise money to compensate the victims. It was such a select field there was talk in the press of naming it the British League Cup: Rangers and Sunderland were the respective league champions, while Celtic and Everton had been the runners-up. The winning club was to receive the magnificent Glasgow Exhibition Trophy, won by Rangers in 1901 when they had defeated Celtic in a tousy final, and insured by them for £100.

Celtic's 5–1 demolition of Sunderland's 'team of all the talents' and an under-strength Rangers' equally impressive feat in overcoming Everton set up expectations of another keenly contested match. The final between Celtic and Rangers was held at Cathkin Park on 17 June 1902 before a crowd estimated at 7,000. Willie Maley moved young Jimmy Quinn from left-wing, where he had played indifferently at times, and tried him at centre-forward again. At least one director had wanted him to be sold but Maley still had confidence in Quinn whom he described as 'the hardy collier-breed player'. He felt that his problem as a winger was a lack of genuine pace and crossing ability, and Maley thought that Quinn's strength, dash and 'rummle-'em-up' approach would be better employed in the spearhead position. Maley's gamble paid off, as Quinn netted a hat-trick, the winner coming two minutes from the end of extra-time. Accounts of that goal differ, but the authors prefer the memory of one supporter who recalled for a newspaper years later exactly how Jimmy

Quinn – all 5 feet 8 inches of him – jumped on inside-left Tommy McDermott's shoulders to head home a corner-kick.

Thus, Celtic took the Glasgow Exhibition Trophy to Parkhead, apparently to the surprise and chagrin of Rangers who, for some reason, had expected it to be returned to Ibrox at the conclusion of the tournament. Several times in the next few years, up to the outbreak of the First World War in 1914, Rangers approached Celtic for its return or suggested that the trophy be put up again for competition. Each time Celtic declined. A *Football Weekly* writer who visited Celtic Park in 1936 to interview Willie Maley discovered why. He found out that the splendid cup (won 34 years earlier) was locked inside a huge safe in the office. The reporter was startled by the vehemence of Maley's response to his question as to why Celtic did not put the trophy up for competition: 'No, no! The cup is ours. We won it outright. We regard it as a treasured possession and, unless some very special occasion arises, we do not intend to risk losing it.'

Despite the success in the Glasgow Exhibition tournament, the directors were becoming less willing to conceal their disquiet about the team's inconsistency in the league championship. Increasingly, the Board was becoming disenchanted with the acquisition of experienced 'personality' players, magnetic but mercenary performers such as Dan Doyle who became notoriously less amenable to discipline. There was a whiff of sulphur about the outburst of chairman McLaughlin in the *Glasgow Examiner* of 23 December 1899 after a series of spiritless performances: 'enough to make the directors inclined to clear the whole crowd of players out if they could, and get an entirely fresh lot to represent the green and white'. The *Glasgow Observer* was just as blunt in February 1902, accusing the Celtic directors of 'paying fancy wages for fancy players'.

Willie Maley, who later admitted that he had introduced 'a considerable number of strangers', had been facing a difficult situation since the start of his managerial career in dealing with players of his own generation – men signed from English clubs, with big reputations and who fitted uneasily at times into the Celtic scheme of things. He delivered a scathing verdict on one import, a half-back from Aston Villa with three FA Cup medals who lasted only eight months at Parkhead: 'Jack Reynolds came really on a seven years' old reputation. His stay was short . . .'

Willie Maley was being economical with the truth, for the conduct of Reynolds and some Celtic players was proving a source of embarrassment to the club, as this *Scottish Sport* revelation suggests: 'A woman named Sarah Byng, belonging to Birmingham, has obtained £20 damages from Reynolds, the ex-Aston Villa–Celtic half-back, for loss of services through the seduction of her daughter. It transpired in the evidence that Reynolds had been betting on horses and losing heavily along with two other prominent Celtic players.' (12 August 1898) Little wonder that Willie Maley would soon be given the opportunity to put his call for a youth policy into practice.

The transition was far from painless. Even the Scottish Cup had stubbornly refused to provide much consolation. Indeed, in 1901 and 1902, Edinburgh sides dealt an unexpected double blow to Celtic's aspirations. Despite a gallant fightback to draw level with Hearts in the 1901 final at Ibrox, Celtic succumbed by 4–3 when keeper Dan McArthur, one of the finest of the club's early goalkeepers but rather shaky on the day, fumbled a Bobby Walker shot and Bell dashed in to net the winner. A year later Celtic failed to profit from the final being played at Parkhead as a consequence of the Ibrox disaster, and fell to another late goal when McGeachan took advantage of slack marking at a corner-kick to give Hibernian a 1–0 win.

Willie Maley gave vent to his frustration when he complained how, all through 1902–3, 'our team showed a lamentable lack of brain and finish'. Such performances were providing ammunition for Maley's contention that the only way forward for the club lay in getting younger players: 'Get them straight from the junior ranks, gather them in unripe, and find out for oneself by nursing, training and coaching whether they are likely to succeed or not.' During the early 1900s he had patiently begun to assemble the nucleus of an outstanding Celtic team, a process which had the active support of his directors. James Kelly and Michael Dunbar, respected as former players and now directors, often turned up at training sessions to dispense practical advice, and assisted the manager in selecting the team.

Few among the critics were taking much notice as a procession of promising youngsters headed towards Celtic Park. The modest Jimmy Quinn from Smithston Albion arrived in 1901, despite his protestations that he was not good enough for the senior game; Alec Bennett and Jimmy McMenemy, inseparable members of Rutherglen Glencairn's inside-forward trio (which included a one-armed inside-left in Albert Underwood) joined in 1902–3.

But everybody had to pay attention after 16 April 1904, when the present (third) Hampden Park hosted its first Scottish Cup final.* Rangers went into an early two-goal lead as Speedie took advantage of some disarray in Celtic's defence. The younger Celtic side fought back furiously, their pace and aggression gradually wearing down an ageing opposition after

---

*This was the first national final in which Celtic wore their famous green and white hoops. It seems somebody at Parkhead took a fancy to the strip after seeing it worn by the Glasgow junior club, St Anthony's.

full-backs McLeod and Orr steadied themselves to get the measure of Rangers' sprightly wingers, Walker and Smith. The crowd of 65,000 could only marvel at the perseverance and strength which enabled Quinn to bring Celtic level before the interval with unsaveable shots, his first goal rounding off a solo run.

Celtic pressed continuously throughout the second half, and Quinn accomplished the rare feat of a hat-trick in a Scottish Cup final with another thrilling goal ten minutes from time. Challenged strongly by Drummond and Smith, Rangers' redoubtable full-backs, Quinn staggered and stumbled, but dragged the ball clear of the defenders; as Watson left his goal, Quinn somehow straightened himself up and struck the ball past the keeper. Jimmy Quinn later described his third goal as 'a dash right through the Rangers defence and finishing with a real trimmer which brought us our first Scottish badges and the confidence which made our team for the next six years'.

The legend of Jimmy Quinn had begun. His courage, his physical commitment and pace, his shooting power: combined, these attributes would make him the most feared centre in British football. Destined to be the most prominent figure in a glorious epoch for the club, his likeness would be painted in bright colours on five-foot-square cloth banners, embroidered with cord of golden thread and displayed with pride by the brake clubs *en route* to matches. Ironically, Celtic's hero, despite his fire and passion, was a quiet man who detested the partisanship involved in football, and the Old Firm rivalry in particular.

The club was on the verge of reaping the reward for its organisation on sound principles, most notably the Board's backing of their manager's policy of building a side rich in promise – and for an outlay of only £200, paid largely to junior clubs. This side was starting to blossom into the first outstanding team in the history of Scottish football. Off the field, things were going equally well, for some members of the Board confined themselves to fostering the business side of the club, a notable testimony to their financial shrewdness coming as early as 1898 when one of them, James Grant, had a palatial stand built on the London Road side of the ground and contracted with the club to operate it as a matter of private enterprise. Grant took a percentage of the admission money as a means of recouping his investment. This two-tiered structure, the first of its kind in Britain, had impressive features including padded tip-up seats. Unfortunately, a couple of drawbacks were to affect its popularity in the long run. Its glass-fronted design (to protect the paying customer from rain) had made little allowance for condensation and the windows misted up, thus obscuring the view. Some people also complained that the stairs leading to the seats were too high or steep.

On 9 May 1904 a fire broke out and damaged the pavilion and stand on the opposite side of the ground, amid suspicion of arson; the mainly wooden structure, capable of seating 3,500, was razed, although the pavilion was capable of repair. In view of the drawbacks already detected in the 'Grant Stand', the owner was only too happy to sell it to the club in their predicament. The site of the burnt-out stand was converted into a large barn-like structure (destined to become known after the Second World War, because of its then advanced state of dilapidation and neglect, as 'The Jungle').

The fire was not an ill omen, since fate dealt Celtic a better hand in the season to come. Good fortune tinged the club's first triumph in the league championship since 1898. In 1904–5 Celtic and Rangers finished level in points after the schedule of 26 games. Neither goal-average nor goal-difference was an accepted method of deciding a tie in points at that time – a lucky break for Celtic, since Rangers' goal record was much superior (83–28, as against 68–31). A play-off match was arranged for Hampden Park on 6 May 1905 to determine the title race. After another close, hard-fought battle, Celtic won 2–1 with goals from Hamilton and McMenemy. In view of the controversy surrounding other Old Firm clashes that season – most notably after a Scottish Cup tie at Parkhead had to be abandoned following Jimmy Quinn's tussle with Craig and subsequent ordering-off – the football authorities had taken the unusual step of importing an English referee (Mr F. Kirkham of Preston) to take charge of the match.

Celtic were developing into an outstanding side, a judicious blend of youth and experience, capable of taking on all-comers. The emphasis may have been on teamwork but the squad contained several outstanding individual performers. Davie Adams was a tall and hefty keeper who managed to retain his concentration despite his wry complaints that he got cold doing nothing behind such a sound defence. His claim was backed by his contemporary, Jimmy Brownlie (a Scottish international keeper and once a Celtic trialist): 'About the only thing Davie got to do for years was to take an occasional bye-kick or pick up a loose ball.' At full-back Donald McLeod, sturdy, small and pacy enough to keep close tabs on opposing wingers, was partnered by the side's veteran, Willie Orr, picked up 'for a song' from Preston North End but an 'out-and-out footballer blessed with sound judgement'. The half-back line of Young, Loney and Hay was outstanding: 'Sunny Jim' Young, a lanky but rugged Ayrshireman picked up from Bristol Rovers, used his height advantage to rise above attackers to head the ball away, and he tackled with speed and determination, anchoring himself beside centre-half Willie Loney, an unshowy but highly effective pivot, who was so hard in the tackle and broad-shouldered that he was described as 'a brick wall to centre-forwards'; completing the trio was

Jimmy Hay, signed 'as a discard from Glossop' but who developed into the side's captain, leading by example. Broad-shouldered and deep-chested, Hay was a strong tackler who, despite a small stature and heavy build that made him appear slow, proved also to be a natural player with subtle skills and an uncanny sense of anticipation. Displaying his versatility and astonishing coolness in defence whenever required was Alec McNair, signed from Stenhousemuir in 1904 as 'a handyman' despite being a self-confessed 'thorough Rangers supporter and staunch Light Blue'. While Rangers were dithering about signing him as an outside-left, Celtic stepped in and pinched him. He would develop into a tackler of unerring judgement who invariably thwarted opponents by – in the words of one awed observer – his 'satanic power of being everywhere at once'.

Two other smallish men formed the right wing: Alec Bennett, a winger who could centre the ball with accuracy after touchline trickery, was also a forward with a powerful shot who averaged a goal every three games for Celtic; his partner was Jimmy McMenemy, the classic Scottish inside-forward, a clever dribbler and a supreme playmaker whose sense of strategy earned him the nickname 'Napoleon'. The left wing of this famous forward line was almost a carbon copy of the right, with Peter Somers, a 'will o' the wisp' inside-left providing the sorcery; he could avoid rough-and-tumble challenges to slide through a pass that opened up any defence. Somers was a perfectionist and forever critical of any player with deficient ball control; he caustically claimed of some players that 'if you were to tie the ball to their feet, they would tramp on the lace and break it'. It was claimed that he could assess his wing partner Davie Hamilton's speed to a yard, despatching a pass to him in the certain knowledge that 'The Dancer' would gather the ball, get it under control instantly, and flight over a dangerous cross.

The main burden of goalscoring lay on the broad shoulders of Jimmy Quinn who mowed down defences with powerful dashes through the backs, and whose shots came from every angle, leaving his foot 'with the speed of a rifle bullet'. At Quinn's peak, the England-based *Daily Mail* was forced to acknowledge his stature after his contributions to Scotland's 2–0 win over England at Hampden Park: 'In Quinn they have undoubtedly the finest centre in the four countries – strong, resolute and dashing, sometimes opening the game up for his wings and on other occasions going right through himself, but nearly always doing the best thing possible under the circumstances.' (4 April 1910)

On the field Quinn was totally oblivious to everything except the match; off the field he was quiet and shy, known in his early days at Parkhead as 'Jamie the Silent'. Throughout his career he was so self-effacing that he shunned most forms of post-match celebrations. As one of his

Brother Walfrid

Tom Maley

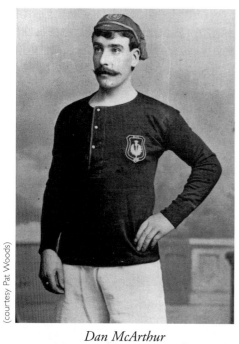

Dan McArthur

Dan Doyle

Bobby Hogg, Willie Buchan and Frank Murphy, stars of the 1930s

The changing face of Paradise. TOP: *Celtic Park, 1900: note the pavilion (extreme left),*
the Grant Stand (right) and the cycling track; MIDDLE: *the Jungle, 1930s; and*
BOTTOM: *the modernised stadium as seen from Janefield Cemetery*

J MC MENEMY

COPYRIGHT
INTERNATIONALISTS

A BENNET

*A famous wing partnership in the juniors with Rutherglen Glencairn
and later with Celtic*

RIGHT: *Raking in the money: a comment on Celtic's financial health* (Scottish Sport, *24 August 1900*)

ABOVE: The Baillie's *view of a 1–1 Glasgow Cup tie between the Old Firm (19 October 1898);* INSET: *an advert dating from August 1896*

W. MALEY, SEC'Y. W. McSTEY. P. SHEVLIN. H. HILLEY M'T. WHITE, CHAIRMAN

P. WILSON. J. McSTEY. J. MACFARLANE. A. McLEAN.

The CELTIC
FOOTBALL CLUB
CUP-TIE AND
LEAGUE TEAM

SCOTTISH CUP WINNERS.
1921-25.
RECORD HOLDERS
WON THE SCOTTISH CUP
ELEVEN TIMES.

P. CONNOLLY. P. GALLACHER. J. McGRORY. A. THOMSON.

(courtesy Pat Woods)

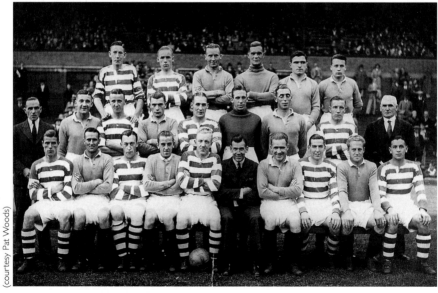

(courtesy Pat Woods)

Rangers and Celtic teams line up for Jimmy McGrory's testimonial, August 1934.
Alan Morton and Jimmy Quinn are linesmen; McGrory is in the front row,
wearing a suit

John Thomson, 'Prince of Goalkeepers', c.1930

*Jimmy McStay leads out Celtic; Alec Thomson and Jimmy McGrory follow the leader,
1933–34*

*Celtic with the Coronation Cup, 1953. Bobby Evans holds the trophy while Jock Stein
(on his left) looks on in delight at his first major triumph as Celtic's captain*

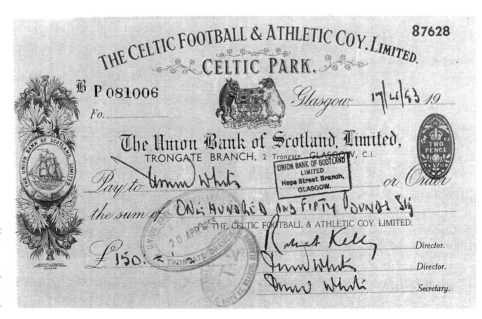

'A family business'

Celtic and Newcastle United, Scottish and English Cup-winners, meet in a 3–3 thriller at Parkhead, 1951. Ronnie Simpson is in goal for Newcastle

Action in a Celtic v Clyde match of December 1946. Seton Airlie, Gerry McAloon, Bobby Evans and Tommy Kiernan are the Celts

Scenes from the 1931 tour to America. LEFT: *William 'Peter' McGonagle, Bertie Thomson and Charlie Napier;* RIGHT: *Trainer Will Quinn and manager Willie Maley discuss tactics aboard the liner* Caledonia (courtesy Tom Grant, Celtic FC)

The Celtic party of 1951 on board ship heading for America. Charlie Tully is at the extreme left; Joe Baillie (standing fourth from left) seems to be auditioning for a part as a gangster (courtesy Frank Glencross)

The 1954 Scottish Cup final: Sean Fallon scores Celtic's winner against Aberdeen

The 1957 League Cup final: Neil Mochan lashes home a shot from a narrow angle past Niven as Celtic rout Rangers 7-1

The 1965 Scottish Cup final: Billy McNeill heads the winning goal against Dunfermline

The 1965 League Cup final: John Hughes sends the Rangers keeper the wrong way to score the first of his two penalties in Celtic's 2–1 win

Celebrating the first league title of the Stein era: McNeill, Johnstone, Lennox, Murdoch, Jimmy Steel, Craig, Clark and Neil Mochan, May 1966

Keeping an eye on the goalkeeper: Jock Stein in charge, July 1971

The pride of Glasgow, May 1967

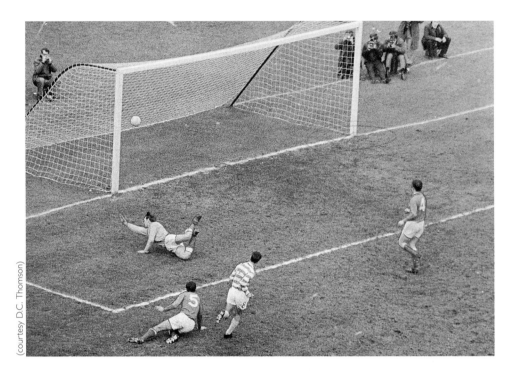

The 1969 Scottish Cup final: Steve Chalmers rubs it in with the last goal in a 4–0 rout of Rangers

George Connelly (third from left) shocks Leeds United with his first-minute goal at Elland Road, European Cup semi-final, April 1970

closest friends, Tom Bute of Kirkintilloch, revealed to a newspaper in June 1914: 'No man has the slightest idea of what Quinn has to endure in a match. The moment a game is over he makes instant tracks for home, and for hours his bruised legs are steeped to the knees in hot water.'

The bare statistics of the squad which would go on to win six championships in a row between 1905 and 1910 do scant justice to a remarkable accomplishment, but they are worth considering: 136 wins and only 23 defeats in 192 matches, and 444 goals scored for the loss of only 153. A constant theme in the press was that, no matter how much praise could be lavished on the team's superlative play, the major credit for the success was due to 'the magnificent judgement shown in the management of the club. Having found a steady, if not brilliant, eleven the Celtic executive have adhered to that eleven, providing always against contingencies by the acquisition of capable reserves, and their perseverance and judgement has this season and last met with the reward the policy deserved. Every member of the present epoch-making eleven can be termed a Parkhead-trained man. No one was gifted with a gilt-edged reputation when acquired; all were fledglings with football in them if the proper means and patience were taken to bring the ability to the surface . . . Celtic players have done well by the club, but it must not be overlooked that the players have been heartened and nursed as they would nowhere else have been.' (*Glasgow Herald*: 27 April 1908) The praise was universal: 'In the matter of management Celtic are considered in Scotland as a pattern to the world.' Thus averred Robert Livingstone, a contributor to Gibson and Pickford's authoritative *Association Football and the Men Who Made It*, published in 1906.

In 1907 Celtic accomplished a unique feat when they became the first club to complete the 'double' of Scottish Cup and league championship. Hearts, the holders of the Scottish Cup, survived Celtic's relentless pressure in the first half of the final thanks only to Allan's inspired goalkeeping. But they had to bow to the inevitable after 55 minutes when Willie Orr converted a disputed penalty for Celtic and two goals shortly afterwards from Peter Somers ended any prospect of further defiance from the Edinburgh side. Both Somers' goals indicated that Jimmy Quinn was more than 'bone-and-muscle': Hearts' defenders closed in on him as he prepared to finish off a move engineered by Bennett and McMenemy, but the centre saw this and neatly dummied the final cross for Somers to score. The second goal was almost a replica, with defenders drawn to Quinn like a magnet, and leaving Somers free to net easily. Overall, it was the display of a side which was stamping its authority on the native game in incontrovertible fashion.

A year later, Celtic retained the Scottish Cup. St Mirren, appearing in their first national final, were little more than lambs to the slaughter, offering scant resistance as Celtic romped to a 5–1 rout. The hapless Saints, whose captain McAvoy won the toss but elected to give Celtic the advantage of the wind, seemed to have approached the contest with the enthusiasm of condemned men awaiting the executioner. Further disheartened by some questionable refereeing, they were simply overrun. Quinn, by most accounts, was clearly offside when netting Celtic's decisive second goal midway through the first half, and the favourites rubbed salt in their opponents' wounds with three more goals after the interval. Alec Bennett, shortly to leave the club for Rangers amid allegations of tapping, scored twice: one goal was a clever individual effort, while the other represented quick thinking on his part when he took full advantage of a collision between Quinn and McAvoy. Jimmy Hay, Celtic's captain, was a model of diplomacy when asked to comment on this most one-sided of finals: 'I thought it was a good game . . .'

One week later, on 25 April 1908, Bennett's ingenuity was again to the fore when Celtic ended Falkirk's challenge for the championship by winning against Rangers at Ibrox to secure the title. In this Old Firm clash Celtic's prospects had looked bleak when Quinn and McMenemy both picked up injuries in the first half; in fact, Quinn had to hobble on the right wing for most of the 90 minutes. Bennett capitalised on an opening just before the interval, however, when he wriggled past Sharp to shoot firmly past the advancing Newbigging for the only goal of the game.

For the second successive season, Celtic had won the hitherto elusive double. Indeed, for the first time in their history, Celtic had won every competition open to them, annexing also the Glasgow Cup and the Charity Cup during that memorable 1907–8 season.

Frustratingly, Celtic were to be thwarted in their bid to achieve the double for the third year in a row – even if the 'failure' was hardly the fault of the players. Once more the Old Firm faced each other in a Scottish Cup final on 10 April 1909, this time before a record crowd of 70,000. With eight minutes left, and Celtic behind by 2–1, Dan Munro, a recruit from the Highlands and briefly Bennett's successor on Celtic's right wing, sent over a cross-cum-shot and Rennie, Rangers' goalkeeper, was perhaps over-stylish in clutching the ball rather than punching it clear; he appeared to step over his goal-line as Quinn rushed in to take advantage of any slip. The referee, J.B. Stark (Airdrie), had a perfect view of the incident, as some Rangers' players sportingly admitted; he immediately awarded a goal on the basis that the keeper had carried the ball over his line.

The match ended in a 2–2 draw, but in the interval between the first game and the replay, the seeds were sown for mayhem on a massive scale. A huge crowd (60,000) watched another draw, this time 1–1, and the trouble started when the referee blew his whistle for time with a number of players, mostly in Celtic jerseys, lingering on the field as if awaiting extra-time to start. Like thousands on the terracings, they may have been misled by a statement by Willie Maley a few days earlier in the *Daily Mail and Record* that the clubs might be seeking this method of settling the final in the event of another draw.

Those players made their way to the pavilion only after a significant delay during which (according to Jimmy Quinn in his weekly newspaper column) 'the referee had no instructions and he cleared off'. Having seen the players milling around before eventually moving towards the pavilion, a large number of spectators grew suspicious of some sort of arrangement; feeling cheated, they surged on to the pitch in their anger. The police moved quickly to halt the encroachment, and the violence escalated. Hundreds then poured on to the pitch, Celtic and Rangers supporters alike, combined in 'an orgy of destruction' which lasted for more than two hours.

The vastly outnumbered police contingent, unable to cope with the invasion at first, had to send for reinforcements. The rioters attacked and pulled down the barricading, gathered the broken pieces and set them ablaze on the track and (so it was reported) fuelled the flames with whisky. The mob set the pay-boxes on fire, uprooted the goalposts and slashed the nets. In short, the authorities were subjected to 'the most inhuman savagery that mortal mind can conceive'. The rioters attacked the police with stones and cinders, they cut the hoses of the fire brigade; they also abused the hapless ambulance men . . .

Inside the dressing-rooms, away from the ugly scenes developing so quickly, players of both sides were ordered by the police superintendent to dress immediately and to leave in their brakes by 'a sort of back way', according to Jimmy Quinn. Outside, the violence continued unabated, and before the mob left the vicinity of Hampden Park many among them marched through the main gate 'brandishing their improvised weapons, smashing windows behind which householders huddled in terror, and breaking every street lamp they saw'.

Public opinion was horrified, and the London-based *Pall Mall Gazette* blasted the hooliganism: 'Saturday's display of savagery shows what a mockery it is to drag the word [sportsmanship] into such an atmosphere. The football craze is one of the most active deleterious influences to which the character of the masses is now subjected, and we cannot too soon set about counteracting it with the wholesome discipline of military training.' (19 April 1909)

No one in the SFA had taken any notice when the *Scottish Referee*, disturbed by the fans' suspicions of 'put-up jobs' in Old Firm Cup matches which required replays, had suggested back in October 1907 that extra-time be played in future replayed finals between the pair. Predictably, nobody in officialdom accepted any responsibility for the Hampden riot.

In the aftermath of the débâcle the clubs (and the SFA) confined their action to 'abandoning the tie', the Scottish Cup being withheld for that season. The SFA contributed £500 to compensate Queen's Park for the damage to the ground, and ordered the clubs to cough up a further £150 each. Given the revenue generated by the final and the replay, these fines were negligible. Indeed, Celtic's players were paid a bonus as if they had won the trophy, since the directors believed that 'they had been unlucky not to win'.

Celtic overcame their disappointment in an impressively professional manner by duly completing their marvellous run in the league championship with a sixth successive title. The finale of the 1908–9 season showed a typical reservoir of character on the players' part – and commendable concentration; to win the flag Celtic had to complete eight fixtures within the space of 12 days and pick up 12 points. Perhaps they really were made of sterner stuff in those days.

But the club was finding that such pronounced supremacy had its financial drawbacks. As 'Man in the Know' later recalled: 'As the Celtic team, unchanged season after season, marched on from victory to victory, the public actually became satiated with the never-ending chapter of Celtic successes. The gates began to dwindle and we were presented with the astonishing spectacle of the world's best football team playing their home games before a beggarly array of empty benches.' (*Glasgow Observer*: 16 July 1927)

That Celtic team from 1904 to 1910 was an outstanding one, a squad of such excellence that in the midst of their dominance the *Glasgow Star and Examiner* of 6 April 1907 reported that Celtic were rumoured to be on the verge of applying to join the Football League (in England). Their accomplishments were surpassed only by Jock Stein's squad more than half a century later. Every great team has to be judged on its complete record, and Celtic's in that period was an impressive one: three Scottish Cup triumphs in seven years, two Charity Cups and five Glasgow Cups. The magnificent league record, with six successive championships, was their crowning accomplishment.

Celtic's marvellous success, though, had been achieved on such a tight, if remarkably talented and resilient, squad that the passage of time would take an inevitable toll. Age and injury started to affect the side, and the transfer of influential players did nothing to stop the decline. In addition to the moves of Alec Bennett to Rangers in 1908 and Peter Somers to Hamilton in 1910, the team's inspirational captain, Jimmy Hay, unable to agree terms, was transferred to Newcastle United in 1911. Celtic made a handsome profit on the deal, receiving £1,250 for a player who had cost only £50 from Glossop nine years earlier.

The problems were made worse by the decision not to field a reserve side, the directorate preferring to operate with a small nucleus of players. The flaws of such a policy had been highlighted by the need to borrow players in emergencies when the cover was inadequate; the most notable example was the loan from Rangers of goalkeeper Tom Sinclair to replace Davie Adams, who had sustained a hand injury at Ibrox in August 1906. The Rangers reserve performed well during his six-week stint at Parkhead, playing in an undefeated side and picking up a Glasgow Cup medal.

Even in the midst of the great league run, Tom Maley (the ex-Celtic player and former manager of Manchester City) had taken the club to task in print in his capacity as a journalist for the lack of proper cover around the same time as the financial statement for 1906–7 revealed that less than 25 per cent of Celtic's income was spent on players' wages and transfers, and that nearly £4,000 remained as a bank balance. This sum had been amassed steadily on the strength of one in-built advantage, as the correspondent of the *Glasgow Observer* noted: 'The Celts never lack generously abundant support' describing it as 'the enormous patronage bestowed on the Celtic "specials" [trains] which conveyed thousands of the club's supporters to such provincial centres as Greenock, Airdrie, Motherwell, Dundee and Port Glasgow'. (19 May 1906) Even with that fervour tailing off, as Celtic's domination threatened to become permanent, the same newspaper could still claim that the club's balance-sheet in 1909 represented 'best value for almost minimum expenditure, and the profit at maximum figure almost'. These figures allowed the payment of a 25 per cent dividend, while the directors trumpeted that £2,200 had been donated to charity since the club had been incorporated as a limited liability company. Given the sum quoted – and considering that 12 years had passed – it was scarcely a justifiably proud boast.

In 1910–11 the defence appeared as solid as ever, but the forwards found it increasingly hard to score consistently. After 15 league matches Celtic had given up nine goals – the lowest total in the league – but the forwards had netted only a miserable 19. The talk centred on bad luck, but it was clear that the vital spark had gone from Celtic's play. The tight matches, won in the past by a late effort, were now slipping away despite the players' valiant endeavours; experience was no longer enough, and the team tumbled from first place down to fifth within the season. When the team suddenly started to look its age, the signs of decay showed.

Nothing could halt such a decline except changes in the line-up and an injection of new blood. Into the team in December 1911 came a most remarkable inside-forward. Young Patsy Gallacher did not resemble an athlete; 'a slight lad with pencil-thin legs' was one typical description. Willie Maley was honest enough to admit later to a journalist that his initial impression of the signing from Clydebank Juniors was not favourable, but he took a chance on the youngster because 'there was strength in his seeming frailness; extraordinary skill in his work with the ball; no handicap in his smallness; rich promise in all that he did'.

The Celtic fans took Gallacher to their hearts immediately, chortling in delight as the slim boy tricked opponents, bamboozling them with his array of dribbling skills. Still, the directors at Parkhead were so dubious of Gallacher's worth, despite his impressive early appearances, that he was not a regular in the side until a knee injury sidelined Paddy Travers in March 1912. McMenemy was moved smoothly over to the inside-left position, allowing Gallacher to be slotted in at the inside-right berth where he quickly demonstrated that he could be neither intimidated nor overawed by any occasion. An admirer on the terracing was once heard to cry out: 'If that ball is ever struck by lightning, Paddy Gallacher will be killed – for he's never off it!'

Andy McAtee from Mossend Hibs later proved to be the solution to Alec Bennett's defection; a strong dribbler, he came with an immensely powerful shot derived from legs made more powerful, like Quinn's, from his mining background. The task of replacing the dependable Loney was given in the end to Peter Johnstone, a Fifer from Glencraig Celtic who had been filling other positions satisfactorily when called upon.

The search continued for a suitable replacement for Quinn; until one was found, Celtic would remain in transition – although they won successive Scottish Cups before emerging with another dynasty to dominate Scotland, starting in 1914. Despite struggling through their worst championship campaign in years, Celtic won the Scottish Cup in 1911 by beating Hamilton Academical 2–0 after a replay at Ibrox Park. The more stylish Celts could not find their form on a bumpy pitch and against determined opposition, and settled for a 0–0 draw. Celtic's greater class showed eventually in the replay. Two goals in the second half – a blistering shot by Quinn after 60 minutes and an equally emphatic finish by centre-half Tom McAteer, yet another product of the coalfields, just before the whistle – brought the Cup to Parkhead for the seventh time, and that without conceding a goal in the competition.

A year later, on 6 April 1912, Celtic faced their neighbours Clyde, again at Ibrox, before a crowd estimated at 50,000. In this final, Clyde put up a stiff resistance but Celtic were in a mood to punish the slightest error. After 30 minutes McMenemy found himself in the clear following a free-kick taken by McNair, and slotted the ball past Grant with his customary coolness. With 20 minutes left Patsy Gallacher, playing in his first final, reacted more quickly than the Clyde defence when he nipped in to connect with a cross from Andy McAtee on the right wing to complete the scoring at 2–0.

Celtic were now marshalling their forces in another bid to regain the summit of Scottish football, and with a side built on a formidable defence.

An outstanding replacement for Adams in goal was secured with the capture of Charlie Shaw from Queen's Park Rangers in May 1913. At 5 foot 6 inches Shaw was far from tall, but he was solidly built and a lively keeper; during his 12 seasons at Parkhead this utterly dependable custodian was to earn shut-outs in more than half his appearances but, remarkably, was never capped at full international level for Scotland. His manager, while granting his steadiness, nevertheless said that his goalkeeper took risks 'which would scare a tamer of wild elephants'.

Shaw formed an admirable partnership with his full-backs, the imperturbable Alec McNair and the more adventurous Joe Dodds, described admiringly in one match report as 'eleven and a half stones of bone and muscle', a physique which contributed to a presence so commanding that goalkeepers playing behind him rarely had to come out for a cross ball.

According to Willie Maley, this triangle introduced a new tactic into Scottish football: 'Shaw, McNair and Dodds understood one another so well that they developed the pass-back into a scientific move of which there have been many imitators but none to equal the originators. It was, indeed, a spectacle to see either McNair or Dodds passing, with unerring accuracy and cheeky coolness, the ball to Shaw two yards away, with the opposing forwards almost on top of them. That was their method of getting out of a corner, which in all probability would otherwise have been fatal.' (*Weekly News*: 25 July 1936)

'Sunny Jim' Young, the veteran right-half and captain, remained as durable as ever; tough and tenacious in the tackle, this ungainly but effective player had turned out to be a magnificent servant for the club. Peter Johnstone, a wholehearted trier signed as the successor to Peter Somers at inside-left, had been converted into a sound centre-half, imbued with a 'they-shall-not-pass' outlook. And Willie Maley enhanced his growing reputation for effective experimentation by changing Johnny McMaster, an unflappable pivot in junior football, into a left-half eminently capable of filling the boots of Jimmy Hay by playing with comparable authority and consistency. This splendidly rugged trio made 'a great stonewall mid-line', the bulwark of a defence which conceded only 14 goals in 38 league matches in season 1913–14, as Celtic carved out the club's third League and Scottish Cup double.

Up front, Andy McAtee's directness and power on the right wing, when allied to Patsy Gallacher's trickery and cantrips, meant headaches for opposing defences. The left wing was a combination of the continuing wiliness of Jimmy McMenemy, pulling the strings with a football brain and positional sense second to none, and the stocky, hard-running Johnny Browning, a winger with a pronounced flair for goalscoring, especially with his left foot.

The only thing missing was a proper successor to the great Quinn, now showing the ravages of his rumbustious style of play – although the old war-horse remained a threat to any defence to the last with his ability to shoot hard with either foot from any position, making it almost impossible for goalkeepers to anticipate his actions. An account of his second-last appearance in a Celtic jersey (against Hamilton Academical in a 3–1 victory) noted that 'he scored a goal on one leg with one of his positional shots which looked simple but gave the goalkeeper no chance'. After his bad knee finally gave way, he was forced to retire in January 1915. The importance of Jimmy Quinn to the Celtic sides of that era could never be exaggerated; upon Quinn's death in 1945, Willie Maley paid tribute to him as 'the keystone in the greatest team the Celtic ever had'. (*Evening Times*: 24 November 1945)

As season 1913–14 proceeded, the search for a replacement was on in earnest. Ebenezer Owers, a Londoner acquired from Clyde during the winter, ruled himself out of contention with a wretched performance in the Scottish Cup final against Hibs at Ibrox in April 1914, missing several clear chances and earning scathing comments from one reporter as 'scampering all over the place, doing nothing, yet threatening to do something big every minute'.

Then, as if to order, a more likely candidate to replace Jimmy Quinn on the field duly appeared. For the replay, held at the same ground on the following Thursday, Owers was replaced by Jimmy McColl, a small, alert forward who did his best work in the penalty area. His quick reactions helped him to snap up two chances within the first 11 minutes and allowed Celtic to settle down comfortably for a 4–1 victory, with Browning adding two more goals in the second half.

The winners' ability to overwhelm opponents at will, emphasised by the ruthless finishing which routed Third Lanark 6–0 in the Charity Cup final a few weeks later, carried ominous overtones for the rest of Scottish football. Celtic seemed certain for another prolonged spell at the top, and their self-belief was underlined by the phlegmatic Jimmy Quinn's comments; shrugging off the winning of yet another double, he observed that 'events had worked out as we had meant at Parkhead'.

These triumphs underpinned Celtic's status in British football; in the view of Lord Kinnaird, the FA President, only Aston Villa could challenge them for the title of the best-run club in the game. In those years, just prior to the First World War, Celtic's prestige was at its zenith. The club remained in great demand on the Continent. From Scandinavia in the north to Hungary in the east, the club's players shrugged off long journeys by train and boat, blisters and bruises sustained on hard pitches under a hot sun, and the frustrations of contentious refereeing to spread the football gospel.

Jimmy Quinn freely acknowledged on behalf of his team-mates the contribution made by the personal enthusiasm and practical knowledge of Willie Maley and his directors, factors which had been central to Celtic's success. He stated that on such continental tours the officials took part in every sing-song and gathering, never attempting to draw an artificial line between themselves and the players. Unlikely as it may sound to modern ears, apparently the players offered to do without their weekly wage in order to make the club's first continental trip, to Vienna in 1904, where Celtic were to play two matches for a guarantee of only £150. That offer on the players' part spoke volumes for the harmony and mutual respect between the directors and the players. In fact, during the tour of Scandinavia in 1912 the manager and directors refused to participate in 'officials only' dinners much to the consternation of their hosts; the result was that invitations were extended to the players.

It was appropriate that the club's five continental tours between 1904 and 1914 had a touch of the imperial mission about them, corresponding to the power and prestige of Britain in that era. Indeed, on crossing from Kiel to Korsar in 1907 on a journey to Denmark, the Celtic party struck up 'The Mariners of England' (!) on leaving the German port. Michael Dunbar, a Celtic director, claimed that it was 'just to show Der Kaiser's subjects that we feared no foe'.

After one appearance in Budapest in 1911 a local newspaper went into raptures about 'the new insight into association football' provided by the Scots: 'Celtic's passing was close and masterly, and they showed football of a kind never before seen.' Unknowingly, that Celtic side was sowing the seeds of future greatness* – in much the same way that a noted former centre-forward was doing in Prague. Johnny Madden spent over three decades in Czechoslovakia (from 1905 to 1938), spreading the gospel of Celtic's short-passing game as coach of SK Slavia. He was so revered in

---

* The Hungarians had absorbed their lessons so well that on a wintry afternoon at Wembley Stadium in 1953 their national side destroyed the myth of English invincibility with a stunning 6–3 scoreline. Among the fascinated spectators was a Celtic party which included centre-half Jock Stein. Later, as a manager, he always maintained that his Celtic sides were modelled on the fluid, attacking style of those 'magical Magyars'.

Prague that he conducted his sessions from a wheelchair in the latter years, before retiring at the age of 73.

The last of the pre-war European tours followed the victory in the Charity Cup in 1914. The continental press were ecstatic about the Celtic close passing and control, the *Berliner Tageblatt* hailing the Scottish 'meisters' as 'the finest team in the world' after the visitors had so demoralised the local Hertha that, late in the game, their players were flatly refusing to go into the tackle for fear of humiliation. Sadly, the guns of August 1914 were to shatter the illusions that football could transcend international relations.

Significantly, the respect that Celtic had earned on the Continent meant that the club was ideally placed to act as a force for reconciliation once the war had ceased. Despite some government opposition and criticism in the press, Celtic became the first British club to tour Germany after the Great War. Indeed, Max Brandl, an official of BFC Preussen, travelled specially to Glasgow to invite Celtic to play a match against a local select in Berlin in May 1922. The German football magazine *Kicker* was prompted to hail the visitors in its report of the 1–1 draw as 'the first swallows of peace' and to delight in the statesmanlike observation of one Celtic official that 'the war is over and it is against the character of the British people to express feelings of political revenge through a boycott in sports'. (7 June 1922)*

On a more parochial level, the Great War was the source of considerable dislocation to Scottish football. The sport could carry on only as the result of a series of adjustments: players not in the services having to seek employment in munitions industries and fixtures being arranged for Saturdays and public holidays only to give but a couple of examples. The Scottish Cup competition was abandoned for the duration but the League decided to soldier on, obviously agreeing with one journalist who insisted, rather patronisingly, that football contributed to civilian morale by 'helping our artisans to do good work during the week by giving them something to look forward to on a Saturday'. The cynics pointed to an element of calculation on the part of the War Office, who had allowed football to carry on in order to boost output; as one commentator put it, football was 'a means of assisting workers to put in overtime and double time in shipyards and munition works'.

The ultra-patriotic, of course, never could understand why fit young athletes should not flock to the colours. Lord Derby, for example, when

---

* Ironically, a boycott of sorts was initiated 46 years later by Celtic's chairman Bob Kelly when Celtic objected to playing against the Hungarian side Ferencvaros after the invasion of Czechoslovakia by the member nations of the Warsaw Pact. On that occasion UEFA was forced to redraw the first round of the European Cup.

presenting the only wartime FA Cup to Sheffield United in April 1915, spoke feelingly: 'It is now the duty of everyone to join with each other and play a sterner game for England.' A few months earlier, the secretary of an unidentified Glasgow club had received anonymously through the mail a bundle of white feathers – the symbol of cowardice. Willie Maley could be excused such an accusation. As a soldier's son, he had volunteered his services but was turned down on the grounds of age – to his fierce indignation.

Maley, in his mid-40s during the war years, was at the height of his powers as a manager, although chafing at being rejected for military service. He had served the club for more than quarter of a century as player, secretary and manager. At the time of his silver anniversary with Celtic in 1913, he had been given a handsome honorarium of 300 guineas, and a contributor to the *Glasgow Observer* in March 1914 praised his part in Celtic's history: 'Willie Maley must of necessity top the poll as the most illustrious of Scotland's sons. Is he not the maker of the world's finest football machine – the super-splendid, unstoppable Celtic?'

Celtic's domination of the Scottish game spilled over into wartime, and gave rise to some unworthy speculation about their commitment to the war effort. In truth, the club 'did its bit', in the parlance of the times. Peter Johnstone, called up in May 1916, made the ultimate sacrifice – killed in action with the Argyll and Sutherland Highlanders at the Arras front in France, reportedly while tending a wounded comrade. Johnstone, according to Patsy Gallacher writing in his weekly newspaper column shortly after the fatality, had always hankered after soldiering; he had been restrained from joining up at the start of the war only by the fact that he was a married man with a family. Gallacher recalled that Johnstone in a visit to Celtic Park in March 1917, just before leaving for France, had told his team-mates that 'he was out to do his bit, and hoped, if he had to go under, he would have the satisfaction of knocking over a German or two before that happened'.

During the bitter and prolonged conflict Willie Maley's eldest son was seriously wounded in France, and one of the manager's nephews was killed in action there.

Shortly after the outbreak of hostilities, Celtic director John Shaughnessy accepted command with the rank of colonel of the Glasgow Citizen Training Force, an organisation set up 'to afford military training to all suitable citizens who desire to obtain that without military enlistment'. (*Glasgow Observer*: 24 October 1914)

Players such as Patsy Gallacher who worked in the shipyards, Joe Dodds in munitions work at Beardmore's, and Andy McAtee and Peter Johnstone (before their call-up) in the coal-mines, were engaged in vital war work. Indeed, the *Weekly Mail and Record* in April 1917 noted that Andy McAtee had worked a shift in the pit before travelling to Glasgow for a league match. One incensed Celtic supporter, 'anxious about the good name of his club', wrote to the *Scottish Weekly News* in April 1916 to complain about the paper's omission of military designations of two Celtic players from the team line-ups in match reports; he wanted proper recognition of Lance-Corporal Joe Cassidy (Scottish Horse Regiment), known as 'Trooper Joe' to the fans, and of the Pioneer status of centre-forward Joe O'Kane of the Royal Engineers, both centre-forwards.

Elsewhere, the manager was thanked by the Scottish Fusiliers Association for the kindness he had shown to wounded soldiers at Stobhill Hospital in Glasgow. In addition, Willie Maley sent footballs to army recruits in training and to soldiers at the Front on behalf of the club. Appeals were made at half-time during matches at Parkhead and at the annual Celtic Sports meetings, asking for recruits to enlist for military service. The Celtic Sports of 1916, for example, staged a reconstruction of trench warfare (including bombs made of canvas and clay) in order to bring the fighting in France and Flanders 'right before the eyes of the people at home'. (*Weekly Mail and Record*: 12 August 1916)

Celtic made a significant financial contribution to war relief funds, initially those for Belgian refugees, by playing, as champions, matches at Hampden Park in 1915, 1916 and 1917 against the Rest (of the League) before crowds averaging over 40,000. When Jocky Simpson of Falkirk scored the only goal of the 1916 encounter, a great cheer went up at Hampden; 'John O' Groats' of the *Weekly Mail and Record* considered the crowd's reaction as a tribute to Celtic: 'The Rest had accomplished what individual clubs had been striving to do.'

Patsy Gallacher was speaking for most at Parkhead when he took a more jaundiced view of the true feelings of those who did not follow Celtic, speaking bitterly after the reception accorded Celtic at the five-a-side competition at Rangers Sports: 'If a team of Huns [Germans] opposed Celtic at Ibrox Park the crowd that "goosed" us on Saturday would cheer our deadly enemies.' (*Weekly Mail and Record*: 12 August 1916)

Like his team-mates, the club's officials and supporters, he might have expected some reflected lustre to shine on the club after Willie Angus, a lance-corporal of the 8th Lanark Battalion Highland Light Infantry, was awarded the Victoria Cross for rescuing his commanding officer from no-man's-land under heavy bomb attack and rifle fire in the trench warfare near Givenchy in France. The hero, who sustained severe wounds and lost the sight of an eye in the incident, received his VC from the King at Buckingham Palace in August 1915. Angus, who had been on Celtic's books before the war, was given a tremendous ovation a month later when he attended a Glasgow Cup semi-final tie at Celtic Park.

The club would make less welcome headlines when Patsy Gallacher was fined by the Glasgow Munitions Tribunal in November 1916 for 'bad timekeeping' in his wartime employment as a ship's carpenter in Clydebank. This punishment was followed by the Scottish League imposing on him the first-ever suspension in its history – from 19 December 1916 till 27 January 1917, a period of six weeks. Some saw in the punishment the familiar 'Celtic-baiting line', as Gallacher himself described it. The incident hardened the suspicions of the club and its supporters that the press coverage was calculated to 'expose their flank to the heavy artillery of their foes' in the midst of another league campaign.

In reality, Celtic's record – at that point – of 16 matches undefeated (for the loss of only four points) suggested they would carry on in their winning way, given the quality and experience of the other members of the squad. In fact, Celtic swept the board that season, retaining the league title, the Glasgow and the Charity Cup and lost only one fixture out of a total of 42 matches; that defeat, in a meaningless game against Kilmarnock, ended an 18-month undefeated league run encompassing 62 matches – still a Scottish record to this day.

Celtic's regulars were a hardy breed, having developed the ingrained habit of putting in that little bit extra when the team was handicapped in any way. In 1915–16, for example, Celtic had used only 16 players (fewer than any other club) to see it through 38 league fixtures, and won the championship in a canter, nobody offering any opposition and Rangers finishing up a distant second. Indeed, Celtic were able to ease fixture congestion by offering to play two matches on the same day in order to complete the schedule on time. Mid-week football had been ruled out by an agreement between the War Office and the football authorities which stated that matches must not interfere with essential war work. So, on 15 April 1916, Celtic lined up at 3.15 p.m. against Raith Rovers at Parkhead (a 6–0 victory, highlighted by three goals from Patsy Gallacher). Immediately after the match, they travelled to Fir Park to face Motherwell for a fixture postponed a few weeks earlier because of heavy snow. Celtic made only one change, Cassidy replacing O'Kane at centre-forward, and finished up comfortable winners by 3–1 (although in fairness it should be noted that Motherwell had also played earlier that day, losing 3–0 to Ayr United at Fir Park).

So pronounced was the club's dominance that the *Glasgow Observer* of 25 March 1916 reported that some bookmakers were leaving Celtic out of their coupons and that others were treating them as the home side in places such as Paisley, Falkirk and Motherwell to discourage the betting on them. In this era such gambling was more prevalent in the West of Scotland than in any other part of Britain. The resulting temptations were considerable, inducing Celtic to seek an investigation of attempts to bribe Scottish players (including an abortive approach to Willie McStay, a Celtic defender). The problem would not go away: in 1924 two former Old Firm players were sentenced to 60 days' hard labour for such offences. Ex-Celt Johnny Browning and ex-Ranger Archie 'Punch' Kyle (once a provisional Celtic signing) were jailed for attempting to induce a Bo'ness player 'to fail to exercise his skill' in a match against Lochgelly United.

By winning their 13th league championship in 1916, Celtic had gained as many titles as the rest of the other First Division clubs in Scotland put together. They were producing a standard of excellence which prompted a writer in *The Bulletin* to laud Celtic as 'the most consistently successful and best-managed professional club the game has ever seen'. (19 May 1917)

'John O' Groats' of the *Weekly Mail and Record* put the situation succinctly after Third Lanark had dealt a fatal blow to Celtic's hopes of a fifth successive championship: 'No greater honour could be paid the Celtic than the desire of other clubs to beat them. The sensation of beating the Celtic is a sensation unequalled by victory over any other club, and thus it is that the Parkhead team finds greater effort put forward against them by opposing clubs than is generated at any other time . . . They go all out to win all the time, and no club does more to keep alive the interest in our greatest sport.' Nevertheless, the writer went on to articulate a widespread concern about Celtic's supremacy; he added that he did not believe that Celtic regretted 'an occasional reverse after the first pang was over' since 'monopoly in football, or anything else, is not for the general good'. (30 March 1918)

Celtic's wartime record was an exceptional one: champions from 1915 to 1917 (extending their run to four in a row), winners of the Glasgow Cup in 1915 and 1916, and winners of the Charity Cup from 1915 to 1918 (completing a sequence of seven triumphs in succession) – and, with the wartime abandonment of the Scottish Cup, the two local competitions assumed greater importance. The record earned the club an anomalous position, however: grudging admiration for its prowess and fighting spirit, but envy and resentment at its seeming invincibility. 'Man in the Know', ever eager to employ military metaphor during the Great War, reminded his readers: 'Whether we like it or not, Celtic teams are like German armies, more feared than loved, respected in a fashion because they have such a winning way with them.' (*Glasgow Observer*. 9 March 1918)

While these high standards were being set, one underlying truth was being virtually ignored or overlooked by Celtic FC and its followers: it was all too good to last . . .

FOUR

The Pure Wine of Soccer

1916–35

It was only as the Great War drew to a close that Rangers, who had been chafing under Celtic's domination, finally emerged from their rival's shadow. The manner of their breakthrough in the championship, however, drew a sharp rebuke from 'Man in the Know' of the *Glasgow Observer*, a notorious partisan where matters Celtic were concerned and undoubtedly echoing the Parkhead club's point of view. The correspondent characterised the new flag-winners as 'the piebald champions', alleging that Rangers had won the title by abusing the Scottish League's 'temporary loan' rule, introduced in the wartime conditions to permit players to move more freely. With customary venom, he had dubbed the Rangers side fielded against Celtic in the Glasgow Cup semi-final on 22 September 1917 as 'a nine-club affair', and ascribed the Ibrox men's 3–0 win to the efforts of Rangers' 'variety troupe'.

Always happier to take the moral high ground where Celtic were concerned, the writer was wont at this period to wax lyrical on his favourite theme, namely that 'to build up is the Parkhead motto, to buy up is the Ibrox way of doing business'. From then on, though – and particularly in the interwar years – no doubt existed about which philosophy prevailed. Rangers' recruitment drive to win the championship in 1917–18 reached a triumphant climax on the very last day of the season; Celtic were edged out by one point as a result of being held to a 1–1 draw by Motherwell at Parkhead, the Lanarkshire men hanging on despite ferocious pressure in the closing stages. Some of the more superstitious fans may have had twinges of anxiety beforehand: that afternoon, the last day of the season and 13 April, Celtic dropped their thirteenth point of the campaign and surrendered the title.

The loss of key players proved too much to overcome, notably the absence of Johnny McMaster (serving in the military) and the long-serving Sunny Jim Young (who had damaged a knee so severely in September 1916 that he never played again). Another recurring problem was at centre-forward where Jimmy McColl ran into fitness problems of the type that elicited the sympathy of one commentator who described McColl as 'an unfortunate player', adding that the centre had 'got as many kicks as ha'pence since he joined the senior ranks'. McColl had barely been restored to the side after an operation for appendicitis in November 1917 before a twisted knee sustained in a 3–1 defeat at home by Third Lanark on 23 March 1918 put him out of action for the rest of the season. It proved a doubly unfortunate day for Celtic as Rangers drew level on points in the race for the championship just when the flag appeared Parkhead-bound again, and McColl took a long time to regain his fitness and confidence.

The consolation for Celtic that season came late. On 4 May 1918 the team gained the Navy and Army War Fund Shield by beating Morton 1–0 through Gallacher's goal, described as 'a delightful piece of forward play', in front of 20,000 at Hampden. The 'trophy' was presented to Celtic 'in spirit' as the silverware was not fully ready; in fact, it remains doubtful if the club ever did receive any silverware for the competition, designed to aid wartime relief funds for servicemen and their dependents. Later in the month came the annual lifting of the Charity Cup; in winning their seventh in a row, Celtic defeated Partick Thistle 2–0 in the final, Gallacher and Browning scoring.

Celtic struck back in the following championship in spite of Rangers' embarrassment of riches. According to 'Man in the Know', Celtic 'had often to fix up a team from eight or nine sound players and a few cripples', while Rangers 'week after week had to choose between ten forwards for five places'. For all Celtic's problems with the non-availability of players for various reasons, that writer exulted in the fact that 'long before Andy [McAtee] came back from the Italian front, some time before Joe Dodds gave over gunning the Germans, a Celtic eleven of a kind got into the way of winning league matches'. (*Glasgow Observer:* 17 May 1919) The colum-nist seemed to be doubling as a war correspondent, both home and away.

Ironically, the sheer depth of the Ibrox squad helped Celtic wrest back the title from their rivals. Scott Duncan, a pre-war signing for Rangers, had been experiencing difficulties in getting into the Ibrox line-up, and he turned out in two fixtures for Celtic. At that stage in the season, early in the New Year, the two clubs were in close contention, and Duncan helped

Celtic notch up successive victories over Third Lanark and Clydebank. The winger had utilised the wartime rule, still in operation two months after the Armistice had been signed, that 'a soldier player' could play two games for another team without asking permission from the club which held his signature. His contribution helped keep Celtic on track for a run of 20 league matches without defeat stretching from mid-December 1918 to the end of the season. 'Man in the Know' could not resist gloating at Celtic's coup in obtaining Duncan's services; mischievously, he ascribed it to a desire on the player's part 'to gratify a wish to be inside a green-and-white jersey once or twice in a lifetime'. (*Glasgow Observer:* 18 January 1919) At the season's end, after Celtic had pipped Rangers for the title by a single point to gain the championship, he exulted in the achievement: 'I cannot find anything to surpass the performance of the haphazard collection which brought the fifteenth championship flag to Parkhead.'

The difference between the youth policy of Celtic and the free-spending of Rangers was underlined at the start of 1919–20 with Celtic's fielding of the teenage Tommy McInally at centre-forward despite reservations about his slight build being able to cope with the rough-and-tumble of the highly physical Scottish game. These fears proved to be unfounded as the youngster from St Anthony's netted a hat-trick against Clydebank at Parkhead on the opening day, and scored twice against Dumbarton two days later at the same venue. Although McInally was to show that he took few things in life seriously – least of all, football – the youngster turned out to be a deadly marksman in his début season, ending up as top scorer with 38 goals in all competitions. With Jimmy McColl struggling to regain form after his illness, McInally's contribution was invaluable; Celtic's confidence in him was such that McColl was transferred to Stoke City in May 1920.

McInally's displays, however, were not enough to prevent the title returning to Ibrox in what had developed into a tit-for-tat struggle for supremacy in the immediate post-war seasons. This time the race was not the close-run thing of the two previous seasons, although controversy played a part – a reflection of the growing intensity of the rivalry, and the feeling of Celtic and their supporters that the club was the victim of prejudice and bigotry. 'The "journalistic experts", or at least nine-tenths of them, are frankly Light Blue and unashamedly partisan,' claimed the *Dundee Catholic Herald* correspondent in October 1920.

Celtic's suspicions that everybody's hand was against them may have been reinforced when Dundee came to Parkhead on 26 April earlier that year for a fixture that the home side had to win to keep in contention for the championship. The match ended in ignominy. The visitors were barracked before the kick-off for 'lying down' in a recent defeat by 6–1 at

Ibrox, and they were unscrupulous in their tackling at Parkhead. The combination of these factors built up such anger and tension in the crowd that the match was abandoned ten minutes from time after hooligans invaded the pitch following a heated clash between Adam McLean, a lightweight winger introduced by Celtic during wartime, and Rawlings of Dundee. Two Dundee players were assaulted by the invaders, and one of them (Raitt) was carried into the pavilion nearly unconscious; the referee also came in for physical abuse. An enquiry into the affair decided that the score (1–1) should stand as the final result, and that Celtic Park should be closed to regular football until 31 August 1920 as 'a deterrent to rowdyism'. Inevitably, the Celtic fans ascribed that verdict to malign influences within Scottish football and society.

During that 1920 close season, significant developments took place, events which shaped the course of Scottish football for much of the interwar period. Bill Struth, Rangers' trainer, took over as manager after the tragic death of William Wilton in a drowning accident near Gourock. Although he had never played professional football, Struth knew the value of fitness, hardness and determination from his days as an athlete. He recognised that Rangers needed toughening up, incredible as it may sound to modern ears, because the club had a reputation for unreliability, being considered a team always liable to break down when apparently set for the major honours; harsher critics accused them of possessing 'a yellow streak'. A martinet, Struth would stress the pride in the club that has characterised most Rangers players since. Everything about the club had to be first-class, including rail travel and seats in cinemas, while a strict dress-code in public was rigidly enforced. In addition, he recognised the need for an entertaining, direct player to keep the crowds flocking to Ibrox; accordingly, in June, he signed the Queen's Park winger Alan Morton, renowned for his superb ball control and an ability to cross the ball at speed.

That same month, Celtic – in direct contrast – gave a free transfer to Jimmy McMenemy, an outstanding inside-forward at Parkhead since 1902. Perhaps McMenemy was past his best, but he still had a lot of football left, as Partick Thistle discovered when he led them to their only Scottish Cup final success a year later. The abrupt release of the player, on the grounds of 'irreconcilable differences' between him and the Board, heightened the speculation that all was not well at Celtic Park. That impression was confirmed by one journalist who was startled by the fearsome sight of Patsy Gallacher emerging from the ground in a foul temper after a stormy interview with Willie Maley over re-signing terms. Unlike McMenemy, the bold Patsy – who really was indispensable – got his way eventually. On and off the field Patsy Gallacher was more than capable of taking care of himself.

For various reasons Celtic and Rangers have long appealed to the public imagination in a way that no other Scottish club does, but there was a keener edge to their meetings in the 1920s, a response perhaps to expectations heightened and appetites whetted by the grim war years. One commentator, John Allan, would later recall that peace brought 'a resurgence of enthusiasm that carried over the country like a fever. The homecoming soldiers and the entire population, seeking the spectacle of football, the colour and romance of the game as a whole, surged back to the game. The desire to see their team win became a passion. Grounds were crammed.'

A crowd of 80,500 had witnessed the Scottish Cup quarter-final at Ibrox in March 1920, won 1–0 by Rangers – a massive boost to the coffers of both clubs. Celtic's prosperity was reported to be 'at floodtide' after a record profit on 1919–20 of £8,275, as the team's efforts to contain a Rangers surge to the title had caused an increase in their own support, which was becoming notably strong in away fixtures. More than a hundred charabancs (a motorised form of transport which had overtaken the horse-drawn brakes) travelled through to Dundee for a league match, won 2–1 by Celtic, in October 1920. The bonds with the Ould Country may have been fraying with the drop in immigration and increasing assimilation into Scottish society, but the *Glasgow Observer* noted that most of these supporters stayed overnight in the Jute City on the Saturday night, lodging in 'various Irish halls'.

In the fierce struggle for supremacy, one which had been becoming more and more lucrative since the cessation of global hostilities, 1920–21 was a pivotal season, the defining one as it were. The momentum had been moving to Ibrox little by little, and the ten-point margin in the league table at the season's end between the sides was suddenly significant. It reflected, as one critic claimed, 'spineless displays' by Celtic which had made Rangers 'a confident, cocksure league force'. The ground was being tilled for the Ibrox club's hegemony of the 1920s and '30s.

In one last, defiant gesture before Rangers took an iron grip on the championship, Celtic hit back in 1921–22 to win their sixteenth title. It had seemed hopeless when Rangers dug in – 'putting down sandbags' as one report had it – for a 0–0 draw at Parkhead on 2 January 1922 which left them three points clear at the top. Celtic's overtaking of that lead owed much to their defensive strength, comprising the old brigade of Shaw, McNair and Dodds and a sheet-anchor in Willie Cringan, the centre-half and captain. The rearguard proved so compact that its near-inviolability at Parkhead earned it the somewhat sacrilegious nickname of 'The Holy City'. Cringan was far from artistic but he had been the epitome of consistency and reliability since joining the club from Sunderland in September 1917; during wartime, the latter club had closed down, and he had played regularly for Celtic. His purchase, for a fee of £600, caused a mild stir among those observers who regarded Celtic as a club which signed juniors and juveniles for token fees only.

Up front, Patsy Gallacher, now a spindly-legged and crouched veteran, still put in a power of work for the team while not neglecting the entertainment that the Celtic fans craved and lapped up. His 'hesitation-stops' were a particular delight, as opposing players were reluctant to be embarrassed by Patsy when he halted in midfield, placing one foot on the ball and inviting opponents to approach and challenge him. Helping to take the weight off him in the football sense was the sprightly Adam McLean, signed in 1917 as a centre-forward from the juvenile side Anderston Thornbank; he was fielded on the left wing where he gained a reputation as an immaculate crosser of the ball.

In a tension-ridden, last-day finish to the league race, Celtic had to secure a draw at Cappielow against a Morton side who had only recently defeated Rangers in the Scottish Cup final. Trouble broke out at Greenock before and during the match, watched by a record crowd of 23,500 with thousands locked outside. The Celtic legions poured into Greenock, blowing bugles, showing their colours and waving Sinn Fein banners expressly forbidden by the local police who were only too aware of the potentially violent religious division which had hardened in Scotland since the Easter Rising of 1916 in Dublin. During the interval, fighting broke out on the terracings and spilled on to the pitch. After the match, the Celtic fans had to run the gauntlet as they hurried back to their brakes, charabancs and special trains; stones, bricks and rivets (the preferred missiles in a shipbuilding town) were hurled back and forth. Sinn Fein banners 'lost' in the skirmishing were set ablaze by triumphant locals.

On the field, Celtic, although badly outplayed in the first half, fought back courageously; with only a few minutes remaining, and following sustained pressure, Morton's keeper Edwards appeared indecisive with a cross ball and Andy McAtee scrambled an equaliser, a goal that secured the championship for Celtic.

When critics stated that the introduction of automatic promotion and relegation that season – a move advocated by Celtic for years – was necessary to reduce the now perennial apathy outwith the supporters of the Old Firm as the season drew to a close, a mood induced by the Old Firm's monopoly, they were only recognising a basic truth. Scottish football had become the battlefield for Celtic and Rangers, but the early 1920s mark a significant shift in the balance of power. Some would argue convincingly that the gap opening up between the clubs was not closed until Jock Stein took over as Celtic's manager four decades later, and made Celtic a club capable of competing consistently on all fronts. The period between the World Wars was marked by the overwhelming supremacy of Rangers, notably in the league championship. It was a period when Celtic lowered their expectations.

The close season of 1922 brought a fateful decision, and the directors had clearly not thought out the implications. The Board decided to dispense with a reserve team, withdrawing from the recently formed Alliance League, apparently on economic grounds. The predictable outcome was to handicap the club by closing down an assembly-line of young players into the first team and undermining the implanting of the club's playing standards at a time when Rangers were going from strength to strength and determined to remain on top. According to Bob McPhail, the famous international who joined the Ibrox club in 1927, Rangers now 'demanded the best and were prepared to pay for it'; Celtic appeared to settle for a 'balance-the-books' mentality.

A few years earlier, Celtic's captive columnist, 'Man in the Know', writing in the *Glasgow Observer* on 6 April 1918, had hinted at the Parkhead outlook when he referred to 'the astute Celtic director' who had pointed out that 'the sixpence of an individual who pays to see the boys go down goes as far towards keeping up the club as the contribution of the most ardent supporter'. Celtic's chairman Tom White would graphically illustrate the attitude of those in charge at this period by his exultant comments upon Celtic's reaching the Scottish Cup semi-final in 1928: 'We're going to make some money from the Cup after all. Let's reach the final now and I'll be completely satisfied – and let the Cup go where it may!' (*Daily Mail and Record*: 5 March 1928) At times, money seemed more important than football glory.

Celtic's parsimonious approach manifested itself most starkly in the shabby treatment of players; disputes concerning basic wages and bonuses, signing-on fees and testimonials became a disturbing feature of the 1920s and '30s for Celtic followers. When the dressing-room was seething with discontent early in 1923–24 following a wage cut, Willie Cringan, the captain, took it upon himself to approach the Board in the person of Tom White to voice the players' concerns. The footballers wanted a bonus of a pound per point won in league matches, and considered it a reasonable request; the directors, in dismissing it peremptorily, described it as 'a demand'. A most unhappy side took the field and lost 2–1 to Partick Thistle, who had never previously defeated Celtic in the league. Cringan, their spokesman, was transferred to Third Lanark within a matter of weeks.

The club could point to the effect that the harsh economic climate was having on attendances. The bedrock of their support was the Catholic community which suffered more than most in those recessionary times as an appalled correspondent from the London-based *Spectator* magazine noted in 1924 thousands of families, their appearance 'stamped and distorted by their miseries', endured a 'life of abjection and squalor for which Glasgow is famous'. The situation was exacerbated by the rampant sectarianism which disfigured the period. 'No Catholics need apply' and 'No Irish wanted here' were sentiments not unknown in the filling of the few vacancies that turned up in the job-market; and, in any interview, the simple question 'What school did you go to?' carried an unusual importance. Many years later, for example, the historian of the Savings Bank of Glasgow would admit that 'until the First World War the staff was entirely male and, until the Second World War, protestant in religious denomination'. Several decades would pass before the members of the Catholic and Irish community could shake off their self-perception of being an under-class; and it would take their football team's greatest era to help their descendants feel truly part of Scottish society.

Rangers FC, which had not been totally exclusive in its recruiting policy prior to the First World War, closed ranks as their religious apartheid proved immensely profitable at the turnstiles in an era of poisonous bigotry. 'Ivanhoe', writing in the *Weekly Record* in August 1927, remarked how, even at five-a-side matches at sports meetings, spectators watched 'beautiful play by the Green and Whites in stony silence, but let a goal be scored against Celtic and great is the joy thereat!'. Nevertheless, Celtic's tunnel-vision penny-pinching response to Rangers' ambition amounted to a virtual abdication of their primary responsibility to the supporters, namely to field the strongest possible side, even if this involved taking a financial risk. The unhappiness of the supporters would be a recurring theme in the letters pages of the press during this extended period of Rangers' domination. It was reckoned at one stage that the Ibrox club had 30 candidates for the 11 first-team places. 'Manhattan', an exile writing from New York, advised his favourites 'to step on the gas' and said how galling it had become 'to see Celtic's name practically every week in the newspapers in the list of defeated league clubs', and wondered, 'What are the world's champions coming to?' (*Glasgow Observer*: 24 January 1925) 'John O' Groats' was right, surely, to accuse the Board of a lack of imagination and foresight – and a basic lack of planning in the matter of team-building – in the *Weekly Record* during December 1924, as was 'Jack O' Clubs' when he remarked sarcastically that 'the Celtic do not believe in paying high fees; they believe in getting them'. (*Sunday Mail*: 29 January 1933) The nine-year period spanning those two judgements, corresponding to Rangers' most pronounced period of dominance, suggests that the Celtic board of that period were loath to make any changes that cost money or threatened dividends.

Celtic's practice of continuing without the back-up of a reserve team meant that the club competed with a squad of no more than a dozen players, plugging the gaps by introducing youngsters from juvenile or junior sides when regulars were injured. It also meant that some promising players were farmed out to senior clubs to gain experience. Clydebank – the first club of that name – was a noted Celtic nursery, a valuable proving-ground for the young Jimmy McGrory in 1923–24.

The disparity in resources in relation to their great rivals determined that joy for Celtic supporters would be largely confined to the celebration of Scottish Cup triumphs, starting with an all-green final with Hibernian at Hampden in March 1923, when a crowd of 80,000 saw two well-matched teams fight out a sterile contest. The only goal of the match was scored midway through the second half when the Hibs goalkeeper, Willie Harper, lost sight of a harmless lob from John 'Jean' McFarlane, a polished performer at left-half for Celtic; Joe Cassidy reacted quickly, and nodded the ball into the unguarded net.

Cassidy, the top scorer for three successive seasons in the early 1920s, was transferred to Bolton Wanderers in August 1924 for £4,000. The substantial fee appeared to be as much a consideration as the unhappiness of a player who, the manager claimed, 'wanted away'. His departure left the stage clear for a striker in the mould of Jimmy Quinn – a man tireless in pursuit of goals, courageous in battle, blessed with a modest, sunny disposition, and a player, through his efforts and accomplishments, destined for the highest place in any Celtic Hall of Fame. That heroic figure, Jimmy McGrory, first came to national prominence with his remarkable goalscoring feats in the Scottish Cup of 1925, including two goals in a 5–0 rout of Rangers in the semi-final at Hampden Park which a crowd of 101,714, the first-ever six-figure attendance at a match between Scottish teams, turned up to witness. At full-time, distressed Rangers fans were seen making bonfires of their brake clubs' banners and flags. The result – and, more particularly, the margin – had come as a totally inconceivable outcome for a press and a football public at large who had established the Ibrox men as overwhelming favourites.

Celtic faced Dundee in the final, played at Hampden Park on 11 April 1925 before 75,137 spectators, and at half-time the unfashionable outsiders led by a McLean goal, netted from a rebound from the crossbar. Dundee, a big, strong side, had started off 'as if they meant to sweep Celtic into the nearby River Clyde' but made the fatal mistake of falling back into defence after scoring, leaving only one forward upfield. In the second half Celtic pressed ferociously from the restart but, despite winning corner after corner, could not get the equaliser. Just when spectators were starting to think of a Dundee victory against the odds, a miraculous intervention from 'the Great Patsy' in the 75th minute turned things around. Even allowing for the conflicting accounts in the newspapers, they convey some flavour of the impact of Gallacher's impish magic after he brought a free-kick from his winger Connolly under control in a crowded goalmouth; the free-kick itself had been awarded after Gallacher had beaten several opponents before releasing Connolly, who was immediately fouled by Thomson. The *Dundee Advertiser* was awestruck by this 'slalom' of a goal: 'The "Mighty Atom" wriggled and pushed his way through a litter of friends and foes to stagger into the back of the net with the leather.' Match reports vary as to how Gallacher ended up entangled in the net, but most versions agree that his last leap was with the ball between his legs and involved a partial somersault. One suggests that Gallacher had brushed aside his own centre-forward Jimmy McGrory as well as opponents in his determination to score. The *Glasgow Herald* described the outcome thus: '[Gallacher] crowned a daring and devious bit of play by throwing himself bodily into the net and carrying the ball with him. It was a positive relief to a great section of the crowd, who were wrought up in an almost painful degree of excitement over the long-continued battle between the Celtic attackers and Dundee's unflinching defenders.' (13 April 1925)

Only Patsy Gallacher could have scored that goal, and the Dundee players themselves sensed that their Cup dream was now over. McGrory threw himself full-length at a McFarlane free-kick a few minutes from time, and his fierce header left Britton helpless. Celtic, with 11 triumphs in the competition, had overtaken Queen's Park and were now the record-holders. Willie McStay, solid and consistent at right-back, spoke afterwards as Celtic's captain: 'Grit did it, Celtic grit.'

Among the grit, Celtic were still unearthing some diamonds despite the lack of a reserve side in which to ground young players properly in the elements of the game. Notable among youngsters thrown in at the deep end who established themselves in the first team were Peter Wilson from Beith in Ayrshire, a smooth, unhurried right-half noted for his excellent long passing; Alec Thomson from Fife, developing into the classic fetch-and-carry Scottish inside-forward; and Paddy Connolly, the natural successor to Andy McAtee and a winger who combined with Jimmy McGrory to pose an almost unanswerable threat to defences.

For over a decade the youthful and cheerful McGrory would remain the most popular player in the side not only as a Celt with an eye for goal but also as a centre who chased every ball with enthusiasm and took on defences despite the odds against him. It was hard for those around him not to be inspired by such an attitude and example. Hugh Hilley, a full-back and McGrory's team-mate, used to walk the three or four miles daily from his home in the tough Garngad district with McGrory in the mid-1920s because neither could afford the tramcar fare to and from Celtic Park for training. Five decades later, he remained awestruck by his friend's commitment: 'Jimmy McGrory was Celtic!'

For a man of his build – relatively short but stocky – McGrory was outstanding in the air. Scottish football has had no more thrilling sight than McGrory hovering in the air to make contact with the ball, or diving bravely to head into the net. Sadly, due to the lack of film footage, the sweeping nature of Celtic's style in this period can be visualised only by listening to elderly supporters recalling from their youth the awesome sight of Paddy Connolly taking the ball out of defence and carrying it deep into enemy territory, outstripping the opposition with his sprinter's stride. The winger, an excellent striker of the ball, could cross with either foot, and most of his crosses were pulled back and aimed at the deadly head of McGrory . . . while the defenders were still turning, after trying to deal with Connolly's run.

With the welcome return of Tommy McInally in May 1925 after a three-season sojourn with Third Lanark following a dispute with Celtic over terms, everything was in place for a real challenge to Rangers in the championship. The gallus McInally assumed Patsy Gallacher's role from the inside-left position, where he acted as Celtic's general in the absence through injury of the 'Mighty Atom'. Now considered injury-prone, the veteran Patsy Gallacher was transferred to Falkirk in 1926, where he gave excellent service for several seasons. Meanwhile, during his time at Cathkin, McInally had evolved, if not matured, into an exceptional play-maker, chockful of guile and conceit. After his return to Paradise, he and Adam McLean formed a superb left wing, playing as if they could find each other blindfolded. Alec Thomson worked like a Trojan to keep his wing partner Connolly and the centre McGrory supplied. From the wing-half positions Peter Wilson and 'Jean' McFarlane controlled the ball 'in magic fashion' and fed their forwards with machine-like precision. Wilson was a particular driving force from his right-half position; a tall and stylish player, he was powerful in the tackle and renowned for the accuracy of his delivery.

Celtic, whose league performances were drawing rarely applied adjectives such as 'methodical' and 'persevering', went on to clinch their seventeenth championship with a comfortable eight-point margin over Airdrie. The provincial club were a formidable enough outfit in those days to finish as runners-up four times in a row to the Glasgow giants (once to Celtic and three times to Rangers) in the early 1920s.

It was a major accomplishment for Celtic to land the championship so convincingly, and to pick up the Charity Cup (for the twentieth time) by beating Queen's Park 2–1 at Ibrox, but the 1925–26 season ended in anticlimax with an unexpected defeat in the Scottish Cup final, the newly crowned champions falling victims to a St Mirren side they had thrashed 6–1 at Parkhead in the league a month earlier.

On 10 April 1926 at Hampden, an excellent crowd of 98,620 turned up, many of them confident of seeing Celtic land the double for the fourth time in their history. Celtic's rediscovered virtues of steadiness and reliability were not to be in evidence at the final as a stuffy St Mirren team refused to allow the Parkhead men to settle. The Paisley side took a two-goal lead after 30 minutes; the loss of both goals was blamed on the smallish stature of Peter Shevlin, otherwise a technically proficient goalkeeper. More accurately, the finger should have been pointed at the Board's policy of operating Celtic on a shoestring, because, when Adam McLean had to withdraw through injury, his place on the left was taken by a virtual unknown, Willie Leitch (who had been on loan to various clubs since joining Celtic). For all Leitch's valiant efforts to impress, the balance of the team was out of kilter and Celtic lost by 2–0; the hopes of the club's first post-war double were shattered in the shock defeat.

As they picked up the pieces the following season, Celtic could find comfort in the phenomenal scoring of Jimmy McGrory. He netted an astounding 59 goals in 41 competitive matches in 1926–27, including four goals at Brechin in the Scottish Cup. This uneasy victory, by 6–3 against a Second Division outfit, convinced Maley that the time had come for a change of goalkeepers. Shevlin was replaced by John Thomson, signed only three months earlier from Wellesley Juniors in Fife; with Celtic not fielding a reserve side, the youngster had been on loan to Ayr United, the only means of allowing him to gain experience, but he was recalled to Parkhead and made his début against Dundee at Dens Park on 12 February 1927 in a 2–1 league victory. A Celtic director, Tom Colgan, sought him out afterwards to console him for his mistake which had cost Celtic a goal, and he was startled at the matter-of-fact way in which the 18-year-old assured him it would not happen again. Young Thomson – 'The Boy Keeper' as the Celtic supporters would call him to the end – had the supreme confidence of the natural athlete.

After only two months in Celtic's goal, John Thomson was given a golden opportunity to win the most prized memento in the national game: a winner's medal in the Scottish Cup. On 16 April 1927 Celtic faced East Fife, and the Parkhead side were overwhelming favourites to thrash the Cinderella club from the Second Division in the first Scottish Cup final to be broadcast on the newfangled wireless. The *Radio Times* quaintly described the programme as 'a running commentary on the Final Tie for the Scottish Association Cup'.

The uncertainty of Cup football attracted a crowd of 79,500 to Hampden Park, including several thousands from the coal towns of the Kingdom of Fife, a region still suffering from the effects of the General Strike of 1926. The economic shockwaves were affecting footballers too, apparently, for before the match Peter Wilson was delegated by his team-mates to approach Willie Maley to find out what bonus could be expected for winning the trophy. The player was promptly sent away with the brusque rejoinder: 'A bonus to beat East Fife? Just get out there and win!'

Celtic duly did so, after overcoming an early setback when Wood headed Edgar's cross past a rather static John Thomson in only seven minutes. Celtic needed that shock to jump-start their effort; within a minute the scores were level after Connolly's low cross was diverted past the Fifers' goalkeeper by a defender. Celtic, the Cup specialists, moved ahead by 2–1 ten minutes before the interval when, in the words of the *Scotsman* correspondent, Adam McLean 'dashed in to snap a cross from Connolly to round off a delightful passing movement that had the East Fife defence completely beaten'. The agony continued for East Fife in the second half; Paddy Connolly, living up to his nickname of 'The Greyhound', sprinted clear of the opposing defence straight from the restart and 'lifted the ball over Gilfillan's head into the far corner of the net' to notch the killer goal.

Two ahead, Celtic were content to turn on the brand of silky football that had become their trademark or, as one critic of the period called it, 'the pure wine of soccer'. The writer for *The Scotsman* marvelled at the gulf in class between the sides: 'The Celtic men appeared to get through a vast amount with effortless ease, whereas East Fife were continually on the run . . . The Celtic played delightful football. From toe to toe the ball travelled with the minimum effort on the part of the players, the half-backs giving their forwards innumerable opportunities which were not turned to account.' (18 April 1927) The team could have run up a cricket score but for this failing as they coasted through the second half. Tommy McInally, fielded as centre-forward in place of the injured McGrory, was the main culprit in Celtic's failure (or reluctance) to increase the margin of victory. He exhibited an infuriating self-indulgence by shooting on sight from unlikely positions when he could have passed the ball to better-placed players; his shots soared high and wide and, unfortunately, he compounded his errors with some unacceptable clowning.

McInally's waywardness might be overlooked in a winning side, but it could no longer be tolerated when a team had to contend with the type of adversity which the club faced after a promising start to the following season, 1927–28. Celtic had a highly skilled squad, but one limited in numbers and reserve strength. Any setback to a key player, whether injury, loss of form or suspension, would affect the team's performance fatally.

Only a week after losing to Celtic in the Glasgow Cup final, Rangers bounced back to beat their main rivals 1–0 in the championship at Ibrox on 15 October 1927. That match was a landmark in the Old Firm struggle for supremacy, as Rangers finally drew level with Celtic in league matches against each other (with 24 wins apiece). This latest Rangers achievement indicated all too clearly that the balance of power had tilted in their favour.

The first chinks in the armour of Celtic's short-lived invincibility could be seen in the continuing indiscipline of Tommy McInally. After Celtic's defeat at Ibrox he was suspended by the SFA for two weeks, having been ordered off in the 60th minute; the referee, W. Bell (Motherwell), rightly objected to McInally's continuous 'narking' about Fleming's goal, disputed by Celtic, just before the interval. A few weeks later McInally was suspended by the club for not turning up to train, but he was restored to the side by the turn of the year. His waywardness – by all accounts, he was the least vicious of men – could be attributed to the player's sense of complacency induced by the absence (self-inflicted) of real competition in the squad. Almost certainly he was the Celtic player who, it was rumoured, failed to return with the official party by train after a cup-tie at Keith in February 1928. He preferred staying behind to sample the Highland hospitality – an indulgence which lasted some three days!

Throughout season 1927–28 Celtic and Rangers were locked in a head-to-head struggle for both the championship and Scottish Cup. The double campaign would reach its climax in April, when Celtic's challenge foundered. By this time McInally had again been in trouble, dropped for missing training sessions; he had been sulking because of a harmless practical joke played on him by his team-mates before an important Scottish Cup tie at Motherwell in early March 1928. The board not only suspended McInally 'for breach of training rules and disobedience' (according to Maley's terse press release), but hinted strongly that the player would never again represent the club. A month later, however, he was restored to the team, apparently because his replacement, Frank Doyle, had not proved effective. Although no points were dropped during that absence – and the team continued to make progress in the Scottish Cup – damage had been done to the morale of the squad.

A crisis duly materialised on 7 April, only one week before the Cup final against Rangers, when Motherwell defeated Celtic 3–1 in a fixture at Fir Park. The loss of two vital points at such a critical stage was bad enough but the worst aspect for Celtic was the injury to William 'Peter' McGonagle, the regular left-back. That most dependable and intimidating of defenders (forbiddingly nicknamed 'The Hooded Menace') was sidelined with a knee injury that later required surgery. Another defeat, sustained two days later at Airdrie, meant that the race for the league flag was now over for Celtic.

Rangers, although burdened by the cumulative memory of repeated failures to win the Scottish Cup during the previous quarter of a century, were determined to take full advantage of the left-back's absence at Hampden on 14 April 1928 – and to end the music-hall jokes in Glasgow. One comedian, George West, had perfected the routine of bounding on to the stage at the Princess Theatre brandishing a replica of the Cup. After gazing at it, he would intone: 'Aye, this is a real antique, a' right. The last name on it is Rangers.' Much depended on the strong-running Sandy Archibald, regarded by Maley beforehand as the most potent threat in Rangers' star-studded forward line. Ominously, from the start, he looked in the mood to roast John Donoghue, deputising for McGonagle. It took a brilliant diving save from Hamilton in the Rangers goal to settle the Ibrox nerves as Celtic raged into early attacks with a strong wind behind them. The massive crowd of 118,115 (the largest officially validated attendance at a club match anywhere in the world at the time) was starting to sense that the first goal would be crucial – and so it proved.

Ten minutes after the interval, following sustained pressure on Celtic's goal, Rangers were awarded a penalty-kick when Celtic's skipper, Willie McStay, had to punch clear a scoring shot from the line. Davie Meiklejohn, the rival captain, insisted on taking the kick – a brave decision on his part. Few of his team-mates could even bear to watch as, amid the hushed silence within Hampden, he approached the ball and drove it firmly past Thomson.

The chains dropped from Rangers; their drive was unstoppable. In 68 minutes McPhail added a second from close range, and Archibald, now running freely on the right wing, scored two more with glorious drives. The hoodoo had been ended in the most decisive manner. Long before the final whistle Celtic had been reduced to a pale imitation of the side that had challenged so long for the double. In the dressing-room afterwards, though, the Rangers players agreed, almost to a man, that Celtic would have won if Meiklejohn had missed from the penalty spot.

The reaction from the Celtic executive was not long in coming. Even Willie Maley, who always had a soft spot for Tommy McInally, had had enough of the player's frivolous misuse of a natural talent. He was transferred once again, this time to Sunderland for £2,500. He was joined a few months later at the Wearside club by his long-time wing partner, Adam McLean, a veteran of almost 12 years with Celtic. A winger considered by Jimmy McGrory to be superior to the great Alan Morton, McLean was almost irreplaceable; and once again the quarrel was over financial terms.

Celtic let it be known that other players were available for purchase, apparently out of a need to raise capital (despite a profit of £2,700 on season 1927–28) to help finance a replacement for the Grant Stand, now in a poor state of repair. The new stand, costing a hefty £35,000, was designed by the Glasgow firm Duncan & Kerr and seated around 5,000 with an enclosure below for standing spectators; the structure would be hanselled on the opening day of the 1929–30 season, with Celtic beating Hearts 2–1.

Incredible though it seems from this distance, the board wished to part with Jimmy McGrory, a move akin to selling the Crown Jewels. For years, English clubs had been interested in the game's most prolific scorer, but McGrory, Celtic-daft from his earliest days, never gave a moment's thought to moving. In the season just completed he had yet again compiled impressive figures: 47 league goals, seven in the Scottish Cup, and another nine in the Glasgow Cup. Maley, however, was instructed by his directors to complete the transfer to Arsenal for what would have been a British record fee; rumour had it that the London club had offered a blank cheque. The player, preparing for a holiday and pilgrimage to Lourdes with his manager and Tommy McInally (who called off after his transfer), was not told about the situation. When McGrory and Maley arrived in London on their way to France, they were met by Arsenal's famous and highly persuasive manager Herbert Chapman; once more, in London on the return journey, they were greeted by Chapman, who again tried every ploy to capture McGrory for Arsenal, without success.

The player would continue to be Celtic's main scoring threat, always marked closely and tackled fiercely; despite the covering, Celtic looked to him to chase every ball, and often he was required to turn out when not completely fit. This utter dependence on their most noted forward was another by-product of Celtic's lack of reserve power, a crucial factor in the failure to win a national trophy over the next two seasons, and so complete their worst spell at that level since the early years of the century.

Apart from McGrory's goalscoring and his lung-bursting exertions, Celtic fans could take some solace in the stylish goalkeeping of John Thomson, a most gallant keeper, who was, however, risking injury too frequently for his own good with daring saves. At that time players wore boots with reinforced toe-caps, and physical protection for goalkeepers was limited. In successive matches in December 1929 he would be concussed as a consequence of his brave – some might say reckless – goalkeeping. At Kilmarnock he dived at the feet of a forward to save a certain goal, and at Tynecastle a week later he clashed with Hearts' inside-right, Chalmers. After this latter incident, he wanted to carry on but the Celtic trainer insisted on hauling him off for medical attention. In the league defeat by

Airdrie at Parkhead shortly afterwards (on 5 February 1930) he was to sustain a broken jaw, a double fracture of the collar bone, the loss of two teeth and a broken rib. Willie Maley complained bitterly that Thomson had been kicked while on the ground and blamed the referee for failing to take action over the incident which sidelined the goalkeeper for seven weeks. After that horrific series of injuries, his brother Jim tried to persuade the young keeper not to be so daring . . .

The gloom over Parkhead began to lighten in May 1930 when the board at last recognised the error of its ways by reinstating a reserve team in the Alliance League. Given the directors' notorious reluctance to take such a step, the move represented a victory for public opinion. 'Ivanhoe' of the *Weekly Record* had reported two years previously that, while many Celtic followers wanted a reserve XI, particularly at a time when low wages and unemployment limited travel to first-team away fixtures, the majority of the club's officials would entertain the proposition only if assured or guaranteed that 'the patronage was liberal enough'. Their obstinacy, if not outright parsimony, was all the more foolish in football terms in view of the report in the *Glasgow Observer* of 28 May 1927 that 'Celtic were quite snug and comfy' with assets of £23,217 – and would be rendered even more absurd with their subsequent profits of £2,070 (1927–28), £5,221 (1928–29), £3,500 (1929–30) despite Rangers' clean sweep that season, and 'a very handsome £5,000' (1930–31).

Despite this encouraging sign, Celtic were not yet ready to loosen Rangers' grip on the championship, although in season 1930–31 they came very close to stopping a fifth successive flag for Ibrox, ending up only two points adrift at the top. The supporters could, however, take satisfaction at the resumption of winning ways in the competition which had brought the club to the fore, the Scottish Cup. With Jimmy McGrory running into rampant form in his favourite competition, Celtic were looking forward with some confidence to the final on 11 April 1931 against Motherwell, a clash anticipated with relish throughout the country. Celtic, clearly emerging from the doldrums, had produced a fine young team bolstered by the ferociously determined Peter McGonagle at left-back, and captain Jimmy McStay, a sturdy tackler and intelligent positional player at centre-half, while the masterly passer Peter Wilson at right-half was still highly influential, his stylishness complemented by left-half Chic Geatons. The manager showed his shrewdness by deploying Geatons' great physical strength to the fullest: the left-half (originally a full-back) was given a defensive remit, but Maley recognised the Fifer's constructive abilities and did not curtail his attacking instincts. Despite the demands of the role, Geatons' strength and fitness enabled him to finish a match full of running.

Motherwell, so often Rangers' only real challengers in that era, were a classic side, popular and respected throughout the country for an attractive, free-flowing style, and a strict no-transfers policy which saw the club repeatedly spurn tempting offers for their players despite having to exist on relatively low gates. With only 20 minutes played, Motherwell were two goals up and, apparently, set for their first-ever triumph in the Scottish Cup. Both goals, shots by Stevenson in six minutes and John McMenemy (the ex-Celt and son of the great Jimmy) in the twentieth, were deflected past a nervous-looking Thomson in Celtic's goal. Celtic forced themselves back into the match, but still had to keep one eye on the ever-dangerous left-wing partnership of Stevenson and Ferrier, and the menacing McFadyen at centre-forward.

Ten minutes from time, with the Cup surely bound for Motherwell, a group of Lanarkshire fans in the crowd of 104,803 started to leave the stadium, eager to return home early by train and acclaim the conquering heroes' arrival in Motherwell with the trophy. There was no live radio coverage of this final, and the population of the Lanarkshire coalfields had been alerted to an impending victory by means of racing pigeons released by jubilant supporters at Hampden Park, and kept informed by bulletins posted up in the office windows of the local newspaper in Motherwell. The editor of the *Glasgow Evening Times* at last gave the go-ahead for the release of the sports edition, its headlines proclaiming Motherwell's triumph. It was said that, behind the scenes, the Scottish Cup was being fitted with ribbons in Motherwell's colours of claret and amber, and that the Celtic directors were already offering their congratulations to their Motherwell counterparts.

On the field, as the minutes ticked away, Celtic still pressed desperately, and Motherwell's defenders were now kicking the ball anywhere out of danger, and giving away an ominous number of free-kicks near their penalty area. With seven minutes to play, Craig, their centre-half, stopped a promising Celtic raid by handling the ball; this time Celtic's clever young left-winger Charlie Napier – known as 'Happy Feet' because of his skill and control – lofted the ball over the Motherwell wall, and Jimmy McGrory half-lunged, half-slid to divert the ball past goalkeeper McClory. The scorer retrieved the ball from the net, spurning congratulations, and dashed upfield with it in order to get the match restarted as quickly as possible. He pointed to the clock on the old Hampden Stand, a gesture that indicated there was still time for Celtic to recover.

His defiance was not lost on the Celtic supporters, massed behind the goal on the King's Park terracing, who shouted themselves hoarse as they rallied behind their team which continued its furious onslaught on the

Motherwell defence, which was now reeling. With seconds left, Motherwell looked like surviving, if only barely, as John Thomson gathered a long ball and prepared to clear downfield; he aimed his clearance in the direction of Bertie Thomson on the right wing. The winger, pacy and often unorthodox, brought it under control smartly, and raced towards the corner flag where he shook off the challenge of Hunter before whipping over a cross into the penalty area. The cross was a swirling in-swinger, bound to trouble Alan Craig, Motherwell's powerful pivot ever wary of the lurking McGrory behind him; too much so, because in a lunging attempt to head it anywhere clear of danger, Craig sent the ball spinning viciously past his own keeper and high into the net.

Celtic were saved! Momentary disbelief on the faces of Celtic supporters – and then sheer bedlam, as suggested by one vivid account: 'Tammies, scarves and banners were flying in the air and, as the final whistle ended the drama, a Parkhead enthusiast was jumping in the air and coming down and breaking a leg that was not his own . . . all the joy in the world was on Bertie Thomson's face as his colleagues threw him to the ground, drowning, smothering him in congratulations.'

The conventional wisdom in those days was that no team ever got a second chance against Celtic in a Scottish Cup replay, and it still held true on the following Wednesday. Motherwell, apparently demoralised, seemed resigned to their fate and went down by 4–2; the men who had rescued Celtic on the Saturday, Bertie Thomson and Jimmy McGrory, each scored twice.

The victory was all the more sweet for the dramatic, fairytale ending to the first match and it meant that Celtic could take the Scottish Cup with them on an extensive summer tour. Forty years after such an enterprise was first mooted at Parkhead, Celtic had at last arranged to tour the United States and Canada where the glimpse of the gleaming trophy took on the aspect of the Holy Grail for expatriate supporters, desperate to see players about whom they could only read and speculate. It was a real adventure for the Celtic party, made increasingly aware of the continuing interest and enthusiasm among the exiles. Tom Maley, the ex-Celt who had joined the party belatedly, would recall the trip as a thoroughly exhausting but enjoyable one: 'railway journeys of a thousand miles or so, uproarious welcomes and hot weather'. Jimmy McGrory observed wryly on his return that 'everyone, it seems, wanted to have their photograph taken with the boys'.

Buoyed up by the unforgettable summer experience, one so far beyond the normal expectations of working-class footballers then, Celtic went into the 1931–32 season like a team given a new lease on life, their early performances so eye-catching in their fluency, craft and precision that their fans were filled with almost feverish anticipation of Rangers' stranglehold on the championship being broken at last. Opponents were not so much being defeated as slaughtered, and the proof lay in 26 goals for Celtic in the opening seven unbeaten games. For once, a fixture against Rangers at Ibrox could be viewed with something approaching pleasurable anticipation . . .

That league match at Ibrox on 5 September 1931 was watched by a crowd of 75,000, absorbed in the tension of an encounter that was heading for a nervous stalemate. But five minutes after the interval came a horrific moment, unforgettable for its tragedy.

After halting a Celtic attack, Rangers broke out swiftly and Fleming released English for a clear run into the opposing penalty area for what seemed a certain goal. The centre-forward prepared to shoot from near the penalty spot, but the scarlet-jerseyed Celtic goalkeeper had dived headlong at his feet at the same split-second the Ranger struck. His head came into sickening contact with English's left kneecap as the Ranger shot with his right foot. The ball trundled past the post, but the players had clashed and John Thomson lay still, while Sam English hobbled over towards him. Suddenly oblivious to his own pain, he called on the trainers to attend the prone goalkeeper, now bleeding profusely from a head wound.

Another Rangers player, 'Doc' Marshall (a medical student at Glasgow University), feared the worst, as he later told a reporter: 'I knew within myself there was little hope. I couldn't say so, of course, for all of us know that while there's life there's hope, but the game for me, at any rate, stopped at that awful moment.' Behind Thomson's goal, the Rangers support began to exult at the prospect of Celtic losing a key player temporarily. But Davie Meiklejohn, Rangers' captain and a figure who commanded universal respect, was another all too aware of the true nature of the injury. Angrily, he strode behind the goal and gestured for silence; a hush gradually descended around the stadium, as the stricken goalkeeper was borne off the field.

After further medical attention inside the pavilion from, among others, Dr Willie Kivlichan – a former player with both Celtic and Rangers – the injured Thomson was taken quickly to the Victoria Infirmary. His relatives in Fife were wired for immediately, and advised to fear the worst. His parents rushed to Glasgow, reaching their son's bedside a few minutes before he died at 9.25 that evening. Despite the best efforts of the staff to relieve the pressure of a depressed fracture of the skull after the injury had been diagnosed at the hospital by a Dr Daly, Thomson had not regained consciousness.

The match had continued without the player, whose place in goal was taken by Chic Geatons, the tall, strongly built and versatile left-half, and the match dragged on to a scoreless draw. The result had paled into insignificance shortly after four o'clock that afternoon . . .

The shocking fatality plunged Scotland into a collective mourning, a grief made all the more poignant when the *Glasgow Observer* later stated that, just prior to rushing off for the match, John Thomson had been writing a letter to a friend in America. The last sentence of the unfinished letter reportedly read: 'Off now to Ibrox to meet the great Rangers, a death or glory affair . . .'

Twenty thousand gathered in brokenhearted silence in and around Glasgow's Queen Street station as mourners departed for Fife in a train which drew behind it a 44-foot-long covered wagon filled with wreaths and other tributes. Hundreds of others travelled by bus or car, and many – being unemployed – walked from Glasgow, a round-journey of almost a hundred miles, and slept rough in the fields there and back. Every current Celtic player was present, and six members of the team carried the coffin the half-mile from his home to the quiet churchyard. From beginning to end, the road was lined several deep with people, and the lane to the graveyard was banked by thousands of mourners. The football world for once was united in grief, because a player had died at the height of his powers – and because this young man was different. A handsome, serious youngster, a clean-living sportsman from a teetotal family in Fife, who read from the Bible daily as members of the Church of Christ, a slim, graceful figure who epitomised all that was best in the national game, and a young man with a glowing future stretching before him. There was not the slightest hint (or awareness) of any irony in the fact that for a couple of decades after the tragedy it was not uncommon for a visitor to enter a Catholic household in Glasgow and see a picture of John Thomson next to a holy water font.

T. Smith from Darvel penned a poetic tribute which captured the mood of those dark days:

> *The athlete rare, who typified all that is best in life.*
> *Your brilliant deeds! The death you died! Our lovely lad from Fife.*
>
> *The unerring eye, the master touch, more buoyant than the ball.*
> *The fearless heart, the powerful clutch, the genius praised by all.*
>
> *The squirrel's leap, the falcon's flight, the clear, quick-thinking brain,*
> *All these were yours, for our delight. Never, alas, again!*

A forgotten victim in the tragic incident was Sam English. The Rangers forward was entirely blameless, as both photographs and newsreel films show, but a most unfortunate response by Celtic's manager to a question posed at the Fatal Accident Inquiry helped to ensure that English would be haunted by Thomson's death during his curtailed career and for the remaining 36 years of his life. Maley's answer – 'I *hope* it was an accident' – should have been withdrawn immediately, but it was not. During the rest of his career, which took him to Liverpool and Hartlepool in England and Queen of the South back in Scotland, English could not escape the moronic cries of 'Killer!' and 'Murderer!' from the terracings.

Willie Maley blamed the tragedy for much of Celtic's misfortunes during the 1931–32 season, commenting in the next Celtic handbook on 'this crushing, staggering blow from which the team never really recovered', one which had set back the clear promise of a return to 'the best days of Celtic powers'.

Irish-born himself, Maley would have further reason within a few months to agree with a later chronicler who observed that 'Celtic, like the race whose name they bear, seem fated to have great joys – and great sorrows'. Peter Scarff, a skilful and industrious inside-forward acclaimed for the strength, punch and power he brought to the forward line, would have to be rested with the early symptoms of the pulmonary tuberculosis that led to his death two years later. At the time they died, John Thomson had been only 22 years of age, and Peter Scarff, another for whom greatness had been confidently predicted, 25.

In the wake of Thomson's death, the league challenge was effectively ended with the dropping of 12 points before the turn of the year. Injuries played their part: Jimmy McGrory, in particular, was sidelined for an extended period with a knee injury and his breakdown early in the Scottish Cup tie at Motherwell enabled the home side, winners by 2–0, to exact some measure of revenge for their trauma at Hampden Park.

Celtic would soon have to come face-to-face with the grim reality that the team in which the club and its supporters had invested such faith and optimism at the start of the season was on the verge of breaking up for a variety of reasons – and not only the customary alleged lack of money. Willie Cook, an Irish international full-back noted for his accurate distribution and his quick tackling, was transferred to Everton in December 1932 to the mutual benefit of club and player: Cook received better terms in England and Celtic gathered in a fee of £3,000. Celtic were fortunate to have an outstanding replacement waiting on the sidelines in the person of Bobby Hogg, who became the youngest professional player in the country when he was promoted to the first team; the teenager, signed from Larkhall Royal Albert, was a tenacious tackler but scrupulously fair. Bertie Thomson, a popular and often match-winning winger, was suspended for breaches of training regulations in the autumn of 1932 and later transferred to Blackpool (where he lasted a year before moving to Motherwell) but progressive deterioration in his health due to excesses in his lifestyle guaranteed a short career, and he died in 1937 at the age of 30. Jimmy McStay, the captain and centre-half, had reached the veteran stage in his career and he departed for Hamilton Academical in 1934 . . .

Willie Maley may have been sensing, too, that his sides needed to adapt to the more pragmatic outlook that had crept into British football with the spread of the 'third-back game' as a consequence of a change in the offside law in 1925. The old-style Celtic artistry could all too often end up enmeshed in a defensive web woven by determined defenders; after Celtic had lost by 3–0 at home to Hamilton on New Year's Eve in 1932, the *Glasgow Observer* hinted that tactical adjustment was required at Parkhead since traditional Celtic craft was being found wanting against visitors described as 'a hefty set of hustling, bustling, tearing first-timers, tackling with fierce tenacity and belting the ball about with a fine freedom that made Celtic's attempts at studied passing seem pinchbeck and futile'. (7 January 1933)

It was not an environment in which arch-exponents of the constructive approach such as Peter Wilson and Alec Thomson could expect to flourish, and it was scarcely a surprise that Willie Maley should be sanguine about their departure to Hibernian and Dunfermline Athletic respectively in the summer of 1934. The manager was now set firm on a course of bringing through a batch of promising young players from the Alliance team who could no longer be denied their first-team chance after displays which left spectators convinced they were watching something special. 'Man in the Know', not always the easiest critic to please, marvelled at the quality of the reserves drafted into the side in an emergency situation that had removed several regulars from a Glasgow Cup tie at Parkhead: 'As a line, these youths played with considerable understanding and enthusiasm, and all were keen as razors to "make their name" against the Rangers.' (*Glasgow Observer*: 30 September 1933)

Their performance, sharpened by the experience gained in the Alliance side, made a nonsense of the fatuous statement attributed to James Kelly in January 1927. Celtic's first captain, now a director, had defended the 'wisdom' of not fielding a reserve side by stating that youngsters would improve their game more by watching first-team players in action rather than by playing together as a unit. Incredibly, the board had actually considered reintroducing the discredited policy in the summer of 1932, but came to their senses before repeating their earlier wrong-headed decision. Otherwise, the footballing public – and Celtic supporters in particular – might have been deprived of enjoying the blossoming talent of several ex-Juniors: the versatile Malcolm MacDonald from St Anthony's, perhaps the purest footballer ever to wear a Celtic jersey; little Johnny Crum from Ashfield, a cocky live-wire of a centre-forward; Willie Buchan from Grange Rovers, a tall, 'brainy' inside-forward blessed with the talent of rounding off moves with cool finishing; John Divers, a tall, rangy inside man from Renfrew Juniors whose height and weight, allied to a fine positional sense, made him a perpetual menace; and last of all, but not least, Jimmy Delaney, a winger of genuine pace from Stoneyburn Juniors who had that rarest of combined talents: the ability to outstrip defenders, to cross the ball accurately on the run, and to cut inside the full-back to have a shot on goal.

The remnants of the old guard still had the time – and the opportunity – to add further lustre to their fading careers at Celtic Park by helping to ensure victory in the 1933 Scottish Cup final against Motherwell, fated to be bridesmaids yet again in that competition. The final was, frankly, an undistinguished one, but the displays of two stalwarts ensured that the trophy was Paradise-bound once more. Jimmy McStay snuffed out the threat of Motherwell's centre Willie McFadyen, scorer of 15 goals in their progress to Hampden, and Jimmy McGrory, now considered a veteran but a man with some seasons left in him, netted the game's only goal three minutes after the interval when he nipped in to turn a rebound into the net when the opposing defenders got themselves into a fankle. The heroic striker played out the closing stages of the final with a knee injury and a swollen ankle – and without two front teeth after a clash in the opening minutes. And, as always, without the slightest complaint as he foraged for goals and ran himself into the ground for his team.

Perhaps the most gratifying display of all for Maley had been provided by American goalkeeper Joe Kennaway, whose alertness had done much to dishearten Motherwell during a period of first-half dominance. In one notable instance, Kennaway astonished the crowd of 102,339 when he saved a vicious 15-yarder from McFadyen by diving and *punching* the shot well clear of the penalty area. The manager had been responsible for bringing the keeper to Scotland, after he had foiled Celtic during the American tour while at Fall River, noted as the toughest of opposition for touring sides. Back then, according to the *Fall River Herald*, Kennaway's work in goal 'brought applause from the crowd several times by his leaping saves', moving their reporter to crow that, if John Thomson (who had mishandled a lobbed shot in the 87th minute to contribute to Celtic's defeat) 'was worth the reported price of $40,000, our own Joe is worth every cent as much'. (1 June 1931) After two deputies had experienced difficulty in filling John Thomson's place in goal, Maley recalled Kennaway's display and invited him to Scotland. Thomson would never be forgotten by the Celtic supporters, but the newcomer had turned out to be a worthy successor to their 'darling Johnny'.

By 1934–35 Celtic had rediscovered sufficient consistency to give Rangers a real run for their money in the championship – and that after a miserable start to the programme when the Parkhead side failed to score in four out of the first five matches of the season. In fact, by early October, Celtic were nine points behind Rangers and had played one match more. The long-suffering support prepared for another undistinguished season but, at that stage, coincidental or not, a transformation took place after the appointment of the old favourite, Jimmy McMenemy, as trainer-cum-coach 'to bring on the youngsters'. He proved a welcome addition to the backroom staff as a father-figure who could impart his practical knowledge and experience in the game to young players at a crucial stage in their maturing process.

Before the end of 1934 Celtic lost only one more match (a 2–3 setback against Hibernian at Easter Road), but real damage, eventually fatal, was done to Celtic's title aspirations by Rangers' 2–1 victory at Ibrox on Ne'erday 1935. Celtic could point to wretched luck as an excuse as Napier had to retire shortly before half-time, having overstretched as he strained to reach the ball. Fifteen minutes from time, Peter McGonagle was ordered off by Mr Craigmyle (Aberdeen) after foolishly throwing the ball at Rangers' Bob McPhail in a fit of temper. McGonagle suspected his opponent of faking a tumble to the ground after his tackle; so incensed and distraught was the defender that the referee had to 'take him by the arm' off the field. Celtic paid heavily for the full-back's tantrum; he missed a critical league match at Pittodrie against Aberdeen which Celtic lost 2–0 during his three-week suspension.

Nevertheless, Celtic were giving their loyal followers justifiable grounds for optimism, instilling the belief that this was a team well worth making the effort to see, however depleted the supporters' finances may be. A touching feature of the Depression years was the determination and resourcefulness of the more dedicated of the club's followers to see their favourites, come what may. Nearly two hundred of them had walked throughout the night from Glasgow to reach Perth in time for the Scottish Cup tie against St Johnstone in January 1932, a round-journey of 120 miles along poorly lit country roads. Three years later, in March 1935, many made the long trip north to Aberdeen for the Scottish Cup quarter-final, starting out on foot and cadging lifts from friendly drivers of fish-lorries. On the latter occasion Celtic were eliminated 3–1 before a record crowd of 40,105 at Pittodrie. One match report compared the team to 'a motor car with one cylinder missing . . . there seemed to be a shortage of that mysterious quality that fans and sports writers call punch'.

Willie Maley may have spent the long rail journey south in a foul temper, livid with rage at some defensive over-elaboration which had contributed to two goals for Aberdeen from the penalty spot. But, deep down, he knew that the gap between Celtic and Rangers had been closing steadily. Rangers had had it their way for too long. Celtic's time was coming . . .

FIVE

Exhibition Stuff

1935–45

Willie Maley, despite his advancing years, was still a commanding figure at Celtic Park. By the 1930s he had assumed full control of the key matter of team selection despite the formality of Board involvement. He rarely laid down specific tactics, though; that was left to a corps of seasoned players who took care of situations as they developed on the field of play. The established players made newcomers instantly aware of the standards expected by those who wore a Celtic jersey. The noted referee Peter Craigmyle had several run-ins during his career with the manager over decisions but, in his memoirs, he insisted that Willie Maley 'had a football brain second to none'. Maley's shrewdness and flexibility was evident in the mid-'30s by the reshaping of the team. A recurring criticism was that Celtic's traditional style had been foundering too often on the formidable 'third-back' defences (most notably Rangers') to which the change in the offside rule back in 1925 had given birth.* The players were now at hand to make Celtic more purposeful and direct than the sides fielded in recent seasons. Maley now wanted a hungry team – and he got it.

Outstanding recruits from junior clubs were determined to make their mark, and had caught the eye with their razor-edge keenness. Thrusting young wingers like Jimmy Delaney on the right and Frank Murphy from

---

* A change in the offside rule in 1925 reduced the number of opposing players required to keep a player onside from three to two. Predictably, the increased freedom this gave to more adventurous sides was countered by the centre-half (hitherto given the scope to venture into attack) being pulled back into defence, positioned between the two full-backs.

Croy Celtic on the left were not content to hug the touchline, but were willing to cut inside and take on defences; inside-forwards such as the scheming Malcolm MacDonald and the deceptively tricky Willie Buchan shared with the evergreen Jimmy McGrory a perception of the quickest route to goal, their preferred weapon being a devastating through-pass – although, like McGrory, they could shoot too; the livewire Johnny Crum, a tiny striker, constantly goaded defences into error with his harrying and acute positional sense.

In spite of all this, it could be argued that a surprise signing at the tail-end of season 1934–35 made the most influential contribution to the renaissance. Maley had been impressed by the ability of Willie Lyon, a sturdy six-footer and Queen's Park's centre-half, to curtail Jimmy McGrory in Celtic's meetings with the Amateurs. He saw him as having the height and weight to stiffen the centre of Celtic's defence (which had sorely missed the influence of Jimmy McStay since his transfer to Hamilton in September 1934). In addition, he was a most resolute pivot, a tower of strength at the heart of any defence but, perhaps more importantly, he had the presence and authority to organise his colleagues and become a great captain.

Lyon's arrival helped to take much of the sting out of the departure of Charlie Napier, transferred to Derby County for the large sum of £5,000; a clever, entertaining forward, he had expressed dissatisfaction with his financial arrangements at Parkhead.

The capture of Lyon suggested that Celtic were ready to re-establish themselves at the top, but the 1935–36 league campaign got off to a rocky start with a 3–1 defeat at Pittodrie, where Aberdeen as usual provided the stiffest of opposition. Celtic's new-look team, however, showing the advantages of having played together as youngsters in the reserves, settled quickly into a rhythm.

The spirit and adventure of those Celtic forwards, allied to swift interpassing and understanding, could open up the stoutest of defences; at times, they simply overran opponents bewildered by their sheer pace, as the defending champions Rangers soon discovered in going down to a 2–1 defeat at Ibrox in September 1935. That Celtic victory, the first league win there since 1921, was fully deserved, although Kennaway had to redeem himself with a diving save from Meiklejohn's late penalty-kick; the pugnacious Celtic keeper had given up the kick by fouling the Rangers captain.

On 28 September – only a week after the visit to Ibrox – Celtic came from behind to defeat Hearts 2–1 at Parkhead; already, they were starting to suggest a certain invincibility in the league, a tenacity which moved one writer to compare them to a runaway train: 'The red light of defeat never showed a greener light all clear to a Celtic team. They simply went ahead brooking no stoppage.'

Now playing with a refreshing abandon, and embarked on an unbeaten run of 18 matches, Celtic travelled to Fir Park a few weeks later and defeated Motherwell on a ground where they had not won in the championship since 1926. The *Sunday Mail* correspondent 'Clarion' marvelled at the performance of the Celtic wingers who 'cut in so boldly that the backs never knew where to hold them. This gave a balance to Celtic's attack, a circumventive menace in threatening at all points which Motherwell never possessed'. (27 October 1935)

Typically, Rangers would not give up their title without a fight, inflicting Celtic's only third defeat in the league that season by coming from behind to win 4–3 at Parkhead on 1 January 1936. In fact, Celtic could start to breathe more easily only after Rangers' narrow defeat at Hamilton in mid-April; appropriately, the veteran Jimmy McGrory released the tension by netting a hat-trick in a 6–0 win over Ayr at Parkhead the following Saturday as Celtic clinched their first league title in a decade.

Jimmy McGrory was the one survivor from the last Celtic team to win the championship and he had been a major factor in the latest triumph; his wealth of experience, his unquenchable spirit and his eye for goal had all contributed to his amassing 50 league goals that season, a total that remains the club record. For once – and the modest McGrory would have been the first to acknowledge it – he had played alongside partners who had done most of the spadework for him. During the season he had set a new British record for league goals, when he scored another hat-trick against Aberdeen on 21 December 1935 to surpass the previous mark of 362 goals established by Hughie Ferguson. Unlike the good-natured McGrory, Ferguson had become a melancholic figure who committed suicide in 1930 at the age of 34 during a state of depression about his lack of success with Dundee.

McGrory, who had virtually carried the Celtic side for many seasons now found himself the spearhead of the most productive – if not the most gifted – group of forwards he had partnered in his 12 full seasons at Parkhead: two fleet-footed wingers in Delaney and Murphy who could pinpoint their crosses, in addition to displaying a healthy appetite for goals – as their combined contribution of 32 out of Celtic's total of 115 suggests; Buchan, considered a 'brainy' player, netted 11 goals, and Crum got nine. Even the pivot Willie Lyon added to the goal feast with six, half of which came from the penalty spot.

Celtic had a well-balanced side of unlimited potential, brimming over with such natural talent and exuberance that Maley's hardest task now seemed to be that of keeping their feet solidly on the ground. Accordingly, the manager was quick to admonish Jimmy Delaney with a magisterial rebuke as the young player left the field at Hampden Park feeling rather chuffed at scoring a hat-trick in a comprehensive 4–2 win over Rangers in the Charity Cup final on 9 May 1936; Maley's 'congratulations' consisted of the words 'Don't let that go to your head!'.

Shortly afterwards, the manager sent this letter to every Celtic player – the men who had won the championship:

Dear Sir,

As already verbally intimated to you before leaving here at end of season, you must on no account play football of any description during the close season. This order includes the casual kicking of the ball so common in the country.

Players must utilise the rest given them by the close season.

Yours truly.

W. Maley, Secy.

Simultaneously curmudgeonly and over-protective they may have appeared, but the manager's instructions were given a certain justification by the hint of complacency (and a certain lethargy) which crept into Celtic's play during much of the following season. The zest and sparkle which had characterised their displays throughout the previous campaign were strangely absent at times. Their stamina was certainly found wanting as the 'superior physique' of champions-elect Rangers came off best in gruelling conditions at Ibrox on Ne'erday 1937, when Celtic went down to a 1–0 defeat in front of a 95,000 crowd. Celtic's fading hopes of retaining the championship for the first time in two decades ended effectively at Pittodrie when they lost by the same score to Aberdeen later in the same month.

That result left only the Scottish Cup as a pick-me-up after their jaded performances in the league so far that season. On 30 January Celtic were jolted out of any complacency at Ochilview Park, the home of Stenhousemuir, a lowly Second Division club; indeed, they were almost ejected brusquely from the competition. Stenhousemuir's refusal to be overawed by their mighty opponents left Celtic most fortunate to be leading after 70 minutes, when McGrory was quick to head home a rebound from the crossbar. Within two minutes, 'The Warriors' had equalised deservedly, and the home crowd howled in vain for justice near the end when Mr Craigmyle, the referee, denied Stenhousemuir what appeared a blatant penalty after Willie Lyon handled the ball.

The toughest hurdle came in the quarter-final against Motherwell at

Parkhead on 17 March. Five goals in the first 20 minutes resulted in a 3–2 lead for the visitors in a tumultuous Cup tie, played before 36,000. Celtic ran out of the tunnel after the interval with sleeves rolled up – but found themselves down by 4–2 within a minute or so of the restart. Celtic, urged on by the large, noisy crowd, applied tremendous pressure and Lyon blasted home a penalty, awarded when Delaney had been upended. In a pulsating finale, Buchan equalised in spectacular fashion with ten minutes remaining; the tall inside-forward outwitted two defenders and, evading pursuing opponents, shot firmly past the advancing keeper. Celtic's nerve – and legendary reputation in Cup replays – held firm at Fir Park, where 35,000 watched another absorbing tie, decided only by another late goal from Buchan to produce a 2–1 win.

For the final on 24 April 1937 Hampden Park bulged with 146,433 spectators; more than 20,000 others were locked out, forced to follow the progress of the match by listening to the excited roars of those inside. The inadequate crowd arrangements owed much to the incompetence of the SFA, a body which had been in existence for more than 60 years but which claimed pathetically that it could not arrange all-ticket matches for successive Saturdays. The Scotland v England international, watched by a world-record crowd then of 149,547, had been made all-ticket and the Cup final not – with the attendant chaos. Officially, it was the largest-ever crowd to watch a club match in Europe and, in view of modern developments in safety and comfort, it is unquestionably an unsurpassable one. The stewarding and crowd distribution, however, was so poor that there appeared to be room to spare on the lower terracing slopes, but such congestion higher up that one observer suggested that 'greater comfort could have been found in an overcrowded cattle truck'.

The opening exchanges in the match itself were brisk, with Celtic first to settle. Several times Geatons made sorties up the wing, troubling the Aberdeen defenders, and it was no surprise when Celtic went in front after 12 minutes; the Aberdeen keeper was unable to hold Buchan's shot, and Crum dashed in to net the unexpected rebound. Celtic's lead did not last long; Aberdeen retaliated immediately and, a minute later, a cross from the lively Beynon was deflected by Lyon past his own keeper for Armstrong to equalise.

Celtic were in the ascendancy for much of the second half, largely due to their iron clamp on midfield. Chic Geatons, so often an underrated performer, was playing magnificently, winning the ball with uncompromising tackles and releasing his forwards with accurate passing. Although recognised more as a solid, dependable player, he showed a finesse that no other player on the field could match. Geatons' performance was complemented by that of the quietly effective George Paterson at left-half; his workrate and accurate passing was no less impressive. Up front, the slick and unexpected manoeuvres of Buchan and Crum posed a constant threat. However, it took the intervention of the veteran Jimmy McGrory to create the decisive opening 20 minutes from time. Afterwards, Aberdeen defenders claimed that McGrory had controlled the ball with his hand before setting Willie Buchan free to outstrip the defence and hit a crisp shot past Johnstone; his low drive skidded into the net off the post for Celtic's second and the winning goal.

The trophy seemed destined for Parkhead again, and for a record 15th time, but Aberdeen – living up to their nickname 'The Wasps' (because of their black-and-gold jerseys) – buzzed around the Celtic goalmouth to mount a last-gasp onslaught that ensured a nail-biting conclusion to the final.

Celtic's greater experience of the big occasion had been a telling factor, re-establishing the club as the greatest Cup-fighters in the land. The club was now regarded as being well placed to celebrate the upcoming jubilee season in a fitting manner, but those prospects were endangered early on in 1937–38 by some indifferent displays – and by the shock transfer of Willie Buchan in mid-November to Blackpool for the substantial fee of £10,000.

Buchan, the scoring hero in the Scottish Cup campaign and regarded as the main fount of inspiration in the attack, left only six months after a bid from Newcastle United was rebuffed by the directors. According to the *Glasgow Observer* at the time of that offer, Celtic 'were not severing their connection with this football genius'. Nearly half a century later, the player retained a vivid memory of being summoned to the Bank Restaurant in Glasgow's Queen Street. Inside that establishment, owned by Willie Maley, he was told for the first time of a deal arranged between the clubs. Buchan had been perfectly happy at Parkhead, but was informed that the transfer was a *fait accompli* – and that he would have no say in the matter.

He was led to believe later on that part of the transfer fee was used to pay benefits due to other players at Celtic Park. Indeed, the Board claimed in the match programme for the next home fixture that finance was the main consideration in the transaction, the directors blaming the supporters for not turning up in sufficient numbers at Celtic Park. To those fans who had been part of the mammoth crowd of 146,433 at Hampden for the Cup final it looked suspiciously like the old practice of selling a player when the opportunity arose to cash in on a young man acquired for a nominal fee from the juniors.

In fairness to the directors, it should be noted that replacements were readily available; the decision to restore a reserve side was continuing to pay dividends in every meaning of the phrase. The transfer created an opening for Malcolm MacDonald, a two-footed natural player, who, along with

John Divers, had been available for transfer earlier in the year. The hard-working and intelligent Divers added height and weight to the attack while slotting in comfortably at inside-left in place of Johnny Crum, now emerging as the obvious successor at centre-forward to that magnificent servant Jimmy McGrory, the greatest opportunist in the history of Scottish (and perhaps British) football.

Jimmy McGrory donned his beloved green and white for the last time on 16 October 1937 for the fixture against Queen's Park, and scored in a 4–3 win; McGrory, a comparatively small man, appeared from nowhere to head-flick the ball over the outstretched arms of the Amateurs' tall goalkeeper, one Desmond White, who would later become Celtic's chairman. It was a goal reminiscent of his heyday. Frankly, no words can adequately convey the contribution of this man to the cause of Celtic on the field, but Archie Macpherson came close in his obituary tribute on BBC television on 20 October 1982: 'He did more than score goals; he converted countless numbers to the belief that football was all there was worth living for – and in the '30s that might not have been an unhealthy supposition.'

Like Divers, Malcolm MacDonald relished the opportunity to leave reserve football behind him for good, and one report enthused about him 'filling Willie Buchan's shoes to perfection'. Celtic motored to the top of the league table on 1 January 1938 with a 3–0 rout of Rangers in front of Parkhead's record crowd of 83,500. Rangers' normally resolute defence was left bewildered by their opponents' sustained attacks from the opening whistle, and Celtic built on that victory to secure the club's nineteenth championship. Who could ever have believed that it would be another 16 years before the next new league flag would flutter proudly above the Jungle? Certainly no one who had witnessed Celtic's performances in capping a landmark season with awesome demonstrations of the resolve and skill which had kept the club at the pinnacle of the Scottish game for most of the first 50 years or so of its existence.

Even Willie Maley, notoriously hard to please, could not fail to be impressed as Celtic limbered up for a prestigious competition, the Empire Exhibition tournament, by competing a hat-trick of victories in Charity Cup finals with an emphatic 2–0 win over Rangers at Hampden Park; the latest triumph came on 14 May 1938 – two weeks short of the half-century since the meeting of the pair in Celtic's first-ever game.

The Empire Exhibition, described as 'an exposition of the work, life, culture and progress of the British Empire', had been devised as a shop-window to entice new industry to Clydeside, which was slowly emerging from the Depression. The Exhibition itself was held at Bellahouston Park and the organisers decided that a knock-out competition featuring the best current sides in Britain would be an added attraction. Celtic, Rangers, Aberdeen and Hearts were invited from Scotland; Everton, Brentford, Chelsea and Sunderland from England. All the ties were to be played at Ibrox Stadium, the ground closest to the site of the Exhibition, and the trophy was to be a replica in silver of the Tower of Empire that symbolised the Exhibition.

A crowd of 53,976 saw the opening contest on 25 May 1938 between Celtic and Sunderland, a match which ended in a 0–0 draw mainly due to the sterling work of centre-half Willie Lyon and the inspired goalkeeping of Joe Kennaway in Celtic's goal. Hampered by injuries, the Glasgow side hung on and survived the 30 minutes of extra-time. Celtic were forced to make changes for the replay, held on the following evening: Matt Lynch, versatile and a fine crosser of the ball, came in at outside-right to replace the injured Delaney, and Malcolm MacDonald took over at inside-right from another injured forward, the clever Joe Carruth (sadly destined to be merely a bit-player in Celtic's history). Heavy rain cut the attendance for the replay to around 20,000, but those present witnessed an enthralling tussle. Celtic rallied after Sunderland had deservedly taken the lead on the half-hour, and lasted the pace better to notch up a 3–1 victory – a result clinched when John Divers, a two-goal hero, sprang the English team's offside trap to chip the goalkeeper deftly.

Once again, Kennaway – the most dependable goalkeeper in the tournament – caught the eye in the semi-final against Hearts before a crowd of 45,403. Apart from Kennaway's saves, Celtic rode their luck; Hearts, outplaying the Parkhead men in the early stages, had a goal disallowed controversially in the first half and missed several chances. The Edinburgh side had to concede – however grudgingly – Celtic's durability, a factor underlined in the 65th minute when Crum scored with a half-chance; Hearts had been punished for their earlier profligacy in scorning easier opportunities.

The final, watched by a crowd of 82,000 on 10 June, fittingly matched Celtic, the Scottish champions, against an Everton side destined to win the English title the following season. Willie Lyon's close marking of the young Tommy Lawton, dreaded by defences for his shooting and power in the air, did much to ensure that a rip-roaring, end-to-end contest went into extra-time without a goal being scored. Everton were handicapped, it should be said, by an injury to their inside-forward Cunliffe which left them increasingly vulnerable to Celtic's swift counter-thrusts.

At last, in the 96th minute, came the vital breakthrough. Johnny Crum recalled that his instinct for reading the play enabled him to snatch a famous victory for Celtic: 'The ball went from Chic Geatons on to Johnny Divers and, with a cute flick of the ball, he sent it through to me; carrying on, veering slightly to the right of the 18-yard line, I let go and Ted Sagar, who made a valiant effort, got his hands to the ball but could not prevent its progress to the net.' *(Celtic FC Supporters Association Handbook, 1955–56)* Crum, always a gallus personality, responded to the delirium of the supporters on the terracing by racing behind the goal to perform a victory jig.

A magnificent occasion, and a splendid team. Matt Lynch, who played in two of the four matches as a replacement for the injured Delaney (and whose name appears in the programme for the final itself) allowed himself to be drawn when asked recently about how that side would have fared against the Lisbon Lions of 1967. His answer: 'We would have done all right, at least until half-time. By then, big Jock would have spotted something, and that would be it.'

A gathering of distinguished Scottish football personalities, past and present, was on hand for a banquet at the Grosvenor Restaurant on 15 June 1938 to celebrate the officially designated golden jubilee of the club. A half-century of tangible achievement was on view in the glistening silver of the Charity Cup, the Scottish League's commemorative shield for the six-in-a-row championships from 1905 to 1910, and in the burnished gold of the 1901 Exhibition Cup, gained from Rangers in 1902 – and most recently, the emblem of Celtic's current standing, the Empire Exhibition Trophy. The Celtic-minded guests present could only derive considerable satisfaction from hearing Sir John T. Cargill, honorary president of Rangers, pay tribute to 'Celtic, the wonderful club and one they could all be proud of'.

The highlight of the proceedings was a presentation to Willie Maley, to honour his long association with the club and his contribution to its fabled successes. That most unemotional of men was seen to have a tear in his eye after hearing the chairman Tom White's fulsome praise: 'The history of Celtic is indissolubly the life story of Willie Maley. Through all his years he has built up one great honour-winning team after another.'

This show of harmony concealed the truth that the Board was seeking the parting of the ways with their veteran manager. Relations between Maley and the players were fraying, and one incident hinted at tensions between the manager and his directors. Shortly after the Empire Exhibition final Willie Lyon, Celtic's captain, was appointed by the players to approach the manager about their victory bonus, promised by John McKillop, one of the directors, of which only 20 per cent had been paid. Maley, staring down his captain, suggested that Lyon take up the matter with the director who, the manager added tartly, would doubtless pay the balance out of his own pocket.

For much of the next 18 months Maley, always preoccupied with money, was embroiled in an undignified haggling with the club over his 'honorarium' of 2,500 guineas. The dispute concerned the taxation (by present-day levels negligible) due on his generous gift – and Maley felt that Celtic, having declared a profit of £7,105 on the year, should be responsible for the tax. The grievances of the manager and the players are even more understandable in view of the club's financial well-being; in the summer of 1939, after another large profit of £4,415 on the season just passed, the shareholders declared a dividend of 20 per cent – free of tax – for themselves, and approved £200 for each of the directors.

The Board, having decided on such a lavish gift for Maley, were genuinely bemused. It had been a generous gesture, although viewed by at least one insider as a golden handshake to induce Maley to retire soon. The directors had run out of patience with the manager's autocratic approach and increasingly uncertain temper. In particular, the memory of one incident at the start of the American tour back in 1931 still festered. Maley had sought an invitation for his brother, Tom, another member of Celtic's original team in 1888, but none was forthcoming. For most of the voyage the manager, apparently in a huff, confined himself to his cabin; on arrival in New York, he took to his bed at the hotel pleading serious illness, and requested the directors to send for his brother to accompany him back to Scotland. As Tom Maley later wrote in the October 1931 issue of *All Aboard* (the journal of RMS *Transylvania*): 'Generously and graciously, I was invited to join. It needed no urge, I was delighted and almost with indecorous haste followed them.' Lo and behold, the stricken manager made a miraculous recovery, in time to greet him as that liner docked in New York.

Maley was never an easy man to approach, retaining a commanding, authoritative air reinforced by his height and military bearing. He habitually gave the impression that a difference of opinion would be treated as an impertinence or, worse, as an insult. Nearly 60 years on, Matt Lynch, one of his players, refers to him in conversation automatically as 'Mr Maley'. One insight into that self-confidence – if not arrogance – was revealed by a journalist friend of the manager. Many people in Glasgow went to the pictures twice a week in the 1930s, and long queues were a common sight. Maley used to ignore any queues, brushing aside commissionaires and heading straight for the box-office to secure the best seats in the house. When the reporter ventured to ask him about it, his cryptic reply was 'Never mind how it's done!'.

Earlier attempts had been made to bridge the uneasy relationship between the Board and the manager. A Celtic director – apparently, Tom Colgan – made the suggestion that Jimmy McGrory, then close to retiring as a player, could 'learn the ropes' as an assistant to Maley, but the older man resisted the idea vehemently. In fact, the mere suggestion so enraged Maley that, when McGrory moved to Kilmarnock as manager in December 1937, he refused to allow the Ayrshire club to register him as a player. Previously, Maley had also survived hints that he might be succeeded by Jimmy McMenemy, the club's trainer.

Despite the turmoil behind the scenes, Celtic made a brisk start to the 1938–39 season. The forwards were in sparkling form and the goals came easily: against Kilmarnock (9–1), Rangers (6–2), Hearts (5–1), Albion Rovers (8–1), Raith Rovers (6–1) and Third Lanark (6–1). The demolition of their oldest rivals must have installed Celtic as clear favourites to retain the league title, so inept had Rangers been in the face of the Celtic onslaught at Parkhead on 10 September 1938. Malcolm MacDonald, although more noted as a creator of goals, netted a hat-trick in a 'needle match' with finishing of the highest order.

However, points were dropped carelessly, particularly at home, and a disastrous slump in form at the turn of the year ended any hope of a successful defence of the championship. Celtic's challenge foundered dismally in the heavy going with three successive defeats in the first week of January. The *Glasgow Observer* pinpointed alarming signs of tiredness in Celtic's lightweight forward line. The side, favoured to win all the honours that season, finished up a distant second in the league, 11 points behind Rangers.

Celtic still had hopes in the Scottish Cup but were doomed to disappointment, failing to heed the warning signs flashing when they squeezed past Hearts in a midweek third-round replay at Parkhead; John Divers' header in the dying minutes of extra-time barely crossed the line before goalkeeper Waugh could claw it back – and the bulk of the 80,840 crowd celebrated noisily. In the quarter-final at Motherwell – admittedly, a tough assignment – Celtic slumped badly to go down tamely by 3–1.

It was a miserable season for the old manager, who had to deal with a highly talented squad cursed with inconsistency. Morale was low throughout the campaign because of the club's failure to resolve the issue of the Empire Exhibition Trophy bonus. Other financial disputes with Chic Geatons and George Paterson, coupled with injuries to key players such as Paterson and Malcolm MacDonald, made things worse, but the most serious blow was the broken arm suffered by Jimmy Delaney on 1 April 1939 against Arbroath. This injury – the result of a nudge by full-back Becci as Delaney went to meet a corner-kick from Murphy – was to put Celtic's winger out of the game for two seasons.

Willie Maley himself was missing for a spell through illness, allowing discipline among the players to lapse to such an extent that the dressing-room regulations had to be enforced more rigorously, with one newspaper remarking enigmatically that 'only directors, manager and trainer' were to be allowed into the players' quarters before and after a match. The manager's iron grip on the affairs of Celtic seemed to be loosening . . .

In June 1940, nine months after the declaration of war against Germany on 3 September 1939, the Scottish League was forced to suspend its operations but, in the meantime, regional leagues had been formed so that some kind of football could carry on throughout the long years of hostilities. Inevitable restrictions on travel and petrol shortages made it impractical for Lanarkshire clubs, for example, to journey to places as far away as Aberdeen, and so Celtic played in the Western Regional Division for the first wartime season. As in the First World War, football continued as a morale-booster for the civilian population, and that only after the immediate threat of wholesale blitzkriegs on the major cities had receded. Sixteen clubs located in the central belt of Scotland eventually regrouped into a Southern League which lasted from season 1940–41 to the end of the war. Players' contracts were cancelled and their wages reduced to £2 a week, plus a maximum bonus of £1, thus forcing them to find 'reserved occupations' in war-related work as a means of supplementing their income. Some expenses were allowed, and clubs could arrange temporary transfers of those players posted to other parts of the nation and unable to travel to their own grounds.

The wartime conditions afforded the Celtic directors the perfect opportunity to dispense with the services of their veteran manager, now 71 years of age, with the minimum of publicity and fuss. Understandably, the focus of everyone's concern was the real threat facing the nation. However, Celtic's graphic decline on the field of play in the opening matches of season 1939–40 was deemed intolerable, and ample justification for the drastic action deemed necessary by the Board.

In December 1939, Celtic – with only a couple of changes in the side that had won the championship and the Empire Exhibition Trophy in 1938 – were mired near the foot of the table, having gained only four points from nine league matches. The *Weekly News* was baffled: 'Never has there been such a mystery in Scottish football as the disappearance of all the things that the name "Celtic" used to conjure up. They've lost the old "will to win" spirit. In fact, nowadays, they are only recognisable by their green and white stripes.' (23 December 1939) The only absentees from the glorious side of 1938 were Jimmy Delaney, sidelined with his career-threatening arm-break, and Joe Kennaway, who had returned to the United States with his sick wife.

Nevertheless, the awkwardness involved in removing the proud, stubborn Maley is not hard to imagine, despite his own occasional hint in the recent past that he might be considering retirement. As the year drew to an end, Maley was virtually given an ultimatum by the chairman Tom White to quit, although the announcement on Ne'erday 1940 of his departure was dressed up as a 'retiral'. The manager was keenly disappointed not to be retained at least as secretary, feeling that he was still capable of making a valuable contribution to the club despite his age. For the rest of his life – and he died in 1958 – the man who had told the Celtic AGM in 1935 that 'life away from Parkhead would be empty' nursed his bitterness about the treatment he had received.*

The post of manager was offered to Jimmy McStay, the former Celtic captain, who had recently completed a highly successful first season as manager of Alloa Athletic. The Board appointed Desmond White, the chairman's son and a chartered accountant, to the position of secretary – a position he continued to hold, wartime service apart, among other responsibilities until his death in 1985 at the age of 74.

Alloa were sorry to lose McStay, as Willie Stanton, their vice-president, indicated: 'He is a man in a thousand. At Alloa he has had our complete confidence right from the beginning. He picked the team himself, and was never subjected to any interference in his work from the Board.'

Unfortunately, after taking up his post at Parkhead on 19 February 1940, Jimmy McStay did not have a chance to be a real manager. Despite being assured by the Celtic directors of a free hand in running the club, he found himself hamstrung in his efforts to keep Celtic going as a force in Scottish football. Sir Robert Kelly, one of the directors (who later became chairman), admitted in 1971 that McStay could be considered 'a part-time manager', and that Celtic had already earmarked his successor. According to Kelly's account, the club were really interested in their ex-stalwart Jimmy McGrory, at that time manager of Kilmarnock. Given his feelings about Celtic, McGrory would certainly have jumped at the chance – and he would not be the last manager of the Ayrshire side to prefer Parkhead. In fact, a *Weekly News* article by Peter Black in February 1940 stated clearly that the only other candidate considered for the position was McGrory – but McStay was given the nod. It does not take much imagination to see that the directors were split on the appointment – and why the new manager was not fully supported by all members of the Board during his tenure.

His appointment (and subsequent treatment) confirms the impression

---

* He chose not to attend a Celtic game at Parkhead until almost ten years later; upon his return to the ground, Willie Maley – obviously then an old man – was touched to be remembered and greeted fondly by so many supporters.

that the Celtic directors had decided that wartime football was not to be taken seriously. Theirs was a serious error in judgement which affected the playing standards of the club for the six war years and, more importantly, for the immediate post-war period. Celtic, in effect, refused to do their best to entertain their support, an attitude which afforded a stark contrast to Rangers, whose manager Bill Struth thought it imperative for clubs to be fully committed to the sport in wartime. Such was Rangers' resultant strength that, in 1941–42, their reserve team joined the newly formed North-Eastern League at the instigation of clubs such as Aberdeen and Dundee United, in order to make the league financially viable.

The stagnation caused by the Board's disinterest was to be spread throughout the club. It was dispiriting enough that the players (like those at other clubs) should have to put up with the conditions forced upon the game by the war: reduced wages, curtailed training, food rationing and the cumulative effects of exhaustion resulting from overtime and night-shifts. Matt Lynch, an analytic chemist at the time, recalls frequently falling asleep on the tram from Yoker, and sometimes missing his stop at Celtic Park.

Sadly, Jimmy McStay, a far from commanding figure like Maley, was unable – and indeed not permitted – to exert the same influence on the recruitment that he had enjoyed at Alloa with such success. This was becoming very clear with the gradual break-up of the famous Exhibition Trophy side for reasons not wholly confined to the wartime situation. Contrary to the accepted mythology, their services were not totally lost to Celtic. Jimmy Delaney, who made a welcome return in 1941–42, Bobby Hogg, always steady at right-back, and Malcolm MacDonald, the most gifted and versatile of players, were all available throughout the war years. As late as August 1941, Celtic fielded the famous Exhibition forward line – and could have done so until the summer of 1942, when John Divers and Johnny Crum, apparently as a result of unrest, went to Morton. Much to Celtic's embarrassment, those two players, aided and abetted by ex-Celt Johnny Kelly, a fast and skilful left-winger, were part of a Morton forward line which took Celtic's defence apart in a 4–0 win at Cappielow on 12 September 1942. Another departure that summer was Frank Murphy, off to Albion Rovers (where a youthful Jock Stein would be one of his team-mates). Celtic had already been hit by John Morrison's move to Morton in the summer of 1940, Chic Geatons' retirement in 1941, and the departure of both Willie Lyon and George Paterson to the Forces in 1940 and 1941 respectively.

The Board – perhaps recoiling from an operating loss of £7,155, the highest sustained by any Scottish club in that first wartime season – did not believe that the best possible replacements available under the circumstances should be secured. Celtic flatly refused to avail themselves of the opportunity to bolster the team by fielding top-class players normally based in England but now stationed in Scotland. Other clubs took full advantage of the situation. Stanley Matthews was invited to turn out for unfashionable Airdrie and Morton, as well as Rangers, and he did so – as was the case with Bill Shankly for Partick Thistle. Hibernian, to cite the most pertinent example, were able to utilise Matt Busby, the Scottish international. The Liverpool wing-half, a Lanarkshire man, found himself posted to Scotland and – as he confirmed to the authors by letter in 1984 – he volunteered his services to Celtic. Jimmy McStay was delighted, realising the beneficial effects that such a personality and player would have on his youngsters. He approached the directors to seek permission to field the player, but to his acute disappointment his request was rejected. Rumoured to be Celtic daft, Busby would continue to train at Parkhead hoping for a game, but eventually Hibernian persuaded him to turn out regularly for them as a guest player. Many perceptive critics trace the Edinburgh side's glittering performances in the immediate post-war seasons to the influence of 'Papa' Busby, as one journalist described the player.

Perhaps the Celtic Board shrank from paying 'inducements' to these guest stars either from tightfistedness or out of a desire not to condone the practice at many other grounds. Whatever their reasoning, in an article written for the *Scottish Daily Express* just prior to leaving for Leicester City, Alex Dowdells, Celtic's trainer from 1940 until 1956, had no doubt that the club's subsequent troubles were caused by that Board decision: 'Not only were the new boys not being prepared, but the standards had slumped. So, when the war ended and football restarted in earnest, we were in a bad way.'

Some useful players from other clubs did turn out for Celtic at this time, notably Willie Waddell from Aberdeen who proved a sound replacement at centre-half for the popular Willie Lyon for a season or two. But at no time did the club field a side which could live up to the proud traditions of Parkhead. This embarrassment was compounded by the unaccountable rejection of the services of former players wishing to wear the green and white again. Frank and Hugh O'Donnell, noted forwards of the 1930s, wrote to McStay in March 1940 offering their services, but the brothers were turned down by the Board. During the war both O'Donnells played for Hearts, Willie Buchan for Stenhousemuir and Hamilton Academical after only one wartime game for Celtic, and Charlie Napier turned out for Falkirk – as did John Fitzsimons, a goalscoring outside-left, better known as the Celtic and Scotland team doctor in later years. Fitzsimons notched a hat-trick for Falkirk in a 6–0 rout of his former club at Brockville in February 1943.

McStay was forced to field makeshift sides using recruits from junior and juvenile clubs, Boys' Guilders and others not ready for senior football.

Jock Stein, the greatest of Celtic managers, was always most insistent that good sides were built around the spine of a sound goalkeeper, a dominant centre-half and a top-class centre-forward. Yet, at the start of 1942–43, Jimmy McStay had to field teenagers (Willie Miller in goal and John McPhail as pivot) in those vital positions, while eight different players were tried (and, Delaney apart, found wanting) at centre-forward during that season.

McStay could point with pride to some notably successful signings: Willie Miller (Maryhill Harp), an exceptional keeper, was signed in 1942 at the age of 17; John McPhail (Strathclyde) also 17 and recently out of St Mungo's Academy was signed in 1941; and 'rufus-haired' Bobby Evans (St Anthony's) joined in 1944 at the age of 17, making his début at outside-left. But, for the most part, the players fielded were not good enough.

An equally depressing scenario unfolded with the Board's refusal to honour its promise in respect of McStay having a free hand in team selection, prompting the exasperated *Glasgow Observer* correspondent 'Blairden' to protest about the tinkering with even a reserve side which lost 3–2 to Hamilton at Parkhead: 'Surely the directors will now be convinced that [John] Conway will not make a half-back, and [Joe] McLaughlin should not be given a further trial at centre-half.' (9 May 1941)

The most significant long-term outcome of this policy of 'drift' was the head-start given after the war to Celtic's rivals, most notably Hibernian, Aberdeen and Rangers, who had spared neither effort nor expense to keep up an acceptable standard during the war. Celtic's failure to compete seriously with Rangers, for example, resulted in the Parkhead club winning only four out of 25 wartime contests – although these matches were not without incident, controversy and, occasionally, farce. The Southern League match of 6 September 1941, won 3–0 by Rangers at Ibrox, was marred by crowd trouble. Frank Murphy's penalty-kick, awarded for a foul on Delaney just before the interval with Rangers leading 2–0, was saved by Dawson but only after the Rangers players had clustered around the referee, W. Webb (Glasgow), protesting his decision at length. The disturbance on the West Terracing – the traditional Celtic end – led to the SFA, on 17 September, closing Celtic Park for a month.

Celtic may have felt hard done by, but one newspaper pointed out that the principle of holding clubs responsible for their fans' behaviour home and away was first endorsed at a conference held in 1922 to discuss football hooliganism. That meeting had been chaired by the SFA's president, Tom White, who was also Celtic's chairman; the Scottish League had been represented by its president, Willie Maley, Celtic's manager. Largely overlooked in the furore was the fact that Rangers, albeit indirectly, were censured by the SFA over the match, being cited as an unfortunate example of the type of dissent with which referees had to contend.

Most bizarre of all, perhaps, was Celtic's 8–1 defeat at Ibrox on Ne'erday 1943. Shortly after half-time Malcolm MacDonald was sent off by the referee, W. Davidson (Glasgow), for protesting Rangers' fourth goal, netted by Waddell from a suspiciously offside position after a George Young free-kick from 50 yards out. A few minutes later, Matt Lynch followed his captain to the pavilion for a foul on Charlie Johnstone. Fortunately, no crowd trouble ensued. The *Glasgow Herald* commented of the low attendance of 30,000 that 'it is to be feared that it [the fixture] has lost some of its appeal'. An unlikely prospect! On the same day as the Old Firm mismatch, ex-Celt Johnny Crum, thriving on a plentiful service from Stanley Matthews (a guest player with Morton), netted six goals in a local derby victory over St Mirren; and another ex-Celt, Willie Buchan, scored twice for Hamilton in their 3–2 win over Motherwell.

For all the club's travails, the supporters continued to turn up in respectable numbers to cheer on the team throughout the war. The slightest hint that Celtic were on the verge of greater things was sufficient to boost the crowd; 87,121 spectators turned up at Hampden in April 1944 to see the Old Firm contest the semi-final of the Southern League Cup, a competition introduced in 1941. Rangers were to dash the rising expectations of the Celtic support, confirming their status as favourites by winning 4–2 despite a thrilling comeback by the underdogs that had Rangers reeling. It came too late to offset a lethargic first half by Celtic, though, or to overcome Rangers' greater experience in such situations. Celtic may have had youth on their side, but Jimmy Smith – in his sixteenth season – produced the goal that killed the contest five minutes from time, when Celtic were pressing hard for an equaliser.

Jimmy McStay, the manager of a famous club which had won only two trophies (the Glasgow Cup in 1940 and the Charity Cup in 1943) during his tenure, became visibly discouraged by his lack of authority, and eventually gave up even his token involvement in selecting the team. Clearly, the directors were looking to replace him, but the club did not handle the dismissal of the manager honourably. While on holiday with his family at Ayr in July 1945, McStay started to learn of the rumours of his impending sacking via the newspapers. Jimmy McGrory met with Kilmarnock's directors on 10 July to inform them that he was considering an offer made to him 'by another club', as the newspapers put it. A couple of days later the press began to hint that McGrory was about to make his long-awaited return to Celtic Park. In the *Sunday Mail* of 15 July, Willie Allison revealed that McGrory was 'as good as at Parkhead as far as my information is concerned. What is more, he will, I understand, have absolute control of the team.'

Tom White, Celtic's chairman, who had approached McGrory and who had to conceal that fact, was embarrassed. On 21 July in the *Daily Record*, 'Waverley' announced that he had been informed (unofficially) that McGrory was due to start as Celtic's manager on Monday, 23 July. This report was officially denied but, to all intents and purposes, it was accurate. Jimmy McStay came back from his holiday on 23 July as manager and met White on his return to the ground. Seemingly, as he alighted from the tramcar at Parkhead Cross, he spotted a newspaper billboard announcing that Jimmy McGrory was slated to take over at Celtic Park. The meeting with the chairman was short, with White asking him to hand in his resignation. Jimmy McGrory took over at Parkhead the following day.

Pointedly, a few days later, 'Jaymak' of the *Evening Times* wished Jimmy McGrory luck in his appointment, but added the following rider: 'No one of common sense is going to be so foolish as to believe that Jimmy McStay was to blame for the way that Celtic had fallen from a time-honoured pinnacle of football skill and renown. In all ways he was well equipped to turn his attention to the job of guiding the team to success from the managerial desk. What he did at Alloa in this respect is sufficient proof.'

Jimmy McStay had fatally compromised his chances of succeeding at Parkhead by not standing up for himself, as can be gathered from a revealing comment in his own version of events in the *Sunday Post*, when referring to the broken promise about a free hand in the running of the team: 'Celtic policy was not moulded to suit my requirements. Rather, my plans had to fit the Celtic programme.' (29 July 1945)

By replacing McStay with the equally diffident Jimmy McGrory, the directors – it seems clear – still did not want to have to deal with a strong-willed and autocratic manager in the mould of Maley. Jimmy McGrory would face two decades of self-discovery, of a gradual realisation that his innate qualities of modesty and gentlemanliness constituted a distinct handicap in the central relationship at any football club, that between a manager and his chairman.

Meanwhile, Matt Busby had been appointed as manager of Manchester United a few months earlier. At his interview he had insisted upon – and obtained – full control of all matters relating to the playing side. Busby was about to embark upon the mammoth task of rebuilding a club heavily in debt and lumbered with a bomb-wrecked stadium. One letter-writer to the *Sunday Mail* of 25 February 1945 bemoaned the fact that Matt Busby's all-round knowledge of the game and his popularity would be lost to his native land; the writer noted Busby's recent statement that he had 'waited almost three years in the hope of a certain Scottish club approaching him . . .'

SIX

Promises, Promises

1945–65

During the immediate post-war period Celtic fielded sides that did not measure up – and their supporters were not fooled. Years later, the residue of bitterness still remained, as an article which appeared in the *Celtic View* of July 1968 reveals. Even at a time when his club was at its zenith, when his team had recently imposed its will on Europe, this middle-aged follower could still look back with a truly jaundiced eye at the past: 'What annoyed me most of all during this lean period was the constant reminder from relatives and friends of the past. The stock saying of this time was "They're just not Celtic class!". For years I wondered if I would ever see a player who measured up to this mysterious "Celtic class" description of ability. Older fans seemed to obtain some perverse satisfaction out of the club's fall from glory, and the fact that the current team had almost been relegated.'

Celtic almost relegated? Not exactly, although the final league fixture at Dens Park against Dundee in 1947–48 has passed into the club's mythology as a life-and-death struggle to avoid instant demotion to a lower division. The match was not of such critical dimensions, since a defeat for Celtic meant that the eventual outcome would depend on the results of subsequent matches involving the club's fellow strugglers. Queen's Park were already doomed, but Morton, Airdrie and Queen of the South (along with Celtic) had a lively interest in the proceedings. Certainly, the threat was sufficient to make the journey to Dundee on 17 April 1948 a tense prospect, with Celtic having to win in order to remove the mathematical possibility of relegation – a fate which had suddenly descended upon them with three successive – and heavy – league defeats in which they had conceded 12 goals.

A most unlikely hero emerged in the person of Jock Weir, signed from Blackburn Rovers only two months previously for a fee of £7,000. A cheerful, bustling centre-forward, Weir had made a scant impression as a goalscorer but, switched to outside-right for this fixture, he netted a hat-trick – including the winning goal two minutes from time – in a 3–2 victory. Celtic could relax in the sure knowledge they were safe, and Airdrie eventually lost out in the struggle to remain in Division A.

Celtic's predicament should have come as no surprise since the 1940s had been a constant struggle, particularly after the resumption of normal competition following the war. The 'years of austerity', the historian's phrase for the condition of post-war Britain, could just as well have applied in microcosm to Celtic. A decade of stagnation, on and off the field, had reduced the once-mighty club to an appalling level of mediocrity – at best. It is difficult to appreciate from this distance the trauma inflicted upon the supporters as Celtic drifted helplessly further and further away from football glory. They had been onlookers as Hibernian replaced them as Rangers' principal rivals in the championship; worse was the realisation that Celtic had failed to make any impact in the League Cup (a continuation of the wartime Southern League Cup) and in the Scottish Cup (where their heroic exploits were fading into distant memory). Indeed, some wondered if the traditional Celtic cup spirit had not evaporated completely, judging by an abject dismissal (2–1) in the 1947 Scottish Cup at the hands of Division B side Dundee at Dens Park. The humiliation of that upset was to be repeated only two years later, this time inflicted by Dundee United, another side from the lower division. The supposedly fitter, full-time Glasgow club was rocked by the determination and stamina of an inspired home team which could afford to shrug off three disallowed 'goals' and still win 4–3.

Stirred into action by the brush with relegation, the Celtic Board, now chaired by stockbroker's clerk Bob Kelly, at last took steps to rectify the intolerable situation. Kelly was an experienced director, having succeeded his late father, James Kelly, on the Board in 1932, and he had moved up to the role of chairman after the death of Tom White in March 1947.

Jimmy Hogan, an elderly Lancastrian who had earned an impressive reputation on the Continent as a coach, was engaged with a view to imparting his knowledge to the younger players in particular. After some signs that his gospel of constructive football might be taking root, however, the influence of this still lively and alert personality soon diminished at Parkhead. Hogan, who would sit at Wembley Stadium as an honoured guest of the Hungarian FA in 1953 to watch the annihilation of England, became just another victim of the insularity of Scottish football. Tommy Docherty, the only Celtic player of that period to make a name for himself as a coach and manager, remembers how the more established Celtic players snubbed Hogan, considering him 'a theory-mad coot'. Apparently, Hogan's stressing of such basics as 'make the ball do the work' and 'use the open space' were felt to be too esoteric for players who had recently 'saved' the club from being relegated.

The focus of attention quickly shifted to the remarkable Charlie Tully, an inside-forward signed from Belfast Celtic in June 1948. Tully, fond of 'a drink' and cigarettes, was an unlikely model for an athlete, but his vibrant personality and dazzling skills made him perhaps the greatest crowd-puller that Scottish football has ever seen, the topic of conversation in pubs and clubs, on trains and terracings, at work and at play. The tremendous lift that his early performances gave to the struggling club was largely responsible for a crowd of 87,000 turning up at Hampden Park on 27 September 1948, when Celtic lifted their first trophy since the war by beating Third Lanark 3–1 in the Glasgow Cup final, as one front-page profile suggested: 'The arrival of Charlie Tully from Belfast a few weeks ago is the most exciting thing that has happened in Scottish football for many a year. Celtic fans in particular, and football fans in general, have welcomed this dainty young Irishman with the dancing feet and the swirling swerve in a way that leaves no doubt as to their feelings. A week ago, at the close of the Celtic–Rangers clash, a crowd of 70,000 – and they weren't all Celtic supporters – lingered behind to applaud the magnificent performance of the smiling Irishman as he walked off the field. Little wonder. His slippery moves, coolness, cuteness, his apparent cheekiness on the ball stamp him as a truly great football craftsman. His very appearance on the field is a signal for a roar from the crowd. His every move is discussed and analysed.' (*Glasgow Weekly News*: 2 October 1948)

Glasgow had rarely seen anything like it. The impact of the young forward was truly extraordinary, sparking off a growth-industry in 'Tully ties', 'Tully cocktails', 'green-flavoured Tully ice-cream', and inevitably – given his own ready wit – 'Tullyisms'. It was reported that pilgrims in St Peter's Square in the Vatican used to point to the balcony and ask, 'Who is that man standing beside Charlie Tully?', and it was confidently asserted in Glasgow that the newly born heir-apparent to the throne had been named after him.

Tully was immediately beatified by the support and, after that performance against Rangers in a 3–1 victory in the League Cup, canonised; unfortunately, those who hailed him as a messiah capable of transforming the club's fortunes overnight were proved sadly unrealistic.

Only a week after his personal triumph in the Old Firm clash, Tully found himself a marked man as Celtic went down to Hibs 4–2 before a record crowd at Easter Road. Acting on instructions from his manager Hugh Shaw, the veteran Sammy Kean shadowed the young Irishman throughout, and Celtic's efficiency was noticeably reduced.

The influence of Tully was missed at the next League Cup match; the club allowed their star player to play for Northern Ireland, and Celtic went down 3–6 to Clyde at Parkhead – and at Ibrox in the return fixture Celtic lost 2–1 to a more determined Rangers. Three splendid victories in the League Cup had been followed by three successive defeats by the same opponents.

In football, alas, those who invest all their hopes in such happy-go-lucky types as Tully are often doomed to disappointment. The contrast with the philosophy and atmosphere then prevailing at Ibrox was memorably illustrated by Willie Waddell, a dour, hard-hitting winger of the 1940s. Twenty years later, recalling the aura of invincibility which surrounded Rangers in the immediate post-war years, Waddell spoke of a contemporary fellow Ranger, Eddie Rutherford, saying that 'Eddie was the nicest character you could meet, the nicest man in the team. He was always smiling. But, when we lost, I used to hate him. "Look at that wee bastard," I used to say. "He's still smiling!"' Defeat was anathema at Ibrox, the loss of a goal (even in matches won) the subject of a post-match dressing-room inquest among the members of their 'Iron Curtain' defence.

While the Celtic half of Glasgow chortled over the cantrips of Charlie, Rangers cleaned up the trophies, including the treble of League, League Cup and Scottish Cup in Tully's first season at Parkhead. That level of commitment and professionalism was simply beyond Celtic sides of this period, for all the talent they possessed: Tully himself, a gifted and brainy player, whose dribbling and cunning passes created chances all too often wasted by colleagues slow of mind and foot; Pat McAuley, who displayed more than a few touches of genuine artistry and intelligence at left-half despite a lack of pace; Bobby Collins, a diminutive but lion-hearted forward, who became an immediate hit with Celtic fans on his début in August 1949 with his courage in taking on the fearsome Rangers left-back, Jock 'Tiger' Shaw; and Bobby Evans, initially a humdrum utility forward, who established himself as a peerless right-half, famous for strong but scrupulously fair tackling, uncanny anticipation and distribution which improved in leaps and bounds. A significant indication of Celtic's weakness lay in the fact that Evans was too often called upon to do the job of three men in overworked defences whose last line was that busiest of all Celtic goalkeepers, Willie Miller, a man who came to the team's rescue time after time with daring saves.

Celtic's inconsistency, and a terminal addiction to individuality, branded them as a team more suited to the glamour and excitement of cup competitions rather than the long haul of the league, where their maddeningly frustrating play ruled them out as contenders. In a manner typical of their waywardness – after 13 years in the wilderness – Celtic finally satisfied their long-suffering supporters' hunger for major success by winning the Scottish Cup in 1951. The triumph was due to the sudden blossoming of a talent that had seemed fated to remain untapped. John McPhail, because of his versatility, had become classified as a utility player since joining Celtic in 1941. However, with the club hovering near the foot of the table early in 1950, he was suddenly converted – more by accident than design – into a centre-forward in the hope that his height and weight could resolve a long-standing problem. He earned an extended run in that position in March 1950 following three goals against Falkirk in a 4–3 win, and four goals against East Fife in a 4–1 rout; in show-business parlance, he never looked back, and achieved hero status through his goalscoring and leadership qualities in the 1951 Scottish Cup competition.

Two early goals against East Fife torpedoed the Fifers' hopes in a replay, won 4–2 by Celtic at Parkhead; in a tense clash with Hearts at Tynecastle his deft chip over a stranded Jimmy Brown for Celtic's winning goal followed a neat bout of inter-passing with Tully (a feat largely overshadowed by the miraculous goalkeeping of George Hunter, a youngster apparently oblivious to the frantic atmosphere on the field and the terracing overspills behind his first-half goal); two more goals in a 3–0 win over Aberdeen at Parkhead in the quarter-final, attended by 75,000 with thousands locked out and hundreds of younger spectators watching from the safety of the track; and, in the final itself before 133,331 at Hampden Park on 21 April 1951, one dramatic moment salvaged an otherwise forgettable match as John McPhail gathered a long downfield clearance and evaded the challenges of Motherwell's outfield defenders before calmly lofting the ball over the head of the advancing keeper, Johnstone, in the 13th minute.

Celtic brought further joy to their delirious support by returning from a close-season tour of the United States and Canada – during which the priceless Scottish Cup itself was almost lost in a train journey between New York and Toronto – and going on to win the St Mungo Cup. This tournament was initiated by Glasgow Corporation as a contribution to the Festival of Britain which was designed as a 'pick-me-up' for a nation only gradually emerging from post-war hardship.

This time, Charlie Tully's influence was paramount in securing the trophy by turning the final against Aberdeen at Hampden Park on 1 August 1951 when, with Celtic two goals down, he sparked the revival with a typically impudent gambit. He converted a harmless throw-in into a corner-kick, after which Celtic scored through Sean Fallon's close-in shot; the cheek lay in the fact that Tully had taken the throw-in himself and played the ball off the back of the retreating Aberdeen defender to gain the corner. With 20 minutes of the contest left and the crowd of 80,600 in a ferment, the outside-left set up the winning goal for Celtic after picking up a neat pass from Baillie and slipping past Aberdeen's other full-back, the hard-tackling Emery; he released the ball to young Bertie Peacock, a recent signing from Northern Ireland – as was Fallon – and an inside-forward 'as eager as a puppy', before catching the return pass right on the bye-line and crossing for another newcomer, inside-forward Jimmy Walsh, to crash home the winning goal after his initial header had been blocked by goalkeeper Martin. Walsh thus completed an impressive record by scoring in every match in the tournament.

Predictably, Celtic could not capitalise in their new-found spirit and inspiration over the next few seasons – a condemnation of the shallow nature of a recovery which owed little to method or planning. It came as no surprise, therefore, that the revival would be curtailed by the lack of depth in the squad when it was struck by injury – or worse. The litany of medical woes seemed everlasting and included John McPhail, sidelined with weight problems; George Hunter, confined to a sanatorium in Switzerland with tuberculosis; and Joe Baillie, a stylish left-half whose Celtic career was all but ended by a serious knee injury sustained at Airdrie in November 1952. Real tragedy intervened when John Millsopp, a youngster who had only recently broken into the side as a half-back, died after an operation for appendicitis.

Celtic's slump back into mediocrity was highlighted by the club's first defeat in a Scottish Cup replay since 1889, a 2–1 defeat after extra-time by Third Lanark at Cathkin in February 1952, and a humiliating exit for the holders at the first hurdle.

The only bright spot – and a most unlikely one – was the arrival in late 1951 of a largely forgotten centre-half from Southern League side Llanelly. The Welsh club's dream of joining the Football League was fading because of financial problems, and the pivot became available at a bargain price of £1,300 – a fee which in hindsight appears all the more remarkable in view of the unexpected role Jock Stein was to play in the next stage of Celtic's rehabilitation. Celtic, perhaps sensitive about accusations of parsimony, asked Llanelly to keep the amount of the transfer fee a secret.

Much to his own astonishment, and due solely to Celtic's injury problems, Stein was immediately pitchforked into Celtic's defence against St Mirren at Parkhead on 8 December instead of 'helping to bring along the youngsters'. As his wry observation later confirmed, 'I thought I was destined for the reserves, but I managed to slip into the first team.' The Celtic supporters, who remembered him as the mainstay of the permanently struggling Albion Rovers, were surprised at the confidence and leadership displayed by the newcomer in more exalted company.

Stein himself must have wondered why a squad containing such famous names and major talents as Fernie, Evans, Peacock, Collins and Tully was not more consistently successful. The 1950s, after all, was a decade in which the honours would go round more equitably in Scotland largely due to a fairly even spread of top-class players in the A Division. For example, Clyde won the Scottish Cup twice, and Hearts won all three major competitions within the period.

It would not have taken Stein long to detect one answer in the unacceptable training patterns of such Runyonesque characters as Charlie Tully. The charismatic Irishman's aversion to training was demonstrated by his practice of lapping the track only when the club chairman Bob Kelly was watching on his daily visit to Celtic Park. As Bobby Murdoch, then a teenager, has testified, Tully was not above using a combination of blarney and subterfuge to avoid the chores of pre-season training. Charlie timed his arrival at Celtic Park to the second on one occasion when the bus was ready to set off for Ayrshire, where the players would be faced with a ten-mile run to build up stamina. At the last possible moment Tully rushed up full of apologies – and with a ready-made excuse: he had been unavoidably detained as a police witness to an incident where 'someone had fallen off a tram-car'. The older hands on the bus assured young Murdoch, about to embark on an ultimately glorious career at the club, that Charlie had probably been peeking around a nearby corner until the bus was pulling out, and then he would sprint up to the bus, knowing all too well that he no longer had time to get stripped inside Celtic Park without holding everybody up.

In fact, Stein was also frequently irritated – as were other Celtic players – by Tully's reluctance to help out in defence when the side was under pressure. Such habits would draw caustic, if private, comments from ex-miner Stein, whose own outlook and work ethic had been shaped by a decade spent down the pit where, in his words, 'phoneys and cheats don't last for long'. One does not have to speculate too long on how Stein the manager would have handled Tully the player.

During this most depressing period – specifically the latter part of the 1951–52 season – an SFA edict diverted attention from the mediocrity on the field. Several cases of misconduct involving Celtic supporters, dating back to the 1940s, culminated in disgraceful scenes at the 1952 New Year's Day clash with Rangers, when the Ibrox side, reduced to ten men through injury, had romped to a 4–1 win on a muddy, rain-swept pitch over a Celtic team languishing in mid-table.

The game's rulers in Scotland were right to be concerned about the violence on the terracings. The Glasgow magistrates met to discuss the situation and made several recommendations which they invited the SFA and the Scottish League to consider. The most controversial was the fourth: 'that the two clubs should avoid displaying flags which might incite feeling among the spectators'. This was construed as a reference to the flag of Eire which flew over one end of the covered enclosure, and some football officials – undoubtedly with a track-record of coolness towards Celtic – chose to use this recommendation as an excuse to bully the club. The tactics appeared to constitute a threat to the club's existence.

After consideration, the Referee Committee of the SFA ruled 'that Celtic be asked to refrain from displaying in its park any flag or emblem that had no association with the country or the sport'. When the full SFA council convened to consider the approval of the committee's report, Bob Kelly of Celtic rose to defend his club's traditions and to move the rejection of that part dealing with the banning of the flag. Not too surprisingly – in view of the lengthy and profitable symbiotic relationship between the two clubs – his motion was seconded by Rangers' John Wilson. The council voted to ignore Celtic's plea, however, – and the battle lines were drawn up.

If Celtic continued to fly the Eire flag in defiance of the SFA ruling – and any misconduct by their supporters took place – the club would face a number of unpleasant options: 'a fine, or closure of the ground, or suspension, or all of these penalties'.

The thought of Celtic being suspended from Scottish football was patently ridiculous, but that threat hung over the club like a pall for the remainder of the season and undoubtedly was a factor in the general malaise.

A clique within the SFA, orchestrated primarily by the secretary, George Graham, continued to press Celtic to take down the flag and submit to the SFA's demands. Celtic had taken legal advice on the subject and were confident about the outcome, but Bob Kelly had to contend with considerable pressure, formal and informal, from his colleagues on the SFA council. He remained unshaken and eloquent in the defence of Celtic's traditions: the club had been founded by Irishmen in the 1880s, the flag was flown to recall and honour that association. The opposition to Celtic's stance fragmented and eventually the furore faded away. The threat had been made, pressure tactics applied – but the likelihood of its ever being translated into action by a now splintering SFA was minimal. If, as many Celtic sympathisers claim, a history of bias against the club exists among football officialdom in Scotland, then the flutter over the Eire flag was probably its last semi-public manifestation.

Given the club's alleged Irish Republican leanings, it was ironic that Celtic should join in the celebrations for the coronation of Queen Elizabeth II in 1953, when eight clubs representing Scotland and England were invited to participate in a knock-out tournament in Glasgow: Rangers, Aberdeen, Hibernian and Celtic from Scotland; Arsenal, Tottenham Hotspur, Manchester United and Newcastle United from England. Celtic were ill-prepared for the competition, having just completed a disastrous season in which their mid-table standing served to hide the fact that they had finished only four points above the second relegation spot; one sportswriter had dubbed 1952–53 'the season of the slow handclap for Celtic'.

In reality, the invitation extended to Celtic owed more to their crowd-pulling power and an excellent record in past tournaments of a similar kind. The obvious solution to their chronic problems was to buy proven players, and Celtic made an offer for Jimmy Cowan, Morton's international keeper, but their low bid was rejected by the Greenock club. One ex-Morton centre-forward was signed in time for the tournament, though; Neil Mochan was captured from Middlesbrough for £8,000, making his début at Hampden Park in the final of the Charity Cup against Queen's Park. He scored twice for his new club, leading Celtic to a 3–1 win on 9 May.

Celtic had been drawn to face Arsenal, the current English champions, in the Coronation Cup two days later at the same venue, and nobody gave the Parkhead side much hope. Arsenal began like real champions but, to the roars of the 59,500 crowd, Celtic drew heart from the confident interceptions of Bobby Evans. They pushed the Gunners back into defence and in 24 minutes Bobby Collins scored directly from a corner-kick, his vicious inswinger deceiving Swindin, Arsenal's veteran keeper. Swindin's inspired performance, though, was the main factor in holding the score down to 1–0 as Celtic, asserting firm control, pinned the Londoners back in their own half in a constant bombardment for most of the second half.

On Saturday, 16 May, 73,466 people turned up at Hampden to see the semi-final between Celtic and Manchester United, the conquerors of Rangers in the first round. Celtic's early pressure was fierce and sustained; in 25 minutes it was rewarded with a goal from Peacock's blistering shot following clever leading-up play by Tully. Mochan sealed Celtic's place in the final with a second goal in the 52nd minute, again set up by Tully; the Irishman brought a clearance from Rollo under control, and then flicked the ball over the head of centre-half Chilton and into the path of Mochan, who raced through from midfield to slip it past the onrushing United keeper, Crompton.

The final was held on 20 May, with 117,060 packed into Hampden

Park to see Celtic take on Hibernian in an all-Scottish clash. Shortly before kick-off the gates were closed, with an estimated 6,000 locked out because the traditional Celtic end of the stadium was already dangerously overcrowded. Those unfortunates were fated to miss one of the most thrilling matches in the club's entire history. Celtic were forced to make one change from the side that had eliminated the two English clubs, Tully having to withdraw after pulling a muscle in the closing minutes of the semi-final. His place was taken by Willie Fernie, a long-striding forward whose mazy dribbling frequently left opposing defences bewildered. Fernie felt he had something to prove in the final; during his four in-and-out seasons at Parkhead, he had frequently been omitted from the line-up because of a perception that he was unwilling to part with the ball. He wanted a chance to establish himself in the side and, although he felt sorry for Tully (a player for whom his admiration is still unbounded), he felt confident about his own ability to seize the moment — like an understudy suddenly thrust into the spotlight. Hibernian had also performed heroics *en route* to Hampden: they had beaten Tottenham Hotspur 2–1 in a replay, and had crushed Newcastle United 4–0.

Celtic immediately put Hibs under pressure, twice forcing goalkeeper Younger to make daring saves at the feet of their forwards, and their sustained effort was rewarded after 28 minutes when Neil Mochan gave them the lead with a glorious shot high into the net from 30 yards, struck with his reputedly weaker right foot. Talking about the goal shortly before his death in August 1994, he recalled that he took three or four steps forward after receiving a 'perfect' square pass from Fernie some 40 yards out, before 'hitting it with everything I had'.

In the second half Celtic's defence performed magnificently against the much-vaunted Hibernian forward line, deservedly labelled the 'Famous Five'. The Edinburgh side threw everything into attack, but their onslaught foundered on the rocks of Celtic's rearguard, marshalled by Jock Stein whose own primary task was to keep a close grip on Lawrie Reilly, a deadly striker. Stein was aided by Bobby Evans at his magnificent best, covering, it appeared, every square inch of the Hampden pitch in both defence and attack — and by a Celtic goalkeeper who confounded his critics with a series of breathtaking saves that ultimately broke Hibs' hearts. John Bonnar, a smallish keeper signed from Arbroath in 1948, had never been fully accepted because of his inconsistency but, on the evening of the Coronation Cup final, he turned in an unbelievable performance. Three minutes from time, Jimmy Walsh rounded off a breakaway by netting a second goal for Celtic — a goal which sent the club's followers into sheer ecstasy on the packed terracings and stands. A marvellous game, and a splendid achievement!

Later, in his days as Celtic's manager, Jock Stein would pause in front of the Coronation Cup when showing it off to visitors to Celtic Park; invariably, he called it 'Mochan's Cup' – but, intriguingly, the late Willie Ormond, the outside-left in a bitterly disappointed losing team, used to insist that the most influential player on a pitch filled with heroes had not been Bonnar, nor Stein, nor Evans, nor Mochan – but Willie Fernie, whose thrilling runs in the first half, and persistent menace in the second, had induced panic in Hibernian's defence.

Celtic, now equipped with a proven striker in Neil Mochan, and possessed of a squad which had discovered the secret of winning during the Coronation Cup, built on their newly found confidence, much to the delight of their followers. The potent unit forged in the Coronation Cup campaign proved hard to beat in season 1953–54 when Celtic won the championship and Scottish Cup double, the first for the club in 40 years.

The fans were quick to sense an omen on 1 January 1954 when Celtic added the craft and guile of Fernie to complement the industry of Evans, Peacock and Collins in notching up a 1–0 win over Rangers at Parkhead through a typical piece of opportunism by Mochan. Excluding unofficial wartime fixtures, that victory was the first over Rangers on Ne'erday in 16 years.

Celtic's sheer momentum overcame a seeming body-blow to their league challenge when Hearts, their closest rivals, appeared to gain a significant psychological advantage through a dubious late winner at Tynecastle on 6 February 1954; Wardhaugh clashed with goalkeeper Hunter and bundled him over the line. Despite Celtic's protests to the referee (Mr J. Barclay of Kirkcaldy), the goal – which gave Hearts a 3–2 win – was allowed to stand.

Thereafter, Celtic channelled any anger or resentment into overhauling the Edinburgh side's lead by running up eight successive wins – the last of these victories, appropriately enough, in another visit to the capital on 17 April 1954. This time, Celtic crushed their hosts with a confident display after a first-minute goal by Mochan, now being fielded just as profitably at outside-left, set up a comfortable 3–0 win over Hibernian before a crowd of 45,000.

One week later, Celtic faced Aberdeen at Hampden Park in the Glasgow club's 25th Scottish Cup final. As befitted a side which had destroyed Rangers 6–0 in the semi-final, Aberdeen put up a stiff resistance but Celtic made the breakthrough in the 50th minute. Neil Mochan, wandering to the right wing in pursuit of the ball, let fly a swerving cross-cum-shot, which was deflected past his own keeper by centre-half Young. Aberdeen's response, as in the final of 1937, was immediate; Buckley converted Leggat's deft pass for the equaliser.

Willie Fernie had often been criticised for holding the ball too long, but he insists that he always followed the advice of one of his Parkhead mentors: 'Don't part with the ball until it's to your team's best advantage.' That piece of advice brought the Scottish Cup back to Celtic Park when the Fifer calmly dribbled the ball along the bye-line, leaving defenders in his wake, before squaring it across for centre-forward Sean Fallon to net the winner in the 63rd minute. Celtic held out for a 2–1 win, resisting Aberdeen's frantic efforts to draw level mainly through the resolution of a formidable half-back line: the tireless Bobby Evans, the beaver-like Bertie Peacock, and the steady, reliable Jock Stein as the pivot and a wonderfully inspiring captain.

Little wonder, then, that at a presentation of medals to the Celtic players at Turnberry Hotel shortly afterwards, chairman Bob Kelly's speech, which dutifully acknowledged the pieces of good fortune Celtic had enjoyed, singled out one player to illustrate the point: 'The luckiest was the day we signed our captain, Jock Stein.' As captain, Stein was already displaying leadership qualities, encouraging tactical discussions and expounding his ideas when the players dined daily at Ferrari's, a city-centre restaurant. And this at a time when training was done virtually without a ball, and the manager was rarely spotted outside the confines of his office. Stein was already absorbing some of the lessons of Hungary's 6–3 demolition of England at Wembley in 1953, and was to observe at first-hand Scotland's chronic lack of preparation for the World Cup to be held in Switzerland the following summer. Both excursions for Celtic (the trip to Wembley, and to the World Cup) were arranged by Bob Kelly, in tacit acknowledgement of the unwelcome realisation that Scottish football was lagging behind the rest of the world.

While his awareness of a football world outside of Scotland was commendable, the interventionist tendencies of the same Bob Kelly were beginning to affect Celtic adversely. His motives may have been sincere and well intentioned but the chairman had fully established an autocracy at Parkhead. For example, he was in the habit of visiting the ground daily to watch the players train and to offer his advice in sorting out any 'problems' they might have. These problems, if they concerned personal matters, should have remained private; if related to football, they should have been the prerogative of the manager. Unfortunately, Jimmy McGrory was manager in name only, and too much of a gentleman to question the chairman's intrusions into his territory.

Bob Kelly's sense of his authority at Celtic Park was to prove calamitous on the playing field for most of the next decade of the club's history – and was manifested in the most bizarre fashion in the realm of team selection. Amateurish tinkering with Celtic's line-up in successive

Scottish Cup finals, undoubtedly at the chairman's instigation, would prove to be a fatal handicap.

In the 1955 Cup final Clyde gained an equaliser in the 88th minute. A corner on the right taken by Robertson was caught by the notorious Hampden 'swirl', and Celtic's goalkeeper Bonnar misjudged it badly although he was unchallenged, allowing the ball to drop and bounce agonisingly into the net.

For the replay Celtic chose to leave out two of their most productive and mobile forwards, Bobby Collins and Neil Mochan, whose pace and energy might have exploited the ageing Clyde defence. Instead, the chairman opted to field Sean Fallon at centre-forward and move John McPhail to inside-left; both men, not noted for speed, were further reduced in effectiveness by the greasy conditions underfoot. Clyde, whose morale was boosted in particular by the omission of Collins, a quick-turning, impudent player, lifted their game from the previous Saturday. Shortly after the interval, Tommy Ring, Clyde's left-winger – and ironically from 'a strong Celtic family' – scored the game's only goal when he cashed in on a breakaway. Afterwards, it was hinted most unconvincingly by a Celtic official that 'Collins was suffering from a lack of confidence following a recent leg operation'; a much more plausible explanation was the known distaste of the puritanical chairman for the little Celt's 'dunting duel' with Clyde's South African keeper Hewkins in the first match. On the morning after the replay the newspapers reported that Collins had been selected for Scotland's forthcoming tour of Yugoslavia, Austria and Hungary . . .

A year later, there would be further cause for bewilderment and anger among Celtic's support when the club was once more on the losing side in the Scottish Cup final, this time against Hearts. There were bizarre antics in both camps in the last hours before the kick-off. To ease some of the pre-match tension Bobby Parker, a rugged full-back and Hearts' former captain (ruled out after a cartilage operation) turned up in the Hampden dressing-room wearing a hula skirt; in addition, Hearts' groundsman Matt Chalmers had donned a bowler hat, old-fashioned frock coat, false nose and glasses! 'When they took the field,' read one Edinburgh-based account, 'the players' nerves were calm.' Bobby Kirk, their right-back, was to reveal (in 1996) that the Hearts players 'laughed' when they heard the Celtic side read out on the tannoy.

Their collective morale must have been higher than that of Celtic. The Parkhead line-up, selected at lunchtime on the day of the match, produced gasps of astonishment and much head-shaking, the choice of forward line simply defying logic and common sense. In place of the injured Collins came an inexperienced youngster, Billy Craig, with only four meaningless league matches to his credit – and absolutely no experience in the Scottish Cup; as his partner, the untried boy had ex-Commando Mike Haughney, the regular right-back who, mystifyingly, had been moved up front 'to spread the play' as an inside-forward. This experimental pairing was preferred to a combination of Jimmy Walsh and Jim Sharkey, two highly rated forwards: Walsh was a seasoned player, a proven goalscorer, and Sharkey had impressed with his ball-control, dribbling skills and a penchant for spectacular goals. But, at Seamill, an alleged misdemeanor was reported to the chairman, and Sharkey was not considered for the final.

Hearts were formidable opponents, boasting an inside-forward unit of Conn, Bauld and Wardhaugh, nicknamed the 'Terrible Trio', and a redoubtable half-back line in MacKay, Glidden and Cumming (who earned plaudits for finishing the match despite a bad head wound). The Edinburgh side, so often suspect in temperament, took full advantage of Celtic's lopsided selection to win comfortably in the end by 3–1, two of the goals coming from outside-left Ian Crawford, on leave from National Service in the army. His crisp finishing and dash contrasted strongly with the guileless Celtic forwards who did not force Duff into one save throughout the entire match. Haughney's only memorable contribution was as controversial as his deployment since he netted Celtic's only goal by charging goalkeeper Duff (legally) and prodding the resulting loose ball into Hearts' net.

A terse comment, made by trainer Alex Dowdells as he departed for Leicester City during the close season, hinted at both an acrimonious parting and the confusion rampant at Parkhead as a consequence of the manager's lack of authority: 'Only when manager McGrory and the directors can make a reasonably consistent first-team choice will they get consistent results. You could be excused for thinking that a team which last season played seven different centre-forwards didn't know the meaning of consistency.' (*Scottish Daily Express*: 19 July 1956) Doubtless, the trainer had in mind the blatant misuse of the goalscoring ability of Neil Mochan. When he was fielded at centre-forward in a 4–1 League Cup sectional victory over Rangers at Ibrox on 27 August 1955, that was only his second appearance in that position in the past two years! Typically, Celtic threw away the advantage gained partly through Mochan's restoration by replacing Fernie, although fully recovered from an ankle injury, with the slimly built, inexperienced 17-year-old Matt McVittie for the return match at Parkhead.

Rangers, notably rugged and vigorous, ruthlessly exploited Celtic's shortcomings and a toll of injuries that mounted during the match to win 4–0 and inflict the heaviest home defeat in the history of Celtic's participation in the League Cup, and to qualify for the next stage of the competition at their rivals' expense. Jock Stein sustained the ankle injury which effectively ended his playing career, and both Sean Fallon and John Bonnar finished the contest limping badly. Understandably, young McVittie was invisible, and Willie Fernie sat in the stand, despondent 'at the worst thing that ever happened to me at Celtic Park', as he recently told the authors.

In August 1955 Celtic had squandered a glorious opportunity to go on and win the one national trophy which had so far eluded them despite a decade of trying. It was a situation which they were to rectify with a vengeance a year later.

Ironically, it took the arrival of the younger brother of John McPhail, the hero of 1951, to inspire the breakthrough which ended Celtic's frustration. Billy McPhail, signed for £2,500 from Clyde in May 1956, was a centre-forward of subtle skills and intelligence, but serious doubts existed about his staying power and fitness; the size of the transfer fee seemed to reflect those doubts.

In the League Cup final replay against Partick Thistle at Hampden Park on 31 October 1956 he netted twice shortly after the interval to decide the contest when it was poised at 0–0. In the 49th minute the alert McPhail took full advantage of defensive dithering to hook the ball past Ledgerwood in Thistle's goal; within another minute or so, he was on hand to steer Mochan's cross into the net from close in. Bobby Collins ended the scoring after 60 minutes by racing clear to fire a low shot past the despairing goalkeeper, while defenders were appealing frantically for offside.

Having ended the hoodoo, Celtic went on to retain the trophy in 1957 with perhaps the most stunning victory in their entire history and a triumph destined to become an indelible part of the club's folklore, celebrated down the years in song and poetry.

On 19 October 1957 Celtic lined up for an unforgettable Old Firm encounter at Hampden Park in the League Cup final before a crowd of 82,293. From the outset, Celtic settled into a rhythm which was to grow into an irresistible force as the match continued. Shots from Tully and Collins rebounded from the woodwork before Sammy Wilson, an inside man recruited on a free transfer from St Mirren in May that year, capitalised on his telepathic understanding with Billy McPhail in the 23rd minute. Wilson took up position within the box to volley home a knockdown from the centre-forward, a player deadly in the air. With half-time approaching, it seemed that Celtic would be heading for the pavilion with only one goal to show for the quality of their outfield play. Suddenly, the ever-dangerous Neil Mochan cut in from the left, outwitting both

Shearer and McColl to blast the ball past Niven into the far corner of the net from a tight, almost impossible angle.

Utterly demoralised, Rangers were to be on the receiving end of a humiliation after the interval as Celtic's barrage continued – a bombardment rewarded by a mounting tally of goals: a gliding header from McPhail in 53 minutes was followed by his close-in finish 15 minutes later; a volley, hit on the drop by Mochan; McPhail, racing through to complete his hat-trick by tucking the ball neatly behind Niven; and finally a last-minute penalty converted calmly by Fernie. The rout – an incredible 7–1 win over Rangers – was complete, apart from the celebrations. Celtic's goalkeeper Dick Beattie turned with his hands raised in salute with seven fingers fully extended, exulting with a Celtic end of Hampden which was already convulsed in the happiest delirium of all. The score still stands as a record for a national final in Scotland, and Celtic's most satisfying triumph ever in a contest with their great rivals.

The astonishing margin of victory owed much to several talents coalescing in rare and triumphant fashion on the day: the man of the match, Willie Fernie, a footballer supreme who strode forward from his right-half position in deep runs, his control and stamina combining to create havoc in Rangers' defence as he brushed aside the physical challenges of the rugged Baird and Davis; Bobby Evans at centre-half, who handled Rangers' infrequent attacks with consummate skill and an ease bordering on the contemptuous; Bobby Collins at inside-right who sprayed a succession of telling passes left and right across Hampden Park; Charlie Tully, now in the Indian summer of his career, who was unstoppable, with his trickery leaving left-back Caldow confused and running in circles; Neil Mochan, so often omitted from the side at the chairman's whim, who utilised his speed and power on the left wing to brush aside the physical challenges of the intimidating Shearer; and, finally, Billy McPhail, lying deep and creating opportunities with his slick passing and cute head-flicks, as he humiliated John Valentine, a centre-half recently signed from Queen's Park and a player on the fringe of international selection. Ironically, Valentine – whose Ibrox career was effectively ended – could have been lining up behind his chief tormentor on that fateful day; he had been the subject of keen Celtic interest when Jock Stein was badly injured two years earlier.

Seventh heaven, indeed! But, sadly, Celtic were brought back to earth within weeks of their remarkable triumph – and fated not to gain another major trophy until 1965.

The cheering had barely died down when that victorious side started to break up through injury, transfers and retirement. A buoyant Celtic side had been consolidating a genuine challenge for the championship, remaining undefeated after the first 11 fixtures; but disaster struck at Parkhead on 21 December 1957 when Partick Thistle won 3–2 in a match which saw Fernie carried off and McPhail badly injured. The consequences were that Celtic had to play without their stars for several weeks. Nobody in their promising reserve side was ready to replace such experienced players at that critical stage in the campaign – and three further successive home defeats over the festive period undermined Celtic's attempts to stay involved in the league race. A few months later, on 1 March 1958, in the Scottish Cup quarter-final, Clyde, the eventual winners, piled on further misery by ousting Celtic 2–0 at Parkhead. A season of high hopes, one during which dreams of the treble had been entertained in the wake of the sensational League Cup triumph, was now petering out in anticlimax.

Celtic's tale of woe did not end there. In August 1958, during the next pre-season public trial match – once a feature of Scottish football – both Billy McPhail and Sean Fallon were injured, and later bowed to medical opinion by retiring from football.

Further distressing news was to follow within a few months with the abrupt departure of Bobby Collins and Willie Fernie when both players were at the height of their powers. It seemed that little effort was made to keep them at Parkhead and they moved to English clubs: Collins went to Everton in September and Fernie to Middlesbrough in December. The club's repeated statement about 'dissatisfied players' sounded just too conveniently self-serving. It was claimed by the more cynical, accurately as it turned out, that the transfer fees – which totalled £40,000 – served to defray the costs of the long-delayed floodlights installed at Celtic Park shortly afterwards. And this at a ground where the holes in the Jungle roof were being patched in an attempt to keep out the rain – and clouds of dust rose from the cinders on the terracing!

The break-up continued in October 1959 with the return of the veteran Charlie Tully to Ireland as player-manager with Cork Hibs. In May 1960 Bobby Evans, a fixture at Celtic Park since 1944, requested a transfer 'for personal reasons' and his wishes were met with a move to Chelsea – a sad finale for his career as an outstanding player. On the eve of his departure to London, he unleashed some scathing criticism. Speaking about the limited role of Celtic's captain, and the paramount influence of Bob Kelly, he stated: 'He has no decisions to take about team changes or tactical changes. The answers to these problems come from the directors' box [i.e. chairman Bob Kelly] to the track – and are passed to the field by the trainer.' (*Scottish Daily Express*: 27 May 1960)

By that time, as a response to the disintegration of a side in which so many hopes had been invested, the club had introduced a youth policy which Bob Kelly – first elected to the Board in 1932 – predicted would replicate the success enjoyed by the youngsters who had emerged from the reserves in the early 1930s. Unfortunately, their Celtic equivalents of the late 1950s and early 1960s were not allowed to serve an apprenticeship, nor nurtured in the painstaking manner and in the same climate of encouragement as the young men who had fostered the remarkable recent success of Manchester United. The praise and acclaim showered on the Busby Babes must have influenced Bob Kelly, but the Celtic chairman did not take into account the fact that Matt Busby had anticipated the decline of a side suffering 'the whips and scorns of time' whilst Celtic were reacting to events in a manner which looked suspiciously like panic.

The impression of a lack of overall strategy is highlighted by the fact that the Celtic youngsters were largely left to their own devices to develop as players – a process akin to Darwinian selection. Indeed, Billy McNeill, who always stood out as genuine 'officer material' after joining the club from junior Blantyre Victoria in August 1957, once described it as 'the survival of the fittest'. He pointed to the burden that was placed – in the wake of the departure of such as Collins and Fernie – on players barely out of junior football. Remembering how he himself was shuttled between right-half, right-back and centre-half in season 1959–60, he states bluntly: 'More was asked of the youngsters than was fair.'

That situation might have been remedied through time, but Celtic allowed Jock Stein, now coaching the reserves after his retirement as a player, to take up the vacant managerial post at struggling Dunfermline in March 1960. Many of the reserves later confessed to dismay at the loss of their coach, recognising instinctively that they had been benefiting from a football education and grooming second to none in Scotland.

When Stein left Parkhead in 1960, he felt that, as a non-Catholic, he could not expect to be considered as a future candidate for the club's managership despite his self-belief and practical knowledge of football. Over the years, a myth was allowed to grow that Jock Stein's move to Dunfermline had been designed and approved by Kelly as 'a learning experience' prior to a return to Celtic Park; in fact, he left with the distinct impression that a recall as Celtic's manager was most unlikely.

Stein proved an instant success in Fife – literally. In his first match as Dunfermline's boss, he watched his relegation-threatened side score in some 15 seconds – against Celtic! Week after week thereafter, the Celtic supporters could read in the newspapers of the former coach's continuing success with humble Dunfermline – and marvel at the Fifers' success in European competition after their Houdini-like escape from relegation. It made bittersweet reading.

Robert Russell of the *Scottish Daily Express* coined the label the 'Kelly Kids' to describe Celtic's reversion to a youth policy. In his report of Celtic's

1–0 victory over Raith Rovers – an accomplishment which followed three successive defeats in the League Cup sectional play, and was materially assisted by an own-goal – he claimed that 'the Kelly Kids had arrived' and that 'they would one day surpass the fame of the Busby Babes'. The fearless reporter 'had no hesitation in forecasting that this team can shortly bring a new flag to Parkhead, and a new pride to Scottish football'. (24 August 1959) Of that Celtic side only Billy McNeill, Charlie Gallagher and Bertie Auld would play in a championship-winning team – and they would have to wait seven years for the honour.

By the turn of the year Celtic were in 11th place in the league, their mediocrity prompting Gair Henderson to comment acerbically in the local *Evening Times* after a 3–2 defeat by Dundee at Parkhead: 'Tonight the unpalatable fact is this – Celtic are being deserted by hosts of their fans. They believe that the SS *Celtic* is in trouble and they have no great desire to stand on the deck of a sinking ship.' (7 December 1959) A crowd of around 10,000 had trudged out of a rain-lashed Parkhead, 'glorying' in its misery after booing the players from the pitch and barracking the directors sitting in their box. One disgusted supporter could still summon up a flicker of wit – upon hearing the tannoy system play the jaunty Irish air 'Off to Tipperary in the Morning' – to mutter: 'If they'll gi'e me the fare, Ah'll no' wait for the morn; Ah'll be aff oan the Irish boat the night.'

Tommy Muirhead of the *Scottish Daily Express* (a famous ex-Ranger and a club manager himself) highlighted the most damaging aspect of the experimentation and lack of direction which characterised 'the seven lean years', as the period was later dubbed: 'Youngsters who showed tremendous promise not so long ago have lost all self-confidence. Or it might be truer to say that the well-meant dropping, reinstating and switching of these boys has undermined their confidence.' (7 December 1959) The journalist had a valid point. Since the start of the season, chopping and changing in the forward line had resulted in Celtic fielding six outside-rights, four inside-rights, four centre-forwards, four inside-lefts and three outside-lefts.

Bob Kelly's intransigence and his infuriating air of self-rightousness in the face of the mounting criticism that his youth policy was bound to fail while he retained the final say in all aspects of its operation served only to fuel the dissatisfaction of the supporters. The fans sensed rightly that the chairman was in full control of the running of the club – and the manager, frankly, a mere cipher. Kelly provoked particular hostility during season 1959–60 by 'advising' his critics to 'stay away and come back in two years, when we will have a good team'.

There was little chance of any of his boardroom colleagues challenging that authority; a noted former player recalls the chairman pointedly showing the door to a fellow director, Tom Devlin, when the latter dared to intrude on a meeting where Bob Kelly was discussing team matters with Jimmy McGrory.

Kelly was equally impatient with players who fell short of the strict code of conduct he imposed on those granted the privilege of wearing a Celtic jersey. For all his advocacy of fielding youngsters as a means of restoring the former glory to the club, he proved intolerant of the transgressions of young men. Bertie Auld, a fearless and promising outside-left, had already shown signs of being fiercely independent in outlook before incurring the chairman's displeasure for a piece of devilment when ruffling the hair of Rangers' Harold Davis after the defender had netted an own-goal at Parkhead in a Glasgow Cup tie in August 1960 – and had been pursued by the Ranger nearly the length of the park. Auld, who years later described his gesture as 'the impulse of youth', was transferred to Birmingham City at the end of the season.

Pat Crerand, a gifted wing-half, was also transferred to England – to Manchester United – in February 1963 after a record of falling foul of referees, and for arguing violently with the first-team coach Sean Fallon in the dressing-room at Ibrox during the interval of the most recent Old Firm match, which had resulted in a heavy defeat for Celtic. Kelly never spoke to Crerand again after the transfer.

Celtic teams of the early 1960s were at once the joy and despair of the supporters, who experienced moments of exhilaration and numbing despair. The sideboard would remain bereft of major trophies, but the fans could take pride in the fact that the club was still providing fast, entertaining football, and producing players who would have stood valid comparison with those in more successful Celtic eras. Billy McNeill was a commanding pivot at the heart of a side whose defence was its strongest asset; the club boasted the finest full-back pairing in the country with the cultured and speedy Duncan MacKay combining with the quick-tackling Jim Kennedy; Pat Crerand at right-half drew gasps of admiration for his inch-perfect passing; Bobby Murdoch caught the eye with his skill and aggression at inside-right; the supporters delighted in the contrast afforded by the outrageously impish dribbling of the tiny, red-headed winger Jimmy Johnstone, and the exciting, powerful runs through the centre or down the left wing of the sometimes inconsistent giant John Hughes . . .

In hindsight, it seems inconceivable that a club with such an abundance of talent at its disposal, raw though it mostly was, should fail so miserably so often in important matches. Bob Kelly, looking back in 1969, attributed the failure and the disappointments to the players believing there was a jinx hanging over Celtic – but there appeared a more fundamental reason for a succession of setbacks. Common threads running through those seasons were bizarre team selections and naïve tactical approaches – and both of these bore the imprint of the chairman.

For example, the team's captain and the most experienced player in the side, Bertie Peacock, was fully expected to resume his left-half berth in the Scottish Cup final against Dunfermline Athletic in April 1961 after recovering from injury. However, the inexperienced John Clark was preferred for that final (0–0) and for the replay, lost 2–0 by Celtic the following Wednesday. Peacock was not even considered for the replay, and had been given permission to turn out for Northern Ireland against Italy on the previous day. In direct contrast, Jock Stein had summarily dismissed a similar request from Belfast for the services of his full-back Willie Cunningham. After the Fifers' shock victory, most of the emphasis was on the inspired performances of Dunfermline's goalkeeper Connachan, but the sheer professionalism of Stein's approach was as much a contributory factor.

For the replay in the 1963 Scottish Cup final against a powerful Rangers side (after Celtic had done well to earn a 1–1 draw), incredible changes were made in the starting line-up. The most upsetting was the replacing of a lively Jimmy Johnstone – whose dribbling and darting runs had caused problems for Rangers in the drawn match – by a sluggish veteran Bobby Craig, a recent signing from Blackburn Rovers. Craig turned out to be the most visible flop in the recast side. To this day, Bobby Murdoch remains angry with the tampering, and winces to recall how Rangers toyed with an understandably demoralised and disorganised team in the second half. His mood was shared with thousands of Celtic fans who could not bear to watch more of the humiliation and left Hampden in droves long before the whistle mercifully ended the match with Rangers 3–0 victors.

Much to the delight – and perhaps surprise – of those same disillusioned fans, Celtic reached the semi-final of the European Cup-Winners' Cup in the following season. The side won many admirers on the way with their buccaneering, swashbuckling style, and in the first leg of the semi-final at Parkhead, built up a 3–0 lead over MTK Budapest. This commanding advantage was squandered in Hungary when the club approached the return leg with the naïve policy of going out for more goals, stemming from the chairman's subsequent insistence that Celtic had 'a duty' to entertain the spectators in Budapest.

At the start of 1965, nobody felt that Celtic could be turned around – at least with the existing set-up; Neil Mochan, by then a member of the backroom staff, lamented in private that 'Celtic are finished'. On the Ibrox terracings that Ne'erday there was palpable anger among the Celtic fans when the team went down yet again to Rangers, this time by 1–0. A rare opportunity to salvage a draw (and some pride) was wasted when Bobby

Murdoch ballooned a penalty-kick high and wide over the bar five minutes from time, a miss all the more galling in view of Celtic having been forced to play the whole second half without Jimmy Johnstone, ordered off for a foolish foul on Beck.

Once more, frustration had got the better of Jimmy Johnstone, who recalled recently one match in his early days at the club when Rangers were giving Celtic a 'chasing'; Johnstone at one point shouted at John Greig and Ralph Brand that 'one day it'll be our turn' (or words to that effect). Unfortunately, Johnstone's words were uttered more in bravado than in confidence, a reflection of his own growing anxieties. A bright future had been predicted for the youngster after the public trial at Celtic Park in August 1962 when he put on a dazzling performance for the reserves in a 4–3 win over the recognised first XI. The correspondent for the *Daily Record* described him as 'a right-wing bomb who should be exploded on Scotland's defences right away'. His immediate opponent, Jim Kennedy – who played Johnstone as clean as a whistle – could only shake his head and agree with the journalist. But now, in the bleak midwinter of 1964–65, both Jimmy Johnstone and Celtic had come to a crossroads . . .

The latest defeat at Ibrox was too much to bear for a long-suffering support, as it came on the top of a defeat in the League Cup final by the same side a couple of months earlier. An out-of-form Rangers had reacted better to developments on the pitch to win by 2–1 against the favourites Celtic at Hampden on 24 October 1964. At a critical stage in the match, when Rangers were in danger of being overrun by wingers Johnstone and Hughes, their captain Jim Baxter had the perception (and the authority) to switch his full-backs to cope with the deteriorating situation. Astonishingly, Celtic had no special ploy to put the hems on Baxter – that swaggering player, and Celtic's tormentor-in-chief during those seasons – leaving him free to roam at will. Such naïvety cost them the match, eventually. Twice, when pushing too far forward, they were caught out on the counter-attack – and twice punished by the deadly Forrest after defenders had lost possession, the winning goal being created by Baxter with a slide-rule pass.

Tell-tale signs were appearing that the supporters at last had had enough – and the economic implications were alarming. Danny Blanchflower, ex-captain of Tottenham Hotspur and Northern Ireland, was an interested spectator at the Ne'erday 1965 match at Ibrox in his capacity as a journalist; he was surprised to discover that the Old Firm scenario which he had been reared on as a boy in Belfast had not materialised. Instead of 'two equal horseshoes of green and blue around the stadium', he estimated that Rangers' fans outnumbered Celtic's by three or four to one in the crowd of 64,500 – and it had not been an all-ticket match. This corroborates John Rafferty's assessment in *The Scotsman*: 'Celtic's support seems to have sunk to the solid corps of die-hard supporters, for it has stuck on or at about 14,000 for some weeks.' (4 January 1965) These were figures that could not be ignored, even by Bob Kelly.

The chairman had to be aware, also, of the crisis of confidence among a squad of players who were totally demoralised. There is a grimly ironic, and unintentional, sense of what might have been when one views a recent (1994) video, *If You Know the History*, which features five members of the Lisbon Lions on a visit to a Celtic Park then in the throes of reconstruction. These legendary players were asked to reflect on their glory days at the club. How many viewers would have guessed that, by early 1965, Billy McNeill had become so discouraged that he intended that season (1964–65) to be his last at Parkhead? That Bobby Murdoch was so disillusioned around that time that he was set on emigrating to Australia? That Bobby Lennox, a promising but inconsistent forward at the time, was reputedly on his way to Falkirk for a modest fee? That Jimmy Johnstone, the archetypal Celtic winger, asked to be dropped after the sending-off at Ibrox because the joy of football had evaporated? And that Bertie Auld, before he rejoined Celtic from Birmingham City on 14 January 1965, had also been attracting the serious attention of Falkirk?

The prospects were truly bleak for what one sportswriter described as 'an anaemic club, badly in need of a timely blood transfusion'. The club's last hope of a major trophy that season, the Scottish Cup competition, had not been enhanced by the draw which decreed that Celtic would face a stiff hurdle in St Mirren at Paisley.

The startling announcement, then, of the club's decision to appoint Jock Stein as manager of Celtic was not the result of long-term planning, as some Celtic apologists have claimed. It arose out of two factors: the truly desperate plight of Celtic as a football club, and Stein's own burning desire to become Celtic's manager.

Since his departure for Dunfermline, Jock Stein had kept in contact with Celtic and with Bob Kelly. He had sought Kelly's advice at various stages in his career: he had spoken to the chairman about his prospects at Parkhead before leaving for East End Park; he had discussed his options in March 1964 when Hibernian had approached him to take over at Easter Road. Jock Stein was the man who had initiated these meetings because he wanted Celtic to remember him as a possible candidate for the manager's job at some time in the future. Once again, he met Bob Kelly for lunch, this time at Glasgow's North British Hotel in mid-January 1965, to mull over an offer from Wolverhampton Wanderers. At this meeting, with Stein hinting that he was considering the move to England, Bob Kelly at last asked him if he was interested in coming back to Celtic Park.

Finally, Celtic's chairman had come to the realisation that the policy and practice of the past seven years had been an abject failure. It was the tacit admission by a chairman, weary and worn out by the stress of running an unsuccessful club, that the task of revitalisation was a job for a younger, more vigorous man and one of unquestioned stature within the game. The chairman's intense involvement in all things Celtic, and the attendant personal aggravation which accompanied the club's decline as a force in Scottish football, had been taking a toll on his health; Bob Kelly was to live only another six years to enjoy and savour Celtic's success under Jock Stein.

Inevitably, the transition was not the seamless affair that the club and the newspapers suggested. Jimmy McGrory was not as sanguine about the abrupt loss of his job as it appeared, although he dutifully accepted it, the blow being softened by the creation of a post of Public Relations Officer for him. In the years ahead, McGrory – whose health had been also affected by the strain at Parkhead – started to enjoy his football again.

A potential hitch developed with the initial desire of the chairman that Jock Stein and Sean Fallon (the man whom Kelly had been grooming as Jimmy McGrory's successor) form a dual managership, a ludicrously impractical proposal. Bob Kelly was forced to abandon the 'plan' after Jock Stein put his foot down, a stance hinted at discreetly in the new manager's column in the match programme of 13 March 1965: '[I] did not become Celtic's manager until after the directors and myself had come to an amicable agreement as to my position. I have been handed the reins of management, and I alone have to do the driving.' Sean Fallon was appointed as assistant manager, in which capacity he proved to be an ideal lieutenant with his knowledge of the ways of the game and his total loyalty to Celtic.

A press conference was called for the afternoon of Sunday, 31 January 1965, at Parkhead, the day after a meagre crowd of 14,000 at the Celtic–Aberdeen league fixture was astonished at Celtic's performance; the players, as if sensing that the rumours sweeping the football world could be true, gave a dazzling display on an icy Celtic Park to rout the visitors 8–0. The burly John Hughes, wearing suction-soled training shoes, kept his feet like a ballet dancer to net five goals. The journalists, crowded into the oak-panelled boardroom at Celtic Park, heard Kelly try to justify the changes as if they represented the unfolding of some masterplan; in truth, the changes had been the final consequence of years of failure – over which he had presided, but for which he was not prepared to accept the blame. As Brian Meek of the *Scottish Daily Express* noted, Bob Kelly 'had signed his own abdication certificate, while still retaining his throne'. (4 February 1965) It would be up to the two men, Bob Kelly and Jock Stein, to determine the outcome in Shakespearian terms: *King Lear* or *All's Well That Ends Well.*

Hibernian were devastated by the loss of a manager who had transformed the Edinburgh team 'from a dispirited bunch of bunglers to a slick, successful side in ten months'. William Harrower, their chairman, had acknowledged his club's loss by rounding off his (earlier) press conference with the wry remark, 'There should be a transfer fee for managers too.'

Now Jock Stein was expected to revive the fortunes of yet another ailing club, but one where, as John Rafferty of *The Scotsman* observed on the eve of the new manager taking over at Celtic Park, 'The sky will be the limit.' He added the intriguing comment that 'there is an underlying belief that he could even outgrow Celtic'.

Great expectations, indeed.

SEVEN

The Big Man

1965–67

The return of Jock Stein to Celtic Park on 9 March 1965 was hardly greeted with a fanfare of trumpets; instead, he received a warm handshake from Bob Kelly and a greeting: 'It's all yours now.' Everybody accepted that the destiny of Celtic could not be entrusted to more capable hands, but few could have predicted the scale of the transformation that he wrought, for all that he had returned to Parkhead with the reputation of being 'The Miracle Man'. Within two years Celtic would rise from the status of a middling club in a minor football power to a world ranking – and all without lavishing the fortunes deemed necessary to compete at the very highest level.

Billy McNeill recalls his impression of Stein's arrival as 'a breath of fresh air', and still shudders at the thought of what might have happened to Celtic had the dynamism of a gifted manager not been introduced at that time. McNeill points out, however, that the new manager, remembered by the captain as absolutely bursting with enthusiasm and energy, did not have to search very far for the raw material with which to build his side: 'Everything was, more or less, in place; all of the players who were to become the Lisbon Lions, Willie Wallace apart, were already there. It needed someone to make it gel, to give us confidence and belief in ourselves.'

Despite that array of talent, the public perception of Celtic in recent seasons had been an unflattering one: an ultimately feckless aggregate or, to put it more bluntly, a team of losers. For the supporters, the agony was increased by an awareness of the potential at Parkhead, and the knowledge of repeated failure in crunch games. The players knew it too, and took the first available opportunity to impress their new boss; the day after the handover, Celtic celebrated his return with a 6–0 romp at Airdrie, and Bertie Auld, at the time an orthodox winger, scored five of the goals. The rumours of Stein's move back to Celtic Park – dubbed 'The Second Coming' by the more irreverent – had already inspired greater enthusiasm from the side, and Celtic had reached the semi-final stage of the Scottish Cup. Before finishing up at Easter Road, Jock Stein had performed one major favour to Celtic; Hibs, with Stein in charge for the last time, knocked Rangers out of the competition on 6 March.

Motherwell, Celtic's opponents in the semi-final at Hampden, drew on their own notable cup tradition and forced Celtic to a replay with a deserved 2–2 draw; both their goals were scored by centre-forward Joe McBride, a goal-hungry striker who was recognised as Celtic daft. In the replay, Motherwell were overwhelmed by Celtic's pace and aggression and went down by 3–0.

Stein had asserted his authority backstage, passing a crucial test of his power by informing the Board tactfully at their first meeting that he would not be picking the side until shortly before the upcoming match. In similar vein, when the chairman learned that Bobby Murdoch (who had been spotted by him when playing in a public park as a schoolboy) would be fielded at right-half in the Scottish Cup final, and protested by growling that the player was an inside-forward, Jock Stein's response was both pointed and polite: 'Well, you'll see on Saturday what he is . . .'

That Cup final, before a crowd of 108,800 at Hampden Park on 24 April 1965, was the first big test of Stein's leadership and resolve. Celtic lined up against Dunfermline Athletic and, given their strong challenge for the championship in which they ended up only one point behind Kilmarnock, the eventual winners, Dunfermline should have been the favourites. But a sudden last-minute surge of bets placed on Celtic changed the odds dramatically in the days preceding the match. It may have been a sixth sense on their supporters' part, but the confidence in the new manager's astuteness was not misplaced.

Gone were the haphazard 'preparations' of the recent past, and in their place assessments of Dunfermline's strengths and weaknesses. Stein's victory plans involved the shrewd deployment of resources – for example, John Clark was detailed to mark closely Alec Smith, the Dunfermline playmaker, and other players were given equally specific instructions.

At half-time, the manager had a crisis to face: Dunfermline had gone in 2–1 up at the interval, having struck a psychological blow just as the half was ending with McLaughlin's goal; and Celtic's youngsters must have been thinking of past heartbreaks. The more historically minded spectators were noting that no side had ever recovered from twice being a goal down in the Scottish Cup final. Jock Stein quickly went to work in the dressing-room: 'Don't worry. Just keep plugging away, and the rewards will come.' A couple of tactical adjustments apart, that was the gist of Stein's message, one which sent his players back on to the pitch determined, and with a spring in their step.

Within seven minutes of the resumption, Celtic equalised when a brisk interchange between Bertie Auld and Bobby Lennox left Auld sprinting clear to shoot neatly past Herriot.

The initiative had been wrenched back by Celtic, as that intuitive journalist John Rafferty had suspected might happen when previewing the final in *The Scotsman*. He acknowledged the Fifers' assets of method and organisation, but he felt that 'efficiency and craftsmanship are cold qualities, and the Hampden field today could well be for the emotional, for roused men fighting for a cause, stimulated by the occasion, by the new manager, by the feeling that great days are just ahead, and that a surge of spirit will add devastation to their play'.

That heady concoction materialised, as if on cue, eight minutes from the end. The tireless Lennox again put the Dunfermline defence under threat with his speed, following Stein's instructions to wear out opponents with strong running and the width of his play. This time, he gained a corner on the left which inside-forward Charlie Gallagher prepared to take; Gallagher, an unsurpassed striker of the ball, swung over a perfectly flighted ball which enabled Billy McNeill to evade the attentions of Alec Smith, his marker in such situations. In recent matches McNeill had been encouraged by Stein to come up for corners, and he had sprinted upfield to connect with the cross and send his header raging into the net.

A stunning goal! And the winning goal, with Celtic ahead for the first time at 3–2! A roar like no other ensued from the tremendous crowd. The din continued minute after minute, with its prevailing note fluctuating until the final whistle: the immediate jubilation switching back and forth into anxiety as the stubborn Fifers set about retrieving the situation. At the end, the euphoria broke out again and grown men were seen emerging from the Hampden stands and terracings weeping tears of joy. The *Scottish Daily Express* observed that McNeill's strike had not just been a winning goal, but 'the official seal on a return to greatness . . . Parkhead is Paradise once more'. (26 April 1965)

It was a moment to savour, the launch-pad for the greatest era in the club's history. Jock Stein knew the importance for himself in this breakthrough in the Scottish Cup and, as if to emphasise the point, for years afterwards the largest framed photograph in his office at Celtic Park showed Billy McNeill carried aloft on the shoulders of his jubilant team-mates at the end of the match.

Delighted though he was, Jock Stein was not blinded by the victory. His conviction that much hard work and dedication was still needed before talk of Celtic's revival became a reality was borne out again only four days after the final when his team travelled to East End Park on league business and lost 5–1 to Dunfermline. Part of him must have been pleased because it gave him the opportunity to blast his players – justifiably. Nobody escaped in his scathing post-match analysis. All of them knew now what was expected of them – every time they pulled on the Celtic jersey.

Better than most, Jock Stein knew from his playing days at Parkhead how Celtic were prone to lapse back into complacent mediocrity after a Cup triumph, and he was determined to add a harder, more professional edge to alter the team's mercurial image. The transformation became apparent in Stein's first full season in charge, a season which saw the emergence of a reshaped club. Celtic were to bear the unmistakable imprint of Stein's personality as he strove to make consistency of performance and success the hallmarks of the new Celtic. Bobby Murdoch had been identified by at least one sportswriter as 'a born soccer general' before making his début as a youngster in August 1962; up until Jock Stein's return, he had experienced only disappointment as a player at Parkhead. He recognised early on how Celtic's competitive streak was being enhanced by Stein's emphasis on pace and ballwork, and speaks feelingly of the training sessions and practice matches organised by the new manager: 'Quite often I used to go home from Barrowfield with bumps and bruises', but adding that 'the spirit of the Big Man got through to us'.

After a shaky start to the 1965–66 League Cup, Celtic rallied to qualify and advanced to the semi-final against Hibernian at Ibrox, an epic cup-tie in gruelling conditions on a rain-soaked pitch with Celtic's salvation coming through a last-gasp equaliser (2–2) from Lennox; the 30 minutes' extra-time provided thrills but no more goals. In the replay, a rampant Celtic thrashed their opponents 4–0, thus qualifying to play Rangers in the final five days later, on 23 October. Their manager was already prepared: minutes after the jubilant players, whooping and shouting, entered the Ibrox dressing-room, Jock Stein burst through the door apparently enraged, his demeanour shocking his players into silence. With clenched fists he glared at them, and asked repeatedly, 'Do you want to win on Saturday?' One by one his players nodded in agreement. A superb piece of psychology! Stein knew that Celtic's recovery required the overturning of Rangers' post-war ascendancy . . . and nothing less than a monumental effort in this match would do.

Celtic fielded the same side against Rangers at Hampden before a record crowd of 107,609 for a League Cup final. Within a minute or so of the kick-off right-back Ian Young, showing how psyched-up Celtic were for the battle, scythed Willie Johnston with a crunching tackle. The referee, Hugh Phillips of Wishaw, chose to give the defender the benefit of the doubt by not sending him off. He booked him – as he did Johnston (for retaliation). But the tone had been set for a short-tempered and bickering final, summed up by one reporter as 'a day of hate, sheer naked hate'. Young's tackle showed Rangers that Celtic were no longer going to be intimidated physically on the pitch, unlike in the recent past. Jim Baxter, Rangers' captain in the early 1960s, has frankly admitted that the likes of Harold Davis and Bobby Shearer (nicknamed 'Captain Cutlass' by his team-mates) had frequently been used by the Ibrox side to instil fear into some Celtic forwards.

Ronnie Simpson, a veteran keeper signed from Hibernian a year earlier for £2,000, showed his vast experience in narrowing the angle to foil the dangerous Forrest during Rangers' early rush, and gave Celtic breathing space to settle down. Soon, John Hughes was running riot on the left wing, racing past Johansen and troubling the rest of the defence with his dangerous, pounding runs. After 18 minutes John Clark lofted a free-kick into Rangers' penalty area, and McKinnon, despite a considerable height advantage over Joe McBride, unaccountably used his hand to clear the ball, an astonishing lapse. Hughes sent Ritchie the wrong way and scored comfortably from the spot. Ten minutes later Celtic were awarded another penalty, this time in more debatable circumstances; Jimmy Johnstone, weaving past Provan, was tripped by the lanky full-back in the area and, despite Rangers' protests, the referee pointed to the spot. Again Hughes scored, although the keeper guessed correctly this time and got a hand to the ball.

Rangers may have felt aggrieved at the latter decision but they could not complain about the worth of Celtic's two-goal lead. In the second half, the Parkhead men revealed a new level of maturity by concentrating on a solid defensive performance rather than on the reckless pursuit of more goals. Rangers did score six minutes from the end when Simpson's palmed clearance bounced off Young's head and into the net for an inconsequential own-goal. Sadly, Celtic's half-lap of honour to show off the trophy to their fans ended in chaos when Rangers supporters, mostly youths, invaded the pitch, some clearly intent on causing physical harm to the Celtic players.

The next battle of the giants took place on an icy surface at Parkhead on 3 January 1966 with both clubs level on points in the championship, ordained by Stein as the primary target. Celtic's new-found professionalism was revealed by Stein's preparation for the match. He personally inspected every area of the pitch, and then decided that his players should wear training boots on the heavily sanded surface. Rangers relied on more conventional footwear, and their players seemed more ill at ease in the tricky conditions. That attention to detail helped Celtic to grow in confidence the longer the match went on, and, allied with an irresistible will to win, enabled them to brush aside the setback of a first-minute goal by Wilson for Rangers. The Ibrox men held out until the interval, but the second half ended in a 5–1 rout for Celtic, the goal-procession being led by hat-trick hero Steve Chalmers. Stein harnessed the non-stop running, speed and intelligence of the 29-year-old forward alongside the bustling Joe McBride, snapped up from Motherwell for a bargain fee of £22,500 in June 1965. Celtic now had a potent spearhead in attack with these two goalscorers, who netted 46 league goals between them that season. Indeed, some consider Joe McBride to be the most explosive Celtic striker since the great McGrory. Billy McNeill, paying tribute to a player whose career at Parkhead was cut short by injury, describes McBride as 'tremendous in the air for a smallish man, and a marvellous finisher in the penalty box'. McBride's record of 86 goals in 94 competitive matches bears out the praise.

However, just when Celtic seemed ideally placed for their first-ever domestic treble, being pace-setters in the league and favourites to retain the Scottish Cup (and with their sights also on the European Cup-Winners' Cup), they began to ship water in the championship by dropping points in a fashion which suggested that the players had still to appreciate fully the demands that their success was making on them. Stein had to apply all his considerable powers of motivation, and to exercise his tactical virtuosity, especially his theory of 'horses for courses' in order to stimulate competition among his players and to exploit the resources of the player-pool to its utmost. For example, Charlie Gallagher and Bertie Auld (nominally a winger) alternated at inside-forward to meet the varied challenges posed by fixtures played under the changing conditions of a long Scottish season. An added refinement, typical of the manager's fertile brain, and remarkably daring in its timing at such a crucial stage in the campaign, was an experiment destined to reap considerable benefits in the future and involved the deployment of Auld behind the forwards – though still wearing No. 11 on his shorts – in the Scottish Cup semi-final against Dunfermline at Ibrox where he and Bobby Murdoch formed 'the mainsprings of an efficient mechanism [which] rapped passes to all points of the field'. (*Glasgow Herald*: 28 March 1966)

Displaying an instinct for public relations which no Scottish manager has matched since, Stein had begun a process of educating supporters through his regular column in the recently launched club newspaper the *Celtic View* on the need for more responsible behaviour, and for patience and understanding as their team strove to compete successfully on several fronts. In its pages the players could be reminded again of long-term planning; he stressed the importance of concentrating on 'doing well in every single game and not on allegedly more important ones in the weeks ahead'. (3 November 1965) How accurate that warning proved in the early months of 1966 when unexpected away defeats by Hearts and Stirling Albion suddenly tilted the championship race in favour of Rangers – and this was an Ibrox side stacked with players experienced in the means of winning titles.

Jock Stein had to extract the maximum from his players while maintaining a calm front under pressure. Not all the pressure was imposed by the immediate need to win football matches; other unwanted distractions, the price of being in charge at such a high-profile club, were intruding.

Stein, who was still feeling his way at Parkhead to a certain extent, had to contend with a chairman who still exerted considerable influence over every aspect of the running of the club. In discussions with Stein, Bob Kelly was not backward in chipping in his opinions about team selections. In fact, the manager felt it prudent and politic to drop Jim Craig, a highly mobile full-back recently introduced into the side, after the chairman had expressed his anger at the player's sending-off in Tbilisi against Dynamo Kiev in a European tie. Stein decided to omit the player from the side against Hearts at Tynecastle in January 1966. When another director, Desmond White, learned of the pressure being exerted by the chairman (which included a demand that Craig apologise for his transgression), he raised the matter informally with fellow directors and the experience may have subdued the chairman – temporarily, at least.

Celtic lost that match 3–2, but the defeat in Edinburgh was due more to another aspect of the chairman's involvement. Celtic's return flight from Georgia lasted a horrendous 48 hours, an ordeal caused by problems which surely would not have arisen had the chairman not stubbornly insisted on using Aer Lingus as the club's carrier, despite the objections of the Soviet bureaucracy. This insistence meant that the journey had to be rerouted through Moscow, a fact which added hours and hundreds of miles on to a trip already plagued by the aircraft's mechanical problems. Eventually, Bob Kelly insisted on a replacement jet being brought in for the final leg of the journey from Stockholm; apparently, Kelly reached that decision only after overhearing the pilot say to a colleague, 'I don't want another Munich on my hands' – a reference to the 1958 air-crash which almost destroyed Manchester United. While the jet-liner was grounded in the Swedish capital, Kelly held a meeting with the club's secretary and fellow director Desmond White; their deliberations resulted in the decision not to formally request that the League postpone that Hearts fixture although the party did not return to Glasgow until late on the night before the match. Upon arrival at Glasgow, the players and coaching staff headed straight to Parkhead for a loosening-up session, and the team members did not get home to their own beds until after midnight. Billy McNeill remembers that, after the travails caused by the delays and the various time-zones involved in the trip, he went to bed with his body feeling as if it was 5 or 6 a.m.!

The consequences of that journey behind the Iron Curtain, one which boosted the image of Scottish football, could have been costly for Celtic. Rangers took full advantage of Celtic's defeat at Tynecastle with a 4–1 romp over St Mirren at Ibrox to draw level on points at the top of the table.

Celtic would need all of Stein's leadership, enthusiasm and guile in the closing stages of the campaign when their season threatened to fall apart as a result of a shock 1–0 defeat at the hands of Stirling Albion at Annfield in late February which left Rangers two points clear at the top. Stein's influence on his players was such that one commentator memorably described it: 'If the wagon-train were surrounded by Indians, Stein would be the man to get you out!' That aura of reassurance, allied to his ferocious determination, helped Celtic bounce back quickly with a 5–0 win over Dundee at Parkhead only two days after the reverse at Stirling. The side recovered its momentum, if not its early-season fluency, in the league race, and were poised to take full advantage of Rangers' disastrous results in March – when the Ibrox club cracked under the pressure, drawing with Hearts and Kilmarnock and losing to Falkirk and Dundee United. The dramatic turnaround in fortunes allowed Celtic to establish a five-point lead at the top of the table, although Rangers had a game in hand. By 14 April, when Celtic defeated Liverpool 1–0 in the first leg of the Cup-Winners' Cup semi-final at Parkhead, Rangers were three points behind but the margin was reduced to two with Celtic's 0–0 draw against Hibs two days later.

In the return leg at Anfield on 19 April Celtic were bundled out of European competition by Liverpool in the most controversial of circumstances. A goal by Bobby Lennox in the last minute – one which would have levelled the tie on aggregate at 2–2 – was disallowed by the referee (Josef Hannet of Belgium) who admitted later – after studying the TV film – that the match officials had been deceived by the sheer speed of the Celtic forward . . . but his decision provoked ugly scenes among Celtic fans incensed by the injustice of it all. That same night, by winning 2–1 against Motherwell, Rangers drew level with Celtic at the top – although the Parkhead side had a game in hand.

The Old Firm met in the Scottish Cup final on 23 April 1966 in front of a crowd of 126,552 at Hampden. As a nerve-wracking season drew to a close, Celtic had been exhibiting signs of stress and fatigue; that shattering defeat at Liverpool had drained the side of its usual confidence and seemed to be a factor in the 0–0 draw against Rangers, a result seen as a moral victory for the Ibrox men, given their underdog status (a rarity for them in the early '60s). In the replay 96,862 watched an enthralling contest dominated by Celtic throughout, but 20 minutes from time Rangers stunned their rivals with a goal from right-back Kai Johansen. Celtic attacked furiously until the end but the attacks were too hurried, and time ran out. One observer compared the dramatic outcome to a boxing match in which an outclassed, outpointed slugger manages to land a knock-out punch late in the fight for victory.

Jock Stein had to rally his forces after two morale-sapping defeats in major competitions inside nine days – and he was facing the problem of coaxing 'an extra bit' out of a team that had failed to score in four successive matches. The league fixture at Greenock three days later was going to be a test of nerve, with Rangers revived after their unexpected triumph.

One more slip by a jaded-looking Celtic could prove fatal, and the team started tentatively at Cappielow. Morton, locked in a bitter relegation struggle with neighbouring St Mirren, had their own incentive to get a result and were far from overawed. Indeed, right on the half-hour the home side were presented with a golden opportunity to turn the screw on a very anxious Celtic. Fleming Neilsen stepped up to take a penalty-kick; on the Wednesday night, one Dane had destroyed Celtic's Scottish Cup ambitions, and on the Saturday, another was looking certain to deal a potentially mortal blow to their title hopes. Seconds later, Neilsen was hanging his head in shame after he had blazed the ball over the bar. The miss acted as a blood-transfusion to Celtic, with Jimmy Johnstone (who had conceded the penalty) responding in typical fashion. Just before the interval, his shot from an Auld pass appeared to be going wide of the goal when it struck a defender and was deflected in at the post. In the very last minute he sealed Celtic's 2–0 victory when he crossed perfectly for Bobby Lennox to head the ball over Sorensen's outstretched arms. Rangers, however, kept up the pressure by narrowly winning 2–1 at Dunfermline.

In the following midweek, on 4 May, Celtic faced Dunfermline at Parkhead and fell behind to a goal from Alex Ferguson after 30 minutes; at that precise moment Rangers were leading Clyde by 1–0 at Ibrox – and very much back in contention. The last, nail-biting ten minutes at Celtic Park were accompanied by a chorus from the crowd of 30,000 fans screaming for the referee to blow the whistle; when he finally did so, it signalled a 2–1 win for Celtic with goals from the same pair of Lennox and

Johnstone, and triggered joyous scenes around the stadium.

Celtic still had to visit Fir Park on 7 May 1966 and gain one point from Motherwell for an outright win in the championship but the supporters turned the occasion into a green-and-white festival, and their joyful day was complete when Bobby Lennox scrambled in the only goal in the dying seconds. The championship had been sealed, as one account noted, 'in the last minute of the last game on the last day of the season'. Jock Stein's first championship as Celtic's manager had been a near-run thing, a fact which tended to be overlooked in the accumulation of silverware at Parkhead over the next decade.

Four days later, a delighted and proud Celtic party set off on an ambitious 11-match tour of Bermuda, the United States and Canada. With characteristic pragmatism the manager viewed the trip as both a deserved reward and as an opportunity for some sensible experimentation, the establishing of the Murdoch–Auld axis in midfield being the most notable outcome. The unusual locations, the weather conditions, the different types of opposition: all would be useful preparation for the forthcoming European Cup competition which might send Celtic to any corner of the Continent. Celtic emerged unbeaten from the tour, twice defeating Tottenham Hotspur (FA Cup winners the following season), and holding Bayern Munich (winners of the European Cup-Winners' Cup the following season) to a 2–2 draw, thrilling the thousands of exiles who turned out in force to watch them. These had been important bonuses for the manager, but equally important was a growing *esprit de corps* among his players. Nearly 30 years later, Bobby Murdoch can describe that squad as 'still a band of brothers, really'.

Celtic's readiness for the challenges ahead was underlined by a devastating display in a pre-season friendly match on 6 August against Manchester United, a side which included England's World Cup stars Charlton and Stiles, as well as George Best and Pat Crerand. Celtic's 4–1 victory – and the manner of it – sent shivers of dread throughout their opponents in Scotland.

With Joe McBride in sparkling early-season form, Celtic stormed through the preliminary stages of the League Cup to meet Rangers in a final watched by 94,532 on 29 October 1966. The Ibrox men were bent on revenge after suffering two humiliating defeats at the hands of Celtic early in the season: at home in the Glasgow Cup by 4–0 and at Parkhead by 2–0 in the league. The former, highlighted by a superb hat-trick springing from the electrifying pace of Lennox, was particularly satisfying. It dented Rangers' self-belief and undermined some of the Ibrox mystique, exemplified at that time by the psychological ploy of having the pegs in the dressing-rooms attached so high up the wall that players had to stand on benches to reach them; the impression given was that the stadium was inhabited by footballing giants. Rangers' two expensive close-season signings, Alec Smith (Dunfermline) and Dave Smith (Aberdeen), had made little difference in closing the gap with Celtic.

Rangers dictated the early pace in the League Cup final, but Celtic supplied the knock-out punch in 18 minutes with a goal stunning in its simplicity and execution. Auld gathered the ball out on the left side of midfield before slinging over a long, precise cross deep into the penalty area and beyond the back post for McBride to head the ball across the goalmouth where Lennox volleyed it into the net. Rangers huffed and puffed thereafter, but Celtic marshalled their defence superbly to hold out for a 1–0 victory; Rangers came closest to scoring but the certain goal was averted by a goal-line clearance from that unsung full-back Willie O'Neill, the epitome of reliability.

Celtic were wrapping themselves in such an air of invincibility that the New Year was approaching with few signs of anybody mounting a challenge to this formidable machine. Already, they were on target for an unprecedented clean sweep of all the domestic honours, having picked up the Glasgow Cup with a 4–0 win over Partick Thistle nine days after retaining the League Cup. Few would be foolhardy enough to bet against them repeating their championship triumph and collecting the Scottish Cup – and Celtic, in their first sortie in the most prestigious tournament in club football worldwide, had reached the quarter-final of the European Cup.

The manager, however, realised that the club had been in a similar position during the previous season when, as he had said at the end, it had found itself 'going for too many big prizes without the resources to succeed in them all'. (*Celtic View*: 11 May 1966) He made a vital signing to help those unrealised ambitions to come true this time. Hearts' unsettled striker Willie Wallace became available on the transfer market in December 1966, and Stein moved quickly and stealthily. Celtic's manager knew of Rangers' interest in the player and waited until the Ibrox club were in Germany to face Borussia Dortmund in the Cup-Winners' Cup before striking. Cunningly, he had dropped hints to the newspapers that Celtic were on the verge of signing an Anglo-Scot forward from Coventry, and Hearts, financially strapped, were more than eager to complete the formalities with Celtic for the transfer. Wallace himself describes the move to Parkhead as 'like coming back from the dead'.

Indeed, this inspired signing would carry revivalist overtones for Celtic as it came only a few weeks before Joe McBride, the country's leading scorer, played his last match for Celtic that season, falling victim to a knee injury which forced him to undergo an operation in March 1967. Wallace would have the task of replacing a striker who, despite missing the last five months of the season and the ultimate glory of Lisbon, still finished as the leading goalscorer with a haul of 37 goals in 29 competitive matches. This feat, the most impressive sustained burst of scoring in Scottish football history, could not console McBride for the disappointment of having missed out on the latter stages of the European Cup – a source of regret with him to this day.

Everybody expected Rangers to mount the greatest challenge to Celtic in the Scottish Cup, but the unexpected was lurking in wait. At Parkhead on 28 January 1967 Celtic were toying with lowly Arbroath, leading by three goals scored within the first half-hour, but the attention of the crowd at Celtic Park, alerted by a half-time score that hinted at a possible shock, soon began to focus on another Scottish Cup tie. Rangers had been drawn to face Berwick Rangers of the Second Division at Shielfield Park with an earlier kick-off. Some 15 minutes into the second half at Parkhead, the news began to spread like wildfire that Rangers had been knocked out of the Cup in the biggest upset this century; at one incredible stroke, the greatest danger to Celtic in that competition had been removed. The Scottish Cup celebrations were beginning early . . .

Celtic continued to lead in the race for the league championship and only Rangers, still smarting from the Cup humiliation, were in any position to challenge. However, on a muddy Ibrox pitch against a tenacious Rangers side Celtic clinched the title by gaining a 2–2 draw on 6 May 1967 in a fixture postponed from 3 January. Both goals were scored by the diminutive winger Jimmy Johnstone; one was a tap-in after a Lennox shot had rebounded from the post, and the second was a viciously struck shot from 25 yards, taken with his left foot.

One week earlier Celtic had lined up against Aberdeen in the Scottish Cup final after an uneventful stroll to the final, although Glasgow rivals Queen's Park put up a struggle at Parkhead before going down 5–3 and Clyde hung on for a replay and a 2–0 defeat in the semi-final. Aberdeen expressed confidence about the outcome, pointing out that they had drawn both league fixtures with Celtic. Their manager, the dour Eddie Turnbull, hinted that Celtic might be jaded after a European Cup match on the Tuesday only four days before the final. That gruelling fixture in Prague had forced Stein to reconsider his options, the manager toying with the idea of resting Steve Chalmers who had toiled singlehandedly in attack and endured an awful buffeting, but he decided to play the veteran striker mainly on the right wing in the Scottish Cup final as a tactical ploy to allow Johnstone a roving commission to soften up Aberdeen's defence with his close dribbling.

As Johnstone later observed, Stein 'wouldn't hesitate to stick me in the middle of the attack, or switch me over to the left, if he thought it would produce goals'. He added that the manager was not so much a tactician as a superb motivator possessed of a remarkable talent for 'making you feel like the best player in the world' before sending his men out to do battle on the big occasions.

With cruel timing for the Dons, Celtic's two goals were scored on either side of the interval by Willie Wallace, already paying off his transfer fee with interest. The decisive first goal arrived after a short corner on the left allowed Lennox to dribble into the penalty area before squaring the ball across the goalmouth for Wallace to net from only six yards out. The second goal was the result of a clever run on the right by Johnstone who cut the ball back for the unmarked Wallace waiting near the penalty spot.

With all four domestic trophies in the bag, Celtic could now look forward with respect but not trepidation to a European Cup final against the Milanese club Internazionale. Celtic could anticipate the encounter with some confidence because they had already proved themselves invincible at home and battle-hardened abroad – a match for Europe's best, and a side which Stein himself ascribed later to 'an astonishing, coincidental coming-together of great players, the likes of which we'll probably never see here again'. (*The Observer*: 9 November 1980).

In that interview, the manager, characteristically, took little credit for his own immense contribution to welding together such disparate talents and temperaments into a formidable unit. A French journalist, after watching Celtic destroy the highly touted Nantes in whirlwind style, was moved to describe them as 'the typhoon'. His feelings about Celtic Park, a stadium as unwelcoming in an architectural sense as well as a playing one, were graphically described; he compared it to a Dante-esque inferno where visitors would enter as if through a prison gate to which was inscribed 'Abandon hope, all ye who enter here'.

Celtic's forward line was now almost tailor-made to disrupt the most resolute of defences: the diminutive Jimmy Johnstone could demoralise opponents with twisting and turning that left them 'feeling like a tin of spaghetti hoops', as one defender ruefully observed; Willie Wallace, 'the football bargain of the century', a versatile player able to snap up half-chances and ready to take the weight off the likes of Johnstone and Lennox; Steve Chalmers, an all-action player whose style always kept defences on the hop with his ability to be in the penalty area when it mattered; and Bobby Lennox, recognised as one of the fastest and sharpest forwards in Britain, a goalscorer of note and a man who kept defenders on the back foot for every one of the 90 minutes.

In goal Ronnie Simpson was a model of concentration, a veteran who went on to keep a clean sheet in half of his games in his career at Parkhead

(courtesy Frank Glencross)

The 'nearly' men. RIGHT: *George Connelly, retired prematurely;* BELOW LEFT: *Joe Miller, out of favour and transferred back to Aberdeen; and* BELOW RIGHT: *Joe McBride, missed Lisbon through knee injury*

(courtesy The Scotsman)

(courtesy Frank Glencross)

How to win against Dundee United: Charlie Nicholas scores at Parkhead, early 1990s . . .

. . . Frank McGarvey turns away in delight as he nets the Scottish Cup winner, 1985.
United's Gough and Kirkwood are not pleased . . .

. . . and Frank McAvennie's header levels things in the 1988 Scottish Cup final against the Tannadice men (he later got the winner)

It's even better winning against Rangers. McGrain, Lennox and MacLeod join in George McCluskey's celebrations, Scottish Cup final, 1980

The Scottish Cup final, 1977: Andy Lynch scores a penalty against Rangers

The Scottish Cup final, 1973: Kenny Dalglish puts Celtic in front against Rangers

*Triumph! Deans, Hood (hidden) Lennox and Dalglish celebrate victory over
Hearts, 25 December 1971*

*Disaster! Gemmell, Williams, Brogan, Connelly, Macari and Hood leave the pitch after
losing 4–1 to Partick Thistle in the 1971 League Cup final*

Ronnie Simpson (playing for Hibs against Celtic in the Scottish Cup, 1961)

Dick Beattie foils Motherwell, c.1957

Pat Bonner under pressure at Ibrox, 1989, surrounded by Mike Galloway, Paul Elliott,
Terry Butcher, Mo Johnston and Roy Aitken

ABOVE: *Paul McStay opens the scoring in Celtic's 2–1 Ne'erday victory at Ibrox, 1983*
BELOW: *Celebrating the Scottish Cup triumph over Dundee United, May 1985*
(courtesy The Celtic View)

while drawing upon his 22 years as a goalkeeper and an unrivalled awareness of the geometry of the penalty area. His appearance in Celtic's line-up had been nothing less than a football miracle. Drifting out of the game just short of his 34th birthday, he was acquired by Jimmy McGrory in September 1964 as a back-up for John Fallon, and actually made his début for Celtic's third XI in a Combined Reserve match at Barrowfield, the club's training ground, before a mere handful of spectators.

At full-back Jim Craig and the exuberant Tommy Gemmell were tall, strapping athletes, noted for overlapping in attack although both were capable in defence, where they could match any opponent for pace. In an interview years later, Craig was to say that he felt sorry for Willie O'Neill, unlucky to be the reserve full-back. Craig feels that O'Neill had played more steadily than Gemmell or himself, but he believes that Stein was convinced that only defenders with pace and flair in attack could help outwit a top-class European defence.

The cornerstone of Celtic's defence was Billy McNeill, an imposing captain, outstanding in the air and assertive on the ground, and alongside him was John Clark, a sweeper so self-effacing that he was never fully given the praise due to him; Clark virtually imprisoned opposing forwards with his unhurried tackles, interceptions and clearances.

The engine-room of the side was the midfield pairing of Bobby Murdoch and Bertie Auld, whose strength and cunning complemented each other perfectly. For all his muscle and power, Murdoch possessed the most delicate touch in passing; 'He could land the ball on a thrupenny bit,' recalls one of his team-mates reared on pre-decimal coinage, and with only the slightest of exaggeration. Auld, a foxy player, added a new dimension to Celtic's play when shifted to his new role at the end of 1965–66; swarthy in appearance, and with more than a touch of swagger allied to machismo, he may have been the first British player fully equipped to take on the Continentals at their own game.

The team destined to become known as the Lisbon Lions had grown in stature, along with their manager, as the season progressed. Subtle changes were made from time to time to freshen up the side; in fact, the team that won the European Cup in May did not play together until 14 January 1967 against St Johnstone at Muirton Park when it registered a 4–0 win. The next appearance of the same line-up was against Aberdeen in a 0–0 draw at Parkhead on 19 April, by which time the manager had decided on his best formation, the one to carry Celtic forward to an incredible clean sweep at home and abroad.

The players had come to respect Stein's wholly professional outlook, as indicated by his insistence on concentration and attention to detail by everybody involved in a match. It was underlined by an explosion of anger at Joe McBride when the player found out in the dressing-room at Nantes that he had left one of his boots at the hotel. McBride had to make a quick dash back to the team's hotel to retrieve his boot, and get back to the ground by taxi – which got stuck in the traffic; he ended up running through the streets amid fans going to the match. Fortunately, Stein was not a man to harbour grudges, and McBride kept his place in the side (and scored the equalising goal for Celtic in the match). After disposing of Nantes by identical 3–1 victories home and away, Celtic had to journey to Yugoslavia to face Vojvodina Novi Sad in the quarter-final of the European Cup. The first leg was lost 0–1 through a late goal caused by a short pass-back to Simpson and everybody at Parkhead knew the enormity of the task in Glasgow. The Yugoslavs had lived up to Jock Stein's assessment of them as 'physically strong and technically expert'.

The return leg on 8 March was the hardest match for Celtic in the competition. At half-time Parkhead was a scene of gloom: Celtic had attacked but, without the injured McBride and the ineligible Wallace, they were stuttering in attack and the Vojvodina defence had dealt with every raid comfortably. Pantelic, the giant figure in Vojvodina's goal, added to the sense of frustration, irritating the crowd with his time-wasting antics. Celtic attacked constantly in the second half, but with a greater sense of urgency. After 60 minutes the visitors' goal fell and the keeper was badly at fault; he misjudged a cross from Gemmell and Steve Chalmers whipped the ball into the net for the equaliser. The goalkeeper atoned for his error by making spectacular saves later from Johnstone and Chalmers.

Despite the Celtic pressure the Yugoslavs held out, intent on gaining a play-off in neutral Rotterdam if the result stood unaltered. In the dying seconds Celtic gained another corner on the right, and Charlie Gallagher, in a virtual repeat of the 1965 Scottish Cup final, flighted the ball perfectly into the heart of the area where Billy McNeill broke free of defenders to head the ball powerfully into the roof of the net, setting off indescribable scenes in every corner of the stadium. After he scored, and had recovered from the momentary euphoria, McNeill trotted back to his defensive position; with clenched fists, he urged his team-mates, 'Don't lose anything now!' He was quietly told by the ever-watchful John Clark, who had seen the referee signal time-up, 'It's okay. The game's over!'

Dukla Prague posed a different tactical and psychological challenge. In the first leg of the semi-final in Glasgow, Celtic struggled to build up a 3–1 lead after giving up a careless equaliser close to half-time. Two second-half goals from Wallace gave Celtic victory and cheered the crowd of 74,406, but Stein was apprehensive about the journey to Czechoslovakia. He was aware that no British side had advanced to the final, and that several notable ones had crashed at the semi-final hurdle. He could recall the occasion when Celtic had squandered a three-goal lead behind the Iron Curtain when they lost 0–4 to MTK in Budapest in 1964, and he was determined that his team would succeed in Prague, regardless of the method. That afternoon the orders were to defend in depth, leaving only Chalmers as a brave and lonely runner up front. After the match, Jock Stein made a point of seeking out Chalmers to praise him for his courageous performance; and this from a manager who rarely singled out players for particular praise. Celtic closed down every avenue to goal, with the midfield pair in ultra-defensive positions and the other forwards pulled back to help out. Throughout the 90 minutes, although the Czech Army side dominated in a territorial sense, Simpson had only one difficult save to make. Accomplished in such a 'non-Celtic' manner that the chairman Bob Kelly made his feelings plain to the manager afterwards, the 0–0 draw nevertheless put the club into the final. Stein would ensure, however, that on the greatest day in the club's history there would be no compromise with Celtic's traditional style of play: fast, attractive, attacking football.

In the interim he would have to devote some of his energy and cunning to winning a war of nerves with the arrogant Helenio Herrera, the coach of the Milanese side, who had sent his scout Dezso Solti to watch the semi-final against Dukla at Parkhead; Solti, a Hungarian who had settled in Italy, and whose role for Internazionale would later take on a more sinister complexion, dismissed Celtic's presence in the later stages of the European Cup of Champions as 'an aberration', adding that, while Celtic's passion might pose a problem at Parkhead, Inter Milan's class 'would undoubtedly prevail on neutral territory'. He was not the only 'expert' to underestimate Celtic; Ken Jones of the London-based *Daily Mirror* had ventured north and patronisingly summed up Jock Stein as 'a weaver of dreams'.

Stein was fully aware of Herrera's mind-games from personal experience. When Celtic's manager travelled to Turin to watch Inter play against Juventus shortly before the Lisbon final, Herrera had greeted him like a long-lost brother but then reneged on an arrangement to provide Stein with a ticket for admission and transportation to the ground. Unfazed by the ploy, Stein managed to get to the stadium on time, obtained entry thanks to the help of an accompanying journalist, and completed his spying-mission on Inter.

The ruthless Herrera continued to employ other acts of gamesmanship before and during the final. The Inter party took possession of the 'lucky' home dressing-room at the Estadio Nacional, claiming to have won a ballot – one which Celtic knew nothing about. The Italians complained about Celtic using numbers on their shorts instead of on their shirts as was the usual practice in Europe.

The most worrying ploy was Herrera's delay in announcing his side because of the doubts about Luis Suarez's fitness. Inter spread rumours that Suarez, their most influential player, would be fit to play even though he had not left Italy, and Stein remained suspicious that he would be flown in at the eleventh hour. Right up to a few minutes before the scheduled kick-off Stein had not seen Inter's official line-up; he requested the referee to allow him to see it – as he had the right to do. And he informed the German official that Celtic would not be taking the field unless he saw that list first!

On the eve of the European Cup final itself he reminded his players that a unique opportunity for football immortality was beckoning and he urged them to perform 'as if there were no more tomorrows'. So impressive was Stein's conduct and management of Celtic's European campaign in every aspect – and the more so in the full glare of media attention just prior to the final – that, within a few hours of the final whistle, he would be approached by two Italian journalists to take charge of one of Italy's top clubs.

If the manager's comments hinted at the club having a date with destiny on 25 May 1967, the chairman's actions confirmed it. For the most important match ever played by Celtic, he arranged for representatives of the Marist Order to be guests of the club; Brother Walfrid would surely have approved . . .

And what a boost the Celtic players got when, half an hour before the kick-off at the Estadio Nacional, they emerged to inspect the pitch and received a delirious welcome from the thousands of Scots who had poured into Lisbon by air, sea, road and rail. Jock Stein was so clearly buoyed up and moved by the reception that he told a journalist as he entered the dressing-room for the final preparations: 'They are all Celtic supporters! It's inspiring!'

One other task remained to be done. Celtic had been assigned a bench beforehand, but the Inter background staff had occupied it, claiming it as theirs. The Italians were quickly removed with a suitable show of force, and as he sat down with the substitute goalkeeper, John Fallon, and the backroom staff, Jock Stein's work was almost over. As always, it was now up to the players on the field: Simpson, Craig, Gemmell, Murdoch, McNeill, Clark, Johnstone, Wallace, Chalmers, Auld and Lennox.

Battle was about to be joined between the homespun Scottish team – every member raised within 30 miles of Celtic Park – and the highly experienced and sophisticated 'Bank of Italy' side.

It looked like curtains for Celtic when Jim Craig was forced to tackle Cappellini awkwardly from behind to concede a penalty in the seventh minute. Mazzola scored calmly from the spot with practised ease by sending Simpson the wrong way. The most infamous defensive side in

Europe, past-masters in the art of frustrating opponents, then pulled up the drawbridge, intent only on preserving that single-goal advantage, and prepared for a long siege. It was bound to be a risky strategy, for few teams in the world could have given that Celtic side such territorial supremacy and not expect to concede goals. Celtic's approach was revolutionary for that time, insofar as Stein did not adhere to the current orthodoxy of playing only three forwards; apart from the goalkeeper and central defenders McNeill and Clark, every Celtic player was committed to attack at one time or another during a match – and Billy McNeill was always a threat at set-pieces.

The verdicts of the respective captains bear graphic testimony to the subsequent developments. Billy McNeill stated that 'Once Inter scored, John Clark and I could have gone and sat in the stand for all that we were needed'; Giacinto Facchetti, regarded as the finest attacking full-back in the world, lamented how 'countless times I tried to get forward but, when I played the ball and ran, I didn't get it back. Really, we were five men against 11.'

Half-time arrived with Celtic still behind, but Stein got to work calmly in the dressing-room, reminding his players that the way to beat that packed defence was by turning it. He asked that the ball be cut further back from the wings to create opportunities for shooting from longer range; to this end, Johnstone and Lennox had not been deployed as wingers exclusively, but asked to take on defenders through the middle, leaving the wings free for Craig and Gemmell to surge forward.

One member of the Italians' backroom staff – like a boxing trainer desperately trying to revive a struggling fighter – had been fully occupied since the interval dousing his players with water from the touchline as they hung on. The sunshine and the temperature should have favoured the Italians, but Celtic continued to attack and attack.

At last the Celtic pressure harvested its reward in 62 minutes after Murdoch sent the ball out on the right to Jim Craig, who had joined his forwards in attack. Craig started towards the corner of the penalty area as if he was going to force a way through, but rolled the ball back for the other full-back Tommy Gemmell who struck the ball magnificently from just outside the area, some 20 yards out. The brave Sarti made only a token gesture at stopping the drive from the hardest shot in Scottish football as it raged into his top right-hand corner.

The equaliser spoke volumes for Celtic's spirit, stamina and sheer boldness. Tommy Gemmell had actually disobeyed his manager's instructions just prior to scoring the goal because Stein had insisted that, if one full-back went forward, the other should remain in defence. Sheer frustration had got the better of Gemmell as the breakthrough just would not come, and so he moved into attack . . . to score the goal of his life.

That goal had been scored with such authority that it seemed but the prelude to more. Celtic's pressure continued minute after minute as Inter wilted, but hung on tenaciously. The Italian keeper Sarti – ironically identified by Stein before the contest as a potential weak link – was inspired and pulled off a series of larcenous saves to deny Celtic. But five minutes from the end he had to admit defeat again.

Close to exhaustion when he scored the equaliser, Tommy Gemmell continued to make lung-bursting sorties down the left wing, despite pleas from Stein on the touchline to hold something back for the looming probability of extra-time. This time, he pulled the ball back to Bobby Murdoch, an inspiration in midfield despite an early knock to his ankle, and he let fly another shot; the ever-alert Steve Chalmers, perfectly positioned around the six-yard box, diverted it neatly past the stranded keeper for the winner. It may have looked a simple goal, even a lucky one, but it was both a piece of quick thinking on Chalmers' part and a product of the training ground; Jock Stein's practice sessions regularly involved players in wide positions firing in angled shots for forwards to 'get across' defenders and deflect the ball into the net.

Writing in the *Daily Mail*, Brian James, that fine English journalist, marvelled at the resolution that ultimately won the European Cup and brought the trophy to Britain for the first time: 'Celtic never faltered. Not when their better shots struck the posts, or flew wide; not when their sharpest moves dwindled to nothing in the mesh of Inter defenders, nor when time galloped away, with every minute bringing fresh cause for cursing fate.'

It had been an archetypal Celtic victory, coming from behind to win at the death. John Rafferty's verdict in *The Scotsman* was a masterly piece of understatement: 'In old Lisbon tonight Celtic annihilated Inter Milan by a single goal.' The headline of one Lisbon newspaper, roughly translated, caught the mood exactly: 'Celtic won the match, the Cup, and the hearts of the public.'

It was not only the greatest triumph in the club's history, but also a victory for football itself and one which captivated an estimated hundred million television viewers across Europe. François Thebaud, the correspondent of the French magazine *Miroir du Football*, captured the impact on the neutral follower of the sport: 'Surely, never in the history of world sport has a team created as many new fans as Celtic, never has a victory been more warmly welcomed, nor a winning goal been greeted with such an explosion of joy throughout the Continent.' (June 1967 issue) For all Celtic supporters, as a famous statesman said of another stirring time, 'It was a great hour to live.'

EIGHT

The Best of Times

1967–70

After the triumph in Lisbon the pessimists feared an anticlimax, and that would have been a reasonable assumption. Indeed, a few months into the new season (1967–68) Celtic were to be confronted with the grimmer realities of football at the top.

Rangers had been hyperactive in the transfer market in their desperation to overtake Celtic, acquiring Persson of Dundee United, Penman of Dundee, and Ferguson from Dunfermline Athletic. The other half of the Old Firm and its supporters had been traumatised by the momentous European achievement of their old rivals, a feat which constituted an enormous dent to the Ibrox club's prestige. The German newspaper *Bild Zeitung* had made an acute observation after Rangers' failure to win the European Cup-Winners' Cup in Nuremberg the week after Celtic's triumph in Lisbon: 'Celtic, not Bayern Munich, were Rangers' real opponents in the final.' In stark contrast to Celtic's triumphant return from Lisbon, no fans turned up at Glasgow Airport to offer any greetings or commiserations when a silent and demoralised Rangers party disembarked from a plane nicknamed 'The Mortuary Special' by one unkind journalist aboard. And this only three years after John Fairgrieve (a journalist, and one of their historians) had asserted confidently: 'Rangers are the greatest football club in Scotland, have been so for many years, and very probably always will be as long as the game is played.'

Celtic, under Jock Stein, had turned such notions on their head. Within two years Celtic had taken a quantum leap in status, providing a massive boost to the self-esteem of those who followed a club long associated with the underdogs of Scottish life. Few (if any) clubs in world football have ever been so closely identified with a 'community' as Celtic; and Celtic supporters walked very tall indeed following Lisbon. In addition, the standards of football at the pinnacle of Europe, never mind Glasgow, were being redefined by Celtic much to the dismay of Rangers and their vast army of supporters. One critic observed of the gap now separating the two clubs: 'Celtic learned more in one season in the European Cup than Rangers had learned in ten seasons in European competition.'

Jock Stein knew, however, that he could never afford to relax in his striving to keep Celtic in the ascendant over their old rivals. For too many people in Glasgow, European glory meant little if Celtic lost too often to Rangers, even though Stein could joke about Rangers' desperation to regain their position as Scotland's top club. When an English journalist, Hunter Davies, visited Parkhead prior to the European Cup final, he was struck by the contrast between the grounds of the Glasgow rivals. He felt Celtic Park was representative of an unpretentious club with 'an underprivileged air', while Ibrox Park, cathedral-like, was the home of a club akin to 'the Established Church'. While he was being conducted round Celtic Park by Jock Stein himself, he took in the green motif at the ground: green paintwork, green crests and green ornamental work. Stein remarked jestingly: 'Ach, Rangers are all right, but they still haven't invented blue grass . . .'

Such was the intensity of the interest and feeling which surrounded the first Old Firm clash of 1967–68 that a crowd of 94,168 turned up at Ibrox, with thousands locked out, to watch a League Cup sectional match which ended with honours even in a 1–1 draw. Rangers' goal came from a free-kick taken by Penman very late in the contest to equalise Gemmell's penalty-kick counter in the first half.

Another huge crowd (75,000) was drawn to the return fixture at Parkhead two weeks later on 30 August 1967. They were attracted by the prospect of another titanic clash, one to decide which team would advance to the knock-out stage of the competition and emerge as overwhelming favourites to win the trophy. Rangers drew first blood, although Henderson's goal in nine minutes incensed Celtic's defenders who had been appealing for an offside decision; the referee chose not to consult the stand-side linesman, level with play, whose initial response had suggested some illegality about the goal. The referee compounded Celtic's frustration by disallowing an 'equaliser' by Lennox before the interval, and it seemed that all Celtic's outfield supremacy and sustained pressure on the Ibrox goal would be in vain. Thirteen minutes from the end, after Henderson had broken away again only to be fouled by Clark inside the area, the referee had no hesitation in awarding a penalty. Kai Johansen, Rangers' full-back hero in the Scottish Cup final 16 months previously, strode forward but his fierce rising spot-kick rebounded from the underside of the bar. Celtic had been reprieved, and their following unleashed a barrage of noise in support of a revitalised side.

Within two minutes, they were celebrating a goal from Wallace, who glanced home a header from a corner-kick after the ball from the left had eluded the grasp of Rangers' keeper Sorensen as he collided with Murdoch in mid-air. Only five minutes later, Bobby Murdoch himself put Celtic in front, striding forward with authority before he unleashed an unstoppable drive high into the net past Sorensen from 20 yards. The pressure on the Rangers goal continued minute after minute. In the dying moments Bobby Lennox darted through the middle of a defence in total disarray to add a third goal and put the seal on a truly remarkable victory.

The manager claimed afterwards that it had been the greatest victory achieved under his command, 'given the circumstances', a reference to the indulgent approach he felt had been adopted by the referee ('Tiny' Wharton of Clarkston) towards the crude tackling of some Rangers players.

Jock Stein's tactical sophistication was again in evidence when Celtic capitalised on 'the great escape' by retaining the League Cup. In the final against Dundee on 28 October at Hampden Park, John Hughes (listed at outside-left) was deployed to rampage down the right while Steve Chalmers (listed at outside-right) played through the middle, and Bobby Lennox (usually gainfully employed in the middle) played wide on the left. The adjustments thoroughly confused the Dundee defenders, who must have been boosted beforehand by Jimmy Johnstone's unavailability through suspension. Within ten minutes they had conceded two goals, the first through Steve Chalmers who nodded the ball home after McNeill had headed on a Hughes corner, and the second from Hughes who brushed past three opponents before hitting the ball past Arrol. Understandably, Dundee never recovered from that opening burst although the match evolved into a ding-dong struggle, with Celtic's defence ominously porous. In fact, the Cup-holders were relieved when Wallace ended the resistance from Tayside with Celtic's last goal in the 88th minute to complete a 5–3 win.

That slackness in defence, highlighted by the scoreline, added to the nagging doubts about Celtic's ability to cope with the strain of matching the incredible standards established during the previous season. The sense of a mini-crisis was aggravated by gleeful suggestions in some quarters that Celtic's very success had made a rod for their own back. After opening the league campaign by winning 3–0 over Clyde at home, Celtic lost 1–0 to Rangers at Ibrox and dropped a vital point to St Johnstone in an untidy 1–1 draw at Parkhead. The worst blow came in the European Cup when they faced the formidable Dynamo Kiev (USSR) in the opening round; Celtic were shocked by two early strikes from the Soviet champions, and Lennox's goal in 62 minutes was not enough. In Kiev, Celtic gave a more characteristic performance, and led 1–0 despite having to play with ten men after Murdoch was ordered off for dissent a few minutes before Lennox's goal; shortly afterwards, a seemingly valid goal by Hughes was disallowed. A last-minute equaliser by Dynamo denied Celtic an away victory, and ensured that the holders were out.

Even more disastrous was the fiasco of the three matches with Racing Club of the Argentine in the legs of the unofficial World Club Championship, held in October and November 1967. At Hampden Park the Scottish crowd watched in growing disbelief as the South American champions gave an intimidating and cynical display. Not even Billy McNeill's header in 69 minutes to give Celtic a 1–0 win could dispel the uneasiness about the prospect of a vicious return match in Buenos Aires.

All the worst fears were realised in Argentina, when Celtic lost in a match played in a proverbial cauldron of hate. Before the kick-off Ronnie Simpson was felled by a missile apparently thrown from the crowd and had to withdraw, his place being taken by John Fallon. Celtic's decision to substitute the goalkeeper was interpreted by their opponents and the massive crowd as a sign of weakness, virtually an invitation to violent aggression on the part of Racing. Dante Panzeri, an Argentinian journalist, stated bluntly after the match that Stein had erred, that after Simpson had been assaulted 'he should have pulled his team off the pitch, and Celtic should have packed their bags for home'. Later, this scenario was put to Stein by a French journalist and the manager was honest enough to admit that he had underestimated – and indeed could never understand – the cynicism in South American football. Reasonably and typically he pointed out that he had no right to deprive the paying customers of what they had come to see, a football match – but he left unspoken his underlying fear of the consequences of Celtic abandoning the match in such a volatile and hostile atmosphere.

From the kick-off Celtic were not allowed any opportunity to play football, as the headline for the match report in one European football magazine suggested: 'Racing took the law into their own hands!' Jimmy Johnstone, a potential match-winner for Celtic, was a particular target for thuggery while an indulgent referee, Esteban Marino of Uruguay, turned a blind eye to numerous offences. In the opening minutes Johnstone was blatantly fouled inside the Racing penalty area, and shortly afterwards, when McNeill came up for a corner-kick, he was bundled to the ground before the ball reached the goalmouth. In fact, when McNeill scored the winning goal at Hampden Park weeks earlier, he had received a black eye from an Argentinian elbow for his reward.

However, even Marino could not ignore the blatancy of the offence when goalkeeper Cejas rugby-tackled Jimmy Johnstone in 22 minutes. Tommy Gemmell blasted the penalty-kick past Cejas even though the goalkeeper had advanced several yards from his line as the full-back was approaching the ball. But Racing Club, inspired by the wildly partisan 120,000 crowd, fought back to equalise in the 34th minute; several Argentinian newspapers conceded that the 'goal' was offside although the final header by Raffo was a spectacular effort. There was nothing doubtful, however, about the winning goal, scored by Cardenas shortly after the interval following splendid leading-up work by Raffo.

The rules allowed for a third and deciding game to be played on a neutral pitch, and the Celtic party was split during the debate as to whether to compete any further against opponents who were determined to win by such violent means. Already Celtic's players had had to deal with a variety of brutal and cynical measures, including spitting. Bob Kelly, the chairman, wanted the team to leave for Scotland immediately and thus avoid any further scenes on the pitch; Desmond White, the secretary-treasurer, did not want to withdraw having come so far at such expense; Jock Stein, the manager, wanted his team to have another opportunity to prove themselves the best club side in the world.

Finally, the decision was made to participate in the play-off match in Montevideo in Uruguay, just across the River Plate from Argentina. Some 30,000 Racing fans made the crossing in all sorts of craft; and hundreds of them turned up at 2 a.m. outside the hotel where Celtic were staying to disturb their sleep with a cacophony of singing and shouting.

To nobody's surprise this powder-keg of a match turned into one of the blackest days in Celtic's proud history. Jock Stein was reported to have previewed the contest with an ominous announcement to the press: 'I cannot send my team into the game with one hand behind their backs.' Such was the mayhem – hysterical from Celtic, cynical from Racing – and such was the lack of control by the referee (Rodolfo Perez Osorio of Uruguay) that six players were dismissed. In fact, four Celtic players, Lennox, Johnstone, Hughes and Auld (all of them forwards) were ordered off, although one of them (Auld) ignored the referee's directive by staying on the pitch until the end. The only goal, scored by Cardenas ten minutes after half-time, was almost an irrelevance.

The emptiness of such a victory was underlined at full-time when the Racing celebrations were abruptly cut short by many Uruguayan spectators, enraged at this spectacle, hurling missiles at the Argentinian players and officials as they headed for the tunnel. Several of the Racing players had to seek sanctuary and police protection in the middle of the pitch. As one observer noted, 'Their triumph dissolved in sheer panic.'

The whole affair left a bitter taste for the Celtic players. After participating in matches against brutal opponents 8,000 miles from home in a hostile environment, after being assaulted, kicked and hacked, goaded and spat upon, every Celtic player who had taken the field was fined £250 for their part in the disgraceful scenes. This decision by the Board was not accepted wholeheartedly by the players, despite press coverage to the contrary. One player, uninvolved in any of the trouble, had a heated argument with Bob Kelly about the fairness of the fines. Racing's players, in direct contrast, were each awarded a bonus of £2,000 and a new car. Even Jock Stein, normally so resilient, was shaken and temporarily depressed by the affair, perhaps realising that his strenuous advocacy of playing in the third match had been a mistake. On the long journey home he was seen sitting with his head down at one stage, silent and bowed in despair.

It took another 12 years for any Racing player to admit his team's skulduggery. In an interview for *Soccer Monthly* in December 1979, the goalkeeper, Augustin Cejas, chillingly recalled the mayhem in Montevideo as 'a fairly normal match for us' – in contrast to the 'pure warfare' of their three clashes with Nacional of Paraguay in the Copa Libertadores, the South American Club Championship, which had allowed them to qualify for the matches against Europe's champions: 'I remember in the play-off in Montevideo I was given a "pacific" role. I didn't have to hit anybody, just be goalkeeper. But suddenly, Basile really hit the red-head Johnstone with a hell of a foul, one of the most violent I've ever seen. And the referee sent Basile off. I started walking casually out of my goal with my hands behind my back, and made my way slowly towards Johnstone. He was still on the ground when I arrived, so I kicked him as hard as I could for getting my team-mate sent off . . .'

During Celtic's absence, surprising things had been happening in Scottish football. Rangers were in first place in the league but, through an intermediary, had ruthlessly fired their manager, Scot Symon, the most consistently successful manager in Scotland in the decade before Stein's accession at Parkhead. Indeed, Symon was asked to vacate his home, owned by the club, at very short notice.

In the ensuing consternation, many seemed to lose sight of the fact that Rangers had been given a window of opportunity to reassert themselves as Scotland's leading club while Celtic were struggling to recover from the double hangover caused by their early exit from the European Cup and the ignominious defeat in the World Club Championship. Celtic's reputation and prestige had been damaged, and it was up to Stein to restore dented morale at Parkhead.

Resuming the chase in the league championship, Celtic settled down to closing the gap which had opened up in their absence. Under new management in the person of David White, who had previously taken unfashionable Clyde to a third-place finish behind the Old Firm in 1966–67, Rangers preserved an undefeated record in the league as they went into the clash at Parkhead on 2 January 1968.

Celtic, two points behind, felt they had to win. Despite the rough treatment meted out to Jimmy Johnstone, Celtic proved the much more fluid and inventive side on 'a dead, muddy field'. At half-time the consensus among the majority of the 75,000 crowd was that they should have been leading by more than Auld's goal. The second half started to turn into a personal nightmare for Celtic's goalkeeper Fallon ten minutes after the restart, when he allowed a softish shot to trickle between his legs for an equaliser. Bobby Murdoch restored the lead, swivelling in the penalty area to drive a left-footer past Sorensen's reach. However, only two minutes from the end, Fallon completely misread a shot from Johansen to gift Rangers an equaliser.

The true test of any team is its response to adversity, and this Celtic side would pass that examination of character with flying colours, prompted by Jock Stein's determination to rebuild confidence by stimulating analysis and frank discussion of what had gone wrong. With good habits restored, Celtic would go through the remainder of the league programme undefeated, a shock 2–0 defeat at Parkhead in the Scottish Cup by Dunfermline (the eventual winners) proving only a temporary setback to morale. All the early-season ills were being worked out of Celtic's system as the side took out its frustrations on hapless opponents while Rangers started to show signs of nervousness as the winning post neared.

Celtic continued to turn the screws on Rangers with a zeal bordering on relish as they boosted their goal-average which, at one stage of the campaign, looked a possible deciding factor. Celtic's determination and confidence was growing as they inflicted heavy defeats on sides which had caused them heartache in pre-Stein days: 6–0 at Kilmarnock on 2 March, a 4–1 win over Aberdeen at Parkhead on 6 March, a 5–0 rout of Raith Rovers (also at home) on 23 March, 6–1 against St Johnstone at Perth two days later, 5–0 over Dundee United at Tannadice on 30 March, and a 5–2 win against Dundee at Parkhead on 13 April as the championship built to a climax.

Celtic also drew some comfort, and a fillip to morale, from Rangers' obvious reluctance to honour the clubs' Glasgow Cup semi-final fixture.

Perhaps fearing psychological damage to their title chances, they withdrew from the competition, citing 'a congestion of fixtures' as a reason. Although Rangers were indeed still involved in Europe and the Scottish Cup, the widespread perception was that, in Glasgow parlance, 'Rangers had crapped it!' In the next issue of the *Celtic Football Guide* Jock Stein reiterated his contempt for Rangers' action by noting that Celtic had retained the Glasgow Cup by beating 'all the clubs eligible and prepared to play us'. Rangers' action misfired badly, since the Ibrox club soon had only the league title to play for – and, on the evening that Celtic were trouncing Clyde 8–0 in the Glasgow Cup final, Morton took a vital point from Rangers in a 3–3 draw at Greenock.

Only three days later (on 20 April 1968), however, that same Morton side almost derailed Celtic's hopes. In the closing minutes the score was still tied at 1–1 and, as the news was spreading around the ground that Rangers were leading 2–1 at Kilmarnock, despair was visible on 50,000 faces . . . until, in injury-time, with referee J.W. Paterson of Bothwell looking at his watch, Bobby Lennox lunged at the ball in a goalmouth scramble to snatch the winner. Once again Lennox had produced a vital last-gasp goal for Celtic. Hugh Taylor of the *Daily Record*, in reviewing the season, would recall the scenes when Rangers fans were leaving Kilmarnock, jubilant in victory and in the mistaken belief that Celtic had dropped that vital point: 'The news spread like wildfire. There was pandemonium. Party songs were sung. The fans danced with each other.'

To those fans, the title race seemed all over. Indeed it was – for their own team, which in its final game succumbed 2–3 to Aberdeen at Ibrox, their only defeat in the 1967–68 competition.

Celtic, faced with their last fixture, at Dunfermline, had to lose 16–0 to be deprived of a third successive championship. Three days later, on 30 April, Celtic travelled to the Kingdom of Fife to be crowned as champions. In a clash between the champions (Celtic) and the Scottish Cup-holders (Dunfermline), played before a record attendance at the ground, Celtic won 2–1 in an electric atmosphere. An estimated 2,000 fans forced their way into the packed stadium by charging a gate or by scaling the walls. Supporters clambered on to the roof of the enclosure and perched on 80-foot-high floodlight pylons to escape the crush that twice caused the game to be halted with spectators encroaching on to the pitch.

Celtic entered the following season as the Rolls-Royce of Scottish football, with the Lisbon team now more mature, and continuing to enhance their tactical awareness under Stein's tutelage; the side required only fine-tuning, and the injection of a dose of competition from new signings. Stein confirmed this belief when he strengthened the squad by making two important captures: lanky midfielder Tom Callaghan from

Dunfermline in November 1968 for £35,000, and Harry Hood, a striker from Clyde, in March 1969 for £40,000. A memorable display in the league encounter with Hibs at Easter Road on 30 November 1968 attested to the fitness, tactical flexibility and breathtakingly entertaining football for which Celtic were by now admired and feared. Fifteen minutes from time Hibernian took a 2–1 lead from the penalty awarded after Gemmell had up-ended his former team-mate Joe McBride, sold to Hibs on 5 November. Celtic's reaction was pulverising: Billy McNeill headed the equaliser, then Jock Stein switched John Hughes from the left wing into the middle and Bobby Lennox to the left wing. Hughes tore past the hitherto comfortable Stanton to net twice; Jimmy Johnstone shredded the Hibs defence before flighting over a cross for Lennox to bullet a header past Wilson. Four goals at Easter Road in five minutes against one of their closest challengers! Celtic's ability to step up a gear when under pressure was positively intimidating to their rivals.

The team's clinical finishing had been in evidence from the first day of the 1968–69 season when they began the defence of the League Cup at Ibrox by winning 2–0, with Willie Wallace taking maximum advantage of mistakes by a flustered Greig, once again discomfited by Lennox's pace. A fortnight later at Celtic Park, Wallace scored the only goal of the match to complete a double victory over Rangers in the sectional play.

A fire at Hampden Park in the autumn of 1968 caused the postponement of the final, and it was not until 5 April 1969 that Celtic claimed the League Cup for the fourth successive time. Against a gallant Hibernian team Celtic were at their most brilliant. It was attacking football at its best, with Celtic going through their complete repertoire as they went three goals up in the first half. The midfield tandem of Murdoch and Auld had taken an early grip of proceedings which they maintained throughout. To the delight of most of the 72,420 spectators, the Cup-holders came out looking for more in the second half and finished up 6–2 winners. A breathtaking exhibition of dazzling outfield play and ruthless finishing (especially from Lennox, who netted a hat-trick) overwhelmed the luckless opposition.

The Scottish Cup final on 26 April 1969 was another disaster for Rangers. Approaching the final, they had been so confident of success that they planned to open Ibrox Park for their fans to make the short journey from Hampden Park to watch the players parading with the Scottish Cup. Their confidence was based on the fact that they had beaten Celtic home and away in the league (although once more ending up in second place), and they were given further encouragement when Celtic were forced to play the final without their regular wingers. The temperamental Johnstone was unavailable through another suspension, and Hughes's ankle had not healed after a bad injury at Perth some weeks earlier.

In only two minutes the vast crowd of 132,870 was stunned by a Celtic goal, assisted by elementary errors in defence by Rangers. Billy McNeill came up for a Lennox corner on the left, and was allowed to drift into the penalty area unmarked; his header entered the net off the base of a completely unmarked post while Rangers' defenders stared at each other in total disbelief at the two blatant errors. Alex Ferguson, the Rangers forward detailed to mark McNeill in this type of situation, paid the usual price for such failures in those days at Ibrox; he never played another match in the first team, and found himself in the third team playing against Glasgow Corporation Transport!* The much-maligned John Fallon, restored to Celtic's goal as a result of a shoulder injury to Simpson which eventually ended the veteran's astonishing career, came to Celtic's rescue with a brilliant save from a blistering shot from Persson as Rangers surged forward hoping for a quick equaliser.

Celtic were content to absorb Rangers' battering-ram attacks. One feature of Jock Stein's planning was designed to draw the Ibrox men forward and thus leave their central defence of Greig and McKinnon more exposed to the pace of Lennox and Chalmers. Rangers' vulnerability to such a counter-attack was clearly revealed as Celtic struck like a cobra just before the interval. George Connelly, a 20-year-old midfielder playing in his first major final, intercepted a stray pass to send Lennox clear on a run of 25 yards; the Celt's pace enabled him to draw away from frantically pursuing defenders, and he clipped the ball firmly into the far corner of the net past Martin. Hardly had the tumult at the Celtic end of Hampden died down when Connelly alertly pounced on a misunderstanding between Greig and Martin at a goal-kick to dispossess the Rangers captain, round the despairing goalkeeper, and prod the ball into an empty net.

Jock Stein had great difficulty in calming down his jubilant players as they danced into the dressing-room a minute or so later; even with the manager's obligatory words of restraint, they knew the final was already won . . .

Despite the comfortable lead enjoyed by Celtic, the match continued as a fierce, savage affair, with some players settling private scores. As he limped off in 57 minutes, Jim Brogan could consider himself unfortunate to have been the only player booked by the referee. Cautiously, Stein substituted him with John Clark, the ideal padlock with which to bolt the door on a Rangers comeback. Rangers' misery was not yet over. In the 75th minute, with Celtic coasting to victory, Murdoch chipped the ball beautifully to Auld who in turn released the speedy Chalmers to run free

---

* Undaunted, Ferguson later embarked on a brilliant managerial career with Aberdeen and Manchester United.

down the left before cutting inside; with Rangers' defenders expecting him to square the ball to the better-placed Lennox, Chalmers cheekily netted at the near post with a casual right-foot bender for the fourth goal: 4–0, and the Rangers end was emptying faster than Guinness bottles at an Irish wake.

April had been the month for success in 1969. In between the finals at Hampden, a late goal by Tommy Gemmell earned Celtic a 2–2 draw at Kilmarnock and the point that gave them a fourth successive championship a few days before the Scottish Cup final.

The only disappointment came in the European Cup. Celtic reached the last eight, having survived the difficult hurdles of St Etienne (France) and Red Star (Yugoslavia). Two brilliant performances at Parkhead against those opponents helped to maintain Celtic Park's fearsome reputation on the Continent as no place for faint hearts. St Etienne came to Glasgow nursing a two-goal lead from the first leg, but Celtic put on an awesome display – helped, according to the visitors, by some sympathetic refereeing – to rout the French side by 4–0. Against Red Star in the first leg Jimmy Johnstone, plied by a stream of passes from the incomparable Murdoch, was truly inspired as he turned the Yugoslav defenders inside out to lead Celtic to a 5–1 victory, and make the second leg a formality (1–1). Perhaps Johnstone's form owed something to a private deal between himself and the manager; Jock Stein shrewdly played on Jinky's fear of flying and had promised him he would not have to travel to Yugoslavia if Celtic had established a four-goal lead!

In the first leg of the quarter-final Celtic massed in defence against AC Milan in the San Siro Stadium to hold the Italian champions to a 0–0 score, but at Parkhead a momentary lapse by Celtic's defence – when Billy McNeill made a hash of a throw-in by Jim Craig – allowed Prati to break away in 13 minutes to score the game's only goal. The Italians shut up shop thereafter, and Celtic, deprived of the injured Lennox, lacked the penetration and sharpness needed to unlock a resolute, well-drilled defence.

After the reality of such a bitter defeat had sunk in, there were some mutterings from the terracings about the 'failure' to win the European Cup again, and suggestions that it had been a 'bad' season. And that following the club's second domestic treble within three seasons! The acute sense of disappointment had stemmed from a feeling that this was a Celtic side of unlimited potential, a match for the best in the world. After all, the coach of AC Milan had freely admitted to Stein that his side's victory was completely unexpected. Max Marquis of the *Sunday Times* reinforced this belief when commenting on the Scottish Cup final triumph: 'Celtic's performance – particularly the darting threats of Chalmers and Lennox –

without their two great wingers was impressive enough. What it would be like with them is enough to make the top English clubs think – and think hard.'

That observation would soon be put to the test but, in the meantime, Celtic continued to maintain the Indian sign on Rangers. The desperation of the Ibrox club to rid themselves of a growing inferiority complex was palpable, even though denied by various spokesmen. After a critical League Cup tie at Celtic Park on 20 August 1969, Rangers were still in search of a cure for their neurosis. A week earlier, they had edged out of the shadow cast by their great rivals with a gritty 2–1 victory at Ibrox in the first sectional clash and, two points up, they lined up at Parkhead needing, effectively, only a draw to qualify for the next stage. Celtic needed a win to keep their hopes alive.

Once again, the outcome hinged on a moment of great drama, but it was a controversial refereeing decision shortly after the interval that affected the outcome this time. The score stood at 0–0 when the referee, J. Callaghan of Glasgow, decided against sending off John Hughes of Celtic, already booked in the first half, for an off-the-ball incident with Johnston. Celtic capitalised on an obvious break to reassert themselves and score the only goal of a torrid match; Tommy Gemmell moved forward to throw himself full-length to head the ball into the net after goalkeeper Neef allowed a twice-taken free-kick by Murdoch to squirm from his grasp midway through the second half.

The consequences for the referee – who had been honoured by his selection for the previous season's Scottish Cup final between the Old Firm – were severe. Rangers lodged an official complaint, and Mr Callaghan was suspended by the SFA for two months. This decision would have significant repercussions for Celtic, and one of their most prominent players, when the club reached the League Cup final, to be played against St Johnstone on 25 October 1969 at Hampden.

Stein's problems in team selection for the final involved Jimmy Johnstone and Tommy Gemmell. These players had featured in a tense World Cup tie for Scotland against West Germany at Hamburg in midweek – and Gemmell had been ordered off. The manager decided to replace both internationals by calling up Tom Callaghan and young David Hay, a hard-tackling defender, although he took out an insurance policy by listing Johnstone as the substitute. Clearly, Gemmell had been disciplined by Stein for his sending-off, his offence a repetition of a highly publicised incident in the infamous match against Racing Club in South America. The player was angered by the manager's decision, and by learning of it only when he entered the dressing-room clapping his hands in a gesture of encouragement to his team-mates; he was handed a ticket to watch the game from the stand. Commenting on the episode recently, Gemmell said: 'I noticed Davie Hay getting ready to take my place. I could never really forgive such treatment.'

Although the manager and the player had shared the flight home from Germany, Stein had not mentioned the incident, nor did he do so at any time in the days leading up to the final. In truth, Jock Stein had felt obliged to discipline the player more severely in the wake of the resignation of Bob Kelly from the SFA Referee Committee earlier that week in the aftermath of the Callaghan affair. Stein simply could not embarrass a man who demanded exemplary standards of those who wore the green and white. Shortly afterwards Gemmell requested a transfer, bluntly informing his manager that he would hardly have been dropped if Celtic had been facing Rangers in the League Cup final. His transfer request was eventually withdrawn, but the relationship between the player and his manager was fractured beyond repair.

In the final itself, St Johnstone were given no opportunity to settle down to their task of causing an upset. Bertie Auld scored the decisive goal in only two minutes, netting from close range after the St Johnstone goalkeeper had parried Chalmers' diving header on to the crossbar. Celtic were used to Hampden Park – very much their second home now – and infinitely more familiar with the Cup-final atmosphere generated by the crowd of 73,067. They utilised these advantages to the full to maintain their grip on the trophy, despite the Perth side's gallant late push for an equaliser.

Celtic's 1–0 victory over St Johnstone, their seventh in a League Cup final, established two Scottish records which have yet to be equalled: a fifth consecutive triumph in the competition, and the acquisition of four major trophies within a six-month period. Inevitably, it was viewed as a platform from which to repeat the clean sweep of 1966–67, an annual quest during those heady times. That prospect edged closer to fulfilment when Celtic went through the formality of securing their fifth successive championship with a draw against Hearts at Tynecastle on 28 March 1970 – an early closing of the league programme, even by Celtic's standards. Rangers, who had dropped points like confetti, finished up 12 points adrift as runners-up. The conviction was growing that Celtic were about to realise their dream by adding the Scottish Cup and the European Cup to the haul.

Celtic had already brought further gloom to the ranks of Rangers supporters by inflicting a 3–1 defeat on the Ibrox club in the Scottish Cup quarter-final at Parkhead; the combative Alex MacDonald of Rangers was sent off in a volcano of a match, one which saw the visitors thwarted yet again by a shrewd ploy from Stein. David Hay was fielded in the midfield to neutralise the forward surges of John Greig; Hay did exactly that – and, late in the game, he found the time and space to crack home a shot from 25 yards which put Celtic on the road to victory.

At least one of those dejected Rangers fans had already provided a solution to the stratagems of Jock Stein by suggesting in a letter to the *Daily Record* that Rangers offer Stein £100,000 tax-free and a villa on the Riviera to quit the country: 'If he hadn't been manager of Celtic, Rangers would still have been on top of the heap in Scotland.'

The Scottish Cup final was held on 11 April 1970 and watched by 108,434 – most of whom departed with the feeling that the referee, R.H. Davidson of Airdrie, had played too controversial a part in the proceedings. Aberdeen (4 to 1 outsiders) put up a stubborn early resistance but the favourites gradually took control. Within the space of ten minutes, however, Celtic's composure and self-confidence was shattered by three separate incidents. In the 26th minute, to the surprise of the Aberdeen players and the consternation of Celtic's, the referee awarded the Dons a penalty-kick when the ball struck Murdoch's shoulder as he tried to block a cross. Harper duly converted the award after furious Celtic protests, which led to a booking for Tommy Gemmell, had died down; four minutes later Celtic had a goal disallowed when Lennox was adjudged to have handled the ball while pressurising Clark, a goalkeeper notoriously uneasy when challenged while clearing from hand; and, finally, Mr Davidson waved away Celtic's confident claims for a penalty seven minutes from half-time when Lennox was tumbled in the box by Buchan, the referee signalling that he believed the Celtic player had dived.

Aberdeen, after those breaks, were not to be denied despite Celtic's all-out attacking in the second half, and took the trophy to Pittodrie with a 3–1 scoreline, two late sucker punches from McKay clinching the result as Celtic sought desperately to retrieve the situation; Lennox had given Celtic a glimmer of hope, netting shortly after Aberdeen's second goal seven minutes from time.

Celtic now had to focus their attention again on the European Cup, a competition which had already proved a hectic roller-coaster ride for players and supporters that season. In an early round the renowned Benfica looked to be down and out after Celtic had responded to the ferment on the Parkhead terracings with a passionate display to sweep aside one of Europe's most glamorous sides; the Portuguese defensive plans for the tie were blown to smithereens after only 75 seconds, when Tommy Gemmell's glorious free-kick thundered into the roof of the net. However, Celtic's substantial 3–0 lead from the first leg melted in Lisbon when the Portuguese turned on their own brand of magic to force extra-time with an equaliser well into injury-time. Celtic qualified for the quarter-final after the further 30 minutes produced no more goals, Billy McNeill winning the toss of the coin that decided which club should advance.

This bizarre method of qualifying brought no joy whatsoever to one person in the Celtic camp, the club's chairman, Bob Kelly. When Billy McNeill mentioned to the autocratic Kelly the following morning that he hoped that the players' celebrations in the hotel after the match had not disturbed the chairman's sleep, the reply was brusque and pointed: 'I don't see what you had to celebrate.' True to his principles, the chairman petitioned UEFA for a change in the method of deciding drawn ties; the penalty competition was introduced by UEFA at a meeting held a few hours before the 1970 Champions Cup final in Milan.

A relieved Celtic had no need of luck in the next round, where the cunning of Bertie Auld undid Fiorentina in the first leg before 77,240 spectators (officially, the largest attendance for a European match at Parkhead). This time, Celtic took no chances with a three-goal lead from the first leg, Stein beating the Italian representatives at their own defensive game with a masterful containment strategy which gave up only one goal in the return leg.

The draw for the semi-final resulted in the first-ever meeting in the competition between the champions of Scotland and England, Celtic against the formidable Leeds United. Celtic were written off in the English press, but Stein welcomed that disdain as an opportunity to further motivate his players for the first match at Leeds. Within the opening minute at Elland Road, Celtic had scored: George Connelly (although featuring in all the English club's pre-game plans as a defensive midfield player) controlled a through ball to shoot powerfully from 20 yards, and a defender deflected it past the stranded Sprake. For the whole first half Celtic dominated the play as the team followed Stein's bold plan to get at Leeds from the start before the English side could build up the irresistible momentum that had crushed earlier European visitors that season. Leeds – 'enjoying' home advantage – were forced to defend grimly. Jimmy Johnstone was at his mercurial best, tormenting the English defence and stretching them to the full.

Leeds United, realising they needed a result at home to survive in Glasgow, swept into attack in the second half but the Celtic defence, organised by McNeill, hung on. Lennox and Johnstone waited to pounce on a breakaway; in fact, to underline Celtic's attacking threat, Stein brought on John Hughes (exclusively a forward) as a substitute late in the contest. The match, a memorable and enthralling clash played on 1 April 1970, ended in a 1–0 win for Celtic; it was Leeds who had been fooled!

The all-ticket return was scheduled for two weeks later, on 15 April, at Hampden Park, chosen because of its greater capacity – and the contest, according to UEFA archives, attracted a record attendance for any match in the various European club competitions of 133,961.

Before the kick-off Jock Stein won another round in his battle of wits with the Leeds manager Don Revie. Anxious that his central defence should not be disrupted by the absence of the dominating Billy McNeill, he took a chance on the fitness of the player, who was feeling the effects of an ankle injury sustained in the Scottish Cup final. Stein kept his gamble a secret from Leeds by instructing McNeill (and three other Celtic players) to wear tracksuit bottoms for the warm-up, a stratagem to conceal McNeill's heavy strapping. The plan might have blown up in the manager's face when Bremner brought Leeds level on aggregate in the 13th minute with a swerving drive from 30 yards out which left Evan Williams helpless in Celtic's goal. The 'Battle of Britain' was eventually decided in midfield, where Celtic's pairing of Bobby Murdoch and Bertie Auld gradually wrested control from Billy Bremner and Johnny Giles. As in the first leg, Jimmy Johnstone was in devastating form, forcing Leeds to hoist distress signals in defence.

Such was Celtic's confidence and resolution that, at half-time, defender Jim Brogan spoke for his team-mates when he said, only half in jest: 'Well, they've had their little moment. Excuse me a minute while I phone Joyce [his wife] and tell her to pack my bags and look out my passport for Milan!' Only two minutes into the second half, Celtic equalised. Auld, loitering with intent near the corner flag as Hay prepared to take the kick on the right, collected his short pass and whipped over a curling cross for the diving Hughes to glance with his head past Sprake. Minutes later, with Sprake unable to continue after an injury, his replacement David Harvey had barely taken up position in goal when Murdoch and Johnstone combined brilliantly on the right; Johnstone dragged several Leeds defenders towards him and squared the ball to Murdoch who lashed a low shot into the net. The contest was over, and Glasgow belonged to Celtic as Hampden's vast bowl reverberated to the chants of 'Jock Stein! Jock Stein!'.

Those moments – on 15 April 1970 – may well have been the pinnacle of achievement in Celtic's history. Dare one say that the accomplishment – and the manner of it – was even more impressive than Lisbon? Afterwards, the immense crowd stayed in their places, savouring the moment and saluting the victors. The English press was generous in its praise. Geoffrey Green, writing in that august daily *The Times*, described the epic encounter as 'a monument to human endeavour and skill under great pressures in a match of disciplined behaviour . . . When Celtic did their lap of honour and the Glasgow skies shook, we knew there had been a just and rightful winner.' Brian Scovell, in the tabloid *Daily Sketch* that same day, enthused that Celtic were 'surely destined to become Europe's soccer supremos of the 1970s' . . .

After humiliating Leeds United home and away – as Stein had so much wanted – Celtic were due to face Feyenoord of Rotterdam in Milan's San Siro Stadium in the final on 6 May. The experts, overlooking the dramatic improvement in Dutch football which culminated in Ajax's later European triumphs, installed Celtic as favourites for the crown. Jock Stein made a point of watching the Dutch champions – though only once – and warned his squad against complacency. Unfortunately, his own air of confidence gave the impression that he was paying only lip-service to the threat from Holland.

The Celtic party was accommodated in quarters some 30 miles out of Milan, which afforded suitable training facilities and privacy, keeping supporters at bay. As a result of this, though, the players began to feel detached from the atmosphere building up among the Scottish and Dutch fans gathering in Milan. This distancing from the sense of occasion was increased by another decision by Stein, one which was surprising for a man whose preoccupation with familiarising himself with the arena of play bordered on the obsessional; he chose not to inspect the San Siro prior to Celtic setting off to play there on match day. Also, in stark contrast to the atmosphere at Lisbon three years earlier, when the manager had become visibly agitated by the sight of reserve keeper John Fallon briefly (and accidentally) exposing his head to the sun, several players were photographed stripped to the waist while training or watching team-mates playing tennis at the hotel at Varese. Malcolm Munro of the *Glasgow Evening Times*, in a despatch to his newspaper, sent a few hours before the match, stated that Stein had 'unwound his players to the point of relaxation. Between now and the kick-off he must wind them up again . . .' In his match report the following day the same reporter commented that Celtic's hilltop hideaway had been 'more like a rest home than a training centre'.

When the sides trooped on to the pitch before a crowd of 53,187 the omens seemed to be against Celtic as the supporters greeted their teams, the horns of the Dutch fans drowning out even the roars of Celtic's thousands. Without showing anything like the fluency and urgency which had destroyed Leeds United, Celtic opened the scoring in 30 minutes through a powerful Gemmell free-kick; only three minutes later, however, Feyenoord struck back through Israel's looping header after Celtic's defence had failed to clear their lines decisively.

The equaliser came as a great relief to the Dutch side's coach, Ernst Happel, who had been worried about the impact the loss of the first goal would have on his team. His concern proved groundless, as the rest of the final belonged to Feyenoord, a side much better prepared tactically, mentally and physically. The Dutchmen had Celtic chasing shadows or, as

Bobby Murdoch puts it, 'They seemed to outnumber us whether they were attacking or defending.'

That ascendancy owed a lot to Happel's in-depth study of Celtic's style of play. Ironically, the Feyenoord scouts sent to watch Celtic play against Leeds United had returned to Rotterdam full of pessimism. The gist of their reports was there was no way the Dutch side could win: Celtic were such 'a perfect well-oiled machine' that Feyenoord might as well not turn up. Still, Happel made a point of seeing Celtic in person, in addition to watching them on film, and he detected weaknesses in Celtic's style that could be exploited. Thus, the Dutch midfield clamped down on Murdoch and Auld from the outset to cut off the supply of ammunition to Celtic's front men.

Miraculously, Celtic took the final into extra-time, thanks to fine goalkeeping from Evan Williams and to Feyenoord missing chances as well as hitting the woodwork. Jock Stein made only one change in an attempt to alter the pattern, replacing the tired and injured Auld in 75 minutes with George Connelly; in the opinion of several Celtic players, Connelly's omission from the starting line-up had fatally affected the balance of the midfield. Still on the pitch were Jim Brogan, limping from the early stages, and Jimmy Johnstone, the target of some uncompromising defending.

John Hughes came desperately close for Celtic with a solo burst after only 30 seconds of extra-time, but Feyenoord soon resumed control of the game. Celtic managed to hold out somehow until three minutes from the end when a McNeill slip from a quickly taken free-kick enabled Kindvall to net Feyenoord's second goal – and the winner. Reflecting on the disappointment a quarter of a century later, Billy McNeill is honest enough to describe the result as a travesty: 'It might have been 5–1.'

The recriminations went deep. There was pointed criticism in the newspapers of the potentially disruptive presence of the players' business manager at Varese, although he would not have been there without the sanction of Jock Stein. The manager himself was accused of overconfidence by some of his players – although the charge came years later.

Based on his viewing of Feyenoord's second half in a 3–3 draw with Ajax Amsterdam, Stein just did not believe that Celtic's opponents could compete with the Glasgow side's pace, power, variety and stamina. While the manager went through the motions – in public, at least – of expressing anxiety, subconsciously he may have been reassuring himself that, in theatrical terms, it would be all right on the night. With the whole Celtic party lulled into a false sense of security, it was little wonder that the players on the field were disconcerted to find that Feyenoord were a side packed with strong and determined runners, and that Van Hanegem, the midfield general apparently dismissed by Stein as 'a poor man's Jim Baxter', turned out to be powerful in the tackle, hard to dispossess and intelligent in his distribution.

Somewhere in the three weeks between the semi-final at Hampden and Milan – a period during which Celtic played only one competitive match and two friendlies – the side lost its cutting-edge. It proved too hard to recover the appetite for battle and the concentration required in professional preparation. As somebody remarked, 'It was Lisbon in reverse.'

The European Cup final of 1970 must be regarded as a watershed for the club and Jock Stein. The Big Man's reputation for infallibility had been severely dented, although he would continue to prove himself an exceptional manager in the years to come.

It marked the end of the most glorious period of accomplishment in Celtic's history, a five-year epoch marked as much by style and flair, colour and excitement as by competitive success. The opportunity to establish Celtic firmly in the pantheon of truly great European clubs was lost, the opportunity to join the likes of Real Madrid and AC Milan as a member of the élite was missed. Something in Celtic died that night.

Celtic were now left to pick up the pieces, but the fall-out from Milan would linger as a malignant half-life for several years. The tensions surfaced almost immediately, starting with another trip to Canada, the United States and Bermuda which followed hard on the club's return home from Italy. Morale among the players was low, and the tour would not prove to be the success of the 1966 venture. Essentially, this trip was a money-making exercise, starting with a round-robin tournament involving Manchester United and the Italian side Bari for the Toronto Cup. After Celtic lost their first match, against Manchester United, the remaining fixture against Bari became only academic and of little interest either in Canada or Scotland – until Jock Stein suddenly departed for the airport 15 minutes before the end of a 2–2 draw, a match attended by only 3,000.

He suggested in a statement before leaving that he had to return to deal with a backlog of paperwork, and to resolve a contractual dispute with Jimmy Johnstone who had been allowed to skip the ill-fated tour because of an injury and his fear of flying. Stein's additional explanation that he needed treatment for his own recurring ankle problem indirectly helped fuel the rumours back home in Scotland. The *Evening Times* journalist who tried to interview Stein at Prestwick noted that 'there was no sign of the injury as the Celtic boss strode across the tarmac from the BOAC jet, shrugging off questions about the Celtic problems during the past few days'. (18 May 1970)

Days later, his bewildered players were still asking the sportswriters covering the tour in North America why their manager had left so unexpectedly for home. Not for the first time his name was being linked with Manchester United.

His managerial responsibilities on tour were assumed by his assistant, Sean Fallon, although Desmond White, the senior director in the absence of the seriously ill Sir Robert Kelly, felt obliged to fly out from Scotland to take overall control of the party. Before White joined up with the group, however, two star players had been sent home by Fallon for breaches of discipline. Tommy Gemmell and Bertie Auld, both recognised as 'free spirits', had become fed up with the boredom of a pointless tour and were/ still feeling low after Celtic's recent disappointments.

It also rankled with many in the Celtic squad that Stein, who in their opinion had misjudged Feyenoord's abilities, seemed to lump the blame for the defeat in Milan on his players. Only minutes after that traumatic defeat, Stein had slammed the dressing-room door shut on downcast Celtic players slumped in deep silence, and turned to make an odd and intriguing statement to the scrum of journalists in the corridor: 'Feyenoord played very well and deserved victory. I must say that. We played a bad match. I know why, but will tell my players and no one else. I was surprised, but not by Feyenoord because I knew they were a good team. I was surprised by my own team.' His statement was widely interpreted as suggesting that his players were lacking in terms of commitment or discipline.

The Celtic spirit was being found wanting . . .

NINE

Merely Champions!

1970–78

On 10 August 1970 at Hampden Park Stein started a process of rebuilding, based on what Billy McNeill acknowledges as 'an incredible wealth of talent in the pipeline'. The Glasgow Cup – a competition now carrying minimal prestige, and held over from the previous season – provided Stein with the opportunity to experiment before the start of the regular season. In the final against a full-strength Rangers side he fielded a relatively youthful team, containing three players more generally recognised as reserves. Celtic convincingly won the match 3–1, an early indication to the playing staff that changes could be made successfully.

An incident just before the kick-off throws an interesting light on the dynamics at Celtic Park. The chairman, Sir Robert Kelly, made a point of visiting the dressing-room to impress upon the Celtic players the necessity of 'good sportsmanship'. He was reacting to the SFA's displeasure in the wake of the last Old Firm battle six months previously in the Scottish Cup. Jim Craig recalls the chairman's words, and Jock Stein's reaction. The manager listened in respectful silence, as did the players; he then ushered Sir Robert towards the door and closed it. Turning to his players, he growled: 'Well, you can forget all about that for a start . . .'

Despite Celtic's impressive start to the season, suggesting that they were shaking off the disappointment of Milan, the approach of winter brought hints of uncertainty and a shading-off of the former authority. Celtic would make their annual League Cup final appearance, but they had reached that stage without convincing. Their opponents in the final were

Rangers and the Parkhead side, as semi-permanent holders of the trophy, were firm favourites – especially when John Greig, Rangers' wholehearted and often inspiring captain, was ruled out through injury. In front of a crowd of 106,263 at Hampden on 24 October 1970, however, Celtic gave another below-par performance, and did not mount a sustained offensive until too late, while Rangers displayed a ferocious determination to hold on to a one-goal lead. Derek Johnstone, a youngster of only 16, scored with a fine header in the dying minutes of a first half in which the Celtic defence had been all but overrun by the lively Rangers forwards, most notably the pacy and tricky wingers, Henderson and Johnston. Despite a late rally from Celtic, nobody could question the validity of Rangers' victory.

It marked Celtic's third defeat in a major final inside six months and, although he had embarked on a process of transition, the nature of this latest setback stiffened the manager's resolve to break up a team which had served the club well. No longer could he hold on to older players for loyalty's sake or sentiment; not while members of a reserve team known as 'the Quality Street Kids' clamoured for places. In the buoyant atmosphere of Parkhead in the late 1960s these youngsters (the likes of Danny McGrain, Kenny Dalglish, Lou Macari and Victor Davidson) had been given a solid grounding in the traditional values of both the game and the club by Jock Stein and his backroom staff. They were taught (and developed) good habits and gained invaluable footballing lessons by training beside such a talented and experienced group of players as the Lisbon Lions. Jock Stein often took time off from first-team duties to work out with these promising reserves – an unlikely scenario at other Scottish grounds. In typical fashion Stein speeded up the process of rejuvenation carefully. His first tactic was to freshen up the team by allowing some of his more youthful squad players to make orchestrated appearances. As with his experienced players, his approach was practical: he never asked a player to do more than he was capable of, and with the youngsters he was doubly protective. He fielded them for short, sustained periods and the young players quickly gained in confidence while their more experienced colleagues were forced to keep a watchful eye on them.

However, certain undercurrents of tension might suggest that Stein was 'losing' the dressing-room, at least insofar as the senior professionals were concerned. Jimmy Johnstone and Billy McNeill were both left out of a fixture against Morton on Boxing Day 1970, and John Hughes requested a transfer after a row with the manager over being dropped for a Scottish Cup tie in March 1971. One player interviewed by one of the authors said that for the first five years or so Stein was 'an absolutely brilliant manager' but, referring to what some players perceived as the manager's later tendency to high-handedness, added, 'You know the old saying. Power corrupts . . .'

Perhaps some players had come to resent the press coverage which appeared to elevate their manager to the status of a magician, with the performers inevitably reduced to the role of puppets on a string. Jack Charlton, the ex-manager of the Republic of Ireland's successful side, has observed: 'After five years or so, players become so familiar with a manager's approach to tactics, training and motivation that their relationship will get into a rut.' Thus, irritations which can be glossed over in successful times tend to surface when the team is struggling. Jim Craig, for example, recalls how Stein once refused him permission to wear gloves during a match played on an icy pitch. Craig, a practising dentist in his spare time, was anxious to protect his hands but had to accept the decision; he felt that the old Lanarkshire miner in Stein considered the request effete in the same way that he treated requests by the players that tracksuits be provided for training. Jock Stein was a product of an industrial Scotland where men had knelt in 12 inches of water underground digging out coal. He could recall the miserable days of post-war austerity in the late 1940s, and he was not too sympathetic. At times man-management was not Jock Stein's greatest strength . . .

The manager had lost none of his drive or hunger for success, though. He was determined to keep his team on top, and that was enough to guide Celtic to a sixth successive championship – equalling the club's own record run from 1905 to 1910 – and indeed to another double.

Celtic were the early pace-makers in the race for the flag, but Aberdeen made impressive strides to overhaul the champions with a 1–0 victory at Parkhead on 12 December 1970 in front of 63,000. The northerners had their sights firmly trained on their first championship in 16 years, and were in the middle of a run of 15 league wins in a row. Rangers had got off to a sluggish start, and were well out of serious contention by the time they faced Celtic at Ibrox on 2 January 1971.

Two minutes from the end of that match, Celtic took the lead through a goal by Jimmy Johnstone, a close-in header after Lennox's shot from 25 yards had rebounded from the crossbar. Hundreds of Rangers' supporters started to drift towards the exits in disappointment. With only seconds left to play, Colin Stein grabbed an unexpected equaliser for Rangers. His goal precipitated the second Ibrox Disaster. The most likely cause of the horror is said to have been a stumble on Stairway 13 as the jubilant Rangers' fans poured out of Ibrox, but the resultant crush was described by one horrified eye-witness as follows: 'The crowd caved in like a pack of cards, as if all of them were falling into a huge hole.' In fact, most of the crowd – which had left Ibrox by other exits – were totally ignorant of the developments until they switched on radios or television sets at home. They had assumed that the ambulances and police-cars racing towards Ibrox after the match were in response to outbreaks of hooliganism. Billy McNeill, like the rest of his team-mates, only became aware of the scale of the disaster while listening to the radio on the team bus as it made its way back to Celtic Park. He still recalls how deep an impression the horror made on Celtic's trainer, Neil Mochan, who spoke of it two decades later. Mochan had been roped in to help with the injured and the dying that day.

At the end of the most tragic day in Scottish football – 'Black Saturday' was the headline in the *Celtic View* – 66 fans lay dead and many more were injured. The only consolation was to be found in the fact that the clubs and their respective supporters were brought together in mourning, and through Disaster Fund collections and memorial services. Unfortunately, this period of co-operation was all too brief.

When football was able to resume some semblance of normality after such a tragedy, Celtic got down to the business of retaining their title, and the events on 16 January 1971 proved to be the turning-point. After 12 successive shut-outs posted by Bobby Clark, the Dons lost a goal and, more importantly for Celtic, dropped two points to Hibernian at Easter Road; meanwhile Celtic were making light work of a potentially tricky confrontation against Dundee by winning 8–1 at Dens Park, displaying the ruthlessness of champions. The truly decisive league fixture took place at Pittodrie on 17 April between Celtic and Aberdeen; the northern side led by three points but Celtic had two matches in hand. After only four minutes Harry Hood again showed his excellent positional sense by gliding home a cross from close in. Although Aberdeen fought back valiantly in the second half to earn a draw, the champions were well placed to secure the title, and duly clinched it with a 2–0 win over Ayr United on 29 April in a fixture played at Hampden Park because the stand at Celtic Park was under renovation.

The last league fixture of the season was fulfilled at Parkhead, however, a now meaningless match against Clyde two days later on 1 May. Jock Stein urged all Celtic followers to be there: 'You'll be able to tell your grandchildren about this match,' he promised. In a masterly piece of stage-management he announced his plan to field the Lisbon Lions, Celtic's greatest pride, for the last time. Before an emotionally charged crowd of 35,000 the European Cup-winners of 1967 took the field, led out by the non-playing Ronnie Simpson (who had retired a year earlier). Celtic romped to a 6–1 win. Better than anybody else, Stein knew the fixture afforded the last opportunity to see the Lisbon side because he was arranging the transfers of two of them: Bertie Auld went to Hibernian five days later, and John Clark joined Morton in mid-June.

One week later, on 8 May 1971, a crowd of 120,092 saw Celtic attempt to complete the double in another Old Firm Scottish Cup final.

Bobby Lennox finished off a Wallace–Hood move in 40 minutes by cutting past Miller to slant the ball away from McCloy to give Celtic the lead; although Rangers pressed for much of the second half, Celtic appeared comfortable in dealing with their frantic efforts. With only four minutes left to play, however, Rangers' substitute, Derek Johnstone, pounced on hesitation between Williams and Connelly to equalise.

The replay the following Wednesday attracted a crowd of 103,332. Rangers took a calculated gamble in fielding débutant Jim Denny to replace their injured right-back, Miller. Stein had been furious with the way Celtic had let Rangers off the hook, and he rejigged his front runners, with Macari replacing Wallace, who was named as substitute. But Jimmy Johnstone, who had been under a cloud since Milan, showed the way to victory; taking on defenders at will, Johnstone was back to his jinking, unstoppable best, teasing and tormenting any Ranger who ventured near him. Rangers' defence, with their young right-back under constant pressure from the strong-running Tom Callaghan, was hard-pressed to survive Celtic's probing raids. In 24 minutes Lou Macari scored the opening goal, the nippy striker turning the ball into the net following a corner-kick on the left. Only a minute later, Rangers were hit with another hammer blow when McKinnon, exasperated by Johnstone's trickery, pulled down Celtic's winger for a penalty. Harry Hood converted the spot-kick, and Celtic were in total command. Rangers were thrown a lifeline with an own-goal by Jim Craig in 57 minutes; the match continued from end to end but Celtic always seemed to be playing well within themselves for all Rangers' huffing and puffing.

As Feyenoord had done previously, another Dutch side, Ajax of Amsterdam, posed an insuperable barrier in Europe for a side trying to recover from the trauma of Milan. Celtic had advanced to the quarter-finals of the European Cup against Ajax by easily disposing of the puny challenge of Kokkola (Finland) by a 14–0 aggregate and Waterford (Eire) by a similarly emphatic 10–2. Ajax were something else, and Celtic took caution to extremes in the first leg at Amsterdam before giving up three goals in the last 30 minutes. The Ajax officials were astonished at Celtic's reluctance to 'have a go', and one Scottish journalist condemned Celtic's 'appalling lack of attacking adventure'. Prior to the match, Stein had scoffed at suggestions that Celtic had come to Amsterdam solely to defend, but his side's blanket-cover tactics were designed to stifle rather than create. A new importance had been placed on getting an away goal in European competitions which such a strike now counting double in the event of an aggregate 'tie', but Celtic showed few indications that they had grasped the value of it. Ajax, in fact, had struggled for much of the first hour, but Willie Wallace had been used as Celtic's sole striker and, with Jimmy Johnstone out of touch, Celtic rarely threatened the Dutch goal. The plane had barely landed back in Glasgow before the players were swept past a waiting reception committee of families and friends to be taken to Parkhead and face an arduous training session ordered by a piqued Stein. 'We were already despondent about the defeat, but it was a case of big Jock taking it out on us. Once again, we were getting the blame,' says Jim Craig, who points out in the Celtic team's defence that the Dutch side included the likes of Cruyff, Neeskens and Krol.

In the second leg, held at Hampden because of the demand for tickets (and the continuing renovations at Parkhead), Ajax were content to absorb Celtic's predictable attacks, Jimmy Johnstone's goal after 28 minutes merely putting a better gloss on the aggregate loss by 1–3. The League and Scottish Cup double apart, the defeat by Ajax was another dent to the club's self-image as a top European side, and the hardest knock in a difficult year for the manager, starting with the defeat at Milan and the frustrations of a North American tour that nobody wanted thereafter, least of all himself. Privately, he had spent considerable time pondering his own future. Manchester United were anxious to land him as their manager, and they had sounded him out. It was a tempting prospect with the security of a lucrative contract and the prospect of fresh challenges. His secret discussions with the English club culminated in a meeting with Sir Matt Busby at a motorway service station just outside Haydock on 14 April 1971, only three days before the title crunch match at Pittodrie. As Stein, accompanied by his son George, returned home after watching a Liverpool v Leeds UEFA Cup semi-final tie at Anfield, Busby headed back to Manchester convinced that he had got his man. However, further reflection by Stein on the long drive north led eventually to him phoning the United manager the following day to inform Busby that he would not be succeeding him at Old Trafford. Disappointed and annoyed, Busby initially thought that Stein had used United's interest to boost his own salary at Parkhead, but the decision to stay with Celtic was based on more complex considerations. His wife, Jean, was strongly opposed to moving south; he himself was unmistakably a West of Scotland man; he retained a sense of loyalty to Celtic and their supporters, and there was a reluctance to leave at a time when the club's chairman, Sir Robert Kelly, was ailing.

The most pertinent factor of all was probably Stein's justifiable wariness of the power Busby might still exert even after relinquishing the managership, doubts which had surfaced during their discussions about the future of ageing United legends such as Denis Law and Bobby Charlton. Whatever the reason for staying – and shortly before his own death Stein admitted that he had come to regret his decision as one based on 'misplaced loyalty' – the fears of the Celtic supporters were not allayed until the eve of the title decider at Pittodrie on 17 April. It was not done in the manner of Stein's choosing. He informed his employers at Celtic Park of his intentions to remain at Parkhead, but wanted to reveal the news exclusively in his newspaper column in the *Sunday Mirror* on the day after the match at Aberdeen. His plan had to be changed thanks to the initiative of John Quinn, a reporter on the local *Evening Times*. Assigned by his editor to uncover the truth about the rumours linking Stein with Manchester United, Quinn called at the office of Desmond White in Bath Street on Friday morning, 16 April 1971. During the final stage of Sir Robert Kelly's illness, White was the acting chairman of the club, and he surmised wrongly that the reporter had been tipped off about Stein's decision to remain. Reluctantly, White briefed Quinn about the latest developments 'off-the-record', enabling the reporter to file his scoop, based on 'insider' information.

The news appeared on the front page for the first edition of the *Evening Times*, which appeared on the streets at lunchtime. Stein was obliged to clear the air sooner than he had intended, but he turned the situation to his advantage by telling his players in a pre-match pep talk at their Stonehaven hotel that 'I want to be in that European Cup next season – with Celtic'.

It had not been the first attempt to lure Jock Stein from Celtic Park. In the late 1960s an even more intriguing possibility had briefly arisen. Two men from Ibrox – director David Hope and almost certainly Willie Allison, Rangers' PRO – had approached him informally and on separate occasions to determine the possibility of Stein's moving to take charge of Rangers. Stein took the secret of these approaches to his grave but, interestingly, he did not appear to have rejected them out of hand, inconceivable though such a switch would have been at the time. After the failure of Manchester United's latest bid for his services Jock Stein would now remain with Celtic for as long as they wanted him.

Stein knew, though, just how difficult a season Celtic were facing when he admitted in the *Celtic View* of July 1971 that 'the price of success comes high, and has taken a heavy toll of our players'. He acknowledged injury and age were of increasing concern as unsettling factors – despite the spectacular success which the club had enjoyed. But even he must have been startled at just how quickly his fears would come true, and how surprisingly and with such public embarrassment . . .

Celtic's tremendous early-season form had seen them thrash Clyde 9–1 at Parkhead on the opening day of the league campaign, and progress to the League Cup final after two sectional victories at Ibrox over Rangers. In the first match – which should have been Celtic's home tie but for the on-going renovations at Parkhead – young Kenny Dalglish made his Old Firm début and converted a penalty-kick with impressive coolness. Celtic seemed incapable of losing at Ibrox and completed a trio of victories there within a four-week period with a 3–2 win in the league on 11 September 1971 when Jimmy Johnstone outjumped (!) the Rangers defenders to head the winning goal.

It was no surprise, then, that the crowd of 62,740 which turned up at Hampden on 23 October 1971 to see Celtic play Partick Thistle could envisage only one winner. The correspondent of the *Glasgow Herald* was only representing of the football consensus when he previewed the match by suggesting that 'merely by reaching the final, Thistle have achieved an improbable success'.

The absence of McNeill, ruled out through a muscle strain, was regarded as a minor inconvenience before the kick-off, but it left a vacuum of authority at the heart of Celtic's defence. Partick Thistle, the rank outsiders, were full of running from the outset, driving hard at a sluggish rearguard through the middle and on the flanks. Thistle tore Celtic's defence to shreds and after 37 minutes were leading by 4–0. In newspaper offices around the country, reporters and office-staff gathered in front of the teleprinters in sheer disbelief. Celtic managed to pull back a goal in the 70th minute through young Dalglish, but Thistle's nerve held for them to pick up their first major trophy in half a century. The full-time score of 4–1 caused such incredulity throughout Britain that an obituarist, writing of the death of Len Martin in August 1995, claimed that it was the only score that the veteran announcer felt obliged to repeat in 37 years of reading the Saturday afternoon results on BBC TV's *Grandstand*.

Jock Stein was generous in defeat in public, but he applied immediate and radical surgery to freshen up the squad. A mere two days later, he signed Dennis Connaghan from St Mirren to provide competition for Evan Williams; Stein considered Williams to have been too much of an onlooker in the final. A few days after that signing, he completed the transfer of John 'Dixie' Deans from Motherwell for £17,500; Deans, a stocky and brave striker but a chronic disciplinary problem at the time serving a six-week suspension, proved to be an inspired capture as he knuckled down to Stein's authority in training and thrived on the service provided on the pitch.

Billy McNeill – although dismayed at the time by the departure of his room-mate and friend Willie Wallace, transferred along with John Hughes to Crystal Palace only a few days before the final, and in advance of Tommy Gemmell's move to Nottingham Forest in December – now concedes Stein's singlemindedness in restructuring the side by bringing in fresh blood from the reserves or through the transfer market. McNeill's description of his boss as 'a master at bringing talent through the ranks' was fully vindicated by the emergence of Kenny Dalglish and Lou Macari during the period of experimentation. Originally, it had been the manager's intention to move Dalglish, Macari and Davidson, a highly potent inside trio in reserve football, straight into the first XI as a ready-made attacking unit. Unfortunately, Victor Davidson – despite the elegant touches that suggested a great future in football – did not develop at the same rate as his colleagues and was hampered both by injury and a falling-out with the manager. Still, the combination of Macari, a specialist in the penalty box, and Dalglish, masterful as a striker or while operating in midfield, looked set to become Celtic's attacking spearhead for years to come.

Aberdeen, well drilled and methodical, maintained a dogged challenge to Celtic in the championship, but the holders had too much flair, resilience and experience to be caught after taking over first place. Celtic duly assumed the lead in the table following a visit to Firhill on 27 November 1971 during which they exacted retribution on the League Cup-holders by thrashing them 5–1 before a crowd of 35,000. The champions had embarked on an impressive run which extended to 27 league matches without defeat; this level of consistency prompted the *Daily Record* sportswriter Hugh Taylor to assert that 'Celtic are so far out on their own that they can win the flag without looking around'.

European success was still out of reach but Celtic progressed much further in the Champions' Cup than might have been expected after an abysmal display in the first round in Copenhagen when they went down 2–1 against the part-timers Boldklub 1903. At Parkhead in the second leg Celtic could relax only in the last five minutes after Wallace scored a third goal to give a 3–0 win. Those stuttering performances had largely been forgotten by the spring of 1972 when Celtic resumed hostilities with Inter Milan in the semi-final, buoyed with optimism about the return of the trophy to Parkhead following the dismissal of the highly rated Hungarians of Ujpest Dozsa in the quarter-final. Abandoning the caution which usually marked their approach to tricky continental assignments, Celtic had gone for the jugular from the start at Budapest, and snatched a priceless 2–1 win with a goal scored in the dying minutes. The goal was a perfectly executed lob by Lou Macari, one of several impressive performers from among Celtic's youngsters, and the result prompted Jock Stein – never a man to go overboard about one performance – to state: 'At this level, and when you consider the age of the team, this was probably Celtic's best European Cup display since Lisbon.' Celtic completed the task with a hard-earned 1–1 draw at Parkhead in the return fixture, when an old favourite, Jimmy Johnstone, came on as a second-half substitute to calm the nerves after Dunai's early goal; the player that the Hungarians feared the most unsettled their defenders with his willingness to take them on in his inimitable style, and he disrupted their self-assurance sufficiently for Maurer's nervous back-header to be intercepted by the live-wire Macari. Another delicate lob by this youngster eased Celtic's passage into the last four.

Internazionale, however, were made of sterner stuff, perfectly content to be as cautious at Parkhead on 19 April as Celtic had been in Milan two weeks earlier – and willing to gamble on achieving (and winning) a penalty shoot-out. After 210 minutes of goalless football over two legs, the semi-final duly went to penalty-kicks in front of 75,000 fraught spectators at Celtic Park. Dixie Deans had felt confident at the end of extra-time about having to take Celtic's first kick, but in the eerie silence that enveloped Parkhead he froze and sent his shot high over the bar – and his was the only miss in a sequence won 5–4 by the visitors. Recently, Deans provided fresh insight into an episode which still haunts him: 'I don't want to name names, but there were a few big stars in that Celtic team in 1972 who weren't having any of it when it came to the crunch.' (*The Sun*: 19 July 1994)

After the match, a philosophical Jock Stein made a point of consoling the player, advising him to get his head up again as Celtic's failure to reach the European Cup final was not his fault. Three days later Deans emerged from the tunnel for the next home fixture, against his former club Motherwell, to be greeted by the crowd roaring out his name in encouragement, and the chants were raised good-naturedly again when Celtic were awarded two penalties (converted by Bobby Murdoch) in their 5–2 win.

On 6 May 1972 Deans repaid the faith of his manager and the supporters with one of the most sparkling individual performances ever produced in a Scottish Cup final. Hibs were fated to be on the receiving end of a Celtic team in irresistible form, determined to end the season on a high note with the completion of a second successive double – and to erase the lingering disappointment of missing out in Europe.

Only two minutes had elapsed when Billy McNeill turned a Callaghan free-kick past keeper Herriot with his right foot from six yards out. Although Hibernian fought back gamely to equalise in 12 minutes, Deans outjumped full-back Brownlie for Murdoch's free-kick in 23 minutes to net with a strong header. Celtic clung to that precarious 2–1 lead until the 54th minute, when Deans opened the floodgates with a truly spectacular goal. He swooped on a misdirected header before rounding the onrushing goalkeeper Herriot and advanced on goal along the bye-line; he sidestepped Brownlie and Herriot once more but delayed his shot; after what seemed an eternity, finally, he fired the ball into the empty net before rounding off his feat by somersaulting in his happiness to acknowledge the delirious cheers from the Celtic supporters behind the goal. Hibernian were broken by that goal and in 74 minutes Deans completed his hat-trick by running on to a through ball from Callaghan. In the dying minutes Lou Macari finished the rout with two goals from close range, both coming from moves involving Jim Craig (appearing in his last match for Celtic prior to playing in South Africa). The 6–1 scoreline was the biggest Scottish Cup final victory this century, equalled only by Renton's drubbing of Cambuslang in 1888.

It was a memorable day for Celtic and the crowd of 106,102, the vast majority of them Celtic supporters revelling in that quintessential scenario of success for their team: a spring day, and the sun on the players' backs creating the perfect stage and mood for the spraying of passes throughout Hampden's broad acres. Celtic had given a majestic display, and most of the danger had stemmed from the power and precision of Bobby Murdoch in the midfield. At least one journalist (John Blair) was somewhat in awe of Celtic's performance: 'a cold, clinical, sometimes cruel annihilation of Hibs at Hampden . . . [Celtic could claim] and not for the first time, the title of the brightest and best soccer entertainers in Britain . . . Hibs had no excuses. They met Celtic on a day when no team in Britain would have stood up to them – Leeds included.' (*The People*: 7 May 1972)

The warmth of that memory was in danger of being chilled the following season; Celtic, who had established a new Scottish record with their seventh title in as many years, would find their monopoly under threat from Rangers, suddenly rejuvenated. The Ibrox club had seemed only a negligible force in the championship race until a dramatic reversal in form around the turn of the year which coincided with a worrisome dropping of points by Celtic in the early months of 1973. Rangers kept up the pressure until the last day of the season, having lost only one point after their challenge gained lift-off with a last-minute 2–1 win over Celtic at Ibrox on 6 January 1973. At that time, Celtic were hit by a series of blows: a flu epidemic which resulted in the postponement of a couple of fixtures, the confinement of Jock Stein in the coronary unit of the Victoria Infirmary for a fortnight and his subsequent convalescence – and the transfer of Lou Macari to Manchester United.

Clearly, Stein, by temperament a restless figure, had been working himself into the ground in his determination to keep Celtic at the top. His zeal incurred hours of involvement above and beyond the normal call of duty, as he would frequently drive long distances to attend midweek matches in England, and turn up at reserve games in Scotland unexpectedly. Asked about the latter practice once, he replied, 'You never know what might catch your eye.' Only now, with the benefit of several years in management behind him, can Billy McNeill appreciate the pressures on Stein to sustain the level of consistency and success at Parkhead season after season. 'Looking back,' he says, 'it must have been a terrible drain on him over the years – and he was a man who didn't know the meaning of the word relaxation.'

As another former player puts it, 'Jock slept with his eyes open, thinking about football.'

Stein's commitment to Celtic and to football was taking its toll. Self-imposed and hectic it may have been, but it was a level of dedication which had forged Celtic into one of the most famous clubs in Europe and would sustain that reputation even in a period of comparative decline. He was only too aware of the paradox that success can be even more stressful than failure, that achievement brings in its train the problem of having to maintain that standard or (for the perfectionist) the setting of one's sights even higher. No matter how heavy the load, he had no intention of quitting, something he would do only, as he told a journalist later, when he no longer felt the positive pressure of his job or the adrenaline of the big occasion. Curiously enough, Jock Stein always seems to have found it difficult to come to terms with the immediate aftermath of his many triumphs as a manager. Apparently drained by his absorption in preparing the side (and having to watch from the sidelines), he was rarely seen joining in the public after-match celebrations wholeheartedly, nor was he photographed too often carried away by happiness.

The medical advice for Celtic's manager to take things easier was not the first intimation of a sense of his own mortality in the recent past. At Ibrox on 2 January 1971 he had been personally involved in bearing the injured and dying on stretchers at that fatal Old Firm match; the memory of that occasion had visibly affected him for some time.

In his hospital bed Stein listened in some anguish to the radio commentary of Celtic's defeat at Ibrox, a setback which was followed at full-time by the announcement of Lou Macari's wish to leave the club. Twelve days later, the player was transferred from Celtic to Manchester United for £200,000. Earlier, in 1971, Macari had requested a transfer during a contract dispute and he had been restless since his promotion to the Scotland squad in 1972 under Tommy Docherty. At Old Trafford he linked up again with Docherty, who had quit the national post to take over United in the interim.

Macari was typical of a new generation of players whose mingling with Anglo-Scots (Scottish players based in England) at international gatherings had made them only too aware of the greater opportunities available in England. Unlike many others who had been exploited at Celtic Park because of their love of the club, Macari was determined to cash in on his talent. Stein simply did not believe the player was worth the signing-on fee demanded by Macari in order to seal a new contract. Macari turned down Celtic's offer of an extra £5 per week, feeling that a club which had recently attracted huge gates for European ties and cup finals should fork out more than a 10 per cent pay rise for an established player. In his column in *The Sun*, a lucrative by-product of the move, Macari claimed to have quadrupled his weekly wage by going to England by having his basic raised to £200; he also suggested that the question of pay had been a constant source of friction between him and the manager.

While paying tribute to Jock Stein's 'unparalleled knowledge of the game' and his brilliance at 'using a player's skills to the best advantage', Macari clearly believed that the manager had too much power. He felt that Stein disliked Macari's tendency to speak his mind: '[Stein] couldn't have really trusted players, because he never treated us like anything other than children.' (24 January 1973) Significantly, perhaps, none of Macari's more experienced colleagues interviewed by the authors were resentful of the player's reasons for leaving Parkhead. Pervading the whole issue was the suggestion of a growing generation-gap between Stein and his squad.

Celtic, minus their effervescent striker, survived a few scares during their wobbly period, before steadying themselves for the run-in in the manner of true champions. The team travelled to Edinburgh on 28 April 1973 needing only a draw to retain the title, but responded to the pressurised situation with a flourish. The atmosphere in the ground was highly charged, some 45,000 having been shoe-horned into Easter Road, but Celtic swept Hibs aside with a superb display, at once professional and stylish, the 3–0 win being highlighted by clinical finishing from the leading scorers, Dixie Deans and Kenny Dalglish.

The winning of the championship for the eighth season in a row, however, was not enough to hide the cracks which had begun to appear. Nowhere was a certain loss of verve and conviction more evident than in the major cup competitions. A month after Ujpest Dozsa had taken ample revenge for the previous season's defeat in the European Cup by trouncing Celtic 3–0 at home to go through 4–2 on aggregate, Celtic's defence was pulled apart in similar manner by Hibernian in the League Cup final. A crowd of 71,696 turned up at a wet and windy Hampden Park on 9 December 1972 to see the Edinburgh side torment Celtic, although it took an hour for them to open the scoring. Stanton controlled a free-kick flighted over a nervous Celtic wall to volley past Williams; five minutes later, the same player crossed intelligently for O'Rourke to net the second. Dalglish's goal for Celtic shortly afterwards sparked a late rally but was not enough to stave off Celtic's third successive defeat in a League Cup final. The tournament – after a spell of notable success – was once more becoming an embarrassment for the club.

Those defensive shortcomings were fatally exposed again by Rangers in the Scottish Cup final on 5 May 1973 when the last six-figure attendance at the event (122,714) saw the Ibrox men snatch the trophy after Celtic had battled back to draw level following two lapses in concentration which had given Rangers a 2–1 lead. Dalglish had opened the scoring after 25 minutes from a finely weighted pass by Deans, but sluggish reactions by Connelly allowed MacDonald to cross from the bye-line for Parlane's headed equaliser. At no time in the contest did Rangers allow Celtic to settle, a policy most vividly illustrated less than a minute after the second-half restart, when Conn outpaced the Celtic defence to score. Then, after Connelly's equaliser from the penalty-spot and the dubious disallowing of a goal by Johnstone for offside, Rangers defender Tom Forsyth ran forward unchallenged to prod home the winning goal after a team-mate's header had come back off both uprights.

Celtic had lost their way in cup finals, and an undercurrent of disenchantment was clear in a letter published in the *Celtic View*'s 1973 summer issue, which took the manager to task for that recent record. The letter may have been considered a trifle ungrateful, but there was no doubting the tone of concern and dismay which hinted that the palates of Celtic supporters were becoming jaded with mere championship success: 'The day the fans really love is Cup final day. It should be a day of rejoicing but Celtic have not given us many such days over the past two seasons. We have been in six finals, and only from one could we walk away smiling. Eight leagues are great, but losing five out of six Cup finals is like climbing a mountain just to fall off.'

The Celtic support could be sure that Mr Stein – as the writer respectfully addressed him – needed little reminding about that situation, but for the remainder of his managerial reign at Parkhead he would be increasingly preoccupied with the type of problems which had simply not impacted on the club during the glory years, with the possible exception of Macari. Rumblings of discontent and unhappiness among players would come to the fore. Clearly, something was wrong when George Connelly, who had developed into a most gifted performer either as a sweeper or as a midfielder – and who had just been voted Scotland's Player of the Year by the country's football writers – 'disappeared' at Glasgow Airport before he was due to board a flight to Switzerland for an international match in June 1973. The quiet, introspective Fifer had been signed as a teenager, but behind the calm exterior of a young player used to playing at the highest level (and who had scored in two Scottish Cup finals against Rangers), all was not well. A sensitive man, Connelly found it hard to come to terms with the freer spirits in the dressing-room, which can be a cruel place at times. Indeed, he told people at the club that he would rather have driven a taxi-cab, or a lorry (like one of his friends). He was talked into a return in November 1974 after quitting, but for the rest of his 'in-out' career at Parkhead George Connelly – frequently compared to Franz Beckenbauer in skill and control, and designated by Stein as the natural successor to Billy McNeill in Celtic's defence – played under a shadow, never fully attaining his potential in terms of honours.

Connelly's closest friend at Parkhead, David Hay, a highly aggressive and mobile midfielder, would obtain no satisfaction in his quest for financial security at Parkhead. An outstanding player for Scotland in the 1974 World Cup in Germany, he too requested a transfer, and eventually moved to Chelsea in the summer of 1974 for £250,000. Absurdly, Stein would tell Mike Langley of the *Sunday People* that both Hay and Lou Macari had 'fancied the bright lights'. Stein's observation was hardly fair to Hay in particular, because the player was only trying to achieve a greater degree of security at Parkhead, and should have been given better terms commensurate with his growing stature at international level. In the 1974 World Cup he had not looked out of place among the élite of the game.

Bobby Murdoch was transferred to Middlesbrough in September 1973. A Celtic great by anybody's reckoning, Murdoch found himself 'expendable' as Stein tinkered with the line-up in a bid to rediscover the elusive blend. In May 1973 the manager had signed Aberdeen's gifted midfielder, Steve Murray, an all-purpose player. Murdoch, after 12 seasons at Parkhead, admitted his own need for a fresh challenge and concluded that the signing indicated a change of emphasis on the part of the manager – a running rather than a passing game. During 1973–74 Murdoch played a crucial part in helping unfashionable Middlesbrough win promotion to the First Division.

Stein would also have to contend with the erratic Jimmy Johnstone, whose lack of appetite for the game was becoming increasingly apparent to the manager, who bluntly sought more dedication from his wayward star. The troubled player's attitude caused an exasperated Stein to confess openly his bewilderment at the enigma that Johnstone had become: 'In the shadows for much of the season, he suddenly takes a tumble to himself and there's all the old artistry and ball skills in full flower.'

Despite the turbulence, Celtic kept a steady course to win the championship for the ninth season in a row, equalling the world record for successive domestic titles. Like a troupe of actors in a long-running show, Celtic went through their well-practised routines to ensure the continuation of the ritual springtime plaudits. Once again, they had too much quality and flair when it mattered for their rivals in a campaign which saw the champions drop only two points in total against their closest challengers, Hibernian, Rangers and Aberdeen. As so often happened during the Stein years, Celtic chose Easter Road to remind their rivals that they were still the team to beat. Hibernian had emerged as legitimate pretenders to Celtic's title, but the champions took a decisive step towards retaining it with an emphatic 4–2 win on 23 February 1974. The boost of that result kick-started Celtic's sprint towards the tape.

The match report in *The Scotsman* two days later underlined the belief that Celtic were still in a class of their own on the domestic front. It pinpointed the strengths of the side: McNeill's authority, Connelly's composure in defence and his confidence in pulling down and controlling the ball before distributing it with panache, and the intelligent athleticism of Hay, Murray and Dalglish, working as one in the midfield engine-room by 'becoming available for each other, running as decoys, running in support, running all the time but with purpose'. Kenny Dalglish was singled out for praise in the report, which commented on his ability to tame the ball in the midst of the fiercest action and beat an opponent before slipping a subtle pass to a team-mate: 'On Saturday he was a world-class player, skilled, sophisticated and yet strong and determined.' And yet, within the space of little more than three years, that nucleus (McNeill, Connelly, Hay, Murray and Dalglish) had departed from Celtic Park for various reasons, an exodus which resulted in a decline in playing standards.

As a measure of Celtic's magnificent consistency between August 1965 and May 1974 it should be noted that out of the 306 league matches played, Celtic won 235 and lost only 26, scoring 868 goals and conceding just 258. Perhaps the most sincere tribute would come from an unexpected source; in 1995, with Rangers on the way to seven successive titles, their manager Walter Smith, desperately keen to emulate and surpass Celtic's feat, stated, 'My admiration for Celtic's nine-in-a-row grows with each season because I know how difficult it is to achieve that kind of consistency.' (*The Scotsman:* 8 February 1995) Latterly, however, Celtic were becoming economic victims of their own success, with home gates dropping by an average of 10,000 compared to the late 1960s when the competition was admittedly much fiercer.

Celtic did not have things all their own way in Scotland that season – a campaign marked by a couple of early hiccups in cup play. Another defeat by Hibernian in the pre-season Drybrough Cup was followed four months later by further disappointment in the League Cup, a competition whose recent change in format saw Celtic face Rangers three times on their way to the final. In the sectional play – from which two teams advanced – the clubs shared victories, before Celtic won the 'rubber' by emerging 3–1 winners in the semi-final at a rain-swept Hampden Park, where Harry Hood achieved that coveted rarity – a hat-trick in an Old Firm match. He climaxed the feat in unforgettable fashion 15 minutes from time by moving in from the right, spotting Rangers' giant keeper McCloy starting to leave his line, and then curling the ball past him with his left foot – before, in his own words, 'running like a madman back to the halfway line'.

By eliminating Rangers, Aberdeen and Motherwell, Celtic appeared to have done the hard work, but the League Cup final against unfancied Dundee proved a dismal affair. The match took place in an eerie atmosphere on 15 December 1973 on a pitch rendered so treacherous by snow, sleet and ice that both clubs virtually played under protest. However, the referee R. H. Davidson of Airdrie (Stein's frequent adversary) had passed it as 'playable'. A paltry 27,974 turned up, trudging through slush and water several inches deep in the approaches to Hampden Park, while others stayed away in expectation of a postponement or the likelihood of abandonment or because of the inconvenient kick-off time of 1.30 p.m., designed to permit extra-time in view of the government ban on the use of floodlights during the power crisis, which had arisen from an industrial dispute with the miners.

Celtic's display matched the gloom, with Dalglish, Hood and Wilson creating few chances because of the tight marking of Dundee's defenders; and the frustration was complete when Dundee, always the more dangerous side on the day, scored the only goal of a miserable final. Fifteen minutes from time Wallace chested down a free-kick lofted into the penalty area and, although surrounded by three Celtic defenders, swivelled to hit the ball low past a blameless Ally Hunter.

Equally memorable for all the wrong reasons was the first leg of the European Cup semi-final against Atletico Madrid on 10 April 1974. The Spaniards' tactics were clear from the outset, as they made little attempt to play constructive football while hacking, kicking and spitting at their opponents, with Johnstone a particular target for their bodychecking and scything tackles. The Turkish referee, Mr Babacan, could not handle the situation, although probably no referee should have been put in such a position. Before the end he had booked seven of the Spanish side, and ordered off three for violent play. That only two Celtic players were booked amid the provocation was commendable. For all Celtic's pressure, they could not make their numerical superiority count, and the tie finished 0–0. The sheer mayhem and intimidation practised by the Spanish champions proved the most important factor in Celtic's frustration because of the frequent, prolonged stoppages in play.

A few weeks before the fixture Jock Stein, apparently in jest, had observed to pressmen: 'Well, they've got half a dozen Argentinians in their pool, and the manager's one – so that means a riot for a start.' His observation had proved to be sickeningly prophetic, but UEFA predictably refused to expel Atletico Madrid from the competition, nor did they order the second leg be played at a neutral venue. Instead, they later levied a risible fine on the Spaniards, and automatically banned the three players sent off at Parkhead, only one of whom – the cynics noted – was a regular member of the first team.

After some internal debate Celtic decided to travel to Madrid two weeks later to fulfil the requirements of the second leg. Not for the last time would a Celtic board of directors succumb to the vague threat of UEFA sanctions – either imposed as a fine or as a ban from European competition. And this surrender was despite the moral support generated by the genuine revulsion throughout Europe at Atletico's brutality. The Madrid club brazened it out, bolstered by a mentality typified in the Spanish daily *Marca* which billed the return leg as 'Atletico versus Celtic and UEFA'.

The atmosphere in the Spanish capital was tense: the players were confined to the hotel grounds under suffocating security, surrounded by armed policemen, and riot trucks were in evidence at the stadium. Jimmy Johnstone – always a marked man – received a death threat over the hotel phone, and proper facilities for training and relaxation were simply not made available. The Spanish press, latching on to violent scenes in the tunnel as the players were leaving the Parkhead pitch, had stirred up a hate campaign against Celtic. Not too surprisingly, the visitors eventually went down to two late goals. At the final whistle the Celtic players stood in the centre circle and applauded Atletico and their fans; this perfect response mingled dignity with contempt in equal measure. Atletico Madrid thus advanced to the final of the European Cup (where they were beaten 4–0 by Bayern Munich in a replay).

Celtic's season ended on a happier note when, on 4 May 1974, they completed another double, their fifth of the Stein era, by lifting the Scottish Cup for the 23rd time. In the semi-final against Dundee, Jimmy Johnstone had rediscovered his old magic to tease and torment his opponents and lead Celtic to a 1–0 win; the victory enabled Celtic to take on Dundee United in the final, and stroll to a 3–0 triumph. So overawed did the Taysiders appear that the final took on overtones of a contest featuring 'city slickers' against 'country bumpkins'. A crowd of 75,959 saw the favourites underline their supremacy with two quick strikes midway through the first half: through Hood's neatly judged header over a stranded goalkeeper, and then Murray rounding off a defence-splitting move by Johnstone and Hood. United's pre-match strategy, geared to preventing an early lead for Celtic, was in shreds. Any hopes of a comeback ebbed away after Connaghan had pulled off a spectacular save from a header by Andy Gray, the talented young striker upon whom the Tangerines were over-reliant. Latterly, it was all too easy, and there was something apologetic about Deans' last-minute counter, scored after he had latched on to a deft pass from Dalglish.

Celtic's comprehensive victory may have seemed the perfect riposte to those critics who were starting to say that Scotland's top team was losing its gloss. Nobody could deny that a certain staleness had crept into their league performances of late, but there was no perceptible lessening of Jock Stein's resolve to maintain Celtic's domination. More than anybody, he would have dreaded hearing the increasingly prevalent whispers of 'all good things must come to an end' but there seemed no need for pessimism at Parkhead when Rangers got off to their now customary bad start to the league season by dropping a point in a 1–1 draw at Ayr while Celtic were crushing Kilmarnock 5–0. Celtic's performance was so convincing that the fans were streaming from the Jungle at the end chanting raucously their latest mantra: 'It's magic, you know – oh – oh, it's gonna be ten in a row!'

Nobody watching Celtic's demolition of Dundee at Dens Park by 6–0 on 14 December 1974, orchestrated by Kenny Dalglish who scored a hat-trick, would have envisioned a change in the status quo . . . yet, a mere three weeks later, after entering the New Year with only one defeat in the first half of their league programme, Celtic were in deep trouble as Rangers powered to a 3–0 win at Ibrox. The setback was due in part to the failure of Celtic's strikers to cash in on a series of chances created by the pace and ball control of the mercurial forward Paul Wilson, a youngster who never really lived up to the expectations aroused by this performance.

Rangers, now under new management in the shape of that hard taskmaster Jock Wallace, a former 'jungle-fighter' with the army in Malaysia, took full advantage of Celtic's failings in that Ibrox encounter and, having nosed in front on goal-difference, continued to make life difficult for the champions. Too difficult, because Celtic revealed a capacity for self-destruction, wilting alarmingly under pressure and dropping 12 points out of a possible 18 in the next nine fixtures. The five losses suffered in that dismal run were more than Celtic had sustained in any entire season during the compilation of the nine successive league titles. The championship was lost, and lost without a fight – not the way Jock Stein would have chosen to relinquish the title. Billy McNeill, for one, believes that the strain of keeping Celtic at the top had got to some of the players, and felt that the team still had a great deal of quality in it; however, the departure of the tigerish David Hay to Chelsea had left a void in midfield, especially in tense, physical matches.

The signs of vulnerability had been evident earlier in the season when the club was knocked out in the first round of the European Cup by the unrated Greek side Olympiakos, suggesting that too many Celtic players were past their peak – and that the conveyor-belt of talent from the reserves was slowing down. After a 1–1 draw at Parkhead, Celtic fell behind at Athens in only three minutes and all hope evaporated with a second goal from the Greeks in 25 minutes; there were no fresh faces on the bench capable of retrieving the situation. Mike Langley, an English journalist covering the match for the *Sunday People*, already sensed the end of an era: 'A club that could only be conquered by the cream of the cream – the Feyenoords, Milans and Benficas – temporarily can't rout a gang of Greeks.' (6 October 1974)

The let-down in Athens was but the latest in a series of distressing performances against lesser continental sides; it reinforced the growing belief that Celtic had been slipping steadily as a European force since the débâcle in Milan in 1970. The unblinkered fans could see that the flair, elan and authority that marked the team in the late 1960s had been ebbing away in recent seasons as Celtic struggled to overcome moderate opposition in the Champions' Cup. Yes, Celtic had reached the semi-final stage in 1972 and 1974; however, a club widely regarded as the most attack-conscious side in Europe had failed to score in these four key matches, home or away, Atletico's excesses notwithstanding. Doubts had crept in about whether the hunger for success was still there. The side's captain, Billy McNeill, hinted at the declining standards when, after sitting grim-faced and silently fuming for a couple of minutes on the team coach after a defeat at Basle in February 1974, he could take no more of certain other players chatting and joking, and erupted in anger: 'What have you lot got to laugh about? Don't you realise we lost tonight?'

An early exit from Europe and a distant third-place finish in the league marked a sad end to the greatest decade in the club's history – but Celtic gained consolation in the major cup competitions. One trophy made a welcome return to Parkhead on 26 October 1974 when they defeated Hibernian 6–3 in the League Cup final at Hampden Park. Only a week earlier Dixie Deans had netted a hat-trick at Parkhead against the Edinburgh side in a league fixture; he compounded Hibs' misery with a similar feat, a harvest of goals which owed much to the devastating wing play of Jimmy Johnstone and the superb distribution of Kenny Dalglish. But the glory – as in most fixtures against Hibs – went to Dixie Deans; he capped another memorable performance in a major final with a truly astonishing goal when he dived, McGrory-like, to head a ferocious shot from Johnstone – one screaming across the goalmouth, wide of the target – past a startled Hibernian goalkeeper.

On 3 May 1975, before a crowd of 75,457 at a sun-drenched Hampden Park, Airdrieonians, the rank outsiders, went into the Scottish Cup final with some degree of optimism, hoping to exploit the uncertainties that had been characterising the recently deposed league champions.

Celtic's early pressure brought its due reward in 14 minutes when Paul Wilson, left alone in front of goal, headed in a cross from Dalglish; but Airdrie fought back with determination to snatch an equaliser in 42 minutes. Celtic went straight up the field and gained a corner; Lennox took the kick and Wilson, again unmarked, headed home the veteran's cross. When Lennox was fouled in the penalty box in 53 minutes, Pat McCluskey, a burly defender, competently converted the penalty with a well-placed, low shot to settle the resting-place of the Cup. Billy McNeill, the captain, a supporter's scarf draped around his shoulders, was borne aloft on the Hampden pitch with the Scottish Cup, savouring the moment of his retirement as a player; Jock Stein, the manager, was seen heading towards the tunnel, rubbing his hands and smiling with satisfaction . . . but already giving the impression that he was starting to plan for future glory.

The value of Jock Stein to Celtic was all too soon revealed in the cruellest way – by his absence. Driving his Mercedes back to Glasgow from Manchester Airport after a summer holiday, he was involved in a head-on collision with another car coming the wrong way on a notorious stretch of the A74 near Lockerbie. Unconscious and seriously injured, Celtic's manager was rushed to hospital; after another brush with mortality, there were serious doubts about Jock Stein ever resuming his fabulous career.

Sean Fallon, Stein's long-time assistant, suddenly found himself taking over the management role for which he had once been groomed by Bob Kelly. Of course, that most loyal of servants, of whom somebody once said that the word Celtic was engraved on his heart, had an impossible task in stepping into the shoes of a colossus. In the absence of the Big Man throughout 1975–76 Celtic struggled, and for the first time since 1963–64 failed to win a trophy. Fallon was unlucky in having to deal with absent players and inconsistent play from some regulars. It should be added that he was not helped by the less than wholehearted co-operation of certain experienced players. The most grievous blow of all, perhaps, was George Connelly's walking out on the club, prompting an exasperated Sean Fallon to inflict an indefinite suspension on the troubled player for whom sympathy was by no means as widespread in the dressing-room as it appeared.

Greatly missed too was the influence and authority of Billy McNeill; ironically, McNeill was coming to regret his 'premature retirement', revealing later that he felt he still had a couple of seasons left. His decision to quit had been brought about by a vexation with training at the time; more and more, the heavy-duty training required of a big man had become a chore for him.

In this, the first season of the Premier League, the major product of a reorganisation of the Scottish League, Celtic shaped up well in the early stages, despite a 2–1 loss at Ibrox on the opening day, before a record Premier Division crowd of 69,594. Approaching the Ne'erday clash with Rangers at Ibrox, Celtic led the table by three points but went down to a 1–0 defeat. Having slugged it out with Rangers for most of the season, Celtic seemed to run out of steam in the last quarter, dropping ten points in their final seven matches to finish six points adrift of Rangers. The latter had won the title with steadiness and resolve; that same Ibrox efficiency had gained the League Cup at Celtic's expense in October 1975 when Alex MacDonald's header, culminating the sole piece of inspired play in a drab final, separated the sides.

The only encouraging feature was the scintillating form of Kenny Dalglish and Danny McGrain, both of whom were approaching their peak. McGrain was a model of consistency throughout, a skilful and determined full-back, and Dalglish – appointed captain in August 1975 after McNeill's retirement – performed heroically in scoring 32 goals in 51 competitive matches although not playing as an outright striker. Kenny Dalglish had matured into a naturally gifted and brave player who combined feints, flicks and deft touches with superb close control (particularly with his back to goal or to a defender); even when tightly marked and taking any amount of rough treatment, he was rarely shut out of a game – and he was always prepared to attempt the unexpected shot. Dalglish was Celtic's playmaker, fulfilling the role memorably described later by one of his team-mates at Liverpool: 'He's the GPO. We post the letters, he sorts and delivers them. That's what happens when we give him the ball.'

When Jock Stein resumed the managership for 1976–77, other administrative changes were made at Parkhead. He was given a new assistant in Dave McParland, the former manager of Partick Thistle, and Sean Fallon was put in charge of youth development. The effects of his near-fatal accident precluded Stein from the tracksuit involvement which he had always deemed essential to get close to his players. McParland now assumed that role but the old fox, who watched intently from the touchline, had lost little of his cunning. Detecting a weakness in the spine of his team, somehow he talked Hibernian into parting with Pat Stanton in exchange for a young Celtic defender, Jackie McNamara; later in the same month of September 1976, he bought Joe Craig, a striker from Partick Thistle, for £60,000. They were inspired signings. Stanton, a canny veteran and an intelligent reader of the game, was employed as a sweeper behind the young pivot Roddie MacDonald, to bring stability to the heart of the defence. Craig was a proven goalscorer, and his strength took much of the weight off other forwards as well as helping to create space for Ronnie Glavin, signed from Thistle in November 1974, to power through from midfield.

With the balance of the side now restored, things were turned around in the battle with Rangers. McGrain and Dalglish continued to sparkle and flourish as they responded to the new managerial régime. Danny McGrain always posed a threat to opposing defences with his speed and intelligent raiding down Celtic's right wing; Kenny Dalglish was a delight wherever he was fielded. As a midfielder his passing was incisive; as a striker his finishing was lethal.

Celtic's surge to the league title was built on a mid-season run of 14 Premier Division fixtures without defeat (with only one point dropped), including 1–0 victories home and away over Rangers, the current champions. Dundee United, making the first of their serious bids for the title under Jim McLean, visited Parkhead on 26 March 1977 and had their hopes dashed with a 2–0 win for Celtic. By the end of the league season, Celtic had extended their winning margin at the top to nine points over Rangers.

Only 54,252 turned up on 7 May 1977 on a rain-soaked Hampden Park to watch the first Scottish Cup final to be sponsored (by Scottish and Newcastle Breweries). The bad weather and the live TV coverage had done much to reduce the appeal of the occasion – even if it was an Old Firm final. Enormous speculation had been aroused about the appearance of Alfie Conn in Celtic's hoops at the same ground and on the same occasion where, four years earlier, his goal had helped Rangers to the trophy at Celtic's expense. Sensationally – and mischievously – Jock Stein had signed the forward from Tottenham Hotspur for £65,000 two months before the final.

In an undistinguished match, played under grey skies, Celtic, without the injured Glavin, were determined to give absolutely nothing away; Rangers had little success in breaching a solid defence where the predictable threat of aerial power was thwarted by the height of MacDonald and Edvaldsson, the Icelandic international. With Pat Stanton standing by as sweeper to mop up, Latchford in Celtic's goal was rarely troubled.

Of course, being an Old Firm clash, controversy was in the air and matters boiled over in the 20th minute when Mr R.B. Valentine (Dundee) awarded Celtic a penalty. Following a corner taken by Conn, Johnstone of Rangers scrambled a shot from Edvaldsson off the line and appeared to use a hand in doing so. The referee was well placed to view the incident and had no hesitation in giving his decision, but Rangers' protests were frantic and long-lasting. After the delay Andy Lynch stepped forward to drive the ball low past Kennedy at his left-hand post to give Celtic the winner. Lynch, a former Hearts player and a winger turned full-back, had won the penalty-kick competition at training the previous day – and this was his 'prize'. Remarkably, he had shown no hint of nerves, although this was the first penalty he had converted successfully at the top level, having missed two when a Hearts player.

It seemed that normal service had been resumed at Parkhead, but Jock Stein was fretting about the continuing unhappiness of Scotland's outstanding player, Kenny Dalglish, who had renewed his request for a transfer. Dalglish did not travel on Celtic's 1977 close-season tour of Australia and the Far East, and Stein, upon returning, made strenuous efforts to persuade his star to remain a Celtic player. Kenny Dalglish was equally determined to leave for England, and reluctantly Stein had to phone Bob Paisley at Liverpool to tell him of Dalglish's availability – as he had promised to do; Liverpool had been trailing the player for some time and, because of the affinity between the clubs born of the friendship between Stein and Shankly, the Merseyside club effectively had first option on a performer regarded by Paisley as the best all-round footballer in Britain.

Only three days before the 1977–78 season opened, Dalglish was transferred to the English champions for a fee of £440,000. The amount, a record sum between British clubs, drew a lot of criticism in England but the Liverpool manager knew that he had got a bargain. Intriguingly, as Bob Paisley later testified, the Celtic Board was only too eager to accept Liverpool's initial offer of £300,000, but thanks to Jock Stein's intervention the fee rose to its eventual level. This eagerness might suggest not only naïvety on the directors' part but also reflects the lack of unanimity among them of the true worth and influence of Kenny Dalglish; the bookmakers, however, knew his importance as the current odds of 4 to 7 on Celtic for the Premier League title immediately lengthened. So too did a depressed Jock Stein who acidly informed one journalist impressed by the size of the transfer fee that 'It's all right saying we've got £400,000, but where do you find any player like him?'.

Although newspaper speculation had prepared Celtic supporters for the worst, the transfer, when it happened, came as such a bombshell that Desmond White, the Celtic chairman, was forced to maintain that 'Dalglish had the wanderlust in his bones' and that 'it had got to the stage where he was practically incapable of giving his best to Celtic'. Uncomfortable as it was to accept, many supporters were now concluding that Celtic Park was now no more than a staging-post for the truly ambitious player.

Jock Stein's demeanour at the Dalglish's transfer hinted at impending disaster, and his own last season proved to be both disappointing for the club and disastrous by his own standards, a blot on an otherwise wonderful record. Apart from the departure of Britain's outstanding player, a loss both distressing and dispiriting for the manager, other factors wrecked his hopes of the squad achieving its potential.

Two key players were badly injured on the opening day of the season, a league fixture against Dundee United at Parkhead (0–0), and had to leave the field. Alfie Conn was scheduled immediately for a knee operation, and made only 16 more appearances throughout the season, failing to score in any. Stanton's knee injury was more complicated, requiring exhaustive tests, but eventually he too had to undergo an operation. The veteran struggled to regain full mobility but was unable to play during the rest of the season.

With Celtic receiving a record fee for Dalglish, Stein might have expected more money to spend on a replacement or for new recruits to boost morale after the injuries. However, during the season he spent – or was allowed to spend – less than a quarter of the money received from Dalglish's sale. Whatever the reason, his ventures into the transfer market were largely unsuccessful, and must have confirmed Dalglish in his perception that he had left a declining club with whom he had gone as far as he could. Journeymen players, such as £25,000 John Dowie, a midfielder from Fulham, and Joe Filippi, a defender from Ayr United, bought for £15,000 plus a young Celtic player, could not compensate for the loss of Dalglish, nor enthuse the supporters. Eyebrows were raised when Frank Munro, a defender with Wolverhampton Wanderers, was acquired, initially on loan, for £20,000. Appointed captain for his match début, against St Mirren on 15 October at Parkhead, Munro suffered the mortification of netting an own-goal in St Mirren's 2–1 victory. The player never did look completely fit during his time at Parkhead, and was given a free transfer at the end of the season. Stein could claim only one successful purchase, that of Tom McAdam from Dundee United for £60,000; signed as a striker originally, the player later achieved considerable acceptance as a reliable central defender.

The palpable sense of disintegration posed questions about the manager's sense of judgement and powers of motivation. Several people close to him, including his friend Tony Queen, a well-known Glasgow bookmaker and a passenger in the car crash two years before, feel that the accident in 1975 had taken more out of Stein, mentally and physically, than the manager would ever admit. The change in his manner was striking; after his convalescence, Jock Stein would be a less dominating personality, a figure robbed of the vital edge that had made him a manager supreme. There was, for example, an unexpected mellowness during a TV interview after Celtic's fourth successive defeat, at Aberdeen in mid-January 1978; in the past, such a result, one which left Celtic flirting with relegation, would never have been accepted with such equanimity by a manager whose reactions had often bordered on the volcanic.

He could have been forgiven for that approach. Player after player was sidelined through injury. Danny McGrain's absence was the most serious – and mystifying; his ankle injury, sustained on 1 October against Hibs at Parkhead, left him out of action for over a year, and McGrain was discouraged as it failed to respond to various treatments and at one stage threatened his career. He was not the only long-term victim: Johnny Doyle, a winger signed from Ayr United, was absent following a cartilage operation, and Andy Lynch was hospitalised with appendicitis.

Celtic's performance in 1977–78 was abysmal. In the championship, a fifth-place finish with as many losses (15) as wins; the first defeat in 29 years of Scottish Cup campaigning at the hands of a lower-division side, in a replay at Kilmarnock; losing after extra-time by 1–2 to Rangers in the League Cup final; and elimination from the European Cup in the second round after a wretched display in Austria against SW Innsbruck – a loss which left a depressed-looking Stein almost speechless.

One of the most painful aspects of this melancholy time for the club – and no secret to Stein – was the fact that, informally among themselves, certain directors were discussing (and, in at least one case, advocating) the manager's removal from the position he had held with such distinction. He was fully aware, as chairman Desmond White made clear in the summer of 1978 in his reference to 'football being a young man's game' for managers as well as players, that the Board were now looking for a more vigorous manager.

The shake-up at Parkhead in May 1978 involved the appointment of a new manager, Billy McNeill, and an assistant, John Clark. In the reshuffle Sean Fallon's connection with the club was severed after 28 years, and Dave McParland, who had played a major role as coach in 1976–77 and who was seemingly being groomed as the next manager, also found his employment terminated. In an interview in 1985, Stein hinted to the noted broadcaster and football historian Bob Crampsey that he had carried on beyond his sell-by date at Parkhead: 'It's probably a mistake to stay too long anywhere in football. You are maybe still saying the right things, but they'll have stopped listening.'

Despite what has been said elsewhere, Jock Stein initially accepted the offer of a seat on the board of directors, a position to be ratified at the formality of an AGM later that year: 'The job became a bit more difficult recently when I couldn't get about the field as much as I'd have liked. I'm more than happy to be going on to the Board.' (*Daily Record*: 1 June 1978) At a press conference held at Parkhead to announce the changes, the chairman insisted that the former manager would be welcomed because 'his name can open many doors and attract many ideas from many directions'.

Unfortunately for Celtic, given the level of football knowledge and experience he would have brought to the appointment, Jock Stein changed his mind during the summer. In August 1978 he was lured back into football management when Leeds United offered him double his Parkhead salary. Apparently, Stein's second thoughts stemmed from a vaguely defined offer from Celtic of 'a working-directorship', in which the former manager judged his commercial role to be 'a ticket salesman' – in his own words. Typically, he was not slow to inform Desmond White of his dissatisfaction in a fraught interview.

The tone of that meeting seemed to typify the relationship between Stein and White, an uneasy partnership which had never been close nor as fruitful as the one he had enjoyed previously with Sir Robert Kelly. Stein felt he had much to offer football still, and he needed a closer involvement in the game than such a directorship offered. He had seemingly anticipated a general manager position at Celtic Park, the sort of responsibility which Sir Robert Kelly had surely envisaged for him when he said on his death-bed in 1971: 'I know that those in authority at Celtic Park in the future will always have a place for him there even when his active days of participation in football are over.'

The seemingly botched handling of Stein's departure inevitably fuelled speculation that the Board's offer, which would have made Stein the club's first non-Catholic director, could not be regarded as a serious one. Certainly, to his dying day, Stein carried a deep sense of hurt at his treatment by Celtic, a feeling that his loyalty to the club had been betrayed. When he later took over as Scotland's manager, he was surprised that the SFA – a body about whom he had entertained the deepest suspicions as Celtic's manager – turned out to be a more generous employer.

Much the saddest aspect of the whole shabby affair was the awful sense of anticlimax to the end of Celtic's greatest era, a mood which was not dispelled even by a bumper testimonial match at Parkhead in August 1978 when 62,000 watched Liverpool, captained by Kenny Dalglish, defeat Celtic 3–2.

A lingering bitterness about the episode pervades the pertinent chapters of Stein's authorised biography, written by journalist Ken Gallacher in 1988; the comments of members of his family circle and friends are dotted with references to that Board as 'they', 'these people', and 'that Celtic mob'. In this work, no mention (complimentary or otherwise) is made of any Celtic director by name, not even Desmond White and Tom Devlin, people with whom Jock Stein had been associated in various capacities at Parkhead for over two decades; indeed, the only director mentioned is Sir Robert Kelly, and that as if to emphasise that the latter appeared as a giant among pygmies.

Whatever the rights and wrongs, no one could deny Jock Stein's indelible contribution to Celtic's history. In 12 years in charge at Celtic Park (excluding 1975–76) the club won ten Scottish League championships, eight Scottish Cups, six League Cups and the European Cup of 1967 – an unparalleled record, and one unlikely to be matched, much less surpassed. His great rival of the 1970s, Jock Wallace of Rangers, paid Stein a sincere tribute recently, on the tenth anniversary of his death: 'Stein was the greatest manager ever to draw breath. As a football man, there was no one who came anywhere close to him. He eclipsed Shankly, Busby and all the other legends in the game. He was in a class of his own.' *(The Sun:* 8 September 1995) Wallace, that most archetypal of Rangers men, conceded that Rangers' feats of the 1990s have been underpinned by tremendous amounts of money spent on top international players – while noting that Celtic's were achieved by 'a wonderful side' comprising native talent, and by Stein's incomparable ability to make those players perform at their very best.

In general, Stein's players' respect for him as a person remains qualified by the uneasy manager-player relationship, with its in-built tensions arising from the insecurity and uncertainty which is part and parcel of the game. Inevitably, differences of opinion and conflict arose at Parkhead, and there were a number of strong-willed characters on the playing staff then! None of them will deny his great strengths, however: the utter certainty of success which he projected, and the authority he conveyed with his commanding presence and intimidating build. One player who experienced life at Celtic Park under Jock Stein describes him as 'part bully, part psychologist and part genius'; he enjoys recalling how Stein handled referees, describing how the manager would observe within earshot of the officials, invariably while the boots were being inspected: 'You'll get nothing from this referee today.' Billy McNeill, his captain and on-field lieutenant, describes him as a revolutionary: 'Frankly, without Big Jock we would have muddled along, perhaps winning the odd trophy. He electrified the club, just as he had done at Hibs and Dunfermline. Just look, for starters, at how he reorganised our training and tactics. He put a stop to all that running dozens of laps around the track, then going our own way out on the pitch. We were going nowhere until he came back to Parkhead.'

Bobby Murdoch, another stalwart of the Stein years, is even more pointed in his assessment, once telling the authors: 'Let's face it, Big Jock saved Celtic . . .'

Stein's total dedication to the job was unprecedented in Scottish football, and his absorption might best be exemplified by his 'manipulating' of the media, which gave Celtic the most favourable coverage the club has ever enjoyed. Ken Robertson, a respected journalist who covered the whole of Stein's managerial career for the Scottish *Sunday Express*, likens Stein to a human computer: 'So little of what was happening in the football scene passed him by. He was the best listener I've ever met.' Robertson still marvels at the natural flair Jock Stein exhibited in arguing Celtic's case (often forcibly) through interviews, press conferences, telephone calls and the 'planting' of stories: 'He saw it as one of his missions in life to keep Rangers off the back pages. I can recall calling in at Parkhead after visiting Ibrox and, sure as fate, Jock would take in your news from there, assess it, and then with that sly grin he would say, "I'll give you a better story" . . .'

His philosophy that the team best prepared to face and overcome all eventualities during a match will win, may appear obvious and simple but, when uttered by a man who had absorbed the lessons of community and team spirit as a miner working down in the bowels of the earth, often in utter darkness, his pronouncements carried force. Prior to his arrival on the managerial scene, the off-the-cuff approach had been the norm – and one found notably wanting when Scottish clubs ventured into Europe. Stein's gift was to harness the spontaneity of the Scottish footballer within a disciplined framework.

So comprehensively equipped was Stein the manager, so remarkable his achievements, that his legacy for Celtic has been both enduring and ambivalent. Ten years after his death on duty with the Scotland squad in Wales, Celtic faced Aberdeen in an important televised league fixture at Pittodrie and lined up wearing black armbands in tribute. Unlucky to be two goals down early in the match, that Celtic side put on a thrilling display to win by 3–2. It was a performance exciting and skilful enough to be compared favourably with one of Jock Stein's sides. At the end, the Celtic supporters packed into the stadium broke out into a spontaneous chant of 'Jock Stein! Jock Stein! Jock Stein!'. It was a reminder that each of his successors cannot escape from being measured against the near-impossible standards he set. As the beleaguered Lou Macari said in January 1994, 'The problem for us is that Big Jock and his players spoiled it for everyone who came after them . . .'

TEN

The Will to Win

1978–83

Billy McNeill had found the siren lure of Celtic Park irresistible but, although he looked forward to taking charge of Celtic, he harboured some reservations. Quite apart from suspecting that such a high-profile job might have come too soon in view of his limited experience as a manager, McNeill had genuine regrets about leaving Aberdeen where he and his young family had settled comfortably in a city with a less frenzied football atmosphere than Glasgow. In fact, he was close personally to Dick Donald, Aberdeen's chairman, who wished him well on his departure, but added sagely, 'You'll not be as happy at Celtic as you were here.'

After the exhilaration of taking Aberdeen close to a league and Scottish Cup double in his first full season in charge, McNeill's early impressions on his return to Parkhead were of dismay. Within a single season the team itself had slid into the apathy and complacency of a middle-of-the-table side; his impression was that some players were self-satisfied and no longer motivated. One of his earliest statements could be construed as an implicit criticism of his inheritance from Jock Stein: 'My first task is to bring pride back to the club. I want the players to have ambition.' (*Daily Record:* 2 June 1978)

McNeill saw clearly that the squad urgently needed an infusion of new blood as much to restore confidence as to strengthen the side, and he enhanced his growing reputation as a shrewd judge of a player's worth by two early signings: skilful Davie Provan from Kilmarnock for £120,000 and industrious Murdo MacLeod from Dumbarton for £100,000. Both were young but vastly different in style: the 22-year-old Provan was a genuine winger, perhaps the last in a long and distinguished array at Celtic Park, and 20-year-old MacLeod proved to be a vigorous, hard-driving midfielder.

The League Cup was McNeill's initial test and Celtic, for the first time in 15 seasons, did not reach the final. Celtic could not shake off a persistent Rangers side in a fiercely contested semi-final at Hampden on 13 December 1978, and ran out of luck. After the Parkhead side took the lead early in the match, Doyle converting an excellent pass that culminated a 50-yard run from Tommy Burns, Rangers equalised after 25 minutes from a most doubtful penalty. Rangers' winger, Davie Cooper, had clearly overrun the ball when he stumbled in the box, but the referee (H. Alexander of Irvine) awarded a spot-kick. Tommy Burns, a talented midfielder, made his feelings too plain to the linesman and was ordered off; at that stage in his career, the young, red-headed Burns was cursed with a fiery temperament.

The match took on a predictable pattern thereafter, with neither side giving any quarter in a highly physical struggle as a fired-up Celtic made light of their numerical disadvantage and shortly after half-time Miller, Rangers' midfielder, was dismissed 'for persistent fouling' after another flare-up. Tom McAdam put Celtic 2–1 up in 65 minutes but, just when it looked as if Celtic would hang on, Rangers' determination paid off with ten minutes remaining. A shot from centre-half Jackson was deflected past Baines in the Celtic goal. The winner was equally unfortunate for Celtic: seven minutes from the end of extra-time, a shot by Johnstone was diverted past the unlucky Roy Baines by the leg of a hapless Celtic defender, Jim Casey, a young midfielder back helping out in defence after coming on as a substitute.

The result was a setback for a manager desperate to re-establish Celtic's winning ways, but it had been predictable as the team's form had slumped after a bright start to the season. By Christmas, the halfway stage in the campaign, Celtic had won only one match in their 11 league fixtures since the end of September; in that period they had drawn five and lost five. Any challenge from Parkhead for the title was not so much drifting as rushing headlong towards the rocks.

Help arrived from an unexpected source. The bitter winter of 1978–79 saw many matches postponed – a factor which proved to be a blessing in disguise. The resultant backlog of league fixtures brought a welcome halt to Celtic's downward spiral. Had he been aware of it, Billy McNeill could have taken some comfort in the assurance of one of his predecessors (Willie Maley), who wrote in the *Celtic Football Guide* of 1937–38 of his conviction that 'a guiding hand' was looking after the club and that, 'when things looked darkest', would sweep away the clouds 'and bring us the "blue heavens" of success again'. The odds still favoured Rangers for the championship, such was the injection of self-belief at Ibrox following their ousting of Juventus and PSV Eindhoven, two of the favourites for the European Cup; these feats, after a horrendous start to their season, had been accomplished by an impressive mixture of style and resolution.

Because of the Siberian conditions, Celtic could not resume league competition until 3 March 1979, but they were now better prepared to tackle the challenge. At Parkhead Celtic eked out a 1–0 win over Aberdeen, but the match was as much important for the boost to morale in the restoration to the ranks of Danny McGrain after an absence of 16 months, one appearance in September 1978 against Burnley in the Anglo-Scottish Cup apart (and a couple of games in the early rounds of the Scottish Cup). He would not be quite the McGrain of old, that overlapping full-back *par excellence*, but a player utilising his experience to build play from the back and, as captain, to bring reassurance to the younger members of the side. As Davie Provan puts it, 'His stature in the game made him a hugely assured and influential figure in the dressing-room.'

Despite improved form, Celtic's quest for the title seemed over on 5 May 1979 when the Old Firm met at Hampden Park in Rangers' 'home' game, that venue having been chosen to accommodate the largest possible crowd while Ibrox Park was undergoing an early phase of reconstruction. Rangers, the more purposeful side throughout, could have won by several goals, such was their superiority over a remarkably subdued Celtic, but seemed content to settle for a 1–0 victory. That win left Rangers one point clear at the top of the table, and seemingly poised to retain the title.

Those who had written off Celtic, however, were badly mistaken, says Davie Provan: 'There was a real hunger for success in that team. We had a useful blend of experience and youth – the backbone of the side was provided by experienced guys like Danny McGrain, Peter Latchford, Andy Lynch, Johannes Edvaldsson and Bobby Lennox. But there were also youngsters like myself, Roy Aitken, Murdo MacLeod and George McCluskey, all desperate to make a name for ourselves.' Their drive and determination would simply not be denied, despite an admittedly serious setback.

Only two days after the defeat at Hampden, Celtic went to Firhill and, although falling behind to an early goal, fought back courageously to win 2–1 over Partick Thistle. Later in the same week they faced St Mirren at Ibrox (as the Paisley club's ground was also undergoing renovations) and won 2–0, the decisive second goal coming from the head of evergreen Bobby Lennox; the veteran, the only playing survivor of the Lisbon Lions, remained a living reproach to any Celtic player who gave less than his all in terms of commitment and enthusiasm for the club.

After winning a nerve-jangling struggle with Hearts at Parkhead by the narrowest of margins (1–0), Celtic now had only one match left, the postponed clash with Rangers due to be played on Monday, 21 May, at the same venue. A Celtic win would bring the title to Parkhead, but a draw would suit Rangers, who trailed Celtic by three points but still had two matches in hand as a consequence of a Scottish Cup final against Hibernian which had gone to a replay.

In a frenzied atmosphere, the 52,000 onlookers saw Rangers manage to hold on to a 1–0 half-time lead, the product of their more direct play earlier on. Rangers had survived tremendous pressure for much of that first half, and there had been little change in the pattern of play after the interval until ten minutes into the second half. Johnny Doyle, a great favourite with the Celtic fans for his wholehearted play, was ordered off in 55 minutes by referee E. Pringle of Edinburgh for lashing out in sheer frustration at Alex MacDonald, an equally combative player. Doyle, the victim of some crushing tackles throughout the match, considered his opponent guilty of time-wasting by feigning the seriousness of an injury after being fouled. The Rangers fans were exultant; there seemed to be no way back for Celtic now . . .

That incident was the turning-point. The encounter had become even more ferocious than clashes in the normal run of Old Firm matches; one Celtic player could smile later and claim to have won standing ovations for gaining throw-ins. Rangers found themselves being forced back. Roy Aitken and Murdo MacLeod in midfield had become elemental forces of nature, winning every ball through willpower and determination, urging on their team-mates by example. Celtic surged forward, willed on by the roars of the majority of the crowd, and in 67 minutes Aitken, the most prodigious worker afield on a night when every Celt was a hero, netted the equaliser from close range; a smart McCluskey–Provan interchange created the space for Aitken to check, turn and slip the ball past McCloy. Players and supporters knew that a draw would not be enough, and so the onslaught on Rangers' goal continued minute after minute to a rising chorus of encouragement from the terracings. The full-backs, McGrain and Lynch, were joining in the attacks, stretching Rangers' defence with their lung-bursting overlaps. Another shot by Aitken was blocked but the ball broke to George McCluskey and the talented striker rifled it savagely into the roof of the net behind McCloy to give Celtic a 2–1 lead with 15 minutes left.

To their credit, Rangers pulled themselves together again and put Celtic under pressure immediately. After a corner taken by Cooper, Bobby Russell gathered the ball and manoeuvred for position in a crowded penalty area; he tried a shot for goal and the ball squeezed in at the far post for the equaliser. At that moment Davie Provan feared that 'it might not be our night', as Rangers once more had the upper hand in the title race, but Celtic stormed back into attack within seconds of the body blow, and McCloy saved in spectacular fashion yet another header from Aitken. Rangers were living dangerously again. With only seven minutes left Celtic took the lead with a bizarre goal. McCluskey, whose clever footwork had troubled his opponents throughout, hit a viciously spinning cross-shot; the keeper managed to push the ball out but it skidded off Jackson, a heroic defender for Rangers, and into the net. Astonishingly, the ten-man Celtic side continued to attack ferociously and, with pandemonium already reigning in the Celtic sections of the ground, Murdo Macleod strode through the middle of a shell-shocked defence to unleash a raging shot from 20 yards in the very last minute to seal a 4–2 victory – or, more accurately, *the* 4–2 victory.

A jubilant Billy McNeill could barely contain his emotions at the end, and heaped praise on his players; some years later in an interview with one of the authors he smiled as he described their achievement as 'something out of *Roy of the Rovers*, wasn't it?'. It was a far cry from his emotional outburst seven months earlier at Tynecastle after Celtic had lost by 2–0 to a Hearts side widely touted as favourites for relegation. On that occasion he had roasted his players for an inept performance, as he later expanded: 'I was angry because I had seen our support let down, and I wanted the players to realise that I was not going to stand for that kind of display from them any longer. I was with Celtic when there were black days, and for a club as great as this one is there cannot be any thought of returning to those days ever again. It won't be allowed to happen.' In true Celtic tradition, his players had risen to the challenge with a vengeance. Celtic chairman Desmond White – generally regarded as a dour figure – was so overcome by the emotion of it all that, during the after-match celebrations, he told the players it had been 'Celtic's finest night since Lisbon'.

In winning the championship Celtic had accomplished miracles by honest effort and spirit rather than skill, and aided by the awareness that they were rated as outsiders. Now, as champions, Celtic were expected to re-establish themselves as a major force at home.

As McNeill suspected, though, his squad did not have the depth to challenge for the domestic treble and the European Cup. After disposing of the Albanians of Partizan Tirana (who refused access to visiting supporters and journalists for ideological and political reasons), and struggling against the Irishmen of Dundalk (whose part-timers may have lulled Celtic into a false sense of security with stories of a relaxed approach to the Glasgow tie, stories which featured the quaffing of copious draughts of Guinness),

Celtic advanced to the quarter-final of the most prestigious tournament in club football. At that stage in the competition they would face a meeting with one of the most famous names in the game, Real Madrid.

On 5 March 1980 Celtic squared up to the Spanish champions in an atmosphere redolent of the great nights in Europe in front of a 67,000 crowd that taxed Parkhead's capacity, but for much of the first half Real Madrid effectively dictated the pace of the match and frequently threatened on the counter-attack. In the second half, however, urged on by the crowd, Celtic hammered at the Spaniards' goal. Celtic's fitness and aggression carved out an excellent opportunity of reaching the semi-finals after an absence of six years; Celtic scored twice through goals from George McCluskey, who took advantage of a goalkeeping blunder, and Johnny Doyle, who outjumped the visitors' defence to power a cross from Sneddon past a startled and helpless keeper.

Buoyed up with a two-goal cushion from the first leg, Celtic seized the early initiative at the Bernebeu Stadium two weeks later, and George McCluskey should have put things beyond the home side's recall in the fifth minute but he fluffed a clear opportunity. A vastly relieved Real celebrated their escape by exerting pressure throughout the half. Just on the interval, they were rewarded as Celtic started to wilt. Even before the match Billy McNeill – after talking with the manager of an English club – was privately entertaining the darkest suspicions of the referee, Karoly Palotai of Hungary, and doubtlessly he felt vindicated, although in the most unwelcome fashion. In the last minute of the first half, with the Celtic bench praying for the whistle, goalkeeper Peter Latchford was pulled up and penalised for time-wasting; the indirect free-kick led to the home side snatching a much-needed breakthrough just when Celtic appeared certain to reach the haven of the dressing-room unscathed, the referee permitting a goal by Santillana to stand although the scorer had clearly impeded the Celtic goalkeeper. Confidence now dented, inexperience at such a rarefied level would be the downfall of a young side in a pressurised situation. In front of a crowd estimated at 120,000, Real equalised ten minutes after half-time; it was inevitable that the home side were going through to the last four, their aggregate winner coming with only seven minutes left. Davie Provan admits that the strain was too much: 'especially playing in front of that gigantic crowd got to us'.

The backwash almost wrecked Celtic's season. That quarter-final had been a desperately close contest, and the disappointment bit deep as Celtic's hopes of European glory had been soaring after the first leg at Parkhead. Initially, Celtic still appeared well set to retain the league flag, holding a healthy seven-point lead over Aberdeen. The trauma of Madrid appeared to be little more than a bad memory on 2 April when Celtic overcame Rangers' resistance with a late goal headed by Frank McGarvey. The goal was netted four minutes from time by the newcomer, signed three weeks previously for £250,000 from Liverpool. However, three days later, in another home match, Aberdeen began to gnaw at Celtic's confidence with a 2–1 win which authenticated their challenge. Theirs was a methodical and disciplined performance, though the balance of the Celtic side was severely disrupted when Tom McAdam, a resolute central defender, had to retire at the interval suffering from concussion. Aberdeen survived a penalty-kick taken by Lennox halfway through the second half, Clark's save denying Celtic a point at least. The race was on in earnest.

Two visits to Dundee within a fortnight destroyed Celtic's hopes. The nerves were clearly jangling when United won by 3–0 at Tannadice, but the real damage to Celtic's collective psyche was inflicted by relegation-bound Dundee on 19 April 1980 at Dens Park. There was a touch of unreality about the unfolding situation as Dundee, seemingly down-and-out after Roy Aitken's early goal, went on to win by 5–1; astonishingly, the home side – without too much possession – appeared capable of scoring at will against a non-existent Celtic defence. Billy McNeill could only shake his head in disbelief as his players trooped off the pitch in a state of shock. 'My worst-ever day since I joined Celtic,' a distraught manager told the waiting journalists.

The erosion of Celtic's self-belief was confirmed four days later in another defeat by Aberdeen at Parkhead (1–3), a result which put the Dons in pole position. Aberdeen signalled that a new force had arrived in Scottish football by holding on tenaciously to their narrow advantage. The more obdurate of Celtic's fans were to insist that the final destination of the championship flag turned on a bizarre refereeing decision in Celtic's last league fixture at Paisley on 3 May 1980. Celtic still hoped to put pressure on Aberdeen, and with 12 minutes left and the match deadlocked at 0–0 Tommy Burns was blatantly up-ended in the penalty area by a St Mirren defender. The referee (A. Ferguson of Giffnock), close to the incident, immediately awarded a spot-kick, but was surrounded by protesting home players and persuaded to consult a linesman (whose view of the tackle was a more distant one), and he changed his mind. A successful conversion of the kick, and who knows? A Celtic victory would have meant that Aberdeen, 5–0 winners over Hibernian on the same day, had to avoid defeat in their final match against Partick Thistle at Firhill, a ground where the champions-elect had foundered on the opening day of the season.

With the pressure off, though, Aberdeen settled for a 1–1 draw, a result which officially brought the title to Pittodrie for the first time in quarter of a century. Commendably, Billy McNeill refused to blame a refereeing decision for Celtic's failure, and pointed instead to 'indifferent performances in the final four weeks when we tossed away the big points-lead we had'. McNeill could reflect ruefully on the fact that his side had finished as runners-up after going from mid-December to early April without defeat; but more than half of those 13 matches had ended in draws, the team's lack of killer instinct eventually proving fatal.

Celtic now faced a real test of their mettle in the Scottish Cup final against Rangers on 10 May 1980, particularly as both regular central defenders, Tom McAdam and Roddie MacDonald, were ineligible because of suspensions. Celtic's makeshift rearguard prevailed by digging into their resources of energy and commitment. The youthful Mike Conroy, normally a midfielder at the heart of Celtic's defence, coped well with the menace of Derek Johnstone; Roy Aitken, a sturdy defender, was anchored beside him to help deal with Rangers' aerial power. Rangers could make little headway in midfield either, where Provan and MacLeod worked hard to supplement the craft of Tommy Burns as he shuttled tirelessly between defence and attack. Rangers' defenders were forced to keep a wary eye on the elusive and unpredictable McGarvey. Celtic's relentless running and constant challenging – on such a warm day, a tribute to their fitness – kept Rangers from building up any kind of sustained momentum . . . and, in extra-time, turned the final their way when Danny McGrain dashed forward from defence at a Provan corner to latch on to a clearance from Dawson of Rangers. McGrain fired in a shot from some 30 yards which goalkeeper McCloy seemed to have covered until Celtic striker George McCluskey neatly diverted the ball into the other side of the goal.

That goal decided the outcome of an absorbing final and a fascinating tactical duel, but the occasion was overshadowed after the whistle by events other than football. The Celtic players moved towards the King's Park end of the ground to be saluted by their supporters, now in full voice after the victory. Some of those fans – in the notable absence of the customary level of police presence – jumped the fence to congratulate their team; that proved a signal for many Rangers' supporters to pour on to the pitch at the other end of the stadium. Within a few minutes the 'Second Hampden Riot' was on, and the skirmishing ended only with the intervention of mounted police wielding batons, reportedly their first operational use in public since the General Strike in 1926. Incredible though it seems, the Celtic players, now inside the pavilion celebrating their triumph, were unaware of these scenes. Davie Provan, for one, did not realise what had happened until he arrived home some hours later and saw the spectacle leading the TV news.

The Secretary of State for Scotland, George Younger, chose in Parliament to condemn as 'provocative' the action of the Celtic players in greeting their supporters; Willie Harkness, the SFA president, had been even quicker to blame the Celtic players' 'exuberance' for fomenting the trouble which ensued. Both Rangers and Celtic were fined £20,000 by the SFA, an amount which many felt was light in view of the television evidence, beamed around the world. Celtic, and Desmond White in particular, felt that the club had been made a scapegoat for deficient policing outside the stadium's perimeter.

Still, victory in a Scottish Cup final against the old enemy – despite the gloss taken off the triumph by the events after the whistle – was pleasant, if not ample consolation for the collapse in the latter stages of the championship. Billy McNeill, though, was far from satisfied, reflecting that Celtic's harrowing experiences in March and April could be 'redeemed' only if they served as a learning process for the younger members of the squad: 'We have to be harder and more professional, more capable of dealing with the pressures at the highest level.'

He must have wondered if his message was falling on deaf ears when, at the halfway stage of the next league campaign (1980–81), Celtic were apparently slipping out of contention for the championship, three points behind Aberdeen, the holders, who had a game in hand and who, on 27 December 1980, routed Celtic 4–1 at Pittodrie. It was a defeat as comprehensive as the 3–0 triumph of Rangers over Celtic at Ibrox at the start of November, when an ageing Ibrox outfit, inspired by Willie Johnston (approaching his 34th birthday), simply ran over the top of the league favourites. Celtic supporters had to start doubting if their team, characterised by one observer as 'a bunch of timid, undisciplined, unco-ordinated players', had sufficient powers of recovery to sustain their challenge for the league.

It took all of Billy McNeill's motivational skills to inject new life and spirit into his side, a process described by one journalist as similar to going to work 'with the urgency and efficiency of a boxer's seconds patching up the damage between rounds'. The manager, as had his predecessor in similar circumstances 13 years earlier, took steps to halt the downward spiral by holding some frank discussions with his players which had one constant refrain on his part: 'Second places are no good to Celtic.'

The most crucial outcome of these exchanges was an increased emphasis on sharpness and speed on the training ground. The change was reflected on the field of play where one adjustment allowed the pairing of the precocious teenager Charlie Nicholas and the tireless grafter Frank McGarvey to blossom into a potent strike force. It was a sheer joy to watch the tousle-haired Nicholas, a gifted player with a sixth sense in front of goal and an uncanny ability to beat defenders at will, being given such freedom to express his skills. The most exciting young talent to emerge in Scotland since Kenny Dalglish, he was already being hailed by Billy McNeill as a footballer in the mould of the top-class continental forwards, and 'a special player' whose regular selection had been delayed only by his manager's understandably protective instincts. A decade later, Kevin McCarra of *Scotland on Sunday* would conjure up a vivid image of the young Nicholas, recalling his apparently carefree and nonchalant manner after forcing his way into the team through brilliant performances in the reserves: Nicholas, he wrote, had an inclination 'to treat the game as one long invitation to take the ball and torment another player'. If overshadowed by his partner's flamboyance, McGarvey's contribution was just as significant. Davie Provan smiles when recalling the stiker's style: 'Frank might have been unpredictable even to his own team-mates, but he was a real nightmare for defenders to play against with his running and close control.'

The transformation was startling. In boxing terms, Celtic picked themselves up off the canvas, going on to confound the other contenders by building up an irresistible momentum. Such a dramatic recovery on a running track would have prompted a drugs-test, but it was simply yet another example of the traditional Celtic spirit manifesting itself. Only one point was dropped in the first 14 league matches of 1981, a run which claimed Rangers as notable victims home and away. Charlie Nicholas, a persistent threat to the Ibrox men in his first spell with Celtic, netted three of the four Celtic goals in those matches, won by 3–1 at Parkhead and 1–0 at Ibrox.

Both Rangers and Aberdeen had been reduced to helpless bystanders by the time Celtic travelled to Tannadice on 22 April to face Dundee United. Tommy Burns clinched the match – and the championship – when he took a pass from the industrious MacLeod bursting through from midfield and turned two defenders as he weaved to create a clear sight of goal; at that point, Burns transferred the ball to his left foot before sending it into the top left-hand corner of the net. Gazing at the pandemonium on the terracings at full-time after Celtic's 3–2 victory, United's manager, Jim McLean, was heard to murmur, 'With supporters like these, how can you fail to become champions? They are just incredible; they're part of the team.'

Celtic went on to create three records during the Premier League campaign of 1980–81: most points in a season (56), most victories (26), and most goals scored (84). By the end of the campaign Celtic had extended their lead over Aberdeen, the runners-up, to a commanding seven points.

However, McNeill's apprehensions about the lack of depth in his squad were borne out by Celtic's relatively disappointing showings in the major cup competitions, marked by semi-final defeats in both League Cup and Scottish Cup by a resolute Dundee United. In Europe, Celtic made an exit in the second round, falling to Politecnica Timisoara of Romania after letting them off the hook at Parkhead. After the setbacks at Ibrox and Pittodrie earlier in the season, McNeill had bemoaned the fact that he was working with a 'tight pool' which gave him little scope for freshening up a struggling team; after the 1–0 win at Ibrox on 18 April (which all but sealed Celtic's 32nd championship) he again spoke of the need to strengthen his squad. His words hinted at frustration in his dealings with the Board. Emphasising to his interviewer, Alec Cameron of the *Daily Record*, that the right time to boost a team is in victory, he added, 'You have to keep moving in football.' (20 April 1981) Cameron's assessment that 'McNeill is not the kind of man to stand still' did not suggest that Parkhead would be an oasis of tranquillity while the manager's demands went unrequited . . .

In contrast to their performance in response to Celtic's runaway title victory in 1980–81, Aberdeen showed much greater resilience during the closing stages of the next campaign. The Dons were again considered the major threat to Celtic's title hopes and the press had singled out their clash at Pittodrie on 30 January 1982 as the decider, and Celtic looked every inch champions as they brushed aside the loss of a goal in the first minute to win with some style by 3–1. The clinching goal came from a 17-year-old Paul McStay who looked a natural to fill a creative gap on the right side of midfield for many years to come. At that stage, few could have envisioned that the contest would come down to the wire and, by the end of February, Celtic, the front-runners from the opening day, had stretched the lead to six points over Aberdeen.

After that defeat, however, Aberdeen lost only one of their remaining 20 matches, a sequence which included eight successive victories at the end of the league programme. The consistency showed clearly the influence of Alex Ferguson, a ferociously ambitious manager who motivated his squad by constant references to the West of Scotland media 'bias' against his club.

Meanwhile, injuries – and a genuine tragedy – had taken a cumulative effect. Celtic had managed to overcome the absence at various times of such stalwarts as McGrain, Provan and Burns but the club suffered a tragic loss in October 1981 with the accidental death by electrocution by a domestic appliance of Johnny Doyle. Doyle, a performer for whom the word 'wholehearted' appeared custom-made, had remained a popular figure with players and fans alike, despite having drifted out of the first-team limelight; a Celtic man through and through, he had rejected offers from Hearts and Motherwell for his services.

In January 1982 Charlie Nicholas broke his leg in a reserve fixture and was sidelined for an extended period, and late in March Frank McGarvey was also put out of action for the rest of the season with a similar injury sustained in the team's 2–0 win over Dundee United at Tannadice. Under the circumstances, the manager had to gamble with reserve players and he came up trumps with the contribution of Danny Crainie who scored all of Celtic's goals in a 3–0 win over Partick Thistle at Firhill; in fact, the youngster netted seven goals in as many matches, none more vital than his first-minute opportunism against Rangers at Parkhead which set up a 2–1 victory on 10 April. The win over Rangers did much to shore up Celtic's confidence after a 1–0 loss at Parkhead to Aberdeen two weeks earlier, and the injury to the hard-working McGarvey four days later.

On 15 May 1982, the closing day of the season, with the title race in the balance after Celtic had seen a nine-point lead over Aberdeen melt away, a crowd of 39,699 turned up at Parkhead to watch their team's closing bid for the championship. Tension was high because Celtic had dropped three points in a goalless draw at Parkhead with St Mirren and a 3–0 loss to Dundee United at Tannadice, as Aberdeen continued to apply the pressure. So tight was the race that, if Celtic lost by a single goal and Aberdeen beat Rangers by five goals at Pittodrie, the championship flag was heading back north.

St Mirren, with keeper Thomson defying Celtic, held out to half-time. As the deadlock continued at Celtic Park, thousands in the crowd were listening in to their transistor radios with mounting consternation as Aberdeen built up a 4–0 lead over Rangers (a declining league force in the first half of the 1980s) before the interval. A collective shudder ran through the ranks of the Celtic fans massed in the Jungle, and the ripples of apprehension lasted until midway through the second half until MacLeod's forward pass to Burns was alertly flicked on into the path of George McCluskey, and the striker went through alone to drive the ball past Thomson. The goal owed much to the fact that McCluskey and Burns had grown up together on the Parkhead ground-staff and over the years had developed an intuitive understanding of each other's play. The tension evaporated, Celtic moved in for the kill, and struck again ten minutes later when McAdam's header from a Provan corner-kick was rightly judged by the referee to have crossed the line. McCluskey's second goal 15 minutes from time was again derived from Burns's understanding with the striker and settled the matter.

Relaxed and at ease, the supporters could now enjoy listening to Aberdeen's rout of Rangers at Pittodrie as Celtic cruised on the way to a 3–0 victory. A hugely relieved Billy McNeill, who had seemed to be kicking every ball in the dugout before the crucial first goal, had been sufficiently composed at the interval to focus on the essentials. He remembers the palpable nervousness in the dressing-room: 'The players were anxious to know the Pittodrie score, but I told them that didn't matter. What did matter was how they performed in the second half . . . and, to be fair, they did the business all right.' Billy McNeill recently told the authors that one player, sidelined through injury, had inadvertently let slip the half-time score at Pittodrie before his team-mates took the field again.

Much less palatable for an exacting manager were early exits in the cup competitions. Celtic failed to advance from the sectional play in the League Cup, fatally handicapped after losing 1–3 to St Mirren on the opening day of the season when a new signing from Aberdeen, centre-half Willie Garner, made his début; he was doubly unfortunate in conceding two own-goals at Parkhead. In the Scottish Cup later in the season Celtic fell at the second hurdle, losing 1–0 to Aberdeen at Pittodrie as the home side dug in hard during a frantic second half to hold on to their early goal.

More easy to accept was defeat by the Italian club Juventus in the first round of the European Cup. Celtic went to Turin holding a precarious 1–0 lead from the first leg at Parkhead, and only the heroics of Pat Bonner in goal postponed the inevitable. The young Irishman, Jock Stein's last signing for Celtic, defied the home side (and his countryman Liam Brady) with a series of full-length saves and timely deflections as Celtic eventually went down by a 2–1 aggregate score. A more horrific ordeal awaited many Celtic supporters after the match, when they were savagely attacked by local fans and had their supporters' buses stoned.

Celtic rectified the cup situation during the following season in one tournament, at least. Their progress to the League Cup final was unchecked in the early stages: the opposition from lower divisions, Dunfermline Athletic, Alloa and Arbroath, had been routed with such ease that the aggregate after the six matches was 29–3 in Celtic's favour, and Partick Thistle were swept aside in the quarter-final with an aggregate of 7–0.

Charlie Nicholas, celebrating his return from injury, was a physically stronger player after the strenuous recovery programme he had been put through. He remained in rampant form throughout the tournament with 13 goals in ten matches, laying down a marker for a season in which he seemed to be waging a one-man campaign against Scottish goalkeepers. He secured Celtic's place in the final with an opportunistic goal against Dundee United at Tannadice in the dying minutes after Tommy Burns had split United's defence with a cleverly weighted pass; the goal gave Celtic a 3–2 win on aggregate.

On 4 December 1982, in the League Cup final at Hampden Park, Celtic set about Rangers from the start, aided by the wind and rain behind them. They opened fluidly and confidently, and Rangers' defence remained under constant bombardment for the first half. In 22 minutes, and following leading-up play by McStay and Provan, Charlie Nicholas held the ball on the edge of the penalty area despite the close covering and waited, delaying his shot until a slight gap had appeared in the defence; his strike was snake-like in cunning and execution, taking the startled keeper totally by surprise. Nine minutes later, the pugnacious Murdo MacLeod latched on to a partial clearance from a hard-pressed defence and hit a typical thunderbolt into the roof of the net from 20 yards.

Rangers hit back immediately on the resumption through Jim Bett's free-kick but, despite their frantic attempts to get on level terms, Celtic held on, although giving their soaked fans on the terracings some anxious moments in a contest which was becoming too close for comfort. At the end, as he greeted his players as they trooped off, Billy McNeill looked like a man making an advert for happiness. The 2–1 victory marked Celtic's first triumph in the competition since 1974. It had been a long wait . . .

The trophy was all the more welcome in view of the fragmenting of a dream a month earlier. For one brief but glorious moment in the autumn Celtic had stirred the support with the expectation that the club could revive its proud tradition in the European theatre.

Drawn against Ajax Amsterdam, Celtic and their supporters savoured almost every moment of a magnificent first leg at Parkhead, studded with fast, flowing football from both sides; but, ominously for Celtic because of the away-goals rule, it ended as a 2–2 draw. Billy McNeill was annoyed that his young side had shown altogether too much respect to the legendary veteran Johann Cruyff, who was permitted to display many of his old, subtle touches. 'If that was him supposedly past his best,' says Davie Provan, 'I'd have hated to play against him at his peak. A fabulous player . . . and just look at the other big names in that side – Olsen, Lerby, Molby, Vanenburg. And they had Van Basten in reserve!'

In Amsterdam on 29 September 1982, however, Celtic refused to be overawed by reputations – and produced their last performance of note against top-class opposition on the Continent to date. Nicholas led the way in the 34th minute with a goal of stunning virtuosity, sidestepping two defenders before taking a return pass from McGarvey to round off the move by flighting the ball past the goalkeeper, Schrijvers, who was taken completely by surprise with the sheer cheek of it. That touch of gallusness set the tone for an uninhibited Celtic approach, and a refusal to buckle when Ajax equalised midway through the second half. The Dutch side now had only to sit tight to qualify for the next round on away goals.

The fates seemed to have conspired against Celtic when the woodwork kept out McGarvey's header with only a few minutes left. Undaunted, Celtic stuck to their task, and were rewarded deservedly when Nicholas created an opening for substitute George McCluskey, lurking with intent on the edge of the penalty area, to move forward and strike the ball into the corner of the net for an aggregate victory of 4–3.

Sadly, it was but a moment in the sun, for all the hopes of a lengthy run in Europe crashed to the ground in the next round when Real Sociedad, having snatched two late goals in Spain (both deflected past Bonner by his own defenders), visited Parkhead and found Celtic's defence wide open in 25 minutes. Celtic did win the second leg through Murdo MacLeod's two goals, but that momentary slackness had given up a vital away goal to Real. Once again, Celtic had fallen to Spanish opponents in European competition. It was becoming a familiar story, but despite the bitter disappointment, the supporters were drawing comfort from a belief that the maturing skills of a young striker like Nicholas would lead to a breakthrough at the highest level in the near future.

The seeds of Celtic's downfall in the other competitions had already been sown by a fatal tendency towards self-indulgence. On a high after their midweek triumph in Amsterdam, Celtic's lapse into exhibition-stuff football allowed a two-goal lead to evaporate and permitted Dundee United to snatch a point in the dying minutes at Tannadice. Ominously, that trait was still in evidence after their first Ne'erday victory at Ibrox in 62 years of regular season play (wartime football excepted), Celtic all but invited Dundee back into the game and almost threw away both points at Parkhead with their over-elaboration. Tommy Burns highlighted Celtic's attacking prowess with a stunning goal when he played a one-two with McStay and then Nicholas before unleashing 'a shot of such quality that if his No. 10 had been on a yellow jersey and the whole thing had been manufactured in Rio, the television companies would have action-played it until the film ran out'. (*Evening Times*: 4 January 1983) It was a strike which eclipsed the memory of Charlie Nicholas's dazzling winner at Ibrox only two days earlier, and illustrated the potency of Celtic's attack as vividly as the bare statistics of 147 goals in 55 competitive matches. Such ease in goalscoring appeared to have an unhealthy effect on Celtic's concentration as a vastly relieved Dundee manager Donald MacKay pointed out: 'The Celtic players seemed to be running a competition to see who could score the most spectacular goal.'

After their League Cup triumph, Celtic's pursuit of a domestic treble would come to grief as a result of that 'indiscipline' within a period of eight days in April. On 16 April 1983, Aberdeen, playing the Roundhead to Celtic's Cavalier, eliminated the Glasgow club from the Scottish Cup in the semi-final at Hampden Park by 1–0; it was a tousy, bad-tempered affair in which Celtic played without McGrain – under suspension – and Nicholas, a surprising absentee with a mysterious injury.

Celtic v Aberdeen matches in the early 1980s had become ferocious affairs, particularly after Aberdeen acquired a touch of arrogance more readily associated with the Old Firm. They had taken on some of the rancour of these clashes too, a Celtic player on one occasion pursuing an Aberdeen opponent into the dressing-room after being called 'a Fenian bastard'. The close marking and tough tackling were all too evident on this occasion, with Celtic the more noticeably aggressive side. Perhaps their vigour had been utilised to offset Aberdeen's more organised approach, but it was always unlikely to disturb the composure of a side on the brink of a notable success in the final of the European Cup-Winners' Cup.

At Parkhead in midweek, Celtic faced Dundee United, the other north-east contenders for the championship. Twice Celtic fought back to equalise and in 58 minutes United's young defender Richard Gough was ordered off after clashing with Provan. Celtic looked in complete command after their second equaliser (in the 73rd minute) but threw caution to the winds and allowed United to go ahead by 3–2 with five minutes left. Milne had time enough to bring a cross under control and steady himself before lobbing the ball over Bonner's head. Davie Provan admits that Celtic 'were caught by a sucker punch when chasing the game, but we only know one way to play.'

Celtic would not recover from this setback, and there were indications of an emotional hangover when they travelled to Aberdeen three days later and went down 1–0 – the third defeat in as many matches within eight days. Commendably, Celtic stuck to the task and were still in a position to retain the championship by the time the title showdown took place on 14 May 1983.

Like Aberdeen, Celtic were one point behind leaders Dundee United but both Aberdeen and Celtic were more experienced in such sudden-death situations. The programme for the last Saturday of the league had thrown together some fascinating fixtures: Dundee United had to face neighbours Dundee at Dens Park, Aberdeen were at home against Hibs, and Celtic had to go to Ibrox. Everything was still to play for . . .

At the interval, Celtic appeared totally out of it, as they trailed 2–0 to Rangers at Ibrox while both Aberdeen and Dundee United were in front. Numbed with despair, Celtic fans could only hope that their team could salvage some respectability from the match, and soon found themselves doing their best to lift the roof off the Broomloan Road stand with their impassioned roars. Celtic tore loose in the second half, scoring four times without reply from Rangers, including two penalties expertly converted by Charlie Nicholas. That burst of goalscoring was in vain, as Dundee United held on at Dens Park to win by 2–1 and lift the championship. Some Celtic players can recall the agitation of Billy McNeill late in the match as he shouted at his men to get forward as quickly as possible from throw-ins. A glance at the league table explained the manager's urgency: had Celtic notched one more goal, and Dundee equalised, the Parkhead men would have been champions for the third time in a row.

The agony of the Celtic fans would extend into the close season. Banners unfurled at the Celtic end of Ibrox carried heartfelt pleas for Charlie Nicholas to remain at Parkhead although, deep down, the supporters knew that the player was set on a move south after it became known that he was irritated at prevarication on the part of the Board in offering him suitable terms to stay. Although he might admit nowadays that he should have stayed at Celtic Park, Nicholas has always insisted that Celtic's offer was so low that it constituted 'an incitement to leave'. Intriguingly, Nicholas would depart with a sense of failure despite ending the season with close to a half-century of goals (48). He showed a self-critical streak in an interview with Gerry McNee in the wake of his departure: 'Mark McGhee [of Aberdeen] scored far less, yet won European and Scottish Cup medals. He was the success.' (*Scottish Daily Express*: 5 March 1984) Charlie Nicholas should 'have been a household name in Europe with his natural ability', according to Davie Provan, but he was never the same player thereafter for various reasons.

Little did those impassioned supporters know that, on top of the loss of the championship to Dundee United at the last gasp and Nicholas's eventual transfer to Arsenal (at a reputed fee of £750,000), an even more traumatic development was in store.

A crisis loomed now that Billy McNeill had come to an impasse in his efforts to obtain some sort of assurance about his position at Celtic Park. His relationship with the Board, most importantly with the club's chairman, Desmond White, had been deteriorating steadily over his five years as manager as a result of continual arguments with the chairman. The manager's unhappiness, and the directors' reaction to the overall situation, reflected irreconcilable perceptions. For his part, McNeill viewed the Board as one which was content to be standing still, comparing it unfavourably with the progressive set-up at Aberdeen. The regret that he expressed to the authors that ground improvements had not come near to matching the club's place in football is echoed in one of his early signings, Davie Provan: 'Compared to the facilities at Rugby Park – and Kilmarnock, remember, was not a wealthy club – the dressing-rooms and training ground were a disgrace for a club of Celtic's stature, and the showers were unbelievably antiquated.'

The directors, on the other hand, chafed at what they considered the manager's impetuosity; certainly, he annoyed members of the Board by his envious remarks about Rangers' new stadium at one post-match conference at Ibrox – and that was only one source of irritation for them.

McNeill dreaded his regular meetings with the Board throughout his tenure as Celtic's manager. Impatient for the club to be successful at the highest level, he sensed that the directors did not share his ambitions and he doubted their capacity to restore Celtic to the pinnacle attained by the club when he was a player. He recognised that the job of manager of a club such as Celtic was the focal point of many people's dreams – and that was difficult enough without having to contend with the interference of directors, or their fickleness. As he observes wryly today: 'When the team hits a slump, it's the manager's responsibilty – nothing to do with the Board.'

The matter had been threatening to come to the boil since the previous summer. On the eve of a pre-season tournament in Rotterdam, McNeill had made no sectet of his increasing frustration at being denied money to enter the transfer market in search of experienced players to boost his squad. His immediate requirements were a central defender and a mid-fielder, to act as cover and to correct what he saw as an imbalance in a young side. McNeill pointed out that no club could compete successfully in Europe with a youthful team, particularly against the top continental sides whose average age hovered around 28 or 29.

He stressed the importance of involvement in that theatre: 'Success in Europe is an all-embracing factor. It's good for the club, the players and, most important of all, it involves and can attract back spectators we thought were lost to the game.' The implications were clear: the Board would have to take financial risks and the club would have to speculate in the transfer market. There was no mistaking the tone of McNeill's sentiments which were not calculated to repair an already fragmenting relationship with his employers. 'I wanted to strengthen the team at the start of last season – but going into Europe this season without back-up is a distinct disadvantage.' (*Daily Record:* 6 August 1982)

In any event, his appeal seems to have fallen on deaf ears, and he had to admit he was making no progress in his discussions with the chairman about the backing he needed. McNeill's persistence was not the only facet of his character to incur the displeasure of the Board. *En route* to a European tie back in 1980, he had participated in a heated argument with a journalist about the refereeing in a recent Old Firm match – and during the scuffle, the journalist, Gerry McNee, had been struck. Within the space of a few weeks the directors twice disciplined McNeill: first they censured him and imposed a fine of £500 for the original incident with McNee, and later they rebuked him publicly for refusing to acknowledge the journalist's questions at a press conference after a match at Paisley. The 'feud' between the manager and the reporter had been simmering since McNee's criticism in a newspaper of McNeill's decision to transfer the experienced (but disenchanted) Icelandic defender Jonnes Edvaldsson at a crucial stage of the previous season's unsuccessful title race.

The manager would again infuriate the directors by a touchline confrontation with a referee, Mr A. Waddell (Edinburgh), during a match against Aberdeen in October 1982 at Parkhead in which Danny McGrain was ordered off. After the *contretemps* with Mr Waddell (himself no stranger to controversy over the years), McNeill was fined £200 and 'severely reprimanded' by the SFA

Thus, the chairman and his fellow directors were not at their most sympathetic when Billy McNeill had to face them in June 1983 after it became known through the press that he had been approached by Manchester City to take over at Maine Road following their relegation to the Second Division. McNeill denied that a concrete job offer had been made, but the Board suspected that the manager was playing one club off against the other. On Monday, 27 June, they held another meeting with him, after which Desmond White issued a press release so terse that it spoke volumes for the relationship between Board and manager: 'Mr McNeill's requests for a contract and wages increase have been unanimously rejected by the Celtic Board of Directors.'

Press sympathy was clearly on the side of McNeill, with a significant emphasis on speculation, apparently well founded, that Celtic's manager was earning considerably less than those of Rangers, Aberdeen and Dundee United – none of whom had been as successful domestically as Billy McNeill.

The Board's attitude only hardened, and one reaction to the barrage of criticism backfired. They decided to reveal the manager's earnings at Parkhead and details of an interest-free loan he had received from the club at a time of financial difficulty (in the wake of the collapse of a major business venture). McNeill was taken aback by the ruthless streak displayed by the Board in disclosing private financial transactions – a tactic which contradicted the club's much-vaunted 'family' image. It was a sharp reminder of where the real power lay at Celtic Park. Accordingly, a short time later, he left for Manchester, reportedly for twice the amount of his salary at Celtic, after telling the *Glasgow Herald* that 'it was perhaps the security of being offered a contract that was the vitally important factor in my decision'. (1 July 1983)

Doug Baillie claimed that 'The directors took umbrage at McNeill's lack of secrecy in negotiating with them by making it virtually impossible for him to stay at Parkhead . . . a state of affairs, it must be said, which didn't appear to perturb them too much.' (*Sunday Post:* 3 July 1983) The journalist's comment suggests that McNeill had provided the Board with an ideal opportunity to dispense with his services – and that was certainly not an outcome beyond the wiles of Desmond White.

Did he fall or was he pushed? Whatever, for the first time in living memory, the club had chosen to wash its dirty linen in public, and the Board could not claim to have emerged from the experience whiter than white.

The criticism clearly got under the skin of the directors, to judge by a revealing comment in an official publication: 'Celtic, we believe, were made to look penny-pinching and miserly before the whole football world.' (*Celtic Football Guide: 1983–84 issue*)

The episode had sent shockwaves rippling through the Celtic support, and the Board had manifestly forfeited a great deal of respect among the fans by their seemingly perfunctory treatment of a football man – a manager with a proven record of success: under McNeill's leadership, Celtic had won a major trophy every season. The newspapers were highly critical of the Board's actions; the directors found themselves compared to 'feudal barons', and pilloried in letters to the press for 'gutter behaviour'.

One such letter, published in the *Glasgow Herald* of 7 July 1983, remains in the mind not just for its description of the Board as 'a small but self-perpetuating élite that is impervious to criticism and sees the supporters as a means of finance and nothing more'. The writer, a Gerard J. Higgins of Shawlands, closed his scathing attack with a remarkably prescient warning to the régime then in power at Parkhead, should the club continue its decline: '. . . the last words will be with us, and they will be loud and clearly unmistakable. The wind had most clearly been sown, and the whirlwind awaits reaping . . .'

ELEVEN

The Nearly Men

1983–87

With the close-season upheavals dominating the headlines, Celtic had to move quickly to reassure supporters about the stability of the club. Celtic's choice as McNeill's successor was their ex-player David Hay, who had guided Motherwell to promotion in 1981–82 but later resigned at Fir Park in expectation of heading for Florida and a coaching post in the United States. That plan eventually fell through because of problems in obtaining a work permit. Instead, he acquired a pub in Paisley as a more viable business concern, and the down-to-earth Hay admitted candidly that he had had to delay giving Celtic an immediate decision in order to sort out the matter of its management.

Oddly, ignoring the convention that a manager chooses his own staff, the directors had already appointed Frank Connor, a former Celtic goalkeeper of the 1960s, as assistant manager. Connor had managerial experience with lower-division clubs and as a former coach of Celtic's reserve side; in fact, the Celtic Board had wanted to employ him in place of John Clark before Billy McNeill had left.

Celtic would start the new season with a new and untried managerial team, and without the striking duo of Charlie Nicholas and the graceful, if sometimes languid, George McCluskey, who had been transferred to Leeds United, the fee of £160,000 being established by tribunal. With such departures, some supporters feared that Parkhead was becoming little more than a nursery for top English clubs.

The mood among the supporters was a bleak one, despite new

signings. Brian McClair of Motherwell, Billy McNeill's last acquisition for Celtic before moving south to Manchester, would prove a bargain at a mere £70,000, but the fans did not warm to either of Hay's initial purchases. Brian Whittaker, a full-back from Partick Thistle, in a part-exchange deal valued at £50,000, and Jim Melrose, a striker from Coventry, for £100,000. Neither Whittaker nor Melrose made much impression in their brief careers at Celtic Park, nor did John Colquhoun of Stirling Albion, a right-winger signed for £60,000 in November 1983. For the supporters it was all too reminiscent of the 'trading down' which characterised the signings after the departure of Kenny Dalglish five years earlier. One disgruntled fan wrote to a newspaper, describing the practice as 'selling high and buying cheap', a lack of investment in genuine quality which caused unrest in the dressing-room to such an extent that a 'jersey player' like Tommy Burns was induced to seek a transfer from a stagnating club.

Celtic would find it difficult to come to grips with the new threat presented by an Aberdeen side now on the crest of a wave after its stunning victory in the European Cup-Winners' Cup final over Real Madrid. Aberdeen was a club set to stamp its authority on Scottish football for the next few seasons before Alex Ferguson's departure for Old Trafford. The Dons were now setting the standards, once the exclusive prerogative of the Old Firm, and in 1983–84 surpassed Celtic's 1981 record Premier League points total, as they left the Glasgow clubs struggling in their wake. Celtic, beset by defensive frailties, finished seven points behind, and Rangers ended up 15 points adrift of the record-breaking Dons.

Latterly it was no contest and Celtic would have to look to the cup competitions for their salvation in 1983–84; oddly enough, because of the rescheduling of the latter stages of the League Cup until later in the season, much of the early excitement took place in the European theatre.

Celtic complicated matters for themselves by beating Aarhus of Denmark by only 1–0 at Parkhead in the UEFA Cup, but eventually displayed the genuine difference in class between themselves and the Danes by overwhelming their part-time opponents 4–1 in the return leg. Everyone at the club scented an extended run in the competition after Celtic went on to destroy Sporting Lisbon on one of their great European nights. Down 2–0 from the away leg, Celtic tore the Portuguese apart to win 5–0 with a combination of pace, power, and emphatic finishing which rocked the visitors in the first half and left them for dead in the second. 'Long before the end,' wrote Ian Wood of *The Scotsman*, 'the Portuguese were a spent force, teased by Paul McStay, charged at by Murdo MacLeod, and thoroughly tormented by Burns, Frank McGarvey and Brian McClair.' (3 November 1983) The Celtic side of that era had its critics, but it was a team capable of producing such a quality of play and a level of entertainment that would have many supporters, tired of some utilitarian displays in the mid-1990s, looking back at that earlier period as something of a golden age.

The dreams of European glory evaporated on a wet, dismal December night at Parkhead. Drawn against English opposition for the first time in 13 years, Celtic had failed to convert midfield superiority over Nottingham Forest into goals in the first leg at the City Ground on a frozen pitch more suited to the local ice-skating idols Torvill and Dean. Tommy Burns posed problems for the home defence with his strong running and clever passing, while Celtic's defence shut up shop; Sutton was the busier keeper by far but both Jim Melrose and Paul McStay blasted shots over the bar when well positioned. Amid the euphoria generated by Celtic's performance against one of the sides favoured to win the competition, few noticed the sting in the tail of Brian Clough's admission that Celtic 'were undoubtedly the best team on the night'. The Forest manager knew that his team, twice European champions, had much more experience at that level, and that they would not be intimidated by the passion generated at a capacity-taxed Parkhead.

So it proved on 7 December 1983, when 66,938 saw Celtic defeated, victims of two sucker-punches. In 54 minutes Wigley intercepted a rare loose pass by Burns and strode down the right wing, avoiding two tackles in a 30-yard run, before crossing a low ball into the middle for Hodge to knock past Bonner. Twenty minutes later, Davenport avoided 'committed' tackles by Aitken and McAdam which removed them from the play as he raced down the left wing to cross accurately for Walsh to glide the ball into the Celtic net. Murdo MacLeod's goal, a fine header from a Paul McStay corner-kick, was just too little too late.

After the heroics at the City Ground two weeks earlier, the sense of deflation felt by the home crowd at Parkhead was palpable. The realisation that Celtic had been out-thought, and at times outplayed, prompted Rodger Baillie to describe this latest Battle of Britain in mock-Churchillian terms: 'Never was there so much effort by fans to get tickets to be rewarded by so little.' (*Daily Record*: 8 December 1983)

Celtic had to wait another three months to get the opportunity to retain the League Cup, in an Old Firm final notable for being the first major competition in Scottish football to be decided on a Sunday (25 March 1984). The crowd of 66,369, an attendance reduced by live TV coverage, witnessed an occasion pock-marked with niggling fouls, as indicated by the fact that referee Bob Valentine of Dundee had to book eight players and to award three penalty-kicks.

Rangers' greater hunger on the day spurred them to victory. In McStay, MacLeod and Burns, Celtic had the best midfield in the country, but on this occasion they drifted in and out of the contest whereas Rangers, forced to play without the suspended Prytz and Redford, got every ounce out of a rejigged midfield directed by the accomplished Bobby Russell. As a consequence of Rangers' supremacy in midfield, the supply to Brian McClair, Celtic's most dangerous forward (whose pace frequently threatened to expose Rangers' defence) was badly curtailed. Nevertheless, Celtic did well to come back from a two-goal deficit. McCoist, who had scored earlier from the penalty spot, profited from Aitken's misjudgement of keeper McCloy's long punt downfield in the 60th minute to add a second. Celtic's hopes were revived seven minutes later when Burns delightfully bamboozled the opposition by feinting to square a free-kick to the powerful MacLeod, but instead scooped the ball over the defensive wall for McClair to swivel and volley the ball past McCloy. In the very last minute Celtic were awarded a penalty when McCoist up-ended MacLeod in the box; Mark Reid, a young left-back, fired home the equaliser. Rangers showed more resolve than Celtic in extra-time and McCoist completed an Old Firm hat-trick for a 3–2 win for the Ibrox side; he had been pushed in the back by Aitken, and his penalty was parried by Bonner but the Rangers' striker followed up to net.

David Hay had hinted earlier in the season that he would consider quitting if Celtic ended up without a major trophy; now he had only one more opportunity left – in the Scottish Cup. Aberdeen, out to capture their first double, were stern enough opponents on 19 May 1984 at Hampden Park but after 38 minutes Celtic had more mountains to climb.

After looking the more likely side in the early exchanges, when one MacLeod effort was cleared off the line, Celtic were reduced to ten men through the controversial sending-off of Roy Aitken. Mr Valentine, the referee in the League Cup final, had already been the recipient of heated Celtic protests when he permitted Black's goal in 24 minutes to stand; Celtic defenders claimed that several infringements had taken place, and that Black was in an offside position – but the goal stood.

Fourteen minutes later Roy Aitken became only the second player ever to be sent off in a Scottish Cup final after a vigorous and ill-timed tackle on Mark McGhee. It had not seemed an overtly malicious challenge although McGhee required prolonged treatment from Aberdeen's trainer; the Dons striker was later named Man of the Match by the game sponsors, the Scottish Health Education Group. Hastily reorganised, Celtic summoned up reserves of energy and determination to dominate the remainder of the 90 minutes, and to draw level five minutes from time when Paul McStay's drive rounded off fine leading-up work from Provan and McGrain.

The physical handicap proved too much for Celtic in extra time as

Aberdeen predictably exploited their advantage in manpower to score the winning goal through McGhee in 98 minutes. It had been a brute of a final, with six players booked, and the war of attrition on the Hampden pitch prompted one commentator's acute observation that 'It was not a Cup final, just the seventh meeting between the clubs this season.' Familiarity had indeed bred contempt.

David Hay's wry sense of humour allowed him to claim that Celtic's winning of the BP Youth Cup had relieved him of the necessity to resign although, to be fair, Celtic had finished runners-up in the three major Scottish competitions – and had qualified for Europe because Aberdeen had captured the double. By the end of his second season in charge at Parkhead, however, Hay could bask in the glow of genuine achievement – and one accomplished in the wake of one of the most traumatic episodes in the club's history.

Rapid Vienna, Celtic's opponents in the second round of the European Cup-Winners' Cup, had served advance notice of their cynical and physical approach during the first leg in Austria, where Alan McInally, a striker purchased from Ayr United for £95,000 in May 1984, was ordered off and three of his colleagues booked as the Glasgow side went down 3–1. The tone for this tie had been established before the kick-off in Vienna, as Davie Provan testifies: 'I got the impression that they didn't like the Scots for some reason. I was hassled by one really aggresive official as I went out to inspect the pitch. It was a pretty tense situation, believe me.'*

The return leg at Parkhead on 7 November 1984 turned into a fiasco halfway through the second half. The Austrians had been struggling all night to contain the home side's fast and fluid play which had brought the tie level on aggregate (and had put Celtic technically in the lead thanks to McClair's valuable goal in Vienna). With 48,813 Celtic fans urging the home team on, Rapid Vienna cracked under the pressure in the 68th minute when Tommy Burns raced in to put Celtic 3–0 ahead, taking full advantage of goalkeeper Ehn's nervousness to net a rebound following a challenge for the ball. A few minutes later, Kienast – still incensed by the granting of a goal instead of a foul – was dismissed by referee Kjell Johansson of Sweden for a blatant punch on Burns inside the penalty area which a linesman brought to the unsighted official's attention.

That infringement should have brought a penalty-kick as well, but the

* Violent play has characterised international matches between Scotland and Austria. In May 1951 Billy Steel became the first Scot to be sent off in an international when his side went down 4–0 in the Prater Stadium in Vienna. Four years later, at the same ground, Scotland won 4–1 in a match littered with fouls, leading to two pitch invasions and the sending-off of an Austrian player. Even more horrendous were the incidents at Hampden in May 1963 when English referee Jim Finney was forced to abandon the match after 79 minutes with Scotland leading 4–1. At that stage the visitors were playing with only eight men, thanks to two orderings-off and an injury.

referee's oversight was compounded by further mayhem. The Rapid goalkeeper exacted further retribution on Burns for the third goal by kicking him inside the penalty area. The referee chose to consult the linesman about the incident, and he became embroiled in a prolonged dispute with all and sundry, particularly the visiting players, near the touchline. Amid the confusion their captain, Hans Krankl, seemed set to lead his team off the field, but the UEFA observer, Dr Hubert Claessens, persuaded him not to do so. But the most significant happening in the 12-minute halt in play came when the Rapid defender Weinhofer fell to the ground, and was assisted from the pitch as if mortally wounded. It was alleged later that the player had been struck by a quarter-bottle of vodka thrown from the Jungle but, as one journalist commented sourly, Weinhofer had 'gone down as if hit by the entire Smirnoff plant'. Finally, a penalty-kick was awarded but Peter Grant, a young midfielder just establishing himself in the team, missed the chance. Still, Celtic were through to the next round on a 4–3 aggregate, apparently . . .

Television footage of the incident, played and replayed in slow-motion, cast doubt on whether Weinhofer had been struck by any object at all, but the player had left the stadium with his head swathed in bandages, despite the claim of an ambulance man to have detected no sign of injury. Rapid Vienna demanded either Celtic's expulsion from the tournament or a replayed second leg on neutral territory; UEFA initially threw out these demands and went as far as fining the Austrians £6,000 for their players' conduct at Parkhead, and banning their coach from the touchline for three European matches, but Celtic were also fined £4,000 for the missile-throwing.

Rapid lodged an appeal and, at that hearing in Zurich only a week later, Celtic were represented by their chairman Desmond White and fellow director James Farrell, accompanied by Ernie Walker, chief executive of the SFA. Before departure, Walker said that in his opinion 'it was inconceivable that the Appeals Committee could overturn a decision already made by the Disciplinary Committee'.

Weinhofer and the team doctor of Rapid Vienna both attended the meeting, and were allowed to testify. The rump committee, consisting of only three out of the 21 officials entitled to be present, refused to look at television evidence. UEFA eventually accepted the revised Austrian contention (their third version of events) that the player had been struck by 'a small object' and, as Rapid had already used their two substitutes and Kienast had been dismissed, the Austrians had to complete the tie with only nine men, thus rendering the match 'irregular'. The tie was ordered to be replayed at least 150 kilometres from Parkhead, although in a bizarre turn of events Rapid's original fine was doubled.

Immediately upon his return home, Desmond White, who had almost certainly been lulled into a false sense of security by UEFA's initial verdict – and by assurances given by officialdom in Scotland – brushed aside all talk of Celtic refusing to comply with UEFA's ruling. Another passenger on that plane claimed that White had shrugged it off by saying, 'We'll beat them again!'

As it had done with Atletico Madrid in 1974, the club held to the moral high ground, content to fulminate in public against the Austrians' spurious claims while, at the same time, starting to make arrangements for a lucrative third match against Rapid Vienna.

The infamous 'replay' was held at Old Trafford on 12 December 1984 before a crowd of 51,500, at least 90 per cent of whom were Celtic followers. Many of them were nursing a deep resentment, having been at Parkhead and witnessed a match won fairly and squarely by their team, only to be robbed of the fruits of victory in the council chamber. In a predictably ugly and frenzied atmosphere Celtic lost their concentration in the 15th minute when Aitken's shot rebounded from the upright; so many Celts had surged upfield in the frantic search for a quick goal that the veteran Danny McGrain, not the fastest man on the pitch by any means, was left alone to pursue Pacult as he raced away to secure the only goal of the contest.

Celtic's increasingly desperate pressure simply would not yield the desired result, and helped to create the type of situation which many had feared, if not anticipated. Two England-based Celtic fans, acting independently of each other and at different stages of the match, took advantage of casual policing to approach and attack the Rapid goalkeeper and the goalscorer, prompting Hugh McIlvanney to comment perceptively on the nightmare: 'The fact that Honeyman [one of the assailants] was wearing a green-and-white hooped jersey compounded the air of unreality that pervaded the moment.' (*The Observer*: 16 December 1984)

The comparatively lenient punishment imposed upon Celtic by UEFA (a £17,000 fine and the instruction that the next home fixture in European competition should be held behind closed doors) hinted at UEFA's own embarrassment at their role in a shabby affair.

A more immediate effect was a lingering sense of disappointment which was mirrored in Celtic's fitful challenge to Aberdeen in the championship, the Glasgow club again finishing as runners-up, seven points adrift of the northerners. Celtic just could not put together a sustained bid, an unbeaten run of victories which could have exerted real pressure on the champions.

At times they gave the impression of being a goal-machine: Morton and St Mirren surrendered seven goals, Dundee, Hearts and Morton (again) five . . . However, the suspicion lingered in the mind that an old weakness would resurface. So it proved on 8 December 1984 at Pittodrie in a fixture built up by the press as a pointer to the destination of the flag. Aberdeen had moved four points clear of Celtic, their closest rivals in the league race; but Celtic's hopes were high, having netted 17 goals in their previous three matches and being boosted by the capture in October 1984 (despite the interest of Tottenham Hotspur) of Maurice Johnston from Watford; Johnston, a lively and intelligent striker, was purchased for a Scottish record fee of £400,000. The Dons, however, punctured Celtic's title aspirations with a convincing 4–2 win; three of Aberdeen's goals were netted by players who rose unchallenged to free-kicks or crosses. Six points ahead after that fixture, Aberdeen never looked back.

Another matter was causing concern. Celtic's average home attendance in the league hovered around the 21,000 mark, and followed the previous season's depressingly low figure of 18,000. The figures suggested two things: that the punters remained unconvinced by Celtic's ability to compete with Aberdeen for the championship, and that the Board had not been forgiven for the transfer of Charlie Nicholas to Arsenal and the sacking of Billy McNeill. A strangely muted atmosphere enshrouded too many home matches; 'funereal' would have been an apt description of the atmosphere generated by pitiful attendances at the last two fixtures of the season at Parkhead when 8,815 turned up for the Dundee match and only 6,514 for Dumbarton. Celtic supporters could no longer be relied upon to appear on cue for meaningless fixtures against unattractive opponents.

Without a trophy since December 1982, Celtic badly needed a pick-me-up to rekindle the enthusiasm of their fans, and the one hundredth final of the Scottish Cup provided a perfect stage for that opportunity on 18 May 1985. The clash against Dundee United had been set up by a typical Celtic response to adversity as the team made one last effort to end the season on a high note. After being fortunate to escape with a 1–1 draw against Motherwell in the semi-final, Celtic reacted to the stinging criticism of their performance by killing off the Lanarkshire side's stubborn resistance in the replay with two late goals from Maurice Johnston helping his side to a 3–0 win.

In the final itself, the Taysiders took the lead through Beedie ten minutes after the interval, but they found themselves unable to frustrate Celtic's traditional surge for the equaliser. David Hay recognised the necessity of altering the dynamics of a struggle which was starting to flow Dundee United's way as long as they preserved their more methodical, disciplined approach in the face of Celtic's frantic pressure.

From somewhere, Celtic had to find an extra ingredient and it arrived with a shrewd substitution and a variation in the pattern of play; Hay substituted Pierce O'Leary, an Irish defender signed recently from Vancouver Whitecaps, for Paul McStay and this switch freed Roy Aitken to roam the midfield and surge forward. Celtic were revitalised, and within a few minutes of the change Davie Provan curled a sweetly struck free-kick from 20 yards out past McAlpine's stretching arms high up at the post for the equaliser. The almost mystic alchemy of this moment – only the third Scottish Cup final goal from such a dead-ball situation – proved too much for United. Everything was now falling into place for Celtic: back on level terms, opponents starting to suspect that it was not going to be their day, and a Celtic support in full cry, scenting victory. The scorer vividly recalls the transformation: 'I could see the devastating effect it had on the Dundee United lads. Suddenly you could see the anxiety and fear on their faces.'

There was a sense of inevitability, destiny perhaps, about the winning goal five minutes from time. Roy Aitken, once described as 'a man mountain of a player', powered himself down the right wing to gather a loose ball, and flight over a cross for Frank McGarvey to head past McAlpine. McGarvey half-dived, half-stooped to reach the awkward ball, and crashed to the ground only to look up seconds later to see, in his own words, 'a heaving mass of green and white'.

Mike Aitken of *The Scotsman*, who had remarked upon how the special relationship between Celtic and their fans had backfired in the extraordinary atmosphere of Old Trafford five months earlier, had no doubt about the supporters' contribution here: 'The fact of the matter was that the legions of Celtic supporters who packed Hampden's terracings willed their team to victory in a denouement quite as grand as anything the competition has produced over the years . . . at Hampden the encouragement of more than 50,000 supporters [in a crowd of 60,436] played a crucial role in Celtic's triumph. They inspired stubbornness in their team, who refused to accept defeat.' (20 May 1985) Those supporters would have taken it for granted that their captain – who had to have a painkilling injection for a spasms in his back on the very morning of the final – should have laid on the goal for McGarvey.

That winner would be the crowning glory for Frank McGarvey, a player who had never been given a real chance at Liverpool, and who had turned down a better financial offer from Alex Ferguson's Aberdeen to join Celtic, his boyhood favourites. In fact, when he had been a youth with Kilsyth Rangers, McGarvey had been rejected by Celtic on the grounds (as detailed in a letter to the man who had recommended him) that 'the lad is very slight, and not good enough for Celtic'. Davie Provan, the other goal-scorer, recalls saying to McGarvey – as they revelled in the victory at the final whistle – that they should savour the moment, adding, 'You never know – we might not be back here.' Neither was, for Celtic at least.

Saturday's hero became Monday's reject when McGarvey was informed that his services were no longer required at Celtic Park after he turned down the offer of a new one-year contract with a signing-on fee so 'insulting' that the player immediately formed the impression that he was being pushed out. During the close season, McGarvey, a most unselfish player and at that time the all-time leading scorer in the Premier League, was transferred to St Mirren for a meagre £80,000. In fairness to David Hay, his determination to establish Brian McClair and Mo Johnston as the side's twin strikers was fully justified by their harvest of goals (122 between them in all competitions) over the following two seasons.

It was becoming a habit for Celtic teams of the 1980s to walk a tightrope without a safety-net, and this hazardous undertaking was clearly in evidence during the following season (1985–86). Twice they were sent crashing by Hibs at Easter Road at the quarter-final stages of both major domestic cup competitions. In the League (Skol) Cup Celtic fell in the penalty shoot-out after an enthralling 4–4 draw during which they had led late on; and in the Scottish Cup six months later the Parkhead men lost to a last-minute goal, defeated 4–3 after twice being in the lead. Between those dramatics in Edinburgh, Atletico Madrid took full advantage of the surreal atmosphere of an empty Parkhead to remove Celtic from the European Cup-Winners' Cup in the first round on a 3–2 aggregate after Celtic had gained a highly creditable 1–1 draw in the first leg at Madrid. Celtic found the enforced absence of their fans in the second leg, played behind closed doors, too much of a handicap; UEFA's punishment after the Rapid Vienna affair seemed doubly cruel as it deprived Celtic of the revenue of a home gate, and the oxygen of support on the terracings.

It was shaping up as a bleak season when the team, on a downer following their defeat by the Spanish side, went on to lose five out of the next six league fixtures, a miserable sequence of results which involved heavy losses to Dundee United at home (0–3), Aberdeen at Pittodrie (4–1), and Rangers at Ibrox (3–0). The latter reverse prompted the outwardly placid David Hay to admit to Alec Cameron of the *Daily Record* that he felt so hurt by the humiliation of it all that once again 'resignation crossed his mind' (11 November 1985); the man who had vowed to himself that he would never let the job get on top of him now appeared to be driven to distraction by the mercurial character of his charges. Legitimate questions were being asked about his response to the unhappy state of affairs, most notably when, in early November, he purchased striker Mark McGhee, then playing in Germany, for £150,000 at a time when Celtic's defence was leaking goals like a sieve.

Optimism was still in short supply following a series of indifferent performances during the winter months, prompting Glenn Gibbons, commenting on Celtic's dreary 1–1 draw with St Mirren in a league fixture at Parkhead, to condemn 'the somnolent body currently in control of the fortunes of Celtic Football Club. It seems that from the Board down the various levels of management and playing staff there is a terrible lack of urgency about the old Parkhead club. That must not only frustrate but anger supporters nourished over the 21 years since Jock Stein became manager there by the belief that they followed the most dynamic club in the game.' (*Daily Mail* 10 February 1986) Gibbons attributed the drift or lethargy to 'an apparent lack of application which tends to produce sub-standard displays, a canker which will have to be removed if Celtic are to return to their former glory.'

David Hay, with the support of the Board, had already decided that a backroom change would improve the situation. The relationship with his assistant Frank Connor had never been a comfortable one, and the decision to sack the latter had been made towards the end of January 1986. Connor suffered the mortification of learning about his impending dismissal on Tayside when Celtic visited Dens Park to defeat Dundee 3–1 on 1 February, a situation arising from a leak from the boardroom which had fuelled media speculation before and after the match. Hay was understandably (and acutely) embarrassed by the 'painful' silent bus journey back to Glasgow. He felt it better to put the assistant-manager out of his misery by delivering the bad news in a meeting with Connor in person at Celtic Park the following afternoon.

Despite this blunt resolution of an increasingly acrimonious situation, Celtic's title hopes did not improve significantly as Hearts continued to confound the experts by their tenacity, and consolidated their position at the top by an unbeaten run. This run, which eventually extended to 27 matches, was set in motion by a 1–0 win over Celtic at Parkhead on 12 October 1985. Celtic were going to need help from other quarters to overtake the Edinburgh side and, indeed, as late as 15 March 1986 Aberdeen and Dundee United appeared more credible challengers than the Parkhead men. On that day only a thunderbolt shot in the 82nd minute from Murdo MacLeod, brought on as a substitute, salvaged a 1–1 draw – and prevented Dundee United from becoming the first side to beat Celtic in all Premier League fixtures in a season.

At that stage in the campaign, Celtic had not won a league match since 1 February and morale had been further dented by the 4–3 defeat in the Scottish Cup by Hibs at Easter Road on 8 March. In fact, Celtic were in fourth place, and struggling to keep up with Hearts, Dundee United and Aberdeen. A week after the Dundee United fixture, the bookmakers' lengthening odds of 6–1 against Celtic for the championship looked spot-on when the Parkhead club found itself seven points behind Hearts (although Celtic had two matches in hand) after a memorable 4–4 draw at Ibrox against Rangers in monsoon conditions.

Despite the loss of another point, Celtic had turned a corner with a gritty display which did much to revive their traditional fighting spirit. The wearers of the green and white on that Ibrox pitch dug deep into physical and emotional reserves after being reduced to ten men when full-back Willie McStay (Paul's brother) was ordered off by the referee, David Syme of Rutherglen,* for a rash tackle on McMinn in the 33rd minute . . . and when they stared defeat in the face after Rangers, assisted by the wind in the second half, had moved ahead by 4–3. For the second week in succession Murdo MacLeod came to the rescue, bailing Celtic out, this time with a ferocious drive from 30 yards which flashed into the roof of the net. Celtic's obduracy would keep Hearts looking over their shoulders nervously; the Edinburgh men betrayed their anxiety when dropping a point at home to Aberdeen, the current champions, and then scraping a 1–0 win over relegation-doomed Clydebank.

Despite Hearts' stutters, a point at Dens Park against Dundee on the last day of the season would be enough for them to fly the league flag at Tynecastle for the first time in quarter of a century. Celtic, on the other hand, had to hope for a Hearts reverse at Dundee while securing a victory by three goals at Paisley against St Mirren in order to pip the Edinburgh side on goal-difference.

Celtic's fixture on 3 May 1986 kicked off in a curiously low-key atmosphere, the overcast conditions reflecting the expectations of the bulk of their following in the smallish crowd of 17,557. However, on the pitch Celtic set about their task briskly and to such effect that by half-time they led by four goals, thus turning the screw even more on Hearts, a side unused to the pressure of such big occasions. The third goal was one of such classical vintage that it must be a candidate for the best in the club's history: the sweeping move involved six Celtic players and was executed with such finesse and precision that no opponent could get a touch of the ball as it was manipulated from one end of the ground to another before Mo Johnston's acute positional sense and timing allowed him to appear as if from nowhere to slot the final cross past Stewart.

If the goalkeeper was left helpless by that hypnotic manoeuvre, he was visibly startled late in the contest when, with his side down by 5–0, he was preparing to clear after another Celtic raid; he turned to the crowd in momentary bewilderment as the Love Street terracings erupted into joy. The news was coming through on scores of transistor radios that, with seven minutes to play at Dens Park, Hearts had fallen behind to a goal

---

* Ironically, Mr Syme's grandfather had played in goal for Celtic in 1918.

from Albert Kidd. Shortly afterwards, the same player netted a second goal for Dundee to trigger jubilant scenes at Paisley, and Celtic had pulled off another triumph against all the odds. Tommy Burns, for one, had been taking no chances before the match, telling a radio interviewer as he left a pitch now being invaded by scores of Celtic fans carried away in the aftermath of a miraculous triumph: 'And could I just thank God for answering all my prayers?'

As Hugh Keevins of *The Scotsman* remarked, when commenting on the sensational developments and how Celtic had exacted a memorable revenge for their ordeals in Edinburgh that season: 'Celtic were well qualified to win the title in such a dramatic fashion. They are the side, after all, who scored seven times in two cup-ties this season, and were eliminated by Hibs on each occasion. The unusual comes at no extra cost with this club.' (5 May 1986) Certainly Hearts felt something abnormal had taken place. A decade later one of their players would say, 'You could have envisaged someone from the clergy coming into Tynecastle on the Monday to exorcise the place.'

A run of 16 matches without defeat in the Premier League, the last eight being outright victories, had helped to bring home Celtic's 34th championship in dramatic manner. It had been accomplished by the very slender margin of a superior goal-difference of +3, as both sides finished level on points.

It was a vindication for David Hay, who had never wavered from his belief that Hearts would crack in the run-in to the title, and had kept that conviction in the minds of his players when they needed a great deal of encouraging. He had apparently survived the dreaded vote of confidence from the Board after axing his assistant back in February. In truth, however, chairman Tom Devlin's statement was in the traditional Celtic mould of unanimity, namely a show of unity described by one of Hay's predecessors as 'the Judas kiss'. At least one director had been harbouring reservations about Hay's seemingly relaxed style of management. Indeed, people in football circles believed that time had been running out for Celtic's manager and that he had been saved perilously close to midnight: in 1985, with Celtic a goal down to Dundee United in the Scottish Cup final at Hampden, he had been within 15 minutes of losing his job; in 1986 at Love Street, he had been only seven minutes away from the same fate . . .

A year later, David Hay was fired by his directors. The manager felt that his dismissal had been mishandled as well as being unjustified; his feeling was that he had been released at a time when he had acquired the necessary experience to perform the job properly. Certainly, he had a right to feel aggrieved about the level of support he was receiving from his employers. A valid complaint about Celtic's performances was a tendency to self-destruct in defence. Hay recognised the fact and had been honest enough to accept some of the responsibility. In an interview in January 1987, after Celtic had given up three goals on successive Saturdays as they struggled to retain the title, he stated: 'The old problem appeared again, and I suppose at the end of the day it all boils down to me, because I pick the team. We are losing bad goals and losing matches we shouldn't be losing, and the bottom line is that I have to sort it out . . . It is an on-going problem that has been with us for three years, and it is up to me to solve that problem as quickly as possible.' (*Glasgow Herald*: 12 January 1987) On a scouting trip to London to watch Joe McLaughlin of Chelsea, however, Hay found himself being informed in the pages of the same newspaper by his chairman, Jack McGinn, that any bid for the central defender would have to be financed out of the manager's own pocket. Hay's other target in England was Steve Bruce of Norwich, who would become a pillar of Manchester United's defence. The manager claimed later that, if he had been allowed to buy two such 'affordable' defenders, Celtic would have matched or even bettered a revitalised Rangers.

By that time, some developments in the Scottish game had become starkly clear – at least, apparent to most people with the exception of the Celtic Board. A revolution was in process at Ibrox Park: a mediocre Rangers, now owned by Lawrence Marlborough, head of the Lawrence Group established by his grandfather (a former Rangers chairman), had shown their renewed ambition late in the 1985–86 season by appointing Graeme Souness, Sampdoria's Scottish international, as player-manager, and had promised him virtually unlimited funds with a view to making Rangers a top European side.

This dramatic move should have sent alarm bells ringing at Celtic Park, but instead served only to reinforce either inertia or a perverse form of complacency. Souness, a charismatic and high-profile personality, bought expensively in the close season, although it took some time for the benefits to be appreciated. Famous English internationals in the shape of Terry Butcher and Chris Woods came to Ibrox, but Rangers continued to drift behind Celtic in the league table in the first half of the 1986–87 season.

At that time, certain Celtic directors delighted in jesting in private about the travails of Rangers, and at least one described their old rivals as 'the Marlborough works team'. But the Board had totally misjudged the true nature of Rangers' ambitious moves. The Ibrox club had not spent millions of pounds for the view advanced by one Celtic director, namely that the vast outlay had been prompted solely by a desperation to catch up with Celtic. In the same interview with the *Glasgow Herald* in December

1986, he rebuffed criticism of the club's 'meanness' by asserting that none of the players was available for transfer and that, indeed, new contracts were being negotiated for Maurice Johnston, Murdo MacLeod, Brian McClair and Alan McInally.

Despite the director's assertions, all of these players were to depart at the end of the season. A decade later, Murdo MacLeod recalled how angry he felt, hinting in the process at chaos and confusion behind the scenes then at Parkhead: 'The way I left Celtic at the end of the season [1986–87] was hugely disappointing. I'd been there around nine years, played 400 games, and my next contract would have taken me into a testimonial. Davie Hay had promised me that would be all sorted out, but then said he couldn't give me the testimonial after all . . . and that hurt. I received calls from two agents in Germany. The second had found a club for me – Borussia Dortmund. And after taking a trip over and looking at the set-up, I decided to take the plunge.' (*The Sun*: 29 December 1995)

The final of the League Cup (now renamed the Skol Cup) between Celtic and Rangers, held on 26 October 1986 at Hampden Park before 74,219, marked a significant turning-point in the modern struggle for supremacy in Scottish football. Rangers' considerable financial gamble was amply vindicated with a victory over Celtic and a major trophy – and accompanied by a corresponding boom at the box office. Money begets money, and success breeds success – and the psychological importance of a Rangers win was widely acknowledged beforehand. Their 2–1 victory was achieved thanks to a hotly disputed penalty awarded to Rangers with only six minutes left to play when the referee (David Syme of Rutherglen) judged that Butcher had been impeded by Aitken, and Davie Cooper converted the spot-kick.

The match ended in considerable turmoil with Maurice Johnston being sent off for an off-the-ball incident; subsequently, Celtic's young midfielder Tony Shepherd was also dismissed by the referee, who thought that Shepherd had struck him on the back of the head. However, Mr Syme quickly realised, after seeing a 50p coin lying on the grass, that he had made a mistake in ordering off the player; he made a point of consulting the linesman before changing the decision. After that incident Shepherd gained a certain immortality in football trivia quizzes in Glasgow pubs as, in his own words, 'the only player shown a red card in a Scottish final, and not to leave the pitch'. David Hay was less amused, telling the assembled press at full-time that 'if it was up to me, Celtic's application to join the English League would be in the post tomorrow morning'. Celtic and their supporters drew no comfort whatsoever from Rangers manager Graeme Souness admitting publicly that the men in green and white had been the better team throughout.

Unlucky in that Skol Cup final, and ousted from the European Cup by the powerful Ukrainian side Dynamo Kiev ten days later, Celtic soon started to slip in the championship after a splendid start which had seen them build up a nine-point lead over Rangers as the competition neared the halfway stage. A 2–0 win by Rangers over Celtic at Ibrox on Ne'erday 1987 brought the home side within striking distance of the champions and confirmed the growing impression that Celtic were losing their way, a judgement that had been echoed by David Hay after a 1–1 draw at Clydebank a few days earlier: 'It would appear that we don't want to win the competition from the front. In fact, if we play the way we did today, we would be better not turning up at Ibrox on New Year's day.'

There seemed little that Hay could do about the situation, his justified grouse about the availability of money for new players apart. At the end of the season he would hint that the malaise went deeper, pointing out after a 1–0 defeat at Tynecastle, 'Possibly you saw some players on Saturday who don't want to play for Celtic. In that case, maybe they'll be better away.' (*Glasgow Herald*: 12 May 1987)

The unrest, apparently, had revolved around financial disputes, but the statement also posed questions about the manager's motivational powers. For his part, Hay felt badly let down by certain players. When he took over as St Mirren's manager in March 1991, he stated bluntly: 'In those days, if the ship was sinking, I would have thrown all 11 lifeboats to the players. Now, I would keep one for myself, throw ten, and lose a player.'

By the penultimate Saturday of the campaign, on 2 May 1987, Rangers were poised to seal their first championship if they managed a point against Aberdeen at Pittodrie. Celtic had to defeat lowly Falkirk at Parkhead – and hope that Rangers would be beaten – in order to push the title-race into the sudden-death scenario with which they were familiar from the previous season's glorious finale. Celtic, who had appeared jaded in the run-in, again could not rise to the occasion; a crowd of only 14,238 – less than half the attendance at the previous home game against Dundee United, when Celtic had dropped a vital point – watched in a sullen atmosphere as Celtic gave a lacklustre performance. It was an ominous indicator when the visitors opened the scoring inside 40 seconds, but not even a McClair equaliser in 60 minutes from a dubiously awarded penalty could rouse Celtic. In the closing minutes, Falkirk's substitute, Gilmour, evaded half-hearted challenges from three Celtic defenders to hit a speculative shot from 30 yards which deceived Pat Bonner.

It was a sad occasion for Celtic and for Danny McGrain in particular. He was making his last appearance before a Parkhead crowd without any prior announcement or fanfare; ten days later, the captain would take his leave of the club with a free transfer, and apparently without a word of thanks from the directors. He was still nursing a grievance about the 'promise' of an assistant-managership that had not materialised. For him and Celtic there had been no consolation in the Scottish Cup either, as Celtic fell at the second hurdle, losing to Hearts at Tynecastle by 1–0 on 21 February after Robertson's free-kick was deflected past Bonner. The Celtic spirit was in need of resurrection . . .

The Board had been set on dismissing David Hay for some months, but with ironic timing they at last allowed Hay to sign the type of central defender who might have shored up the rearguard during the faltering title race. Mick McCarthy, a no-nonsense pivot, was purchased from Manchester City on 20 May 1987 for a reputed fee of £500,000.

Just over a week later David Hay was phoned at home by the secretary of chairman Jack McGinn and asked to report to Celtic Park, and no specific reason for the request was offered. At the meeting which followed, McGinn asked the stunned manager to resign, adding gratuitously that he was 'too nice' to be a football manager. Hay was too proud to submit his resignation as requested by the chairman, who had already contacted Billy McNeill, recently sacked by Aston Villa, to line him up for a return to Paradise. Hay's refusal to resign forced Celtic to abandon the fiction that they had never fired a manager; the reality is that every previous Celtic manager – Willie Maley, Jimmy McStay, Jimmy McGrory, Jock Stein and Billy McNeill – had been firmly propelled towards the door under one pretext or another.

Hay, who had recently rejected a lucrative offer to manage Hibernian (one made while he was embroiled in a salary dispute with Celtic) learned of Billy McNeill's restoration on the radio a couple of hours later. The emotional scars from Hay's sacking were to linger in the mind for some years. As he said later: 'You can't forget completely about all wounds.' The depth of his feelings can be gauged by the comments of his wife Catherine in the *Scottish Daily Express* of 21 September 1989: 'David was in a state of shock. For the next month or so, he and I – and our teenage daughters Allison and Caroline – shed many tears at how Celtic had treated him. He'd given 150 per cent effort to his job, and Celtic had repaid him by tossing him away like a piece of garbage.'

David Hay had every right to feel bitter about the ruthlessness of it all but, as if endorsing the belief of many observers that he was too honest for his own good, he stated later that he had been so disgusted with the intrigues and scheming among the directors that for a time he had not bothered to attend Board meetings even to submit reports.

In addition, after the Skol Cup final in October 1986, the outspoken Hay, still furious at the referee's controversial handling of the match, had suggested to the directors that chairman Jack McGinn should resign from the League Management Committee as a protest. Hay's recommendation sank without trace. Football directors are not animated by a spirit of self-sacrifice.

Hay was an early victim of the instability that beset the club in the years which followed Desmond White's death in June 1985. It was a period characterised by a succession of chairmen who, for various reasons, lacked the authority required at the helm of such a high-profile club as Celtic. Undoubtedly, this vacuum in leadership ultimately contributed to the demise, in 1994, of the boardroom set-up which had been in place for almost a century.

Two long-serving players cast their own perspective on Hay's downfall. Danny McGrain, the club's captain in the Hay era, pinpointed one distinct handicap during the manager's tenure at Parkhead. A knee injury had prevented Hay from personally conducting and taking full part in training sessions; Jock Stein, against whom all Celtic managers are fated to be measured, once said that much could be learned about a player's strengths and weaknesses by being involved with him regularly on the training ground.

Tommy Burns, when still a Celtic player – and five years before he himself was invited to fill the manager's position at Celtic Park – was asked to assess David Hay as a manager and spoke frankly: 'Davie is a hard, hard guy and a lovely, totally straightforward and honest bloke. But I don't think he was the right choice to manage Celtic . . . Basically, I suspect the major problem during his four years in charge of the club was his rather laid-back attitude to the job. It reflected his easy-going personality – although, as I say, he is a fearsome prospect on the few occasions he is roused to anger. Managing a club the size of Celtic or Rangers requires 24-hours-a-day commitment. You don't leave the problems behind you when you walk out the front door, and you don't look forward to a quiet night with your feet up in front of the television. . .

'I suspect he failed to grasp the huge demands involved and, ultimately, paid the price when he was sacked on the return of Billy McNeill. A glance at the workload of the truly successful managers of the 1980s provides an idea of what is involved. Billy McNeill, Alex Ferguson and Jim McLean are workaholics and it is the only way to survive in a hard business. They are forever turning up at midweek matches. No distance is too far for them to travel to watch a player. They have a network of contacts to keep them in touch, they care passionately about the game and they are completely ambitious for their clubs and themselves.' (*Evening Times*: 21 March 1989)

A characteristically honest assessment from Tommy Burns who was observed by a journalist to be distressed on the day that David Hay was so brutally axed by Celtic. Typical, too, that Burns' high regard for his mentor was revealed in his early appointment of David Hay as Celtic's Chief Scout, 'with worldwide responsibilities'. For David Hay, a Paradise Lost had been regained . . .

TWELVE

Double, Double, Toil and Trouble

1987–93

'If ever a man was made for a specific club, it was Billy McNeill and Glasgow Celtic. He was never really manager here, or at Aston Villa. His heart was always at Parkhead.' Peter Swales, the chairman of Manchester City, said that in April 1989, and it could have been vouched for by anybody who talked to Billy McNeill during his years of exile in England. His animation whenever the name of his old club was brought into the conversation was an absolute giveaway.

In May 1987 McNeill was still reeling from the impact of his own dismissal by Aston Villa, and had already turned down offers to work in such diverse football outposts as Kuwait and Airdrie. He was in good spirits, though, having recently attended a reunion of the Lisbon Lions at the Normandy Hotel in Renfrew, where he had been accorded a rapturous welcome by the supporters and guests present at the function. Celtic's chairman, Jack McGinn, impressed by this show of support, arranged a meeting with McNeill in a Clydebank carpark. The discussion was brief. McNeill admits candidly that he jumped at the opportunity to return to Celtic Park as manager when McGinn extended the invitation on behalf of his Board.

When he walked through the front door again at Parkhead on 28 May 1987 as Celtic's manager, Billy McNeill expressed delight at being home.

He had lost little of his drive or his ability to motivate, and he had an added incentive to succeed in restoring Celtic's fortunes since the club was entering its centenary season. However, he recognised quickly enough that the customary buzz around Parkhead had disappeared; in his own words, he had returned to 'a dead club'.

He assessed the damage inflicted by the loss of four players, on top of Danny McGrain's retirement: Brian McClair and Mo Johnston, Murdo MacLeod and Alan McInally. The backbone of the side had been badly affected with the departure of the peerless McGrain, and replacements had to be found quickly for the others. McClair and Johnston, a duo who had formed arguably the most potent strikeforce in Britain, left after the expiry of their contracts – as had the industrious MacLeod and McInally, nicknamed 'Rambo' by his admirers, who had never wholly convinced as a striker.

McNeill's early signings were inspired. He captured Chris Morris from Sheffield Wednesday for £115,000, and the speedy Cornishman would function as a right-back who liked to get forward. He acquired Andy Walker, a busy little striker, from Motherwell for £375,000 and that player followed in the tradition of other captures from Motherwell (Joe McBride, Dixie Deans and Brian McClair) by finishing up as top scorer. He then signed Billy Stark from Aberdeen, and the veteran midfielder added a new dimension to the side with his ability to slip unnoticed into the opposition penalty area. Stark, methodical and effective, was a perfect professional; more importantly, he had acquired the winning habit under Alex Ferguson at Pittodrie. At £75,000, his capture by Celtic smacked more of larceny than a transfer.

Later in the season, in October and November, McNeill took further steps to strengthen his squad. Frank McAvennie joined the club from West Ham United for £850,000, a record fee for Celtic at the time, and he was followed by Joe Miller from Aberdeen for £650,000. Miller was purchased to provide more width, an option lacking at Parkhead since the premature retirement of Davie Provan the previous summer after a debilitating illness and prolonged absence, while the quick, incisive McAvennie proved to be more than just a striker. Billy McNeill still regards him as 'the complete centre-forward', a player who took the weight off the other forwards with his unselfish running, his courage and tenacity.

McNeill has frequently commented on the fairytale element that has characterised Celtic's history, and it was now up to him and his players to provide a happy ending rather than a grim one to a milestone season for the club. They got off to an excellent start in the league campaign by defeating Morton 4–0 at Greenock, with the more superstitious among the support viewing this as a good omen; Cappielow had been the venue nine

EUROPEAN CUP
QUARTER FINAL
1st LEG

CELTIC V FIORENTINA
CELTIC PARK WED. 4th MARCH 1970
Kick-off 8p.m.
OFFICIAL ILLUSTRATED SOUVENIR PROGRAMME Price 1'

DOBRODOŠLICA CRVENOJ ZVEZDI
RED STAR BEOGRAD

EUROPEAN CUP 2nd Round 1st Leg
CELTIC v RED STAR BELGRADE
Celtic Park Glasgow
WED 13th NOVEMBER 1968
KICK-OFF 8 p.m

OFFICIAL ILLUSTRATED SOUVENIR PROGRAMME   PRICE 1'

EUROPEAN CUP
CELTIC versus REAL MADRID
CELTIC PARK GLASGOW · 5th. MARCH 1980

SOUVENIR
PROGRAMME
25 pence

Celtic

U.E.F.A. CUP
ROUND ONE SECOND LEG
CELTIC FC
V
1. FC COLOGNE
CELTIC PARK
WEDNESDAY 30TH SEPTEMBER 1992
KICK OFF 7.30p.m.
JOINT MATCH SPONSORS
CLASSIC BUILDING SYSTEMS
and
HUURRE U.K.

UMBRO
OFFICIAL KIT SPONSORS

LISBOA
25 DE MAIO DE 1967
ESTÁDIO NACIONAL
FINAL DA
XII TAÇA DOS CLUBES
CAMPEÕES EUROPEUS

PROGRAMA OFICIAL
PREÇO: 5 ESCUDOS

INTER — CELTIC
ITALIA   ESCOCIA

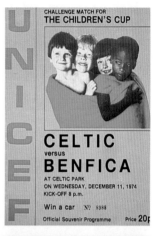

CHALLENGE MATCH FOR
THE CHILDREN'S CUP
U N I C E F

CELTIC
versus
BENFICA
AT CELTIC PARK
ON WEDNESDAY, DECEMBER 11, 1974
KICK-OFF 8 p.m.

Win a car   №. 8988
Official Souvenir Programme   Price 20p

THE
Jungle
BOOK

SATURDAY 13TH MAY

Celtic

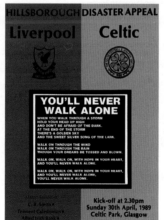

HILLSBOROUGH DISASTER APPEAL
Liverpool   **Celtic**

YOU'LL NEVER WALK ALONE
WHEN YOU WALK THROUGH A STORM
HOLD YOUR HEAD UP HIGH
AND DON'T BE AFRAID OF THE DARK.
AT THE END OF THE STORM
THERE'S A GOLDEN SKY
AND THE SWEET SILVER SONG OF THE LARK.

WALK ON THROUGH THE WIND
WALK ON THROUGH THE RAIN
THOUGH YOUR DREAMS BE TOSSED AND BLOWN.

WALK ON, WALK ON, WITH HOPE IN YOUR HEART,
AND YOU'LL NEVER WALK ALONE.

WALK ON, WALK ON, WITH HOPE IN YOUR HEART,
AND YOU'LL NEVER WALK ALONE,
YOU'LL NEVER WALK ALONE.

Allied Banks▪
C. R. Smith▪
Tennent Caledonian▪
Allied Irish Bank▪

Kick-off at 2.30pm
Sunday 30th April, 1989
Celtic Park, Glasgow

official souvenir programme
CORONATION CUP FINAL
19   53

CELTIC v. HIBERNIAN
Wednesday, 20th May, 1953
HAMPDEN PARK, GLASGOW   Kick-Off 7 p.m.

ABOVE: *Jimmy Quinn and Alec McNair*
BELOW: *Charlie Tully and John McPhail*

Cornered! Pat McGinlay and Simon Donnelly are covered by McPherson and Boli of Rangers, 1994. Celtic won the match 2–0

(All courtesy The Celtic View)

Tommy Burns: a Celt, man and boy

Pierre van Hooijdonk's header wins the Scottish Cup against Airdrie, May 1995

Paul McStay and Tom Boyd debate a point with the linesman at Parkhead, October 1995

ABOVE: *Jackie McNamara and Tosh McKinlay*
LEFT: *John Collins and Pierre van Hooijdonk celebrate Collins' penalty goal at Ibrox, 1995*
BELOW: *Peter Grant*

Andreas Thom scores at Ibrox during November 1995's Old Firm clash . . .
. . . while Andy Goram (and friends) look on as Celtic celebrate Thom's goal in a 3–3 draw

Fergus McCann and (RIGHT) *the new Celtic spirit*

years earlier when McNeill had started off his first, title-winning championship as Celtic's manager.

As the season progressed, perceptive observers could detect a change in style because, without sacrificing an attacking philosophy, Celtic had started to make themselves less vulnerable at the back. McNeill's assistant, Tommy Craig, revelled in being given a free rein on the training-ground, where he played a significant role in developing and perfecting a 'pressing' game. Celtic's forwards were encouraged to put opponents under pressure in the latter's own half of the field in order to snuff out attacks before they could get under way. One player described the approach as 'defending from the front', and it proved highly effective; Andy Walker claimed that 'we didn't allow our opponents to breathe', and pointed out that the method had a cumulative effect on opposing defenders who surrendered a considerable number of vital late goals throughout the season. Celtic's greater discipline was reflected in 28 shut-outs in the 44-match league schedule.

Early exits from two cup competitions forced Celtic to focus on the league championship. Aberdeen eliminated them from the League (Skol) Cup at the quarter-final stage with a 1–0 win at Pittodrie, and Borussia Dortmund of West Germany won 3–2 on aggregate to advance at Celtic's expense in the UEFA Cup.

Celtic were determined to make a real bid for the league, and the clashes with the holders Rangers proved entertaining, controversial and conclusive. The first fixture between the great rivals was at Parkhead on 29 August 1987 when a goal after only four minutes secured both points for Celtic; the goal, a characteristically stealthy one from Billy Stark (who drifted away from his marker to drill McGhee's low cross past Woods) seemed to arouse the more belligerent instincts of Rangers' player-manager Graeme Souness who was ordered off shortly after the interval by David Syme of Rutherglen for a nasty tackle on the Celtic goalscorer.

The most controversial Old Firm clash of recent times took place at Ibrox on 17 October 1987, a match in which Rangers gave the clearest possible indication that they would not be surrendering the league flag without a fight. The Ibrox club set the tone for an unsavoury affair by refusing to take the field side by side with Celtic for this fixture (the 50th meeting of the sides in the Premier League). This unfortunate decision may have been a reflection of Graeme Souness's simmering anger at his ordering-off at Parkhead. That incident had brought Rangers' player-manager to the edge of resigning, and his subsequent suspension by the SFA kept him out of the Ibrox fixture.

At the end of a bruising encounter Rangers had fought back to salvage a 2–2 draw after being two goals down, and with a disadvantage in manpower. After only 18 minutes their goalkeeper Chris Woods objected vehemently to a challenge from McAvennie, and other defenders became involved in the fracas; Woods and McAvennie were dismissed by the referee (Jim Duncan of Gorebridge), and Graham Roberts took Woods' place in goal. Later in the contest, Terry Butcher, Rangers' central defender and captain, was also ordered off for a foul on Celtic's goalkeeper. However, the holders of the league title kept plugging away and Richard Gough's scrambled goal in the last minute earned them a draw. The Assistant Chief Constable of Strathclyde, John Dickson, would describe the atmosphere at the match as being 'as bad as anything I have experienced in 33 years with the police'.

Given those comments, the sequel was scarcely surprising, although it marked the first case of legal intervention in respect of on-field behaviour in an Old Firm match. The clubs might well have anticipated such an outcome as their chairmen had held a three-hour meeting afterwards to discuss the implications. Four players (Woods, Butcher, Roberts and McAvennie) who had been involved in various incidents and actions ended up in court eventually charged with 'conducting themselves in a disorderly manner and committing a breach of peace'. All the verdicts available in Scots Law were invoked by the JP at the conclusion of the trial in April 1988: Woods and Butcher were both found guilty and fined, the case against Roberts was found not proven, and McAvennie was cleared with a not guilty verdict. If 1987–88 were to be a fairytale season for Celtic, this chapter could well have been titled 'Goldilocks and the Three Bears'.

On 2 January 1988 Graham Roberts once again found himself playing in goal against Celtic, this time when Woods suffered a rib injury in a clash with Celtic's youthful defender Lex Baillie at a corner-kick in the second half. Frank McAvennie exacted the full measure of 'revenge' on Roberts, whose court appearance had been occasioned by an alleged assault on the Celtic striker; he rose beautifully to a free-kick taken by Paul McStay and headed the ball past the helpless Roberts. The sight of the rugged Englishman sitting disconsolately in the goalmouth as the Celtic players danced upfield in delight was a sweet one for the Celtic supporters behind the goal. This time Roberts was left to conduct himself with dignity in his side's 2–0 defeat.

The opening goal, on the stroke of half-time, had been scored by the same McAvennie, and it was a memorable one. Paul McStay gained control in the centre circle and considered his options in the manner of an American football quarterback; after shimmying clear of opponents, he cut open the Rangers defence with a glorious pass inside their left-back – a 40-yard pass which found Chris Morris overlapping down the right wing for the Celtic full-back to swing the ball low into the penalty area where

McAvennie arrived with exquisite timing to sweep it past Woods. The correspondent of the *Glasgow Herald* went into raptures over Paul McStay's authoritative display: 'His was a performance to match the balance and grace of Nureyev, the gentle arrogance of Beckenbauer, and the chilling accuracy of a hired assassin.' (4 January 1988)

Celtic rubbed in their supremacy with another victory over Rangers, this time at Ibrox on 20 March 1988. The 2–1 win was a giant step towards winning the championship, with the winning goal coming late in the contest; Andy Walker – described by Billy McNeill as his 'best-ever purchase' – alertly diverted into the net with his chest a header by Celtic's substitute Anton Rogan. The young Irish full-back Rogan, vigorous and wholehearted if not the most skilled performer, was emerging as something of a cult-hero among the Celtic supporters.

The race for the championship was all over bar the shouting – of which there was plenty on Saturday, 23 April 1988, when Celtic faced Dundee at Parkhead before a crowd officially listed as a capacity 60,800, a figure which many would dispute in view of the severe congestion inside the stadium. It is believed that hundreds gained access to the ground without paying but, whatever the reason for the overspill, thousands of youngsters sat on the track during the match. John Quinn, writing for the sports edition of the local *Evening Times*, was awestruck as he described the scene: 'The ground was a seething mass of green and white with the stand full 90 minutes before kick-off! There were astonishing scenes in the minutes before half-time when thousands of supporters were escorted from the west [Celtic] end, where they sat behind Pat Bonner's goal, to the opposite end.'

Chris Morris set off early celebrations when he netted the opening goal in only three minutes after venturing forward in typical fashion from his right-back position, and Andy Walker added a late pair of goals to end Dundee's resistance and seal a 3–0 victory. It marked the club's 35th triumph in the league championship.

Three weeks later, on 14 May 1988, at Hampden Park Celtic put the icing on their birthday cake by gaining the Scottish Cup, and thus completing the double for the first time in a decade. Brilliant sunshine, Prime Minister Margaret Thatcher in attendance to present the trophy and to be 'welcomed' by red cards brandished *en masse* on the terracings (in protest at her presence and politics) by a crowd of 74,000 most of whom were in celebratory mood, all helped to make it an occasion to remember.

Dundee United were Celtic's opponents, and the newly crowned champions had to line up without two stalwarts in Pat Bonner, out with a calf-muscle injury, and the midfield grafter Peter Grant, sidelined with a broken bone in his foot.

The Taysiders managed to contain Celtic's opening surge in a first-half stalemate when nerves got the better of two sides who produced few goalmouth thrills. Shortly after the restart, the speedy Kevin Gallacher, a grandson of Celtic's legendary Patsy, outstripped Roy Aitken through the middle to blast the opening goal past Allen McKnight, Bonner's replacement. It was a goal worthy to settle the destination of any Scottish Cup, and Celtic looked rattled for some minutes.

A couple of inspired substitutions by Billy McNeill helped to turn things round: simultaneously, the vastly experienced Billy Stark and Mark McGhee were brought on for young defender Derek Whyte and striker Andy Walker. The change soon paid dividends when Celtic equalised after 75 minutes; Rogan motored down the left wing for the umpteenth time and, collecting a Stark pass, crossed to the far post where McAvennie rose to head home after the United goalkeeper Thomson misjudged the flight of the ball. Celtic continued to press, but the match seemed destined for extra-time. Chris Morris made another long overlap, this time on the right, to win a corner; Miller's kick was directed towards Stark, loitering on the edge of the penalty area, and the midfielder's shot spun off Narey. With the Dundee United defence in total disarray, Frank McAvennie pounced on the loose ball to crash home the winner.

Sitting in the stand among the celebrating hordes was Matt Lynch, a great Celtic servant of the 1930s and the wartime seasons. For him it was a touch of *déjà vu*, the last-minute drama so reminiscent of the traditional, never-say-die spirit which, as a spectator, he had seen rescue Celtic from defeat in a famous final against Motherwell. Back then in 1931, the reporters had begun to fold their notebooks in the press box, with the referee looking at his watch and Motherwell were still ahead by 2–1; and now, sitting in the stand 57 years later watching a match which had only seconds of normal time left, Matt was aware of hearing the start of a tannoy announcement outlining the details of the anticipated extra-time when McAvennie struck for the winning goal.

The celebrations at the end of the match were only the prelude to a summer 'weirdly and wonderfully Celtic', to borrow a phrase first used to describe a certain event in Lisbon back in 1967. The centre-piece of 'one giant green-and-white party' turned out to be a play, *The Celtic Story*, which ran for two months before packed houses at Glasgow's appropriately named Pavilion Theatre. Another successful venture, virtually contemporary with the play, was an exhibition of Celtic memorabilia in the People's Palace on Glasgow Green; instigated by the club, it attracted an impressive tally of 200,000 visitors.

The club appeared to have revived its proud traditions in full, but the renaissance was to prove all too brief. Gaining that memorable double should have been the ideal springboard for the mounting of a realistic challenge on both fronts, domestic and European, but Celtic's triumphs turned out to be an aberration as Rangers reasserted themselves to fashion a championship momentum which has so far proved unstoppable. Billy McNeill, looking back at a watershed in the recent history of the Old Firm, attributes Celtic's failure to compete with their old rivals to a complacency on the part of the Board. Never a diplomat, McNeill admits to problems in working with his bosses in both his managerial terms at Parkhead: 'Even in my first spell as Celtic manager I have to be honest and say that I didn't get the backing I sought. Too often I was fighting against the directors, not working with them.'

An all-too-familiar scenario was being played out at Parkhead; while the directors were basking in the glow of success, the manager pointed out the need for further improvements. His frustrations surface when he talks about his failure to impress upon members of the Board his view that Celtic had regained only some measure of credibility and respect, and that the club needed to face the challenge of Rangers head on. To take on the threat posed by Ibrox would require Celtic to break with the past by investing heavily in the transfer market, speculations that the conservative Celtic Board would shrink from. As he recently put it to the authors: 'We needed the same quality and stature of player that Rangers were buying – the Terry Butchers and the Chris Woods – and that meant a good few million rather than the million or so made available to me.'

Rangers had, indeed, upped the ante to an unprecedented degree, and no other club in Scotland could compete. Consider the calibre of player that Souness was bringing to Ibrox in a spending spree which saw his nett outlay before leaving Rangers in April 1991 amount to £9 million (once the money recouped from sales is taken into account). Among his other buys would be Gary Stevens (£1 million), Mark Walters (£500,000), Richard Gough (£1.5 million), Trevor Steven (£1.5 million), Ian Ferguson (£850,000) and Mo Johnston (£1.5 million). Souness was determined to make Rangers the best, and it is instructive to note the comment volunteered by ex-Celt Pat Crerand in a conversation with journalist Gerry McNee shortly after Souness's arrival at Ibrox: 'It's going to be murder for Celtic fans up there for the next ten years.'

At that time, while he was in charge at Celtic Park, Billy McNeill had to remain tight-lipped about the failure to consolidate after the double success in 1987–88. He had to be equally evasive about another internal matter which was threatening Celtic's bid to stay on top. From August 1988 until March 1989 the manager sustained a news blackout on Frank McAvennie's four transfer requests; the blond striker had proved to be an exceptional player, but he was chafing under the strains of his goldfish-bowl life in the West of Scotland. He considered Glasgow too divided a city: 'Hardly a day goes by without some wee guy coming up and shouting abuse, even when I'm with my mother.' Billy McNeill finally had to admit defeat in his attempts to keep such a valuable player, until the end of the season at least, after McAvennie – who had denied unconvincingly any desire to leave Celtic – contradicted McNeill's assertion that he had been dropped from the line-up against Hearts at Tynecastle because he was not match-fit.

Celtic made a tidy profit on the transaction: the club received an estimated £1.25 million for him from his former club, West Ham United, in March 1989, after paying out £850,000 for him in October 1987. The profit indicated the value of the player to Celtic; before his departure, McAvennie had continued to make a useful contribution to the fruitless campaign to retain the championship with 12 goals in 23 matches.

However, Celtic had struggled from the early weeks in the league. Two heavy and demoralising defeats at Ibrox (5–1 and 4–1) highlighted the team's defensive frailties, although in both cases Celtic had taken an early lead before Rangers wrested control of the midfield and finished off their old rivals in ruthless fashion.

The first of these humiliations, on 27 August 1988, effectively ended the brief career of Ian Andrews, a goalkeeper signed for £300,000 from Leicester City to provide back-up for the injured Pat Bonner. In fairness to the Englishman, most of the blame for the débâcle should have been attached to a defensive confusion so acute that Tommy Burns confessed on TV the following day that he had been suffering agonies at the thought that Rangers might have equalled (or even surpassed) Celtic's famous 7–1 victory in the 1957 League Cup final. Four days later, an apparently hung-over Celtic were eliminated from the quarter-finals of the Skol Cup by Dundee United at Tannadice by 2–0.

Rangers, leading by ten points from third-placed Celtic, put paid to the champions' aspirations for 1988–89 with a 2–1 victory at Parkhead on 1 April 1989 after Joe Miller failed to convert a penalty-kick for the equaliser in the second half. It was proving to be a most disappointing season, a largely ignominious retreat from the heights of the previous campaign: in the European Cup, another West German side, Werder Bremen, took full advantage of casualness in Celtic's defence to snatch a 1–0 win at Parkhead – and the pragmatic Germans took no chances in the second leg, settling for a 0–0 draw. Earlier in the competition Celtic had advanced by routing the Hungarian champions Honved by 4–0 in the second leg, after losing by 1–0 in Budapest. Only those with eyes closed to the reality of the modern game could fail to see that more and more Celtic were losing touch with those heady days when they could compete regularly with the very best in football's most testing arena.

The club still had one shot at retaining some of their glory from the centenary season, and that was in the Scottish Cup. It would not be the easiest of tasks as their opponents in the final on 20 May 1989 were Rangers, who were going for the elusive treble. The match was watched by a crowd of 72,069 which witnessed a written-off Celtic rise to the occasion by displaying a welcome appetite for the fray at the end of a season that had seen the balance of power shift decisively in Rangers' favour – and without too much resistance from the Parkhead club.

At Hampden, Celtic closed Rangers down by scrapping for every ball and man-marking so tightly that by the later stages Rangers had been reduced to punting high balls down the middle, and adding the weight of Gough and Butcher to the attack. This despairing tactic was dealt with comfortably by Celtic's central defenders Mick McCarthy and Derek Whyte, and the watchful Pat Bonner.

Despite all the pre-match hype, it was yet another Old Firm final in which constructive football was missing, and goalscoring a lost art. For the third successive Scottish Cup final between the clubs, the outcome was settled by a single goal. It came about in the 42nd minute through a catalogue of mistakes by Rangers' defenders: Roy Aitken claimed a throw-in within his own half and took it quickly, catching Rangers by surprise; Peter Grant pumped a hopeful ball into Rangers' penalty area, where Gough headed clear, but not emphatically; Mark McGhee and Butcher jousted below the descending clearance, and the defender won the duel to play the ball over to the unfortunate England international, Gary Stevens, who attempted a pass-back. An alert Joe Miller swooped on the mis-hit pass-back with a low shot past Chris Woods. After the match Rangers' enraged player-manager Graeme Souness hurled his runners-up medal into a corner of the dressing-room with the words: 'I don't collect these!'

In keeping with Celtic's disjointed season, the goalscorer had only recently been liberated from his 'chained role' on the right wing in order to roam through the middle, his favourite position but one in which he was fielded only a few times after his arrival at Parkhead from Aberdeen in November 1987. His chance to play as the main striker came with the unavailability of Frank McAvennie (recently transferred to West Ham) and Tommy Coyne (recently signed from Dundee, but still cup-tied with them).

Before the Scottish Cup final Billy McNeill had apparently taken a significant step in halting Celtic's slide. Alerted by his captain Roy Aitken on the latter's return from a Scotland training session at Gleneagles, McNeill learned that Mo Johnston would not be averse to a return to Celtic Park from Nantes. Quickly, a transfer deal involving a fee of an estimated £1.2 million (available after McAvenney's move south) was negotiated with the French club. On 12 May 1989, only eight days before the final, the player made a morale-boosting appearance at Celtic Park. Paraded in a Celtic jersey for the benefit of the assembled media, Johnston claimed that deep down he always wanted to be back: 'I don't want to play for any other club.'

The next day, he travelled with the team on the bus to Paisley to watch Celtic's last league fixture in 1988–89 against St Mirren – and was greeted joyously by the supporters as he took his seat in the stand. It appeared to be a marvellously astute business transaction: Celtic had acquired a proven striker of quality, and one who was now arguably a more complete player than he had been when he had left two seasons earlier. Not only was Johnston almost four years younger than the recently departed McAvennie, but he was now at the top of his form, having netted six goals in five of Scotland's qualifying games for the 1990 World Cup finals. It would be the perfect riposte to the frequent accusations of 'Celtic penny-pinching' in contrast to the free-spending ways at Ibrox.

Scottish football is essentially a village, complete with a gossip grapevine, and the word soon began to filter back to Celtic Park that the deal could be falling apart only a fortnight or so after the 'transfer'. For instance, two Celtic players had reason to doubt whether the arrangement was watertight after chatting with Johnston at the Scottish Professional Footballers' Association annual dinner at a Glasgow hotel. They had gained the distinct impression that the player was now intending to sign for Rangers.

Rumours were soon abounding in Glasgow of the possible sensational developments, although Johnston's agent laughed off the chances of his client joining Rangers: 'It's a complete fabrication – you can run that story for ten years and it still wouldn't be true.' (*Sunday Mail* 2 July 1989) What was now becoming an issue, openly discussed, was the combination of Rangers' interest and the player's religion, whether nominal or not. Shortly afterwards (on 10 July) Johnston committed 'the ultimate apostasy' by signing for Rangers to become, our research suggests, only the 16th Catholic to wear a Rangers jersey since the club's inception in 1872. The BBC's Ceefax service was wrong-footed, informing its subscribers that this 'sensational' development was 'all the more remarkable as Johnston will be the first Catholic ever to play for Celtic, normally an all-Protestant club[*sic*]'. One Scottish newspaper remarked dryly on the hasty corrective action required: 'Ceefax is now well aware that it has a lot of readers north of the border.'

An orgy of speculation broke out as to the real motives behind Johnston's change of mind. In a highly charged atmosphere (on both sides of Glasgow's football divide) conspiracy theories abounded. The player himself maintained that he had not signed a contract with Celtic, but it was suggested that his move to Ibrox was a piece of inspired devilment on the part of Graeme Souness, eager to put one over on Celtic and having the financial clout to do so. Typical of the hype surrounding the affair was one headline in *The Sun* reading 'Mo got a million in his hand! He couldn't turn it down, says father.' (14 July 1989) One suspects that the controversy still has a lot of mileage. Recently, for example, the player's agent, Bill McMurdo, felt obliged to defend his own role in the matter, blaming the furore on the Celtic directors of that time trying to save face by 'demonising' him as an influential factor in Johnston's astonishing switch: 'Around that time, none of them understood the workings of Freedom of Contract. They had previously let Maurice, Brian McClair, Alan McInally and Murdo MacLeod go out of contract at the same time, which tells you something.' (*The Sun*: 10 December 1994)

Meanwhile, Billy McNeill had been busy in the transfer market. His first acquisition, for a fee of £500,000 in June 1989, was a versatile player from Heart of Midlothian, Mike Galloway. This was followed shortly afterwards by the signing of London-born Paul Elliott, a towering central defender bought from Pisa in early July for £600,000 to replace Mick McCarthy, who had left for Olympique Lyon at the end of his contract.

The signings continued and took on an even more cosmopolitan hue: Dariusz Dziekanowski, a Polish international striker from Legia Warsaw for £500,000 within a fortnight of the Elliott signing. The purchase of another striker suggested that the manager was already harbouring doubts about the effectiveness of Tommy Coyne, signed just four months previously for a similar fee. Some months later, the Pole was joined by a compatriot in the person of the highly competent, if somewhat self-effacing full-back Dariusz Wdowczyk, also from Legia, for £400,000.

McNeill claims that he bought the continental players only because the Board denied him the money to obtain the top-flight British performers that he really wanted: 'I had to go "down market" a bit, since it was virtually impossible at the time to attract the really top-class players in view of Scottish football's poor, small-time image abroad, and Celtic's limited budget.'

Dziekanowski, a crowd-pleaser in the mould of a Tully or a Nicholas, produced an extraordinary solo performance in the European Cup-Winners' Cup tie against Partizan Belgrade at Parkhead on 27 September 1989. Down only by 1–2 from the first leg in Yugoslavia, Celtic looked set to advance in the competition when Dziekanowski, in a display which rekindled memories of Jimmy Johnstone against the more famous Belgrade side (Red Star) 21 years earlier, embarked on a one-man crusade against the Yugoslavs, netting four goals and fashioning another for Walker with a precision cross after taking three defenders out of the play. However, Celtic (winners by 5–4) somehow contrived to end up eliminated, victims of the away-goals rule after a series of naïve defensive lapses at almost regular intervals; the fourth, decisive goal for Partizan came heartbreakingly late after a breakaway in the 89th minute.

Sadly, the impact of the talented striker would prove to be short-lived. During his stay in Glasgow the Polish international, who amassed 70 caps for his country, appeared to exhibit the self-destructive tendencies more readily associated with Scottish players such as Jimmy Johnstone or Jim Baxter. Graham Spiers, writing in *Scotland on Sunday*, looked back on Dziekanowski as 'a dashing Pole of seriously handsome looks and fantastic skills' for whom 'a quiet night in was a prospect of intolerable anguish . . . dance halls, drink and women made for him a cocktail he couldn't handle.' (21 November 1993)

The other Polish international, Dariusz Wdowczyk, was entirely different in temperament. Although a defender, his ball-control and skill shone through. However, the full-back was to play for five years at Parkhead without using his impressive skills to the full; for some reason, he appeared content to play his own position competently without feeling the need – or being encouraged – to influence play in other areas of the field. A particular regret was the fact that his dead-ball capabilities were never fully exploited by his various managers at Celtic Park.

A neurosis of sorts soon descended at Parkhead as Rangers began to exercise an iron grip on the championship by 'spending big and buying quality'. Already installed as red-hot favourites to retain the title, Rangers had strengthened their squad by buying Maurice Johnston from Nantes and Trevor Steven from Everton. Rangers' financial muscle was leaving Celtic more and more ill-equipped to cope with the Ibrox surge, a situation feared and resented (envied, even) at Parkhead.

Soon, a floundering Celtic were struggling in the wake of their greatest rivals, unable to string together a number of victories at crucial phases in the championship. The result was mediocrity, and the bare bones of the statistics bear the most telling witness: a mid-table finish in the league with a mere 34 points garnered from 36 matches; more games lost (12) than won (10); only 37 goals scored and the same number conceded; and in 15 of the 36 matches Celtic failed to score.

Undercurrents of internal tension flared up early in the season during a 1–0 defeat by Aberdeen in the Skol Cup semi-final at Hampden Park on 20 September 1989. Billy McNeill decided to substitute Joe Miller midway through the second half, although the player himself had replaced Steve Fulton only at the interval. Miller, obviously disgusted, came close to throwing his jersey into the dugout in his rage. Later, the player accused his manager of making him a scapegoat and complained of McNeill 'making his life a misery by playing him out of position'.

Miller was one of four players who sought transfers during the first six months of the season. Among them was Roy Aitken, whose departure for Newcastle United in January 1990 for £500,000 created a leadership void which has not been filled adequately to this day. This transfer came as a shock: the manager referred obliquely to 'influences outside this club' as the reason for his captain's insistence on leaving, while the player added to the mystery by citing criticism from members of the media, and 'referees who pick on me'. A later newspaper profile on the player suggested that another reason was Aitken's growing belief that 'those who were there longest were being singled out for abuse if things went wrong'. These words remain surprising, coming as they do from a man who had appeared to be a permanent fixture at Celtic Park.

Another great loss, in December 1989, was Tommy Burns; aggrieved at being denied – prematurely, in his opinion – the opportunity to exercise his craft in a more influential, deep-lying (and less stamina-sapping) role in midfield. He left for Kilmarnock where, as player-manager, he led the Ayrshire side to promotion, and then to survival in the Premier Division.

Celtic's last chance at qualifying for European competition lay in the Scottish Cup, but that ended in the most unbearable of failures. Undoubtedly, the highlight of the campaign was the dramatic manner in which Celtic eliminated Rangers in the first meeting of the Old Firm in the early rounds of the competition since 1970. Rangers, of course, were favourites despite having to play at Parkhead, but the crowd of 52,565 on 25 February 1990 provided a suitable backdrop and accompaniment to another frenzied clash between the great rivals. Celtic's midfield gradually took control with an impressive display of industry and purpose; shortly before half-time Tommy Coyne, largely written off as a striker by management and supporters alike, slid in to bundle the ball into the net after Woods could only partially divert a cross-shot from Joe Miller. Throughout the second half Celtic stood firm against the threat of a Rangers comeback, Paul Elliott and Derek Whyte stonewalling the much-vaunted Rangers strikers McCoist and Johnston.

Unfortunately, Celtic could not reproduce that same brand of inspiration in the final itself on 12 May against Aberdeen at Hampden Park. Many in the crowd of 60,493 watching the tactical stalemate could sense long before the whistle that this was a final heading for extra-time and the first penalty shoot-out in Scottish Cup history. The quality and contribution of two such wholehearted players as the recently departed Aitken and Burns were badly missed by a Celtic side singularly bereft of inspiration, self-belief and invention. Aberdeen duly won the shoot-out at the sudden-death stage by a 9–8 margin after their goalkeeper Theo Snelders dived to his left to tip Anton Rogan's well-struck shot around the post. After giving up only one goal in their 570 minutes in the competition (at Forfar after only four minutes at the first hurdle), Celtic had failed to land the Scottish Cup, falling short of winning the trophy for the third time in a row.

It had not gone unnoticed that Celtic's leading goalscorer, Dariusz Dziekanowski with 19 goals in all competitions, visibly displayed a reluctance to take part in the tense shoot-out, although he converted his penalty-kick with no apparent difficulty. His days at Parkhead were numbered, but there were persistent rumours that a similar fate was waiting for the manager. By his own admission, Billy McNeill had alienated members of his squad by stinging public criticism in a newspaper on the eve of the semi-final of the Scottish Cup against first-division Clydebank. Despite the tough talking on that occasion – the newspaper headline labelled the players as 'duffers' – the action backfired motivationally as Celtic scrambled to an unconvincing 2–0 win. The locking of the dressing-room door after similar poor performances had become a distressing feature of the post-match rituals.

In addition, McNeill's normally sure touch in the transfer market would now desert him at a time when he was under pressure from the Board. In the 1990 close season he spent slightly more than £2 million on three players, and questions were soon being asked about the manager's judgement of two of them. An old favourite, Charlie Nicholas, was purchased from Aberdeen at a cost of £450,000, although many felt he was now well past his best and incapable of lasting the full 90 minutes; Martin Hayes, a midfielder, came from Arsenal for £650,000, but his lack of pace (and a later serious injury) resulted in his making only ten appearances for the club before being given a free transfer 18 months later.

The other signing of that summer was much more successful, although the player did require a lengthy period of adjustment. Midfielder John Collins arrived from Hibernian, burdened with an expensive price-tag as Celtic's first million-pound signing.

Things took an ominous turn for Billy McNeill after Celtic made another indifferent start to a league season, one which had been prefaced by a clear warning from the Board that the manager's close-season purchases had to produce tangible success.

Some months earlier, in May of that year, Brian Dempsey and Michael Kelly had been co-opted on to the Board in a much-needed move to project Celtic as an ambitious, forward-thinking club preparing for the 21st century. At the time, the idea was hailed by both media and supporters alike as a 'dream-ticket'. Michael Kelly, a grandson of Celtic's first captain and the nephew of Sir Robert Kelly, had first come to prominence as a high-profile Lord Provost of Glasgow who had been given much of the credit for the success of the city's 'Glasgow's Miles Better' campaign of the 1980s. Brian Dempsey, the son of a former Labour MP, had earned a reputation as an entrepreneur and property developer. Together and as individuals they appeared to be valuable additions to a Board in need of reinvigoration.

Within the space of a few months, however, relations between the pair had cooled, and it appeared to some observers that, despite the denials, their differences were deeply personal and visceral. The issue that would open up an ultimately unbridgeable split between the two – and which would involve every member of the Board – was Dempsey's persistent advocacy of a plan to have a new stadium built at Robroyston in the north-east area of the city.

The Taylor Report, drafted in the wake of the 1989 Hillsborough Disaster, and UEFA rulings had made all-seated accommodation imperative for major clubs by the mid-1990s. Celtic, as an organisation, had dragged its feet for decades on stadium improvement. Nevertheless, certain members of the Board harboured doubts about the viability of Dempsey's scheme, considering it too speculative. Two, at least, felt they detected a conflict of interest in Dempsey's proposal.

It is not difficult to understand why the scions of families which had run Celtic for much of its history, namely Michael Kelly and Christopher White, described as 'strange partners, [but] both are driven by ambition and need each other' in the *Evening Times* of 27 March 1992, would be deeply suspicious about the long-term ambitions of an outsider, a man whose forthright approach barely concealed his impatience with their continuing antagonism to his vision of Celtic's future. Dempsey, indeed, was so appalled at what he perceived as resistance to change and a lack of dynamism that he reputedly told one of the other directors during a meeting months after his removal, 'I am not your enemy. The truth is your enemy.'

Matters came to a head at the club's AGM on Friday, 26 October, at Celtic Park; after the directors had dined together at the stadium's Walfrid Restaurant, Kelly informed Dempsey that he and Chris White would be opposing his ratification as a director. Prior to the AGM, they had clandestinely mustered enough share-vote power to do so. The success of their gambit removed Dempsey from a position on the Board, but it plunged the club into civil war, a bitter strife which lasted more than three years. The opening salvo in that conflict – and the ensuing turmoil – may have had an adverse psychological effect on the players as they were preparing for the Skol (League) Cup final against Rangers only two days later on Sunday, 28 October.

In that final, after a first half in which Celtic had played the better football without exploiting that superiority, Paul Elliott at last appeared to have tipped the match in Celtic's favour in 52 minutes when he stooped low to head a wayward shot from Wdowczyk past a startled Woods in Rangers' goal. Surprisingly, at that relatively early stage, Celtic opted for a defensive strategy by bringing on full-back Chris Morris for Joe Miller, who was admittedly out of touch. Rangers seized the initiative and equalised 13 minutes later through Walters. Celtic survived into extra-time thanks only to two splendid point-blank saves by Pat Bonner, but in the early minutes of the extra period Dziekanowski squandered an opportunity to put Celtic in front once again when he shot weakly at Woods after being put clear through.

Shortly afterwards, Celtic paid for the striker's miss; hesitancy involving Morris and Bonner in defence allowed Richard Gough, a central defender noted as a menace at set-pieces, to steal round the back and nudge a long free-kick past the advancing Bonner. In Glasgow terms, the result was 'a real scunner' for the Celtic fans in the crowd of 62,817, a defeat symbolised by the sight of Paul McStay, the captain, sinking to his knees in mute despair at the final whistle.

For Billy McNeill it was another body-blow to his hopes of prolonging his tenure as manager particularly in view of the directors' stated expectations of success. After that Skol Cup final Celtic's season was falling into a tailspin. The miserable start to the league campaign, in which the club won only three matches out of the first ten, allowed Rangers to move ahead of Celtic in the table by six points after a 2–1 win at Parkhead on 25 November. Celtic Park no longer held the terrors for the Light Blues that it had for much of the existence of the Premier League. A depressing series of six fixtures without a win around the turn of the year left Celtic trailing 15 points behind Rangers, with all hope for a challenge in the championship abandoned. The more statistically minded pointed out that, throughout the period bracketed by the two New Year defeats which Rangers inflicted in 1990 and 1991, Celtic's league form had been more in line with a side threatened by relegation. In 36 matches – the equivalent of a full Premier League season – Celtic had won 8, drawn 12, and lost 16.

Kevin McCarra, writing in *Scotland on Sunday*, was already reporting that the club was buzzing with rumours of Billy McNeill's imminent sacking. He noted reasonably enough that 'if he is to be judged solely on the displays of his side since the double victory of 1988, he could scarcely expect to survive'. (16 December 1990)

McNeill's fate was almost certainly sealed by a 2–0 defeat at Ibrox on 2 January 1991. After a performance so ineffectual that Celtic gained their first corner-kick only in the last minute or so, James Traynor, writing in the *Glasgow Herald*, was scathing in his match report: 'Celtic have become a depressing sight. They are disjointed, uninspired and short on genuine talent. Gone are the days when they played this game in the most thrilling of attacking styles and, unless better players arrive, Celtic will never recapture old glories.' He ended his report with a blunt warning: 'To be so many points away from the top end of the league is an affront to the supporters, and if they start deserting, Celtic will be left with absolutely nothing. The club has reached a critical point in its history; if the right moves are not made soon, Celtic will be finished as a force. The great sadness, of course, is that few believe that the people running the club possess the necessary foresight and acumen to reverse the downward spiral.' (3 January 1991)

Shortly afterwards those directors gathered in an atmosphere of crisis – the recurring mood over the next three years – for a secret meeting at the SFA offices. Unfortunately, this mood was to recur regularly over the next three years. Given the club's hereditary suspicion that an anti-Celtic mentality lurked behind those closed doors at the SFA, it was a most ironic choice of venue, but the directors felt the need for strict security in view of the increasing press speculation about the manager's future. At the meeting they took a decision in principle to dispense with McNeill's services, subject to an unexpected and significant revival of fortune on the field.

That change of luck duly materialised soon afterwards with an impressive run of 11 matches without defeat, capped by two home victories over the arch-tormentors, Rangers, on successive Sundays in March 1991. The more dramatic and controversial of these triumphs took place on St Patrick's Day when Celtic seemed to take out much of their pent-up frustration on the visitors with a vigorous and skilful performance in a Scottish Cup tie. At half-time they were leading deservedly by 2–0: Gerry Creaney had beautifully volleyed Tommy Coyne's headed flick past Woods, and Dariusz Wdowczyk took full advantage to utilise his under-exploited dead-ball skills with a long-range free-kick deflected by Hurlock past his own keeper.

The second half exploded into mayhem. Peter Grant was sent off by the referee, Andrew Waddell of Edinburgh, shortly after the restart for committing his second bookable offence within a minute, the latter time for encroaching at a Rangers' free-kick. The Ibrox men squandered their numerical advantage through ill-disciplined play which resulted in Hurlock, Walters and Hateley being ordered off by the referee for violent play. Celtic went on to coast to victory before 52,286 spectators, most of whom were ecstatic throughout the second half. A week later, Celtic temporarily halted Rangers' advance towards a third successive league title with an emphatic victory at Parkhead, this time by 3–0. Another Rangers player, Scott Nisbet, further tarnished his club's name by being sent off, and this latest embarrassment helped to hasten the departure of his manager, Graeme Souness, to Liverpool out of disillusionment with the Scottish football scene. Only a few weeks earlier a shamefaced Souness had apologised on behalf of his team for their lack of discipline in the Parkhead cup-tie: 'I never thought we were capable of such a performance.'

Unfortunately, this double victory was in the nature of a last hurrah for Billy McNeill; Celtic crashed out of the Scottish Cup in a semi-final replay with Motherwell. Twice Celtic led and appeared to be comfortably in control of the situation before going down 4–2.

The only thing left to play for was a place in Europe, a target almost overlooked in the public drama concerning the future of Billy McNeill as manager of Celtic. By this time, McNeill suspected an orchestrated campaign to remove him in the form of persistent references in the press to the possibility of the likes of Lou Macari or Kenny Dalglish taking over at Parkhead. Much credit is due to the manager for remaining focused on the immediate task of winning a place in the UEFA Cup, a feat accomplished with a run of four successive wins in concluding the league schedule.

It was far from a routine matter, though, because on the last day of the season, 11 May 1991, St Johnstone took the lead in only 20 seconds at Perth but Celtic fought back to equalise; after falling behind again, they levelled things in 60 minutes. The issue was settled in Celtic's favour ten minutes from time when Tommy Coyne converted a penalty to seal a 3–2 victory; it was the first penalty awarded Celtic in a league fixture since 2 December 1989, a gap of 55 matches.

All this came too late to save Billy McNeill's job: his side had finished well behind Rangers in the championship for the third successive season, had lost the Skol Cup final in extra-time to Rangers, and had been beaten in a Scottish Cup semi-final replay by Motherwell, the ultimate winners of the tournament. It was not quite good enough.

McNeill himself had found it increasingly difficult to accept that the wearers of the green and white in the early 1990s represented the same club which had conquered Europe with such flair in 1967. At Lisbon the European Cup had been won by a home-grown side but such was the current dearth of natural talent in Scotland that his squads had to be bolstered by imports from England and further afield.

McNeill found himself increasingly out of touch with the outlook of too many of the modern players. He became more and more dismissive of the inclination to put forward outside pressures as an excuse for a lacklustre performance; he was scathing about the possible effect of distractions such as the much-publicised boardroom politics, being quoted as saying: 'All I know is that, when I was playing, if someone had told me my house was on fire, I'd go and put it out – but not until the game was over.'

That exaggeration hints at the difficulties being posed by a growing generation gap between the manager and his players. He would not have reacted sympathetically to the reported melodramatic complaint of one player: 'People are starting to laugh at us in the street, and it hurts.' As one of McNeill's former team-mates reflected, anonymously: 'He began to think that the modern game had changed out of all recognition, and he seemed to be at his happiest with old friends reliving old times . . . We were on £60 a week basic wage, and although there were bonuses, it was part of the club's tradition you were never told the size of them until after you had won something . . . I remember the night we played [Inter] Milan in the semi-final of the European Cup and we lost on penalties. There were over 80,000 in the ground, but we never received a penny over our basic wage. Nowadays, very average players are making ten times that amount, and I think he found it hard to come to terms with that.'

McNeill had been finding it impossible to accept another aspect of the modern game, namely the undercutting of managerial authority. The colleague quoted above spoke with some understanding of the changing situation: 'None of us ever had agents or advisers and, of course, there was no freedom of contract. With Stein, you did as you were told. He was a complete autocrat. We didn't much like the discipline he demanded, but we knew it won matches. I don't think today's kids see it that way.' (*Mail on Sunday*. 26 May 1991)

Jason Tomas, writing in the *Sunday Times* of 13 January 1991, felt that the manager had contributed to Celtic's decline by 'sacrificing quantity for quality' in his spending of £7 million in the transfer market after his return to Parkhead in 1987 and the journalist considered that only McAvennie, Elliott, Walker and Stark had represented good value for money. Tomas contended that McNeill's criticism of the squad had soured his relationship with them, and that he had forfeited the loyalty of some key players as a result.

McNeill himself felt that his authority had been undermined by the Board's appointment in December 1990 of a chief executive, Terry Cassidy, a 'troubleshooter' whose previous employment was described by Ian Archer as including stints as 'a professional footballer, nightclub bouncer and managing director of a newspaper chain'. Although he would be credited later, somewhat contentiously, by that same journalist with putting Celtic on a sounder footing in terms of commercial organisation, Cassidy caused offence by an abrasive manner which antagonised some members of the press as well as supporters' groups, sponsors, team managers and eventually his employers, whose patience and good will had been exhausted by the time he was sacked in October 1992. Billy McNeill takes an even more sinister view of Cassidy's appointment, accusing him of 'riding roughshod over the club's traditions' by 'battering people's emotions and feelings for Celtic'.

In that same newspaper article, McNeill recalls how Cassidy would bring together all the heads of department – financial, ticket-sales, catering and so on – and expect the team manager to talk about his plans with them: 'There was no way I was going to discuss the team in public, knowing that the whole world would eventually know about it. There were leaked documents and a whispering campaign. But I knew what was going on. In fact, I took Cassidy aside one day and told him that I knew he talked to certain pressmen. I told him if he had something to say, he should do so to my face.' (*The Sun*: 21 June 1994)

McNeill had sought clarification of his position from his employers in mid-April 1991 without any response. However, he would soon find hints in a tabloid newspaper which published a leaked document on the morning of the critical final league match at Perth against St Johnstone. The memo, drawn up by Terry Cassidy, detailed options for handling a change of manager with the maximum 'damage limitation'. Despite investigations at Parkhead, the identity of the mole would remain a mystery. The rerouting of internal documents at Parkhead was scarcely a surprise; one journalist claimed that 'Celtic had so many leaks that, if it were a ship, it would be renamed the *Titanic*'.

Eleven days later, Billy McNeill was on his way out of Parkhead for the second time, his departure such an open secret by then that one onlooker, observing the press and the knots of supporters who had gathered, indulged in some gallows humour by commenting that he 'half-expected to see a guillotine erected in the forecourt'.

McNeill emerged from his final meeting with the Board not only generously compensated but also, as he later confessed, with 'an incredible sense of relief that all the lies and back-stabbing were over'. Virtually every managerial career ends in dismissal, and that is a fact of football life. Billy McNeill would take some comfort in his record of eight triumphs in major competitions during his combined tenure of nine seasons. He could walk away with his dignity fully intact, telling the waiting well-wishers: 'You support the best team in the world, and you are the best supporters in the world: so, carry on supporting them, because they need you.'

Inside, the club's chairman Jack McGinn was about to hold a press conference to spell out the Board's rationale for the 'harsh and painful decision' that they felt deep down had been unavoidable; he cited the lack of natural progression from the success of 1988 and 1989, a failure that had been reflected in Celtic's winning only 27 out of 72 league matches in the past two barren seasons. The chairman was the same man who had welcomed McNeill back to Parkhead four years earlier as 'the Celtic prodigal – the only man to manage this great club . . .'

Still smarting from the hostile reaction to McNeill's sacking, and much more aware of the poor image it was projecting on several fronts, the Board took some time to choose a new manager. By any standards, the appointment of Liam Brady on 19 June 1991 was a bold and innovative one, widely approved by the supporters at the time. Paradoxically, it represented both a break with the parochial policy of employing former players in the role and a considerable gamble, since the 35-year-old Irishman had no previous experience as a manager. His playing career only recently over, Brady at the time was a partner in a Dublin-based sports agency which had Pat Bonner, among others, as a client. But he had been missing the day-to-day involvement in football and had been sufficiently intrigued after a phone call from Phil Gordon, a sportswriter for Glasgow's *Evening Times*, to apply for the vacant position at Parkhead. Brady's Dublin background had given him an affinity with Celtic, prompting him as a boy to seek the autographs of the Lisbon Lions when they visited his native city in 1968 to play a friendly against Shamrock Rovers. Almost two decades later, when he was at the tail-end of his career in Italy with Ascoli, David Hay had tried to sign him for Celtic, only to learn that Brady had given his word to join West Ham United. He had exhibited a reluctance to enter management, apparently holding some reservations as to whether his personality cut him out for such a post; essentially, Brady was, and remains, a private and reticent person, but he possessed sufficient ambition and confidence to succumb to the temptation, as he later told one journalist: 'There are jobs – and jobs. Normally you would expect to enter management at the very bottom, and work your way up. With Celtic, I'm starting at as big a club as you can find.' Reportedly, he was also starting at double Billy McNeill's salary, and as the first Celtic manager to be offered a contract.

Liam Brady was universally respected in football, with a reputation as a thorough professional who had graced the major stadia of England and Italy as a player with such world-famous clubs as Arsenal, Juventus and Internazionale. His illustrious career as a highly creative midfielder had brought him a record 72 caps for his country. A cosmopolitan figure, articulate in three languages (English, Italian and Gaelic), his intelligence shone through when he was introduced at a press conference at Celtic Park on 21 June 1991. Speaking below the huge portrait of Jock Stein which has become the mandatory setting for photographing the great man's successors, he acknowledged that he faced a daunting prospect in taking over a club like Celtic. He admitted feeling 'a bit scared' when he became aware of the massive publicity surrounding the announcement, and after watching a video charting Celtic's history.

He felt confident, however, that the club could become more successful immediately, but unwittingly offered himself as a hostage to fortune by adding: 'Celtic should be in Europe every year, and win at least one domestic trophy every season.' Rightly believing that the manner of victory, and not just victory for its own sake, was in keeping with Celtic's traditions, he outlined his philosophy of the game: 'My playing ethic is quite simple – I like a skilful passing game, one where the people watching are going to be entertained.'

His baptism into Scottish football came at Tannadice on the opening day of the season. Twice Celtic surrendered a two-goal lead, but still ended up winners by 4–3 over Dundee United, with John Collins netting a spectacular decisive goal just before the end. At the press conference afterwards he asked the journalists: 'Surely not every Premier Division match is like that?'

Already, too, the novice manager had found himself embroiled in the politics of Parkhead, as Gerry McNee later pointed out in his column for the *Sunday Mail*. The journalist recalled how Brady had decided to tell the Board before his first season in charge had even got under way that they had to choose between him and Terry Cassidy. The resignation threat stemmed from a breakdown in their relationship during Celtic's pre-season tour in Ireland, allegedly as an outcome of remarks made by the chief executive to journalists: 'A major rift had developed between the two, but Brady backed out at the last moment and lived to regret it. He was never as strong again.' (21 November 1993)

A few weeks later, he would come face-to-face with the hype that surrounds the doings of Celtic (and Rangers), when his first chance of a trophy disappeared as a consequence of a defeat in the quarter-final of the Skol Cup at Airdrie; Celtic lost in a penalty shoot-out (2–4) following a goalless draw after extra-time. Brady conceded that Celtic's performance had been dreadful, but he drew unflattering headlines by stating that the team had nothing to be ashamed of, citing several factors in mitigation: Airdrie, after all, were another Premier Division club, a hard, physical side difficult to beat on their tight ground at Broomfield, and they had eliminated Aberdeen at Pittodrie in the previous round. Listening to the manager's statement, one journalist murmured: 'Somebody should tell him that Celtic just don't lose cup-ties to Airdrie.'

The reaction in the newspapers must have proved disconcerting to a manager still finding it difficult to adjust to a new career, judging by his observation to an interviewer more than a year later: 'People ask me what time I want the team coach, which hotel we are staying in – the sort of decision I never realised had to be made. As a player, everything is done for you.'

In fact, Liam Brady found that he could not get away from his job in a city like Glasgow, where the intensity of feeling and media coverage surrounding the Old Firm caused him to remark after he left Celtic: 'You have to be a certain type of animal to succeed. It took me at least a year to understand it.' A number of pressmen would attribute that misunderstanding to a lack of rapport with them during Brady's tenure. Equally disturbing, although he would become philosophical about it, was his realisation that there was an unpleasant edge to the rivalry, as he told the visiting London journalist Hunter Davies: 'I was told when I joined about Celtic's paranoia. Now, I know it's true. We are hard done by. Religiously and politically, there are people against us. I meet people who hate me, just because I'm the manager of Celtic. I've had to grow mentally stronger.' (*The Independent*: 20 October 1992)

Liam Brady was already finding himself under scrutiny before the defeat at Airdrie. Questions had been asked about his forays into the transfer market, a crucial aspect of any manager's job – and which he was later honest enough to admit proved to be his Achilles heel. Perhaps his most significant failure was Tony Cascarino, a tall, lumbering striker whose lack of pace and skill made him the butt of terracing wit; one caustic comment from the Jungle comes to mind: 'The last man I saw running like that was Long John Silver.' Brady's first signing, and reputedly the best-rewarded player in Celtic's history up to that time with a signing-on fee of £250,000 and a basic wage of £3,000 per week when he came to the club from Aston Villa for £1.1 million in July 1991, Cascarino was off-loaded to Chelsea after only seven months in a swap for Tom Boyd, an international full-back with attacking flair. The Irishman had scored only four goals in 30 appearances, taking until his 11th competitive match to score his first.

Eyebrows were also raised at the acquisition in August 1991 of Gary Gillespie from Liverpool for £950,000 to replace Paul Elliott, who had joined Chelsea the previous month for £1.4 million. Unlike the rugged Elliott in build and manner, Gillespie was described as 'a footballing centre-half'. However, he arrived with such a reputation for being injury-prone that one newspaper critic dubbed him 'a porcelain pivot'. His tendency to 'stand off' opponents rather than challenge them was a disturbing feature of his performance against Mark Hateley of Rangers who was allowed to wreak havoc on the defence during his side's comfortable 2–0 win at Celtic Park on 31 August 1991, a shattering blow to the home side's morale.

Celtic's first venture in Europe under Liam Brady ended in disappointment tinged with the realisation that the club was still ineffectual even in confrontation with moderate opposition in the UEFA Cup. After disposing of Germinal Ekeren by winning 2–0 at Parkhead and gaining a comfortable 1–1 draw in Belgium, Celtic travelled to Switzerland to face Neuchatel Xamax on 22 October in the second round. It was scarcely the most daunting of assignments, but Celtic gave an utterly naïve tactical performance, one pock-marked by slovenly defending, and were humiliated by a scoreline of 5–1, a result which stands as the worst in the club's three decades of participation in Europe. In the second leg two weeks later, Celtic salvaged some self-respect with a 1–0 result on a rain-soaked Parkhead, but further progress in the competition was beyond them. Ominously, Liam Brady already appeared to be a manager under siege. After the shambles in Switzerland, Ian Archer had written in the *Mail on Sunday* on 27 October 1991: 'To find such a civilised and urbane man as Brady caught in the dark and muddy waters of Glasgow football invites only sympathy and a hope that he will find the necessary solutions.'

The manager moved quickly to shore up that leaky defence by signing Tony Mowbray, a craggy, no-nonsense central defender, from Middlesbrough for £1 million. Mowbray was injured in only his second match for Celtic (against Hearts at Tynecastle on 16 November); the injury affected him for much of the season, and proved troublesome thereafter. Brady could only ponder on his ill-luck in buying a player, notably injury-free throughout a decade in English football, and watch him struggle to regain full fitness at Parkhead. The organisational and leadership qualities that Mowbray had shown signs of bringing to his area of the pitch were badly missed, as Celtic continued to drop points and concede goals. However, the supporters could draw satisfaction from the fact that Brady was intent on fashioning a side that put a premium on entertainment, a reflection of the manager's philosophy. He put it succinctly: 'Too often the enjoyment of spectators seems to come a poor second to a fear of failure.'

Celtic, striving to get back into contention in the league race, were struck two devastating blows in successive fixtures at Parkhead. Rangers visited the ground on 1 January 1992 and inflicted a 3–1 defeat on Celtic, the damage being done late on when Hateley converted a penalty awarded after Celtic's goalkeeper Marshall had unaccountably downed McCoist although the striker appeared to have lost control of the ball; in the last minute, with Celtic pressing hard, Brown sealed Rangers' victory with a trundling shot which deceived the goalkeeper at the far post. Celtic could claim that their rhythm had been disrupted shortly after half-time when

Paul McStay had to leave the field for attention to a facial injury with the score level at 1–1. Little excuse could be offered three days later, however, when Hearts – the unlikely leaders in the table – stole two points at Parkhead by taking control of the match following another injury to Mowbray. Mike Galloway, his replacement in central defence, was ordered off early in the second half for continuing his protests to the referee after a decision had correctly gone against him.

Celtic were now hopelessly out of contention, 13 points off the pace in the championship, but the manager did not win any friends in the boardroom by candidly admitting this fact in public. His task now would be to build for the future, and to concentrate on the Scottish Cup, so often the feather-bed to catch a falling Celtic. It was a better time for the manager: his side embarked on a long, undefeated run in the league, a sequence of 16 matches which included a comprehensive 2–0 victory at Ibrox on 21 March when Celtic gave a fluid, controlled display capped by precision finishing. In the Scottish Cup progress was being made equally impressively in three home matches: Montrose (6–0), Dundee United (2–1) and Morton (3–0).

But Celtic's season virtually ended on 31 March 1992 with a defeat in the semi-final of the Scottish Cup on a wind-swept, rain-lashed Hampden Park under the most bitterly disappointing of circumstances. Naturally, the victors were Rangers, so often Brady's nemesis, who qualified for the final through a goal by McCoist only a minute before half-time. Celtic had every advantage: Hateley, the man most feared by the supporters, was absent through injury; and Rangers were reduced to ten men after only seven minutes when the full-back Robertson was dismissed for a blatant body-check on Joe Miller, who had tormented him in the league match at Ibrox ten days earlier.

Celtic – and Brady, of course – were unfairly castigated by their fans and in the press for not taking advantage of their territorial supremacy. In truth, Celtic were desperately unlucky, especially in a second half which they dominated: a shot from Galloway thudded against the base of the post, another wind-assisted drive from Paul McStay crashed against the crossbar with Goram stranded, a header from Tommy Coyne bounced against the bar . . . and in the dying minutes the referee, Mr Waddell of Edinburgh, denied a confident Celtic claim for a penalty when Brown tripped John Collins inside the box. Victory in that match might well have transformed the whole situation for both manager and club had Celtic qualified for the final against Airdrie – as they should have done.

At the end of his first season in charge Brady could conclude that the club had not enjoyed much luck. His reasoning would have been valid: Celtic produced some glorious football, inspired by Paul McStay in midfield, a player recently recovered from injury but giving his best displays in what many people assumed would be his last season at Celtic Park after his contract expired; the emphasis was on fast, exciting and sometimes breathtaking football with a trio of strikers leading the way. Tommy Coyne, always underrated, scored 15 league goals; Gerry Creaney, a capable young finisher with head and foot, scored 14; and Charlie Nicholas ended up as leading scorer with 21; John Collins added to the goalscoring threat with a useful 11 from midfield. The manager felt, rightly, that a barren season was a scurvy reward for the team's crowd-pleasing passing game, a style he was convinced that the support had appreciated.

Unfortunately, some chilling attendance statistics suggest a certain disenchantment on the part of the supporters. Following the reversal in the Scottish Cup, a paltry 13,236 had turned up on 11 April for the fixture against St Johnstone (won by 3–2), and an even smaller crowd of 12,649 was present to see Dunfermline beaten 2–0 two weeks later. The last home league attendance against Hibernian on 2 May 1992 climbed to a more acceptable 25,527 but many had turned up to witness Paul McStay's anticipated farewell appearance – and in the hope of seeing Celtic gain a European place for the following season. In fact, the home side lost that match 2–1, ending a prolonged undefeated run and finished in third place in the league. Later on, however, Scotland was awarded an extra berth in the UEFA Cup as a result of political uncertainty in the Balkans – and Celtic did get to participate in the competition.

The truth was that Celtic fans were becoming jaundiced by the club remaining in the shadow of Rangers: league winners for the past four seasons; winners of the Scottish Cup in 1991–92, a club enjoying season-ticket sales of more than 30,000, and with a handsome up-to-date stadium already in place. The contrast between the clubs had become even more graphically illustrated a few weeks earlier when the Celtic Board had unveiled their blueprint to build a new stadium at Cambuslang. That announcement – greeted with widespread scepticism – came in the wake of a highly public split in the boardroom. As the old régime lumbered headlong towards self-destruction, two directors, Tom Grant and James Farrell, were threatened with removal by some of their colleagues in the midst of a bitter power struggle.

In the close season Brady, although admitting that Celtic could not compete with Rangers in the transfer market, made further moves to strengthen the squad. Celtic's financial situation had been eased by the removal of a succession of fringe players who had been languishing in the reserves: John Hewitt to St Mirren, Anton Rogan to Sunderland, Dariusz Dziekanowski to Bristol City, Martin Hayes (given a free transfer) and

Andy Walker, off to Bolton Wanderers. The last-named departed after experiencing a touch of the manager's steel, Brady having demoted the striker to the youth team where he played at such remote football outposts as Stranraer and Dumfries. The final indignity came when, as Walker recalls, he was kept sitting on the bench at Stenhousemuir in a reserve fixture and then told by Brady to warm up with only two minutes to play. His outright refusal meant his days were numbered . . .

A transfer spree in August 1992 brought three players to Parkhead who would experience mixed fortunes with Celtic. Stuart Slater, fast and a skilful dribbler, came from West Ham United, where he had played alongside his new manager, for a record fee for Celtic of £1.7 million; Brady predicted he would prove the type of forward who would 'get supporters up off their seats', but his lack of aggression and penetration, highlighted by only three goals in 55 appearances for Celtic, would mark him as an expensive misfit. Rudi Vata, a versatile Albanian defender from Dinamo Tirana, was signed for £200,000, and Andy Payton came from Middlesbrough in a straight swap for Chris Morris (valued at £600,000). Payton turned out to be a reasonably effective striker, notching 20 goals in 46 appearances for Celtic, before domestic problems forced him to return south.

After an impressive burst at the start of the new season, Celtic – unbeaten in their opening ten matches – eventually shattered. They displayed their now familiar Jekyll-and-Hyde tendencies with a dramatic comeback accomplished by ten men at Falkirk from 4–2 down with 15 minutes left to win by 4–5, and followed that result four days later by surrendering tamely to Aberdeen by 1–0 in the semi-final of the Skol Cup at Hampden Park on 23 September 1992. Rather improbably, Celtic then found reserves of mental toughness and passion (and no little skill) in Europe to overcome a two-goal deficit from the first leg in Germany to eliminate Cologne by winning 3–0 at Parkhead; John Collins, who had dominated the midfield and constantly threatened the German goal, scored the decisive third goal in the closing minutes.

And yet, only a few weeks later, the bookmakers, unprecedentedly early, stopped taking bets on Rangers for the league championship after Celtic had outplayed but could not punish a weakened Ibrox side at Parkhead. In the latter stages Rangers were forced to pull back Hateley into central defence after an injury to Gough; Celtic's own defence had been posted missing when Durrant netted the only goal of the contest in 32 minutes.

The New Year clash at Ibrox on 2 January 1993 produced a similar scoreline, and once again after Celtic had dominated the second-half play. A visibly dismayed Brady emerged from the dressing-room to inform a bemused press corps: 'The team was magnificent; that's the way football should be played – apart from putting the ball in the net.' It may have been an attempt to raise the morale of a squad which had suffered a third successive defeat without scoring a goal. But there could be no denying the obvious fact – that, for all Celtic's neat, attacking play and territorial advantage, Rangers had the hardness and the priceless ability to scramble a victory when not playing well.

That result left Celtic trailing ten points behind Rangers, who had two games in hand. Brady had to concede, honestly but perhaps unwisely, that 'the league season is over for us'. There were still four months of the competition remaining. Worse was to follow. Early in February, Celtic travelled to Falkirk's Brockville Park on Scottish Cup business after struggling to dispose of lowly Clyde through a scrambled Tommy Coyne goal in a replay. Falkirk had never beaten Celtic in a Scottish Cup tie in seven previous attempts, but this time the underdogs won by 2–0. The atmosphere among the Celtic supporters was poisonous.

For the first time in 41 years Celtic had no silverware to compete for at that stage in the season. The supporters' growing frustration was demonstrated by the mere 15,561 who attended the next home fixture in the league, against Partick Thistle, a match which finished in a goalless draw at an eerie Parkhead housing its fourth successive crowd of under 20,000. The statistic becomes even more alarming with the awareness that Celtic needed a home average of 25,000 to break even.

Brady's position as manager was now under active consideration by the Board and it was leaked to the press that the directors had asked him 'to review the whole situation . . . and to come back to us with his plan for the way forward'. The episode, a barely disguised rebuke, perhaps fatally undermined Brady's authority in his shaky relationship with the Board.

An obviously disillusioned squad of players was now left to salvage some measure of dignity and self-respect from the wreckage of the season. The outstanding remaining highlight was the convincing 2–1 defeat of Rangers at Parkhead on 20 March 1993, Celtic's only victory in Old Firm clashes that season. Writing in *The Scotsman* two days later, Hugh Keevins posed a legitimate question: 'Where does the level of commitment go when Liam Brady needs it most?' Perhaps Rangers striker Ally McCoist provided a useful clue to resolving the conundrum by suggesting that Rangers' matches against Celtic were 'really hard, because at the moment it's like facing a wounded animal'. An exasperated Liam Brady would have surely shared this assessment a month later after watching Celtic submit tamely to Hibernian by 3–1 at Easter Road, a miserable display he condemned with a cryptic observation: 'What you saw out there was one team with the right attitude and one team with the wrong one.'

A season which had started so brightly ended with Celtic again in third place in the Premier League, 13 points behind Rangers who seemed to be unstoppable in Scottish football. Indeed, they won the domestic treble that season – and came uncomfortably close to emulating Celtic's European Cup triumph of 1967, the jewel in the Parkhead crown.

All in all, it had been a melancholy season for Celtic supporters, who also had to bid a sentimental farewell to one of the most evocative enclosures in British football, a structure that had resounded for decades to the roars of thousands of fans willing their favourites on to victory on many a famous occasion. The Jungle was converted during the close season into an all-seated area. It said much about the perilous state of Celtic FC in mid-1993 that the 19,316 who turned up on the miserable wet night of 1 June for 'the Jungle's last stand' should number only 120 fewer than the attendance at the final home fixture of the season against Dundee two weeks earlier. However, it was indeed a special occasion, for among his fellow Lisbon Lions donning the Celtic jersey to play in a charity match – a little portlier perhaps was the King of the Jungle himself – one Jimmy Johnstone.

Liam Brady, by contrast, could not allow sentiment to intrude. In response to the Board's concern about the team's playing standards, he decided to reshape his backroom staff for the new season by dispensing with the services of first-team coach Mick Martin, a long-time friend and international colleague, and bringing in Joe Jordan, the former Scotland international striker recently sacked as Hearts' manager, as his assistant in place of Tommy Craig. The latter was put in charge of the recruitment and development of young playing talent, while Frank Connor, dismissed by David Hay as his assistant-manager in February 1986, returned to Parkhead to assume responsibility for the reserve team in place of Bobby Lennox. Bobby's removal from Celtic Park broke the last official link with the Lisbon Lions.

Such restructuring was widely viewed as Brady's belated recognition of the need to instil greater qualities of resilience and determination into his players. The sweeping overhaul prompted chairman Kevin Kelly to hail the new set-up as a measure which 'will see Celtic back at the top of Scottish football, and hopefully Europe as well'. That optimism, apparently, was not shared by his cousin and fellow director Michael Kelly who, after the manager had outlined his proposals at a Board meeting, advocated Brady's dismissal in the private discussion which followed. He did not get a seconder for his motion but, to paraphrase Jock Stein's observation of a struggling fellow manager, 'his jacket was on a shaky nail'.

As the new season (1993–94) loomed, Brady was faced with the popular perception that, such were the financial resources of Rangers and the depth of their playing pool, every other team in the Premier Division was competing only for second place. In July, Rangers had just spent an estimated £4 million, a British record, to purchase Duncan Ferguson, a striker from Dundee United; it was a sum which exceeded the total spent by the rest of the Scottish clubs put together that close season. Celtic's manager limited his spending to more modest parameters by purchasing Pat McGinlay of Hibs for £525,000 (a fee fixed by tribunal) to add drive to the midfield. The deal was financed by selling Joe Miller to Aberdeen for £300,000 and Steve Fulton, a gifted young midfielder who had not realised his potential, to Bolton Wanderers for a similar amount.

Shifting the balance of power in the direction of Parkhead was going to be a Herculean task, the extent of which could only be appreciated by considering that Rangers had displayed a remorseless consistency in the previous five seasons (since Celtic had last won the championship); Rangers had won 136 league games and Celtic only 98, Rangers had lost only 25 and Celtic 51. Unpalatable figures to digest, indeed.

The opening matches in the 1993–94 season did not suggest that Celtic had come up with the solution to a now chronic problem: an apparent inability to kill off opponents after taking the lead, especially in home fixtures. In Celtic's first league match at Parkhead, Hibs stole a point in the dying minutes when Tweed, a central defender, found himself unmarked in Celtic's penalty area following a free-kick; he was allowed time to chest the ball down and then drive it past Bonner for an equaliser in the 1–1 draw. Archie Macpherson suggested that the intervention of a psychiatrist might produce better results, such was Celtic's tendency 'to mystify with their fluctuations of mood, which rages from outright confidence and exhilaration to almost childish nervousness in defence'. (*Sunday Times*. 15 August 1993)

Any such analyst would have been kept busy in the next two months since the dropping of five points out of the eight at stake in the opening four home league matches – at a time when Rangers were struggling – did little to alleviate the introspection now enveloping Parkhead, and the club was plunged further into despair when they were defeated by Rangers in the Skol Cup semi-final on 22 September. Because of reconstruction at Hampden Park the tie was played at Ibrox, Rangers having won ground advantage on the toss of a coin. Things seemed to be moving Celtic's way at last in an Old Firm match when Rangers' Dutch midfielder Huistra was ordered off for striking Tommy Boyd after 50 minutes. But, with Celtic exerting control, Galloway's sluggish reaction during a rare counter-attack by Rangers 15 minutes later allowed Durrant to sweep past him and square the ball across goal for Hateley to steer it past Bonner.

For the second successive cup-tie Rangers had triumphed despite playing for extended periods with ten men, and this latest failure on

Celtic's part only hardened the suspicion that the team had an incurable tendency to 'bottle it', that they lacked the cutting edge and mental toughness to win crunch games. The difference in style between the Old Firm rivals became more evident the longer the match continued: Celtic, pretty but ultimately ineffectual, and Rangers, purposeful and determined and winners.

A disappointed manager reflected on the outcome: 'In the end we weren't going anywhere. We just ran out of ideas.' For his part, Liam Brady was running out of time, and he admitted later that the latest loss to Rangers cost him the support of many fans. Up to that point, he felt he had enjoyed a good relationship with them: 'I was desperate to get results, but unfortunately they didn't come – and they [the fans] got frustrated. It was my responsibility that things didn't happen and it was understandable that they lost patience.' (*Celtic View*: 13 October 1993)

A few days after that defeat by Rangers, Brady was brief and to-the-point when commenting on the 'lack of character' displayed by the Celtic side which had gone down yet again, this time by 1–0 to Hearts at Tynecastle. One reporter said that Brady 'at the finish had looked like a man on Death Row'. The manager still felt he could turn things around, despite the atmosphere of increasing desperation he had detected inside Celtic Park; the side had not got the breaks when it mattered, he claimed, but he remained convinced that things were improving and that his team 'had been playing a lot of good football and doing the right things'.

Others were not so sure. Kevin McCarra, writing in *Scotland on Sunday* on 10 October 1993 about Brady's demise, recalled a conversation which questioned the manager's readiness to immerse himself in the nitty-gritty of motivating a team. The journalist had asked him about Steve Fulton, the talented youngster who had failed to establish himself as a first-team regular, and Brady's brusque reply stuck in his mind: 'How should I know? I'm not a psychologist!' Reticent by nature, Liam Brady consistently refused to make himself readily available; it was understood that only one or two journalists were favoured with his home telephone number.

The sudden transfer of Stuart Slater at the beginning of October was more than the public admission of another expensive failure. The player had come to Celtic for a record sum, but was now leaving for only £750,000, less than half his purchase price. He joined Ipswich Town amid persistent and damaging rumours that Celtic were being forced to sell players to placate the Bank of Scotland.

Some critics of Liam Brady felt that his trading in the transfer market was the source of his downfall; but, in fact, his dealings did not incur a massive deficit. He spent an estimated £5.6 million, and took in £5.25 million – although these are figures which take no account of wages or signing-on bonuses. More pertinent to his eventual fate, perhaps, was that in the latter stages of his time at Parkhead he had been denied the cash to strengthen his squad. Brady had been keen to sign a prolific striker from lowly Southend United, but the directors were reluctant to sanction the move out of concern about the club's financial plight – and reservations about Brady's judgement in the transfer market. The player did move on eventually to Nottingham Forest, and later to Liverpool. His name was Stan Collymore . . .

Matters finally came to a head when Celtic visited Perth on 6 October 1993 and lost 2–1. The defeat meant that Celtic had collected only nine points in ten league matches so far that season; surprisingly, however, the team's mediocrity had left them only four points behind the league leaders, Hibernian.

Brady, however, found this defeat from St Johnstone very hard to accept, especially after learning what had happened at Ibrox. Rangers, overwhelming favourites for the title, had been faltering too since the start of the season, and had gone down to Motherwell that same night. But it was an utterly dejected Liam Brady who sat in the team bus going back to Glasgow and came to the conclusion that it was time for him to go. He could no longer shield the players from the pressures: 'It was getting through to me, and it was getting through to them.'

On the bus, he spoke briefly to Kevin Kelly and on arriving back at Celtic Park, he informed the chairman that he was resigning. He became the first Celtic manager to do so entirely of his own volition.

The less charitable might make much of the fact that, under Liam Brady, Celtic had failed to win even a runners-up position in any major competition, but that would be unfair. His approach to the game had been principled for, throughout his tenure, he had been an advocate of 'the beautiful game', always striving to field teams which represented the best traditions of skill and artistry at a club which, above all others in Scotland at least, has elevated football as an entertainment. Unlucky on the field, he deserved better in terms of tangible rewards, but there was no bitterness exhibited by him on his departure. Indeed, with typical sincerity, he still regards his time at Parkhead as an honour: 'To be allowed to manage a club like that is something special.'

Kevin Kelly, the third member of his family to act as Celtic's chairman, acknowledged rightly that the Irishman had comported himself with great dignity in the managerial post. However, and apparently without any awareness of irony, this representative of a Board which was tacitly admitting for the third time in less than seven years that they had made the wrong choice in manager – and still remained in power themselves – added that Liam Brady had done 'the honourable thing' in resigning . . .

THIRTEEN

Sound and Fury

1993–94

By this time, given the turmoil enveloping the club both on and off the field, the post of Celtic's manager, long regarded as one of the most prestigious in British football, was beginning to be viewed as a poisoned chalice. Liam Brady's successor would be the fifth occupant of the manager's office in little over a decade, a stark contrast with the former perception of the club as a bastion of stability in having only four managers in the first 80 years after the first appointment (Willie Maley) in 1897. The reality of modern football, however, is that no shortage of candidates exists for even the most daunting of managerial remits – although by October 1993 a growing belief suggested that one of Scotland's most famous institutions might be too far gone to be turned around.

Tragic it may have been for Celtic, but farce intruded into the proceedings. Within the space of a few days, in the chaos generated by Brady's departure, Celtic had three 'managers'. After barely a day in charge as caretaker boss, Joe Jordan, Brady's assistant, followed the Irishman out of Parkhead, insisting that he was quitting out of principle, saying, 'I'm no vulture'. His statement did not stop the cynics from claiming that he left immediately upon learning that the Board had no intention of considering him for the position on a permanent basis, and that they had already contacted another club about the 'transfer' of their manager.

Frank Connor, now back at Parkhead in a coaching capacity, took over until the situation resolved itself, and earned an honourable mention for himself in the club's annals by being in charge for an unbeaten four-match spell under difficult circumstances.

It became clear very quickly that Celtic's directors were targeting Lou Macari, Stoke City's manager, as a suitable replacement for Brady. Macari, an ex-Celt, had earned a reputation as a manager who could work wonders at clubs with limited financial and playing resources, notably Swindon Town whom he had taken from the Fourth Division to the brink of the First. He would be an ideal manager for a club as cash-strapped as Celtic, some thought.

Macari took over at Parkhead on 27 October 1993, reportedly despite warnings from such as Alex Ferguson and Kenny Dalglish not to touch the job with a barge-pole in view of Celtic's escalating troubles off the field. He was given the security of a three-year contract, and he brought north with him a three-man backroom staff. Many considered that his appointment represented the last throw of the dice by a beleaguered Board – or 'a way out of Bungleland', as one critic described it. Macari, however, had never hidden his ambition to manage Celtic, and there had been recurring suggestions that the interest was reciprocated by members of the Board. Apparently, being embroiled in 'betting and tax scandals' at Swindon Town had prevented him from succeeding Billy McNeill in the early 1990s, as his own rueful comment suggests: 'The tax man cost me the Celtic job.'

The three-week hiatus between Brady's departure and Macari's arrival prompted some sour comments from unsettled Celtic players which showed that Lou Macari would not be entirely welcomed by his new charges. Some players were openly endorsing Frank Connor, the latest caretaker boss, as the best replacement for Brady. There was an ominous ring to the observations ascribed to two anonymous Celtic players by Hugh Keevins in *The Scotsman* on 20 October 1993: 'Macari played 110 games for Celtic, left the club when he was 22 and he spent the last 20 years talking about his days here,' said one. 'If he was that keen on becoming Celtic's manager, he would have been up here by this time,' said the other.

Frank McAvennie, back at Parkhead after being signed by Liam Brady in December 1992, would admit later to having warned the players in advance of the new manager's arrival about Macari's 'safety-first approach' at West Ham United, where McAvennie had played under him. It did not bode well for a happy dressing-room . . .

The squad did not have long to wait for an opportunity to size up their latest manager and his methods. On the eve of the Old Firm league fixture at Ibrox on 30 October, Macari made it plain that he had no sympathy whatsoever with the widespread feeling that the Celtic players were being affected on the field by the boardroom unrest currently at its height: 'For players even to mention it is an excuse for not doing the business on the park. The punters don't care who runs the club! They want results. I want results, preferably good results.'

For this match, Frank Connor was left in charge of team selection, and evidently produced the right permutation when Brian O'Neil, a young midfielder sent on only two minutes earlier to replace Charlie Nicholas, headed the winning goal in the last minute for a 2–1 victory. The win, accomplished after being a goal down, was celebrated by jubilant fans and heralded as a dream début for Lou Macari. The manager, however, had made a mental note to have a word with John Collins about the midfielder's rush to take the corner on the right which led to the winning goal, telling one journalist afterwards: 'In injury time with a point at Ibrox – I'd have settled for that.'

In truth, for all his early talk about not changing Celtic's cavalier approach, Macari's two decades in England had marked him with an ingrained streak of pragmatism. The more utilitarian and cautious values of the Football League – an emphasis on workrate and discipline – had inevitably influenced his philosophy more than the gospel of flair and self-expression on which he had been reared as a young player at Parkhead. When manager of Birmingham City, he had openly expressed his scepticism about the fans wanting style and entertainment, and he appeared to be shocked by the fact that Celtic had been so keen to take the game to Rangers. He reflected that in the south the away side tended 'to set up its stall' and considered itself to have done well if it mounted a couple of attacks. He was on surer ground when he observed in justification of his tactical approach that the Jimmy Johnstones and Bobby Murdochs were not around any longer, and that it was unrealistic to expect lesser players to perform in like fashion.

That win at Ibrox brought Celtic level with Rangers in joint fifth spot, and four points behind leaders Aberdeen. Macari's return, however, did not bring the crowds rolling back to Parkhead; only 21,629 turned up a week after the Ibrox triumph to see Celtic take on Partick Thistle. But a run of 11 league matches with only one defeat under his guidance kept Celtic within touching distance of Aberdeen and Rangers at the top of the table. Celtic were two points behind Rangers, but still had a game in hand over their rivals.

Celtic went into the Old Firm Ne'erday clash at Parkhead with the growing reputation of having the meanest defence in the league, a perception enhanced by the preserving of a clean sheet in six successive home games. Macari was in confident, even combative, mood as he looked forward to the upcoming clash with Rangers, and stated that he would fancy Celtic's chances if 'the match turned into a battle'.

That notion, however, blew up in his face within the first minute;

Celtic attempted to play Hateley offside but the wily Englishman had timed his run perfectly and sprinted through unchallenged to collect McCall's pass and curve the ball past Bonner. Celtic never recovered from that blow, and the defence looked so comatose that it was no surprise that Rangers led by 3–0 after 30 minutes.

The third goal provoked a spontaneous eruption of anger among Celtic supporters: in the stand, that fury was directed largely at the directors' box. Scarves and missiles, including coins and even a pie-case rained upon the directors and their guests. One Celtic supporter, despite the reported presence within the stadium of no less than 788 policemen and security personnel, managed to charge from the front of the stand towards Rangers' goalkeeper Maxwell, but he was seized by two Rangers players before he could attempt any damage. In Glasgow Sheriff Court his lawyer would plead that his client, admittedly under the influence of alcohol, had acted out of 'sheer frustration at what was happening to his team on the field'.

A revival in the second half, sparked by a clever goal from Collins after a free-kick, restored a semblance of respectability on the field. Shortly after that goal, Charlie Nicholas struck the bar with a splendid shot; another goal at that stage could have turned the match around, but Rangers eventually prevailed by 4–2. In the closing stages of the match one stand patron is said to have totally ignored the events on the pitch and knotted his scarf into a noose; turning to the Celtic directors, who sat impassively in their seats, he swung it slowly and menacingly . . .

James Traynor, writing in *The Herald*, accurately diagnosed the ugly atmosphere as having its roots in 'the frustrations which have been mounting since Rangers' revival began more than seven years ago with the arrival of Graeme Souness and then David Murray's money and leadership. The Ibrox side have been collecting trophies, whereas Celtic have been suffering from decades of boardroom negligence.' (3 January 1994)

The humiliating defeat would prove to be a watershed in the fortunes of the manager, but even more importantly in the whole future direction of the club.

The real significance of the events at Parkhead that day had not escaped David Low, a financial consultant who had come into media prominence as one of that disparate band of discontented supporters, broadly identified as 'the rebels'. For the past few years the members of various groups had been actively engaged in attempts to take over the club. Commenting on the mayhem at Parkhead that day, he described the scenes as 'the final nail in the coffin – I think you will find that events will now move to a swift conclusion'. He knew that a final showdown between the rebels and the Board was approaching. It would be the climax of a long saga, a veritable hall of mirrors, whose complicated scenario involved shifting alliances, secret meetings and clandestine deals, intrigue, disinformation and 'dirty tricks'. The full story may only be revealed in the fullness of time, or will surface as more of the participants are prepared to tell their story.

The 'events' referred to by Low brought to an end almost a century of dynastic influence or control at Celtic Park. The dénouement was prefigured by one commentator, Brian Scott of the *Daily Mail*, who, after comparing the ruling families to the last of the Romanovs, went on to state: 'Only fools ignore the passions of the people, however crudely expressed. History is littered with pathetic examples of those who sought to cling to power when public sentiment was violently opposed to their doing so.' (3 January 1994)

One aspect of the role of those families prominently associated with the club needs to be clarified at this point. Contrary to popular belief, the Kellys, Whites and Grants had not been in charge of the club since its inception in November 1887. For all but the last six months of Celtic's first decade, the club was run by committee, since it was not until April 1897 that Celtic became officially incorporated as a limited liability company. As has been shown in an earlier chapter, that change – bitterly contested – was essentially the first takeover.

The most prominent of these families – the Kellys – had enjoyed an association with the club which stretched back to the earliest days. James Kelly, Celtic's first captain, had been elected to the first board of directors in June 1897, served as chairman from 1909 to 1914, and was succeeded as a director on his death in 1932 by his son Bob. This son – later Sir Robert Kelly – also served as chairman, from 1947 until shortly before his own death in 1971; his wish that the Kelly family connection on the Board be retained was granted posthumously when his nephew Kevin Kelly became a director in 1971. Kevin fulfilled another of his uncle's hopes by becoming chairman in October 1991 and held that position until March 1994. Another nephew, Michael Kelly, was less favoured by Sir Robert, it seems, because of the latter's falling-out with his own brother several years previously. However, Michael joined his cousin Kevin on the Board in May 1990 as if to validate a Glasgow version of Divine Right.

A most revealing cameo occurs in the film *Celtic*, reissued in video format as *The Celtic Story* in 1982. In the closing footage, Bob Kelly is seen placing the European Cup on a sideboard, and the commentary links the winning of the most prized trophy in club football with the chairman's father having 'left the famous Renton' 80 years earlier 'to take his chance with the new club, Celtic'. The film – originally commissioned by the Board at Kelly's instigation in 1967 – shows the chairman 'put the

European Cup in the place that, somehow, had been waiting for it ever since'. The impression remains that the scene, staged as it is, appears uncomfortably, if unintentionally, close to an act of consecration.

That sense of the fortunes of Celtic and of the Kelly family being inextricably intertwined was echoed 25 years later when Kevin Kelly, objecting to any takeover bid by 'some conglomerate which might change this, that and the next thing', would characterise his being a party to such a transaction as akin to having 'sold your birthright'. (*Scotland on Sunday*. 13 December 1992) A year later, his cousin Michael described Celtic as 'a limited company, a family business'. (*The Independent*. 20 November 1993)

That quasi-mystical concept did not appear to be shared, publicly at least, by the White family. Their ties with Celtic were less close and more businesslike, and started only in 1906, following the death of John Glass, with the co-option on to the Board of Tom White, a graduate in law from Glasgow University and a director of the *Glasgow Star* newspaper. Tom White served as director and then as long-time chairman from 1914 until his death in 1947; and the White links on the Board were preserved with the accession of his son Desmond, himself the club's secretary since 1940. Desmond White later became chairman in 1971 while Bob Kelly was terminally ill, and he was joined on the Board by his son Christopher in 1981, four years before his own death.

The final third of the trinity of Celtic families, the Grants, could not boast of such unbroken links with the club. James Grant, a Glasgow publican, had been elected in 1896 to the last Celtic committee before the club became a limited liability company. After this incorporation, Grant joined the first board of directors, and served as a member for 17 years until his death in 1914. Thereafter, this family's association with Celtic for seven decades was an emotional one, albeit underpinned by a substantial shareholding. That source of influence was not recognised formally until March 1985 when Tom Grant, a Stirlingshire publican and the great-grandson of James, was co-opted on to the Board at the invitation of the chairman, Desmond White. Some felt that the issuing of such an invitation, so long delayed despite Grant's keenness to become a director, was a tactical ploy on the part of White in anticipation of future power struggles involving the Kellys and the Whites.

An old adage, one often cited in business administration courses, runs as follows: 'The first generation creates the firm, the second consolidates it, and the third destroys it.' This quotation was resurrected when, for the first time, a Celtic board of directors came under serious challenge in the wake of the brusque and humiliating rejection of Brian Dempsey in October 1990. That episode has to be viewed as a tactical error on the part of

Christopher White and Michael Kelly, if only on the basis that differences might be better resolved within the confines of a boardroom than in the glare of publicity, largely negative. Dempsey would remain adamant that revenge was not a spur in his subsequent actions. Len Murray, a noted lawyer on the 'rebel' side, says, however, that the Board's action had made it an 'implacable enemy' of Dempsey. But after he combined with David Low and other dissidents in late 1991, the Board was put on the defensive. Ironically, the man dubbed the 'people's champion' and the 'club's saviour', a charismatic figure who articulated the widespread discontent with affairs at Parkhead, would not be the ultimate beneficiary of the revolution which his dismissal had set in train.

Low's attention to detail and extensive knowledge of company law, combined with a terrier-like, pugnacious approach, was essential to the rebels' guerrilla warfare, a campaign which eventually appeared to sap the will of the directors to fight back. The crucial strategy – the one which unlocked the Board's grip on power – was a clever ploy to circumvent the veto which the Board (or, more accurately, the directors really in control of the club, Christopher White and Michael Kelly) effectively had on the matter of share transfers.

That veto dated back to an amendment to the company's Articles of Association in 1933, designed ostensibly to keep out 'undesirable outsiders'. In practice, it enabled directors to buy up shares to consolidate and strengthen their position. The policy was practised so assiduously that the *Daily Record* was able to note on 20 February 1952 that members of the Board and their relatives held over half the shares, and that 'if a selected number of those who are the heaviest holders were to combine they would dictate the policy to be adopted'. This was a clear reference to the blocs of shares already amassed by the White and Kelly families.

Low's tactic, funded by Dempsey and an ally, was to tap into a considerable vein of discontent among many smaller shareholders. Low made strenuous efforts to identify those disaffected shareholders who had suffered petty (but irritating) slights and a dilution of their privileges over the years. He worked hard, travelling far and wide to establish personal contact, he telephoned and faxed those shareholders – and, in the end, managed to acquire a substantial number of proxy votes to be wielded at appropriate meetings. This strategy provided the ammunition to harry the Board, and ultimately to effect a takeover in March 1994 by an exiled Scots-Canadian, Fergus McCann.

Low was aware, too, of the growing gulf between those in charge of the club and those who supported it. In 1989 the chairman of the club had provided evidence of the 'gulf war' by his reaction to a question frequently posed by readers of the *Celtic View*. The supporters clearly wanted the club's directors to take up the matter of better facilities at Hampden Park with the football authorities. Jack McGinn was asked why Celtic fans always had to stand on the open terracing at Hampden at cup finals and semi-finals, often in miserable weather; the reader wondered why they could not secure access to the covered end of the ground. The chairman, while acknowledging that the 'Celtic end' should be covered as well, simply responded to the legitimate grievance by observing: 'Celtic fans seem to want that [uncovered] end because they know how to get there, and where to park buses etc.' (*Celtic View*: 15 March 1989) Smug paternalism was not the prerogative of chairmen Kelly and White, apparently.

The recent use of the Kelly–White voting blocs by Christopher White and Michael Kelly had ensured the removal of Dempsey, but long before that the same axis had swung into operation to cope with an internal threat to their power. Back in 1947, after Tom White's death, his son Desmond worked out a deal with Bob Kelly when the most logical choice for chairman would have been the senior director Colonel Shaughnessy, a man who had a long-cherished ambition to hold that position. This deal denied the veteran his wish. In return for casting his vote for Bob Kelly as chairman, Desmond White (who had succeeded his father on the Board) not only retained the secretaryship of the club, but also obtained Kelly's agreement that he (Desmond White) would succeed him as chairman – as happened in 1971.

However, as Gerry McNee, a journalist, broadcaster and former Celtic historian, revealed, an undercurrent of rivalry remained between the families. Bob Kelly, it seems, long harboured ambitions for unilateral control of the club. Felicia Grant was the daughter of James Grant, and the inheritor of a large slice of the shareholdings of her father and that of another former Celtic director, Tom Colgan, a relative. She lived quietly in Ireland until her death in the early 1970s, and before that 'Bob Kelly made several visits to Toomebridge, hoping to gain Miss Grant's substantial shareholding. But no amount of sweet-talking could part her from a treasured inheritance. The shares had been in the family for years, and she was determined to keep them there. Had the Kelly family got their hands on the Grant shares, they would have become unassailable.' (*Scottish Daily Express*: 24 January 1992)

It was the fracturing of their voting-power which eventually undid the Kelly–White alliance when it fell victim to the accumulated force of several factors in the early 1990s: a noticeable lack of success on the playing field; a massive piling-up of debt; an informal pincer movement, eventually bringing together various factions within the rebels; and all against a continuing backdrop of heavy criticism in the press.

As hostility to the Board swelled, Michael Kelly, for one, seemed to detect collusion and conspiracy designed to subvert the old order. The fragile unity of the Board came under siege when David Low's plans were set in motion. The situation deteriorated with the public realisation that the directors were hopelessly split on major and minor issues. After engineering Dempsey's downfall, Christopher White and Michael Kelly had alienated themselves from four of the other directors, Tom Grant, Kevin Kelly, Jim Farrell and Jack McGinn. This tension enabled the rebels to target those directors broadly sympathetic to their cause, two of whom, Kevin Kelly and Tom Grant, they were particularly anxious to detach because of the substantial shareholdings under their control.

The long-suffering supporters were stirring, too – and in a manner noticeably different from previous outpourings of discontent in the lean years of the late 1940s and early 1960s. In those days, the word was 'protest'; now the air was thick with talk of 'revolution', fanned by lively and irreverent fanzines such as *Not the View* and *Once a Tim*.

In February 1991 the 'Save Our Celts' movement held its inaugural meeting in a packed Shettleston Hall close to Celtic Park with a view 'to pressure the Parkhead Board into making wholesale changes at directional and managerial level'. The meeting, held only a few months after his ejection from the Board, was addressed by Brian Dempsey, and two Celtic directors, Tom Grant and Jim Farrell, accepted invitations to attend. In December 1991 another body held a similar meeting at the same hall 'to express its concern about the direction of the club'; the group called itself the Independent Celtic Supporters Association. The pressure was mounting on a beleaguered Board.

A third organisation, 'Celts for Change', under the guidance of its articulate principal spokesman Matt McGlone, the founder of the fanzine *Once a Tim*, came to the fore in late 1993. It proved to be a thorn in the side of the Board with a campaign which featured hugely attended public rallies, demonstrations inside and outside Celtic Park, and eventually the call for a boycott of a particular match. This fixture (against Kilmarnock on 1 March 1994) resulted in Celtic's lowest home crowd for many seasons although estimates of the attendance varied, depending on the 'political' viewpoint of the speaker. According to a count arranged by 'Celts for Change', less than 10,000 were inside Parkhead that night. Those who did attend were diverted momentarily by the appearance of a fox on the pitch during the match; as an omen, it may not have compared with those in Shakespeare's *Julius Caesar* on the nights before the assassination, but, only three days later, Celtic's dynasties fell . . .

Even the more conservative element within the Celtic support had begun to join the swelling discontent. On Sunday, 3 October 1993, a delegates' meeting of the official Supporters Association passed a vote of no-confidence in the Board's ability 'to act as the custodians of Celtic Football Club'. This resolution was followed on 31 January 1994 by a similar meeting's decision to send a letter to the Board asking the directors to resign. This stormy meeting took place the day after Celtic had been defeated in a Scottish Cup tie at Motherwell by a goal scored by a Celtic discard, Tommy Coyne – and at a time when the grassroots supporters were uniting in spirit to force the pace of change at Celtic Park as those in power there seemed to retreat into their bunker while support for them ebbed away. Things had changed. In February 1991, almost three years earlier, George Delaney (the secretary of the Celtic Supporters Association, and a man who probably shared the view of those resisting change that the breakaway groups were bandwagons for Brian Dempsey and the rebels) had observed that 'publicly criticising Celtic does not further the aims of the club but, if certain people want to do this, they are perfectly entitled to do so. All I can say is that *my* Celtic Supporters Association will never adopt this tactic.'

Those resisting change perhaps did not appreciate how painfully Celtic's decline was affecting the club's followers. As Brian Dempsey is quick to observe, 'Celtic means so much to so many people – the club belongs to the people, without whose support there is no Celtic.' He, after all, grew up in a community which looked upon Celtic as effectively its only symbol of equality at a time when Catholics felt they were still being denied a square deal in Scottish life; his sense of the acute sectarian tensions and bigotry in industrial Lanarkshire had been sharpened by his father's battle to retain the Coatbridge and Airdrie seat for Labour in the 1959 General Election in a bitterly fought contest with the Tory candidate, who was the sister of the famous ex-Rangers player Alan Morton. As Dempsey notes, football provided 'a level playing-field in the matter of competition'. During the campaign to unseat the Celtic Board, he was reminded of what Celtic meant to many people: 'I was overwhelmed by ordinary Celtic fans – postmen, policemen, you name it – who stopped me in the street to wish me well.'

Increasingly, the members of the Board became vulnerable to the criticism that they had not adjusted adequately to the commercial realities of the modern game, particularly in comparison to Rangers. The Ibrox club's transformation had been symbolised by the rebuilding of their stadium and the expert marketing of their commercial potential. This energy and drive was regularly contrasted with Celtic's comparatively naïve and anachronistic business ways.

The commercial landscape of football in Scotland had altered, sometimes beyond recognition, in the quarter-century since Celtic's triumph at Lisbon. At the very top level, at least, football had moved steadily away in the late 1980s from being 'the people's game' and had become a more packaged form of entertainment, a popular spectacle hijacked by the more affluent, according to Ian Archer: 'If you want the best seats in the ground, then you have to be part of the fat cats circuit, eating poached salmon and drinking chilled Chablis in the executive boxes. You can't any more decide at the last minute to go to a top match, pitch up at the turnstiles, pay a few bob, and wander off on to the terraces. You can't even stand any more. And the carry-out is part of history, just like gaslights. Clubs will play in any colour of strip that the manufacturers believe will attract the kids to buy the replicas. And they'll play at any time of day and night throughout the week at the drop of a TV contract!' (*Evening Times*: 8 August 1995) The pie-and-Bovril era was being left behind.

The fundamental reason for this shift was articulated by Celtic chairman Kevin Kelly, when looking back over more than 20 years as a director: 'It used to be that we budgeted for the next year on what we brought in at the gate the last. Some years you made a profit, some years a loss – but you knew your budget from one year to the next. Then the change in demands of players ended all that. Around the turn of the 1980s, when freedom of contract hit the game, we suddenly found our gate receipts did not cover our expenditure. The gap between income and outgoings has gradually widened to a point where there must be a shakeout in football. Clubs need to take a hard look at themselves.' (*Scottish Football Today*: April, 1993)

In the past, Celtic boards of directors had not been noted for self-examination, and their competence in coming to terms with the requisite financial complexity and sophistication came increasingly into question during the early 1990s. As an unfortunate legacy of the fiscal prudence that had been the club's watchword in a simpler past, Celtic had failed to grow with the phenomenal success of the early Stein era. One commentator described Celtic in the late 1980s as 'a big club run by little people', and many, including Len Murray, felt the institution was still being operated like a corner shop. The sudden and undreamt-of success under Jock Stein had taken the directors aback, and their reaction was similar to the often-expressed sentiments of pools-winners: 'This won't change my life!' Unfortunately, in Celtic's case, that was true. Len Murray, who is scathing about the Board's lack of vision pre-takeover, points out that the club was so 'grossly under-capitalised' that, as he said at an emergency general meeting of the club in November 1993, Celtic's net asset (or paper) value compared unfavorably with Glasgow's two other professional clubs, being one sixtieth of Rangers' and a quarter of lowly Partick Thistle's.

The critics pointed to the piecemeal nature of the ground development as evidence of the Board's attitude. Gerry McNee felt that this sort of outlook reflected the personality of Desmond White, the club's chairman from 1971 until 1985: 'When White succeeded Kelly, he was Celtic chairman, treasurer and secretary, accountable to no one and running a business from a ground with the best part of a hundred turnstiles, none computerised. He dominated, was loud, bombastic, and got his way. His policies kept the club in the black, but there was little re-investment in the business. One must surmise the cash from huge gates was badly used because Celtic paid low wages and sold their best players.' (*Sunday Mail,* 27 February 1994)

Desmond White insisted stubbornly that people wanted to stand at Celtic Park, despite the changed social status of many of the club's traditional bedrock of support. In the 1970s and 1980s, particularly, Catholics had made significant inroads into the legal, professional, political and business worlds in the West of Scotland – and, accordingly, were adopting different tastes and leisure patterns. White simply would not listen when Willie Waddell, Rangers' general manager, returned from inspecting the West German stadia used for the 1974 World Cup finals to tell him that he had seen the future. Waddell's vision was to be realised soon afterwards in the rebuilding of Ibrox Stadium. After he effectively took over the club in March 1994, Fergus McCann would castigate the failings of those who served on the Celtic Board after White's death in June 1985 for not addressing the club's financial plight, holding them responsible for a heavy debt incurred as a result of 'a lack of professional business management, too much short-term thinking and a lack of long-term planning on the stadium'.

Desmond White's conservatism, it has to be said, contained a laudable, if somewhat paternalistic, dimension; he genuinely believed that Celtic had to keep admission prices low for the many he felt were relatively poor, but his legacy was a stadium constantly in need of attention to meet costly modern safety requirements, and a club with a capital base so low that it could not withstand the challenge of a Rangers revitalised by massive cash injections in the mid-1980s.

The custodians at Celtic Park were slow to realise that the times had changed. Indeed, one observer, commenting on their Micawber-like stance, said that they appeared 'to cling to the hope that the revolution at Ibrox would explode through lack of money'. Economic survival at the top level now required the active embracing of market forces, what one commentator has described recently as 'Thatcherism in excelsis': merchandising, corporate entertainment, all-seated stadia and sponsorship.

The latter, for example, was not introduced to Parkhead until September 1984, when a deal was struck with C.R. Smith, a Fife-based double-glazing company; the company's logo was emblazoned on the front of one of the most instantly recognisable jerseys in world football, and one recently identified as that of a 'platinum' club – a strip which sells not merely locally, but nationally and further afield. The company's profile in Scotland rose by nearly 500% as a consequence of the deal (which involved a joint-sponsorship with Rangers over a period of three years); the clubs received only £250,000 each in return. Even that boost to the club's finances, a move which brought outraged references in the club newspaper to 'the desecration of the jersey', was simply a means to help balance the books and did not leave the club in any position to face economic reality.

Celtic's dilemma was summed up by Kevin McCarra: 'Until 1986 Celtic might have been portrayed as a bumbling, unambitious company which shrank from the very idea of debt. In that year Celtic found Scottish football taking an alarming new form as Lawrence Marlborough reinvented Rangers. It is the unsuccessful attempt to meet that challenge which has brought Celtic to their present alarming position.' (*Scotland on Sunday*. 13 December 1992)

Celtic's comparatively modest outlay on players in the period from 1987 to 1989 amounted to £750,000 in real terms (when purchases and sales are compared), an investment designed to contain a Rangers newly resurgent under Souness. The current chairman Jack McGinn admitted in July 1989 that the club was in 'considerable debt' as a result of the development of the stand-side complex having apparently overrun its estimated £2 million cost and of extensive work undertaken on the east terracing (the 'Rangers end') to comply with safety regulations.

McCarra, commenting that summer on the club's plight, noted wryly that '[Celtic] fans continue to cry for the biscuit tin to be opened but, if the directors decline, it may be because they know that the only folding stuff it contains is bills'.

The journalist went on to cite the fears of a prominent and respected player, Tommy Burns, to illustrate Celtic's growing predicament: 'If they [Rangers] had continued to limp along, then Celtic probably would have too. The potential at Ibrox is frightening. There is a chance that they could just run away with the championship for years ahead. Football is unpredictable and we will certainly compete, but you have to recognise the standard of player they are buying. Rangers are littered with established internationals – people with 30 or 40 caps. It's bound to bring down your failure rate. They are signing people for £1.5 million while Celtic have to operate in the £600,000 range. That's just a fact of life. Celtic will always be a different sort of club, but I wouldn't want to see them hiding behind the family image. They have to find ways of competing for the best. There's always room for an exceptional youngster, but I think the Old Firm will be fielding cheque-book teams more and more in the future.' (*Scotland on*

Sunday: 30 July 1989) Everything he predicted came to pass.

Celtic's quandary had begun to attract entrepreneurial attention. The centenary season (1987–88) had been marked by the winning of the double and the generating of a fount of tremendous goodwill from all quarters. That source of possible income, some observers believe, was not exploited fully by the club. However, the directors did look at ways of raising money; in a survey of Scottish football's finances in *The Observer* in October 1988, a Celtic spokesman revealed that the Board had discussed a tax-exempt scheme for investors and even a shares flotation. Significantly, there was no suggestion of any dilution or abandonment of the club's private company status.

Another factor had arrived to complicate the equation in the person of one Fergus McCann. The son of a former headmaster at St Modan's, Stirling, he had started his working life as a trainee chartered accountant in Glasgow. After qualification in 1964, he emigrated to Canada where he obtained a solid grounding in finance and marketing at such famous companies as Seagrams and Pretty Polly before venturing into business for himself with a company handling 4,000 'golfing' clients annually and operated all-inclusive tours, packages which incorporated flights, hotel accommodation, meals and guaranteed teeing-off times at famous golf courses. His approach ran contrary to the accepted wisdom of such organisations as the British Tourist Authority who believed that golf was better sold as part of a larger 'touring package'. McCann insisted that golfers were interested primarily in golf, and put his faith in targeted marketing by advertising in *Golf Digest*, North America's foremost magazine for the sport. That strategy, and an attention to detail which placed customer-satisfaction as the priority, enabled his business to be built up solidly among a clientele of hard-nosed business types. A well-maintained databank, which helped to ensure customer loyalty and repeat business, was a feature of his company.

A Celtic supporter from boyhood, McCann went to matches initially with his father and later with the Croy Celtic Supporters Club; in fact, for much of his five years as a highly active and enthusiastic member of this club, he served as its social convener. A fellow member recalls him as a stickler for detail, and he was also regarded as something of an innovator who ensured that his bus travelled in style and comfort, particularly welcome in those days when long-distance trips were undertaken without the advantages of motorways and bypasses.

Even in those days McCann was not afraid to challenge authority; he had a run-in with the Celtic Supporters Association when that organisation criticised seven members of the Croy club including young Fergus who, in their determination to see Celtic play Elgin City in March 1960, had travelled north with a nearby club (Woodside CSC, Coatbridge) which had fallen out with the Association.

In September 1963, before departing for Canada and shortly before completing his training as a chartered accountant, he flew to Basle to see Celtic play a European Cup-Winners' Cup tie. McCann displayed a flair for negotiation by persuading the venerable *Glasgow Herald* to pay him £12 12s 6d for an account of the match – a report he was obliged to file by telephone from a noisy bar adjoining the St Jakob Stadium, and which appeared under the by-line of 'A Special Correspondent'.

His interest in Celtic did not fade when he settled in Canada. In 1967, while attending a seminar in connection with his work, he listened in to Celtic's European Cup triumph in Lisbon on a shortwave radio, and in 1972 he was given an early indication of how costly it could be to take a financial interest in Celtic. He took the risk of buying satellite time in order to beam the Celtic v Inter Milan European tie from Parkhead live into the Maple Leaf Gardens in Toronto; the match extended into extra-time, followed by a penalty shoot-out, and the additional costs (at the rate of $16,000 an hour plus overheads) left the youngish Fergus McCann close to broke.

In 1988, by then much more secure financially, he approached Celtic, through the chairman Jack McGinn, with an offer: the building of a two-tiered stand (15,000 capacity) with McCann lending the club the money at half the rate of interest charged by the bank, on condition that McCann acquired the rights to a three-year marketing project selling season tickets for the new structure. At that time, it did not appear that McCann was interested in taking control of Celtic, but his advance was still rebuffed: 'I was treated entirely as a threat from day one. The paranoia was there.' (*The Herald*: 9 July 1994)

The authorities at Parkhead underestimated (or misunderstood) McCann in part, at least, on a physical appearance which one director, Michael Kelly, later described as 'eccentric'. To be fair to the directors, they may have shared the natural suspicion of a stranger about whom they knew very little. The brisk-talking McCann may have been considered by the Board members as an unlikely figure to be associated with Celtic, but Bob Wylie, writing in the Toronto *Globe & Mail*, sensed the threat posed to the Celtic Board. This journalist described him as 'a bespectacled, bald man flitting in and out of the lobbies of the Hilton Hotel [Glasgow] . . . just another 50-year-old businessman making deals over pots of coffee and cigar smoke . . . He makes getting straight to the point sound like procrastination.' The writer noted that McCann's business skills and bluntness had been honed in a more direct North American milieu. That outlook would underline the Scots-Canadian's frequently posed question:

'Where is it written that only two families can ever control Celtic?' (18 October 1993) The journalist was quick to detect the steeliness in McCann's make-up. This was a man who would not take no for an answer.

The Board's scepticism was not unilateral, and found an echo in the views of Ian Archer, a prominent local sportswriter: 'Mr Fergus McCann does not possess the proper credentials to take over Celtic Football Club and act as its chief executive. His proposals should be viewed with extreme caution by supporters. He knows exceedingly little about Scotland and its football. His motives may be impeccable. His competence is totally unproven. The greatest modern myth is that sport is a business and that businessmen should run it, a dangerous road to travel. Sport is sport with a need for proper business procedures.' (*Evening Times*: 28 September 1993) He compared McCann's credentials unfavourably with those of David Murray, effectively the owner of Rangers since November 1988 – a man who had played rugby in his youth, sponsored a professional basketball team, and bid unsuccessfully for Ayr United before acquiring Rangers, and described by Archer as 'a sportsman willing to put his entrepreneurial skills at the service of a boys' game, and doubtless make money as well'. The journalist concluded that the Celtic directors, characterised as 'decent men caught in an impossible situation', should be given the benefit of the doubt unless or until they were 'proven to be inadequate protectors of the club's rich and romantic heritage' by failing to provide proper facilities for its supporters.

Two years after his summary rejection in 1988, Fergus McCann, as he recently told the authors, had come to the realisation – 'after all offers of assistance were seen as a threat and rejected' – that the only way forward for Celtic would be through a change of ownership. He would be back . . . but in the interim, and all but forgotten now, there was another bid for control of Celtic, this time by Paul Green, a millionaire Jersey-based property developer. Reportedly, but in the face of official denials and obfuscation in August 1989, he wanted to buy Celtic for £6 million by purchasing the shareholdings of directors Tom Grant and Christopher White, and those of the late chairman Tom Devlin (briefly the successor to Desmond White). These purchases would have given Green a controlling interest of slightly more than 50 per cent and he planned to instal another businessman as chief executive, while offering Tom Grant the chairmanship and Christopher White the continuing role of club secretary. Green's long-term plans included a new all-seated, multi-purpose stadium in the huge acreage available adjacent to the Parkhead Forge complex in which he was a partner. Nothing came of this speculation; Tom Grant, who met Green, insists that no concrete offer was made and, at the time, the club was under no immediate threat anyway thanks to its recent Scottish

Cup triumph and a bright start to the 1989–90 season.

Green and McCann were not the only entrepreneurs interested in Celtic around this time. Gerard Eadie, who runs C.R. Smith (the double-glazing firm which still sponsors Celtic's shirts), has recently admitted that he was thinking 'long and hard' about seizing the reigns of power at Parkhead. Even though the club was ripe for the plucking he eventually 'opted to take a back seat and let Fergus McCann come through.' Eadie had come to the conclusion that for him football and business were different cultures, a realisation that does not diminish his admiration for McCann: 'Fergus is smart, one of the smartest people I've ever met. He is totally focused and in Celtic he saw a great business opportunity – but it was a very high-risk thing and I don't think there are many people who could have pulled off what he has.' (*Daily Mail*, 8 June 1996)

The Board, however, came under scrutiny as it gave the impression of floundering when its own plans for re-development surfaced in the press. In early 1990 it was reported that they hoped to raise £30 million to turn Celtic Park into an upgraded, all-seated stadium by approaching 30 'Celtic-minded' people for an interest-free loan. Each lender would be guaranteed 'privileges' such as being wined and dined at home fixtures. Naturally, the scheme proved a non-starter. Few would welcome the prospect of lending vast amounts to a Board regarded as lacking in business acumen, without being given the opportunity of share-holding and the prospect of having a voice in the running of the club.

The Board then pinned its hopes on both an influx of funding from success on the field and the launching of a space-age development on a 30-hectare site at nearby Cambuslang. This project, estimated to cost £100 million, was announced with great fanfare in mid-April 1992. The scheme was based on a feasibility study carried out by Superstadia, and contained the following features: an ultra-modern, circular and roofed multi-purpose stadium seating 52,000 as part of 'a practical and versatile complex which is economically self-sustaining', comprising a Celtic heritage museum, a 30-lane bowling alley, a multiplex cinema, a 'support-village' containing retail and fast-food outlets, 'business-class buildings', car-showrooms and a petrol station as well as 5,000 parking spaces and enhanced railway and motorway links.

If everything went according to plan, Celtic were scheduled to occupy the stadium during the second half of 1994. Michael Kelly, once so dismissive of a similar scheme for Robroyston which had brought down Brian Dempsey, told Amanda Mitchison of *The Independent* that 'Celtic is being invited to come in. We will have a purpose-built stadium, rent-free. We will just have to turn up and play.' (20 November 1993)

Many doubts remained, sustained by the widespread belief that the directors were not the men to carry out such plans successfully. Kelly's emphasis on 'tenancy' prompted one critic to point out the possibility that the consequences might 'in the nightmare scenario lead to vagrancy' and, in any case, the majority of supporters were reluctant to abandon Celtic Park, considered to be the club's spiritual home. The sceptics among them also entertained doubts about the scheme coming to fruition, given the allegations about the site being contaminated by chemicals. The area in Cambuslang was described as 'a toxic time-bomb', and one wit suggested it be twinned with Chernobyl, the scene of the infamous nuclear accident in 1986.

Questions were raised about the financing of the project, apparently to be made up in a variety of ways: sponsorship, executive-box sales, seating debentures, capital allowances and public-sector grants. Kevin Kelly had the outspoken opponents of the plan in mind when he defended the Board's scheme against 'a non-stop barrage of ill-considered criticism from uninformed people of dubious motivation'. But the directors had little hope of shaking off the widespread perception that the whole venture was little more than a mirage or, as Fergus McCann put it, 'a PR exercise consisting of a house of cards, to be financed by a fairy godmother'. The eventual collapse of that 'house of cards' brought about the fall of the Celtic dynasties.

The critics would always view Cambuslang as a diversionary tactic, an attempt to buy more time until the old order could somehow reassert itself. They pointed out time after time that the Board remained hopelessly split, and claimed that the unveiling of the scheme, shortly after the rebels' first (seemingly abortive) public assault on the status quo, had been an attempt to camouflage the growing schisms in the boardroom. An Emergency General Meeting of shareholders had been convened for 30 March 1992, effectively called by Christopher White and Michael Kelly in an unsuccessful attempt to unseat Jim Farrell and Tom Grant, the two directors who had been courted by the rebel camp. It became obvious during the course of that six-hour meeting that a move had been made by the Kelly–White axis to 'neutralise' Tom Grant. The latter was one director who always seemed to be seeking a genuine compromise, and he was persuaded to vote at the meeting for the ratification of the previous month's co-option on to the Board of David Smith, a Brechin-born, London-based businessman. Smith had earned a reputation as a City high-flyer with his involvement in the £2 billion takeover of the Gateway supermarket group in 1989, and his accession to the Celtic Board had come only on the casting vote of Kevin Kelly. The chairman described Smith, the first-ever non-Catholic director of the club, as 'the boldest and most imaginative appointment ever made to a Celtic Board'. The addition of Smith was a manifest ploy by Christopher White and Michael Kelly to strengthen the commercial expertise of the club in coping with the reduction of the debt and the financing of the new stadium. White and Kelly, recalls Tom Grant, assured the rest of the Board that Smith would 'deliver the goods' when it came to sorting out the club's finances. More pointedly, it was seen by White and Kelly as the enlisting of a heavyweight who could deliver a knock-out blow to the rebels.

The secret agreement to which Grant had been a party was revealed later that summer in the local *Evening Times* as a pact which incorporated the Kelly, White and Grant shareholdings and the tranche held by David Smith into a limited liability company formed under the title Celtic Nominees Ltd. This grouping essentially combined 60 per cent of the club's shares (when those shares held by their families and associates were included) to be mustered for the blocking of any takeover bid. The two other directors, Jim Farrell and Jack McGinn, were omitted, presumably on the grounds that their shareholdings were minimal and their influence relatively small. The pact was also aimed at ensuring loyalty by preventing the participating directors from attempting to remove each other from office; the requirement that the five members vote in unison at meetings seemed to make it a watertight arrangement.

In truth, however, the rebels had won important victories at the EGM: their show of strength had prevented the proposed removal of Grant and Farrell from the Board and, more importantly, they had forced their opponents to resort to an extraordinary measure in order to cement their control. Looking back, Brian Dempsey says that the calling of the meeting gave a focus and impetus to the campaign. It turned the 'rebels' into what he calls a 'legal entity', and provided Dempsey and his allies with ammunition for their campaign in the shape of information from company records to which they were now entitled under company law. That EGM – in the words of Dempsey – 'gave us a standing and credibility we had never previously had and the outcome removed that aura of invincibility from the Board'. Farrell, who had already suggested that the club might be 'technically insolvent', described the pact as 'the refuge of frightened men'. His view clashed discordantly with that of the chairman who claimed that the major shareholders had 'submerged their personal interests to give a commitment which will achieve long-term unity'. Brian Dempsey was closer to the reality when he told the *Daily Telegraph* on 6 April 1992 that 'the movement towards change is unstoppable now'.

Earlier, in January 1992, Kevin Kelly had reacted to revelations in *Scotland on Sunday* about the rebellion being already under way by dismissing the takeover threat as 'rumours', the product of 'naïve kite-flying', and 'unwarranted, untimely and unsophisticated'. He would continue to display an uncertain touch at the helm. In October 1993 he insisted that the cornerstone £20 million financing needed to ensure the green light for the Cambuslang project was in place – despite growing doubts about the viability of a project for which full planning permission had not yet been obtained. Tom Grant, increasingly doubtful about the project despite his membership of the pact, publicly scorned this announcement when he informed the press a month later that the company acting on Celtic's behalf to secure the £20 million underwriting for the first phase of construction had failed to confirm the money's availability in writing: 'They [Superstadia Ltd] seem to be the only businessmen who have Swiss bankers without a typewriter in their office.' In spite of such reservations, Kevin Kelly persisted in his optimism, claiming in the wake of the Ne'erday 1994 defeat by Rangers that 'a major announcement' would be made within a week. The promise did not materialise, however, and yet another vestige of the Board's fading credibility had disappeared.

Kevin Kelly, the man who had hailed the Cambuslang announcement in April 1992 as 'the most exciting day in the history of Celtic Football Club', was present to endorse the project again, a touch more uneasily this time, as 'the best deal for the Celtic and the supporters' on 25 February 1994 when the last rites of that particular saga were enacted at a press conference at Celtic Park, attended by the pact signatories – and without Jack McGinn and Jim Farrell, who had not been invited. David Smith, the club's deputy chairman, announced 'a comprehensive and visionary package of radical measures designed to take the club into a glittering new future in the 21st century'. They included the recasting of Celtic's capital structure by an initial share issue, intended to bring in funds to reduce borrowing (and strengthen the team on the field), which would lead to the club 'going public' via a Stock Exchange flotation by the end of the year. The whole enterprise was to be underpinned by the 'assurance' that the cornerstone financing for Cambuslang was in place, underwritten by Gefinor, an international merchant bank.

This seemingly stunning public-relations coup turned into disaster when the press could not obtain confirmation of the key funding from the Geneva-based bank. Its director, Harold Jupp, denied the existence of any such commitment or formal agreement. The ensuing furore brought wholesale condemnation of the Board and ridicule on the directors: 99 per cent of the callers to a hot-line set up by *The Sun* reckoned the new plan was doomed to failure, and 84 per cent claimed they would not return to Parkhead until the current Board was ousted. A similar poll was conducted by the *Evening Times* on the same day (1 March 1994) and the verdict was the same, with 87 per cent of the callers demanding that the Board 'Go now!'. The last shreds of credibility had been stripped from the directors by a press conference which had now been exposed, it seemed, as a charade or stunt.

All this brought about an intervention by the Bank of Scotland, the club's long-time bankers, who were believed by many, notably Fergus McCann, to have delayed over-long before taking action while the club's position was worsening. Reportedly, Celtic had an overdraft of £15,000 in 1987, but the club was staggering under one estimated at £5 million by June 1993. That situation had seen Celtic Park itself mortgaged as security 'against the debtor's present and future debts to the bank', and led to the drastic step – revealed in October 1993 – of the bank taking out a 'bond and floating charge' which gave that financial institution effective ownership of all Celtic's assets should the club go bankrupt.

Indeed, Terry Cassidy, the club's first chief executive (from December 1990 to October 1992), had no doubt about the bank's culpability: 'In some ways the bank is to blame for Celtic's current predicament. When I was there, I actually told the bank to act. I believe they should have acted before I joined. I told the most senior official the problem was the board of directors had no money. If I decided to open a corner shop tomorrow, I would be asked for a budget and a business plan and projections. But when I went to Celtic, they had none of these and had £5 million of debt. Now that debt has doubled.' (*Scottish Sunday Express*: 6 March 1994)

Banks, it should be noted, have tended to treat football clubs by different criteria compared to other businesses, and have been reluctant to invoke the most drastic measure available to them for fear of negative publicity. Some observers believe that football debts have become untouchable, something akin to Third World loans. Ian Dewar, a partner with Price Waterhouse and a leading analyst on the finances of Scottish football, has claimed that 'apart from not winning any friends, they have to consider whether they would get any money back from that course of action [receivership]. The main assets of any football club are the players and the ground. The players' contracts revert to the ownership of the Scottish League if a club goes into receivership, and there are not many people in the market to buy a football stadium as planning consent would be required for a change of use into a supermarket or housing development. The best solution appears to be to encourage the clubs to act in a more businesslike manner and trade out of the problem.' (*Sunday Times*: 12 June 1994)

Price Waterhouse, in its fifth annual review of the finances of the Scottish Premier Division clubs at the end of 1992–93, showed that nine clubs whose indebtedness was established owed a total of nearly £18 million; Celtic topped this 'league table' with debts of £4.68 million and

Rangers were not far behind with £4.1 million. The difference between the two was that Rangers were unhindered by requirements to spend on massive ground improvements, and the perception that the greater commercial acumen of the Ibrox club would enable it to service the debt even while continuing to strengthen the club's playing resources.

Celtic's situation was aggravated during the winter of season 1993–94 by a cash-flow problem stemming from a lowering in the revenue generated at the turnstiles, a shortfall caused by the supporters' discontent with their club's failure to compete with Rangers on the field and with their palpable sense of dissatisfaction with the Board. As the club struggled to pay wages and cope with meeting operating expenses, Celtic FC found itself up against its overdraft limit. Interviewed on BBC TV Scotland on the day Fergus McCann effectively took over the club, vice-chairman David Smith emphatically denied suggestions that he had misled the Board about the club's financial position. Instead, he seemed to blame the players for the demise of the club's directorate: 'Things were going along relatively smoothly as far as the finances of the club were concerned – in fact somewhat better that we had anticipated – until, I should think, the first two minutes on New Year's Day, plus the Cup tie [defeat] at Motherwell didn't help things at all . . .' (4 March 1994)

This state of affairs coincided with an external battle between two rival consortia eager to take control of the club – and all against 'a background of intense speculation that they [the Board] are now backed into a corner, and radical change is imminent', as Hugh Keevins observed in *The Scotsman* on 17 January 1994. That sense of a régime in the throes of drift and decay was acknowledged even by Mike Stanger, a partner in Michael Kelly Associates (a public relations firm run by the Celtic director and which was used by the club), when he commented on Celtic's image: 'There's no doubt Celtic is a difficult account. That is mainly because there is little pro-active ammunition available.' (*Scotland on Sunday*, 23 January 1994)

Speculation rose to fever pitch when one of the groups, that fronted by Glasgow businessman Willie Haughey on behalf of multi-millionaire Gerald Weisfeld, offered to buy the shares of the members of the now infamous pact at a cost of £300 per share. This would give Weisfeld, whose fortune stemmed from the sale of his chain of What Everyone Wants stores in 1989, outright control of Celtic for an estimated £3.6 million. A report in *The Sun* of 10 February 1994 suggested that Christopher White would receive £887,000 and that Kevin Kelly and Tom Grant would each receive more than £500,000.

In direct contrast, Fergus McCann's investor group – as it was termed – had announced in September 1993 a £17.9 million rescue package to refinance the club with the backing of a new share issue. Their motion to that effect was thwarted by the pact's block-vote at a November 1993 EGM of the shareholders. The views of the two groups opposing the Board were seen as irreconcilable, not least because of the personalities of McCann and Weisfeld, both self-made men and not regarded as 'team players'. A profile of McCann in *Scotland on Sunday* suggested how uneasy any formal alliance would have been: 'McCann has the same lack of affection for consensus and democratic decision-making common to most millionaires – it's My Way or No Way. The current negotiations between McCann and Dempsey, Weisfeld and Co. are not about him joining them, but about them joining him.' (29 August 1993) As three self-made men, it was perhaps inevitable that McCann, Dempsey and Weisfeld would eventually resent playing second fiddle in any set-up.

The outcome hinged on a tug-of-war between the rival factions for the ultimate support of Kevin Kelly and Tom Grant. Both men clung to the commendable belief that the future of Celtic FC, an institution they cherished, was more important than a swift improvement in their own financial circumstances.* Their reluctance to 'betray' their family connections with the club proved crucial when the three other pact members were prepared to sell out to the Weisfeld group. Kelly and Grant were persuaded by McCann's contention that the proposals put forward by Weisfeld did not contain a capital-intensive, long-term business strategy. They also held a strategic advantage because, under the terms of the pact, the other three signatories, when desirous of selling any of their holdings to outsiders, had to offer them first to Tom Grant and Kevin Kelly – and the pact could be dissolved only with the unanimous agreement of the signatories. Thus, by a supreme irony, the 'watertight' pact, conceived to preserve the status quo, became the instrument of revolution.

Still, Gerald Weisfeld was convinced around mid-February 1994 that he had clinched a deal to take over the club after weeks of wheeling and dealing with members of the pact. His interview with the *Sunday Mail* in the wake of the failure of his coup revealed his frustration at being stymied: 'We were told categorically there were only two directors wavering, Kevin Kelly and Tom Grant. The others had agreed to sell. They had had enough. We met the bank. Their representative was instructed not to give us precise details. They wanted us aboard, but they could not initiate that. Then there was talk about upping the price. What they wanted was a device which

---

* In a recent interview with the authors, Tom Grant expressed his belief that the supporters' disillusionment with the Board in the early 1990s was so strong that even success on the field of play would only have delayed the inevitable: 'The punters simply didn't believe in the club anymore.' He felt that the situation had been made worse by a tendency on the part of some Board members to stigmatise all of the critics among the support as 'trouble-makers', 'hooligans' or 'malcontents'.

would allow them to remain in some form or another. Certainly, as far as David Smith was concerned, a deal was done. Then, on Thursday [24 February], I was called by Smith. He told me he would fax details of what was released at the press conference [25 February], saying, "Ring me and I can tell you how you can help." He told me I should underwrite the £6 million they were seeking from a share issue. I asked him what possible benefit there would be for me . . .' (27 February 1994)

Smith had to resort to the resurrection of the Cambuslang scheme at that press conference after Kevin Kelly and Tom Grant, briefed by David Low acting on behalf of the McCann and Dempsey camp, could not be moved from their obstinate stance. The press, who had gathered at Celtic Park in expectation of the Board's collective resignation and a Weisfeld takeover, were stunned and perplexed. The result was a consequence of the stalemate in the manoeuvring within the boardroom. Weisfeld and Haughey afterwards raged about 'double-dealing' and 'betrayal'.

Weisfeld was not finished, though. He returned from a trip to Australia to offer the bank a £3 million guarantee against the club's overdraft, thus saving it from any threat of receivership. This move, ending a period of absence which possibly left him out of touch with developments, appeared to have improved his prospects; indeed, even as the wheels were in motion to bring McCann to power, Weisfeld was still defiant, telling the local *Evening Times* on the day of the takeover that 'I am still in the game' (4 March 1994), an optimism which may have borne fruit had a stalemate of sorts resulted.

The Bank of Scotland was obviously anxious to encourage Celtic directors to reduce the debt more quickly, having noted that only one of the seven home matches since the EGM in November 1993 had attracted a crowd of over 20,000 and that the boycotted fixture on 1 March had produced an official disputed attendance of 10,882.

Kevin Kelly and Tom Grant were by now convinced of the damage done to Celtic's credibility by the continuing fiasco of Cambuslang. They learned that the bank was seeking substantial personal guarantees from the club's directors as a factor in coping with the overdraft, and that decreasing revenue at the turnstiles had brought Celtic closer to receivership.

They persuaded two other directors, James Farrell and Jack McGinn, to accompany them to the bank offices on the afternoon of 3 March and, since the four constituted a majority of the Board, the club's bank manager felt he had little option but to give their preference for the McCann–Dempsey consortium precedence over Weisfeld's offer. He added the condition that a guarantee of £1 million, suitably secured and in a form suitable to the bank, be delivered to his office by noon the following day; otherwise, a receiver would be appointed. The condition was met when

Fergus McCann, alerted to the developing situation, flew in from his holiday home in Arizona and completed the requisite paperwork at the Bank of Scotland's office in Glasgow's St Vincent Street – eight minutes before the deadline. A few days later McCann underlined his position as the major player in the rescue bid by lodging a further £5 million with the bank as collateral to stabilise the club's financial situation.

By that time, Kevin Kelly, acting as chairman, had stripped David Smith and Christopher White of their authority as directors on the grounds that 'the full financial plight of Celtic Football Club had been withheld from the full Board'.

After completing the formalities at the bank offices, McCann had to confront an unwelcome reality if he was to take over the club. He was forced to reconsider his earlier vow not to pay 'one thin dime' in compensation to his opponents, a statement which had endeared him to many among Celtic's support. Despite his strong moral repugnance about rewarding the very people he held responsible for Celtic's decline, he had to compromise by negotiating the buy-out of the shares of Christopher White, David Smith and Michael Kelly and their families – in addition to their resignations.

There is a touch of poignancy about the fact that, only a few days before the takeover, Mrs Greta Kelly – Michael's mother, and Celtic's oldest living shareholder – had celebrated her 90th birthday. Ironically, that same Kelly dynasty was being removed from effective control at Parkhead as a rift continued to develop between the Kelly cousins, Kevin and Michael. The *Sunday Mail* would reveal that the two, who had served together as Celtic directors, had not spoken to each other since the day of the takeover, five months earlier. Kevin Kelly commented on his cousin's sense of betrayal: 'He was among people who felt that, since they were selling out, I should too. They were my shares and it was up to me what I should do with them. I imagine Michael feels a bit sore.' (14 August 1994)

Indeed, Michael Kelly's anger would surface shortly afterwards when he described 'the dirty campaign, conceived in vengeance, born in deceit' which he claims unseated him and other members of the former Board. In a radio interview seven months after the event, he held to that interpretation of his removal by 'a determined group of people that was prepared to damage Celtic in order to obtain their ends'. He cited organised fan boycotts, both of matches at Parkhead and of commercial activities, allied to 'a very, very subversive press campaign that denigrated the Board personally'. He reserved a fair amount of bitterness and bile for those directors who, he believed, had panicked at the bank's 'bluff' in threatening receivership. As a consequence of their final actions in 'the struggle for Celtic's soul', he contended, 'the Celtic ethos and the Celtic personality' were now dead.

There was absolutely no sympathy for that viewpoint among the several hundred Celtic fans who were on hand outside Celtic Park, standing in the pouring rain, when late on Friday, 4 March 1994, Brian Dempsey emerged from the main door to announce, after the protracted final negotiations between the two camps: 'The battle is over – and the rebels have won!'

A new dawn was about to rise at Parkhead . . .

FOURTEEN

The Whirlwind of Change

1994–95

Fergus McCann paused only briefly to celebrate and savour the triumph, and then he buckled down to the challenge of restructuring the club to his satisfaction, a huge task characterised by Terry Cassidy – the former chief executive – as 'like turning the *QE2* around'. Privately, McCann was disturbed to find that Celtic's plight as a business was worse than he had anticipated. In his role as managing director and chief executive, he was to put in long hours, reportedly until 8 p.m. most evenings, in order to evaluate the real nature of the club's finances and to put those finances in order. He had the added incentive of working to protect his own personal stake in Celtic, reported to be about £9.3 million. It would not be long before his new and exacting standards would claim a prominent victim.

Most supporters believed that Lou Macari would be placed under some form of probation after the takeover, especially after he had been seen as backing the former Board by describing the Cambuslang venture in its final form (and ramifications) as 'a step in the right direction'.

The supporters were not surprised that the manager struggled to come to terms with Celtic's deficiencies on the pitch. The disturbing feature of the team's play in recent seasons – a tendency for confidence to drain away, almost visibly, when things started to go wrong – had duly manifested itself in the wake of the shattering defeat by Rangers on Ne'erday 1994. Two away defeats, to Partick Thistle (1–0) and Motherwell (2–1) inside the next 11 days, meant that Celtic were slipping hopelessly out of contention in the league race. Macari was making little secret of his chafing at the financial restraints under which he had to operate, telling Hugh Keevins of *The Scotsman* that the supporters could see for themselves what the team needed: 'I surely do not need to have to tell seven directors what that is, do I?' (10 January 1994)

His complaints were legitimate: he could point to the inexperienced players on the bench against Sporting Lisbon in his second game in charge (a 2–0 away defeat which eliminated Celtic from the UEFA Cup). He could indicate the lack of competition for places, a fact which he attributed in part to the club 'from youth level upwards' not having 'looked after itself for years'.

Macari was handicapped in his attempts to offload surplus players because of their lucrative contracts with Celtic, and he admitted that he would have to wheel and deal in the transfer market, a situation he had been made aware of before his return. His rummaging in the bargain basement could hardly be expected to capture the imagination: Wayne Biggins, a 32-year-old 'target man' signed from Barnsley in November 1993 in a swap deal (plus £100,000 in Celtic's favour) for the unsettled Andy Payton, made only ten appearances in four months without scoring before he departed for Stoke City for £125,000; Carl Muggleton, a third-choice keeper at Leicester City, signed for £150,000 in January 1994 while at Sheffield United on loan, played in 13 matches before being transferred to Stoke City for £200,000 six months later; Lee Martin, a full-back signed from Manchester United in January 1994 for £350,000, the fee determined by tribunal; and Willie Falconer, a midfielder-cum-striker, signed from Sheffield United for £350,000 in February with the odd 'endorsement' from the new manager that 'no one will be drooling over him'.

Ironically, it was a Celtic reject who torpedoed Macari's hopes of redeeming a season falling apart in tandem with the death throes of the old Board. Tommy Coyne took revenge on Celtic in the Scottish Cup tie at Motherwell on 29 January 1994 by turfing his old club out of the competition with an opportunistic header over Muggleton's outstretched arms ten minutes from time after a free-kick had looped into the penalty box following a deflection. While Macari may have complained in private to a journalist about his predecessor's 'folly' in transferring Coyne, he himself had sold an out-of-favour young striker to Portsmouth for £500,000 only three days before the cup-tie which Celtic lost at Fir Park. Macari claimed that he was compelled to sell that player, Gerry Creaney, to help finance his transfer dealings. After his departure, Creaney would fulminate at being latterly deemed a substitute, and at being played out of position. He would decry the motivational powers of a manager who, he claimed, was rarely seen on the training ground on Mondays and Tuesdays.

'Lou Macari,' he said, 'took care of Lou Macari first and foremost. He never had Celtic's interests 100 per cent at heart.' (*Daily Record*: 17 June 1994)

Other players later joined in the swelling chorus of criticism: the acerbic Frank McAvennie would liken Celtic's new style of play – which bypassed the midfield and the creative Paul McStay and John Collins – to 'head tennis'. Peter Grant was quoted by Alex Gordon of *Scottish Football Today* as saying, 'There were occasions when the players had no idea of the formation of the team even 15 or 20 minutes before kick-off. It was an intolerable situation and one that obviously affected the performance of the team. We rarely worked on set-pieces, corner-kicks, free-kicks and so on. There was a great element of off-the-cuff about it all. In this day and age you need a game plan. Banging the ball from back to front is just no good in the Premier League. Basically, Lou was hardly ever there. When you wanted to speak to him, you were told he was down south.' (July 1994)

It was reported that Tom Boyd, an attacking full-back, was deeply unhappy at being advised not to cross the halfway line, that the goalkeepers were being instructed not to throw the ball out to start attacks, and that defenders were ordered to clear their lines at any cost. Allen McKnight, the former Celtic goalkeeper, speaking to the *Daily Express* about his experiences under Macari at West Ham, put the boot in further, commenting bitterly: 'He is a strange organiser of football tactics, and he never took people's emotions or personalities into account.' (3 January 1996) In fairness to Macari, he could argue that the side was playing in a way that the club's current resources permitted, and that he was seeking a framework of basic organisation within which players could express themselves to the utmost of their ability.

It seems clear that Macari never appreciated the intensity of hostility among the supporters towards his employers. He was taken aback, apparently, by the difference in press coverage about Celtic's affairs; since his stint as a player at Parkhead two decades previously, the reporting had become much more aggressive and critical, fuelled in particular by a circulation war between two tabloids.

A series of unconvincing displays by the side and the manager's tendency to criticise the squad only worsened the situation. Macari's outbursts were tinged with *déjà vu*, eerily reminiscent of Brady's frustrations and McNeill's anger; the predictable result of this exasperation was the departure soon afterwards of the manager who uttered them.

Peter Grant's candid admission in *The Sun* reflected the decline in morale among the players at Parkhead, although it also said little for their standards of professionalism: 'I wouldn't have paid to watch us last season.

They [the fans] were being cheated, paying money to see players who chucked it so easily.' (13 August 1994) It was ominous that Glenn Gibbons, writing in *The Observer* during a spell in which Celtic under Macari had thrown away the lead on four separate occasions, commented on the indifferent attitude of certain players who had 'already decided that their contracts will not be renewed at the end of the season, [and believe] there is little point in shedding buckets of sweat for a cause which will soon no longer be theirs'. (17 April 1994)

Tom English, writing in *The Sunday Times* (Scotland), went even further, alleging a more sinister dimension to the players' part in Macari's demise after such a short period in charge: 'In the dressing room Macari's players plotted against him. They criticised his style of play and made sure McCann heard about it. The backroom boys too had their say. Suggestions to offload Macari were ignored at first, but eventually McCann became convinced that his manager should go . . . The only conclusion you can draw is that Macari was the victim of a concerted campaign, and McCann fell for it. The players, instead of concentrating on winning games, whipped themselves into a frenzy, and convinced each other that the reason they were getting thumped by Partick Thistle and Kilmarnock was because of the style Macari was insisting they play. Their manager had become their latest alibi for failure, and the stories almost immediately started to appear in the tabloid press.' (19 June 1994)

Celtic's fitful form against the other Premier League sides continued. Under Lou Macari, Celtic's league record consisted of 12 wins, 6 losses and 14 draws. The team finished up mired in fourth position, without a place in Europe for 1994–95. Lack of success on the field is usually the main catalyst for change, and Michael Kelly came closest to identifying the most plausible reason for the demise of the former Board when he stated in his account of the struggle (*Paradise Lost*, 1994) that 'After five years of Rangers victories in the league, Celtic fans would have seen the club sold to the Ayatollah Khomeini if it gave a glimmer of hope of success on the park.' If Boards could be replaced, mere managers had no protection in the face of poor performances by their players.

The only ray of hope for the future was provided by the precocious displays of a teenage forward, Simon Donnelly, whom the manager compared – perhaps unwisely – to the young Kenny Dalglish. Certainly, the youngster showed promise and displayed a sharpness allied to self-confidence, but the premature publicity served only to set up unrealistic expectations which later affected the player's form in addition to highlighting the general level of Celtic's mediocrity.

Macari could only wonder at the performances against Rangers, when Celtic continued to win and do well in the unimportant fixtures. At Ibrox at the end of April 1994 as the season drew to a melancholy close, his side dug in admirably for a 1–1 draw, highlighted by a superbly flighted free-kick goal from John Collins. The match itself was played out in an unreal atmosphere caused by the ban imposed by Rangers on Celtic supporters attending, as a consequence of the Parkhead club refusing to stump up compensation for alleged vandalism at an earlier fixture.

Macari started his rebuilding programme at the end of the season by informing five first-team players (McAvennie, Gillespie, Wdowcyzk, Nicholas and Bonner) that they were no longer needed, although Nicholas and Bonner were to be reinstated. He hinted that a similar number of imports would be necessary to strengthen his squad, but the manager himself would not remain at Parkhead long enough to see his plans fulfilled because, the day after he bought Andy Walker back from Bolton Wanderers for £550,000 on 14 June 1994, Macari's reign as Celtic's boss ended, only eight months after his arrival. Reportedly, he was sacked over the phone by Fergus McCann just as the Macari family was about to set off for the United States. McCann cited the following grounds for dismissal: that Macari had 'failed to attend to his responsibilities at Celtic Park, including adequate direction and supervision of the various departments in his charge'. The sacking prompted newspaper speculation that the manager had spent too much time at his family home in Stoke, and had not kept a promise to move to Glasgow. Fergus McCann stated: 'A football manager's job is not nine to five, and that is reflected in the money he receives. It's not a half-day job or two days a week at Celtic Park. Being on the phone does not get things done.' (*The Sun*: 17 June 1994) A 'hands-on' manager, he added, was essential.

Naturally, Lou Macari disagreed violently. He could point out that his trip to America was not just a holiday and that it afforded him an opportunity to watch the best players in the World Cup. Sensing perhaps that he had been fated to be another victim of the recent power struggle at Parkhead, he pointed to personal animosity between himself and the chief executive, telling the *Scottish Daily Express* on 2 November 1994: 'Fergus McCann made up his mind to sack me from day one.' Macari hinted later that the real reason for his dismissal was that he had clashed regularly with McCann, and had told the new owner not to interfere in his job as manager.

Macari eventually sued Celtic for breach of contract, for a failure to give him two years' notice of termination of employment and for dismissing him within a year of his appointment; Celtic countered Macari's claim for £431,000 with a demand for £727,000 from him, an amount calculated to reflect the money lost by the team's failure to qualify for European competition in 1994–95, and the money 'wasted' in recruiting him from Stoke City in October 1993. At the time of writing the dispute has not been resolved.

The manager was not the only departure from the Celtic scene that summer. The saying goes that every revolution devours its own, and the figure who was regarded as its torchbearer, Brian Dempsey, found himself increasingly at odds with the new régime and took leave of his former comrade in the takeover struggle for which he had been the catalyst: 'Mr McCann is taking the club in the wrong direction. It is because of this that I have decided I will not be back at Celtic as part of his team for the future.' (*Sunday Times*: 19 June 1994)

He was one of a number of former rebels who remain dissatisfied with the outcome of the campaign they fought alongside McCann. Dr Hugh Drake, an academic and shareholder, expressed his views to the authors as follows: 'I became a rebel to help save the club my ancestor helped to found. [He is a descendent of John O'Hara.] Alas, rebels rarely steer their rebellion through. There's a line I recall from G.K. Chesterton about those rebels "who, while waiting for daybreak, do not think so much about the noon of that day". And that seems to sum up pretty well the anxieties I expressed before the coup. What did noontime bring? Only an autocracy in place of a pact-oligarchy! Not what I'd envisaged at all . . .'

Further boardroom changes that summer signalled the transition to the more corporate Celtic which was effectively formalised at an EGM held on Thursday, 15 December 1994, at Celtic Park, when the Celtic Football and Athletic Company Ltd was re-registered as a public limited company, Celtic plc – although the former name lives on as a subsidiary of the new company.

The decision, or perhaps the necessity, to retain four members of the *ancien régime* had been viewed with distaste and anger by many supporters who shared McCann's general denunciation in *The Herald* on 9 July 1994: 'All those Celtic people who were supposed to be doing their best for the club were not doing that at all.' The new supremo, while aware of the lingering resentment, had to acknowledge the pivotal role of such as Kevin Kelly and Tom Grant in his coming to power. It was no surprise that the remnants of the old Board were forced to come to terms soon with the changed situation at Celtic Park. For the most part, they bowed to the inevitable. First to go from the directorate was Jack McGinn, although he was 'retained' as the club's Legislative Adviser; he was followed a week later by Tom Grant, although he remained at Celtic Park as the stadium director; Kevin Kelly left, holding the title of Chairman Emeritus and President of Celtic Boys Club.

Only James Farrell chose to fight to retain his place on the Board but he lost his bid to retain his seat at an EGM on 13 September by a vote of

29 to 12. Ironically, Farrell, an acquaintance of McCann's parents, had spoken favourably of McCann when the latter's approaches had been the subject of Farrell's former colleagues' scepticism and suspicion. His departure, after nearly 30 years as a director, set the seal on the liquidation of the old order; the legal firm Shaughnessy, Quigley and McColl of which he was a senior partner had incorporated Celtic in April 1897, thus setting in motion the dynastic control which had recently crumbled.

Into their places came the following: Eric Riley as financial director, Patrick Ferrell as marketing director, Willie Haughey, John Keane (an Edinburgh builder) and Michael MacDonald (Gerald Weisfeld's stepson). This brought the number of members of the new Board to seven, as Dominic Keane, a former banker (and adviser to the winning consortium), had already joined McCann at the takeover.

If the above changes went through without any hitches, the appointment of Tommy Burns in Macari's place as Celtic's manager brought the outspoken McCann into open conflict with Scotland's football authorities, and caused Celtic financial grief. The furore served only to confirm McCann's growing conviction that the sport in Scotland was moribund, hide-bound by antiquated rules and regulations: 'There are too many non-investors around inside Scottish football. We're over-populated by too many clubs, who are subsidised by larger clubs, and they don't want to stop.' (*Daily Record* 5 October 1994)

In view of the subsequent uproar over his appointment, it is surprising to note that Tommy Burns did not appear to be Celtic's first choice as manager. Well-informed reports suggest that approaches, not necessarily by McCann, were made to Kenny Dalglish (then manager of Blackburn Rovers), Ivan Golac of Dundee United, recent winners of the Scottish Cup, and Bobby Robson, the former England manager currently in charge of Porto. Indeed, Robson admitted speaking to Fergus McCann during the summer of 1994 when the latter was sounding people out: 'I was flattered but it wasn't the right move for me at the time.' (*Scotland on Sunday* 14 May 1995)

The initial delight among the supporters over Burns' appointment and return to Celtic Park turned to dismay five weeks after he had taken over from Macari. On 18 August 1994, Celtic were fined £100,000 for an alleged illegal approach to their former player. The amount of the fine – 20 times higher than the previous highest sum levied by the League for a comparable offence – was decided unanimously by the Scottish Football League's management committee for 'a serious and blatant breach of the rules'. The League's secretary, Peter Donald, did not expand on precisely where Celtic's interpretation of the rules and the committee's differed. Celtic lost their appeal against the verdict itself at an acrimonious special general meeting on 29 September by a 69–1 majority (when a representative of a lower-division club 'got mixed up', thus preventing another unanimous decision). At the same meeting, Celtic also lost a further appeal against the size of the fine by a vote of 65–5.

Peter Donald, responding to the assertion that Rangers had been fined only £5,000 for their 'approach' to Duncan Ferguson of Dundee United, pointed out that Ferguson's case consisted of an alleged inducement of a player whereas 'this case was more complicated'. Unfortunately, he did not provide further enlightenment about the nature of the complexity. Fergus McCann, understandably perplexed, noted that he would have anticipated a fine of that severity in a court of law for 'a serious offence with a death involved, and it was an alternative to five years in prison'. He remains incensed about the club's never having received an acceptable explanation for the magnitude of the fine, all the more so since he is adamant that 'He [Burns] applied for the job, but we're deemed to have induced him.' (*Sunday Mail* 12 March 1995) His analogy, taken from the business world, that this affair was simply a case of a man in a managerial position changing one job for a bigger one with greater prospects, cut no ice with the game's governing body at the SFA's appeals committee on 12 October 1994. Their endorsement of the League's decision was described as 'final and binding' by the organisation's chief executive, Jim Farry. Celtic could not resort to a court of law, given the SFA's powers of expulsion from all organised football, and the likelihood of a civil court's upholding the right of a governing body to administer a sport as it saw fit.

At the SFA's AGM, held in May 1995, a Celtic motion – seconded by Rangers – to introduce a right for clubs to have recourse to law, should they be dissatisfied with the verdict of an SFA tribunal, was heavily defeated on a show of hands. Shortly afterwards, on 22 May 1995, Celtic were ordered by such a tribunal to pay Kilmarnock £200,000 for taking Tommy Burns and his assistant Billy Stark from the Ayrshire club. This brought to an end an 11–month wrangle between the clubs during which Celtic, in the person of Fergus McCann, had been condemned by one writer for 'behaving arrogantly and dictatorially'.

The last word in this saga should go perhaps to Brian Scott of the *Daily Mail*, who detected more than a whiff of hypocrisy in the whole affair: 'Tapping of players and managers may be against the rules, yet there cannot be a club so pious as to plead that they have never indulged in it. Most take the precaution of employing middlemen as, at the risk of blowing his cover, a venerable colleague in journalism would testify. He has tapped more managers and players than a shipyard worker has rivets.' (29 April 1995)

The emotional appeal of Celtic had proved irresistible for Tommy Burns, and, although he may have harboured fears that he was still too young for such a job (a reservation shared by one of his predecessors, Billy McNeill, some years before), he realised that this represented an opportunity that might not arise again. Tommy Burns was a man raised in long-demolished Soho Street (once described by him as 'only a free-kick away from Celtic Park'), and a Celtic player who had taken a highly emotional leave of the supporters in December 1989 in a friendly against Ajax. At the conclusion of that match, he had thrown his boots into the Jungle and blown kisses to the crowd: 'I didn't want to cry, I wanted to leave the field with a smile on my face – and I just made it.'

On his appointment as Celtic's manager on 12 July (!) 1994, Burns expressed optimism about arresting and reversing the situation at Parkhead. He ascribed the decline in part to his belief that 'Celtic has been missing from Celtic'. His first task was to lift the morale of the oft-maligned players he inherited: 'Celtic are on their knees right now; so it's my job to bring back credibility and get the players believing in themselves. It's all about pride and passion. There are a lot of good players here, but that seems to have been forgotten somewhere along the line. And, instead of knocking them, I'll encourage them in what is going to be a long, hard, uphill struggle.' (*Daily Record:* 13 July 1994)

His resolve was to be sorely tested during a campaign he was to describe at its end as one of 'unbearable pressure'. As his first season in charge drew to a close, he would admit with commendable frankness that he had not appreciated the extent of the task which faced him in the wake of the upheavals of the recent past; nor had he been fully aware of the frenzied expectations of the supporters. He told Hugh Keevins of *The Scotsman:* 'Players had been here for too long without having a future with the club, and there was no sign of a youth policy anywhere. It was like walking into the middle of a cyclone and being expected to stand there, looking unruffled by it all.' (17 May 1995)

Only two weeks into his first season (1994–95) Celtic fans were given grounds for optimism in thinking that the corner might have been turned, when Celtic travelled to Ibrox and won convincingly by 2–0 over a Rangers side which contained their two most recent expensive signings: Basile Boli from Marseilles and Brian Laudrup from Fiorentina. John Collins netted the first goal with another glorious free-kick from 20 yards out when he curled the ball around the Ibrox wall; Paul McStay added the second with his first goal at Ibrox in six years by netting in off the post with a well-struck shot from 25 yards. At that early stage in the season, Rangers were in considerable disarray: knocked out of the European Cup by AEK Athens, surprisingly ejected from the Coca-Cola Cup by Falkirk, and now humiliated by Celtic at Ibrox.

Celtic's confidence grew with the capture of Phil O'Donnell, a young midfielder acquired from Motherwell for a club record fee of £1.75 million in September 1994. The young international was bought to add a new dimension to Celtic's attack by complementing the craft of McStay and Collins with his energy and industry in getting forward into areas where he could hurt the opposition. The newcomer made an impressive début against Partick Thistle at Firhill, scoring both Celtic's goals in a 2–1 win – and putting the club in first place in the Premier League standings.

As has been frequently observed, though, the league championship is a marathon and not a sprint. Soon, Celtic began to reveal tell-tale signs that the early optimism was unrealistic. The unfortunate tendencies of recent seasons started to reappear. The supporters again had to endure the sight of lapses in concentration in defence, and a most frustrating habit of giving up a lead when apparently in control of a contest. This inconsistency was scarcely surprising in the case of a team playing under its third full-time manager within a year. Celtic FC, as a team as well as a club, was still sorting itself out after the long drawn-out trauma. In addition, the team's temporary home during the rebuilding of Celtic Park was Hampden; both manager and players would complain of the lack of atmosphere in the national stadium.

Three defeats within a short period sealed Celtic's fate in the championship and left them struggling to catch up in a bid to obtain entry into European competition: at Tynecastle they went down 1–0 to Hearts after a pedestrian display; at Hampden they were defeated 2–0 by Falkirk while playing inept and lethargic football throughout; and on 30 October at the same venue a Rangers side, minus six or seven key players, swept past Celtic by 3–1 when Laudrup, relishing his roving commission, left defenders bewildered and reeling in his wake. The humiliating nature of this defeat, in a fixture played on a Sunday and televised live, led to *The Independent*'s David McKinney concluding that the six-point gap between Rangers and Celtic in the league table 'was fuelling the suspicion that Tommy Burns has merely papered over the cracks since he replaced Lou Macari . . . Burns needs money for players and requires it quickly, if they are to build on the success in reaching the Coca-Cola Cup final.' (31 October 1994) The championship, a competition revamped with three points awarded for a win, was now a forlorn hope as the Rangers juggernaut rumbled on.

Celtic were beginning to anticipate that Coca-Cola [League] Cup final against humble Raith Rovers of the First Division with some trepidation. Suffering from a slump in form, Celtic could no longer consider the match a formality – even against a club which had been on the brink of receivership nearly six months earlier. As overwhelming favourites against opponents who had started the competition as 150–1 outsiders, Celtic would gain little glory from a victory, though even that could no longer be considered certain.

That a crisis of confidence was engulfing Celtic on the pitch was revealed by John Collins after a 2–2 draw at Tannadice against Dundee United, a result which dropped Celtic into fifth place. Emerging from a dressing-room inquest, the midfield player, who had twice put Celtic ahead in that league encounter, spoke about his frustration at the way in which Celtic had managed only three points out of a possible 18 from their past six league fixtures: 'We were a shambles, and a performance like that is not good enough for a club like Celtic. The players should be in twice a day for training until we learn to pass the ball properly. The bad run we are having has nothing to do with effort or determination. It is about a poor quality of possession. How can you get anywhere if you keep giving the ball to the other side?' (7 November 1994)

Four days later, after an insipid league performance against Partick Thistle in a goalless draw at Hampden Park, Celtic were jeered from the pitch by those supporters who had elected to stay till the final whistle. Tommy Burns, inwardly seething, barely succeeded in his attempt to be stoical at a perfunctory press conference afterwards: 'We suffer in silence . . .'

In the days leading up to the final, Celtic's increasing nervousness was being exposed despite the almost choreographed expressions of confidence: Charlie Nicholas let the mask slip when he spoke of 'the nightmare scenario' if Celtic were to lose, and Tommy Burns responded tetchily to a query about his players' frame of mind with a revealing 'I don't know. I never went five years without winning a medal'. (*The Scotsman:* 19 November 1994)

Before an all-ticket crowd of 45,384 Celtic and Raith Rovers lined up at Ibrox on 27 November 1994, and from the outset Gordon Dalziel, Raith's striker, sensed an upset could be on the cards when, by looking at his opponents just before the kick-off, he could see the signs of tension among the Celtic players.

The Kirkcaldy side, described as 'a team of free-transfers, YTS boys and lower-division stalwarts', started off brightly and took the lead in 18 minutes when a corner on the left by Broddle was not cleared decisively; the ball broke to Crawford, who brought it under control in a crowded penalty area and drove it through a forest of legs past Gordon Marshall. Celtic, galvanised into action by this impudence, hit back immediately and equalised on 30 minutes when Boyd's cross from the left to the back post was headed across the face of the goal by Galloway for Andy Walker to dive low and head the ball past the keeper.

Celtic dominated the remainder of the match with unrelenting pressure on the Raith goal in the second half, and appeared assured of victory when Nicholas stabbed the ball over the line after Walker's shot had rebounded off the post. It marked Charlie Nicholas's 125th goal in 250 appearances for Celtic, an impressive symmetry which now looked certain to be marked by a winner's medal for a darling of the fans. There were only six minutes remaining . . . but, three minutes later, Dair was allowed to advance from midfield and shoot from 20 yards. Marshall, notably idle through most of the final, failed to handle the shot cleanly and the ball bounced awkwardly out of his hands into the path of Dalziel who 'headed' the equaliser. Later, the Raith hero was honest enough to admit that he had scrambled the ball into the Celtic net more with his nose than with his head.

Celtic were crestfallen, as Tommy Burns would admit some months later: 'I looked at my players and I knew that it was as if a dagger had been plunged through the heart of each and every one of them.' (*The Scotsman*: 17 May 1995) Raith Rovers, spirits raised by the unexpected gift of the equaliser, held out fairly comfortably during the extra 30 minutes. They carried that momentum into the penalties decider, a nerve-wracking course they had already been over when defeating Airdrie in the semi-final. For the Celtic players, however, it was a relatively unknown journey, and one made worse by the weight of expectation, and the fear of the unthinkable now looming much closer. After each side had converted the regulation five penalties, and Raith had edged in front once more with their sixth, Celtic came to grief; Raith's keeper Thomson threw himself to his right to save Paul McStay's effort. James Traynor, writing in *The Herald,* captured the numbness of defeat for Celtic as McStay, hands over his head, stood inconsolable in his agony: 'All around the same stadium in which Celtic fans had rejoiced after the extra-time win over Aberdeen last month, people in green and white wept. Men and children sat heads bowed, unable to walk away, perhaps afraid they might crumble under the weight of their despair.' (28 November 1994)

A pall of depression settled over Parkhead after an event described hysterically by one newspaper as 'the blackest day in the club's history'. Some speculated that a devastated young manager might buckle under the strain; Burns admitted later that he had gone home after the match and prayed for the strength to handle the disappointment and embarrassment of 'a cruel twist of fate'. A few days later he snapped at a journalist who asked about the possibility of an expensive new signing coming to Celtic Park: 'What's the point? The other ten would only bring him down to their level.'

Certainly, the psychological damage inflicted on Celtic by this humiliating defeat was profound and prolonged. Such was the trauma that the team and its supporters might become overwhelmed with self-pity: one player suggested the club might never recover from 'having the cup we thought was ours snatched from our grasp', and one fan complained in the *Celtic View* about 'the anti-Celtic feeling' prevalent throughout Scotland: 'Suddenly, every second person you meet seems to be a Raith Rovers supporter.' The sports writer Kevin McCarra wrote of the need for a sense of perspective in the face of such derision: 'Anxious, angry and filled with disgust, everyone at the club has to embark on a search for patience.' (*Scotland on Sunday.* 4 December 1994)

Fortunately, the club's chief executive – and the first official in Celtic's history to have made a truly substantial personal financial investment in the club – had already taken a major step towards steadying the ship by asserting that the blow would not deflect him from his course: 'There were 38 other clubs who did not even make it to Sunday's Coca-Cola Cup final. We need to make changes but we are not in crisis.' He rebutted the rumours that he was ready to quit in the wake of the defeat: 'I didn't come here for five minutes or five weeks. I am here for five years to face the many challenges the club has to meet.'

McCann's statement may have sounded merely defiant, particularly as it came at a moment when a most critical stage of Celtic's revival had been reached. The upcoming share issue, designed to bring in much-needed capital to secure the club's future on and off the field, appeared to be compromised by the climate of defeatism. Indeed, a prominent official of the Celtic Supporters Association was quoted shortly after the final as saying that he would not be buying any of the new shares.

The cynics were given further ammunition when the side, described by some as 'the worst in Celtic's history', went on to create an unwanted club record, a run of 11 league matches without a win. Most of those games were draws but, with only one point awarded for a draw, they had to be considered miserable results. The sequence was eventually broken with a 2–0 win over Falkirk at Hampden on New Year's Eve 1994.

Launching an ambitious share issue in these circumstances, and just before Christmas, seemed hardly propitious, especially when the minimum stake required was a substantial £620. A major boost would come, however, with the announcement of a £4 million investment in the shares on the part of Dermot Desmond, a Dublin-based 'tycoon and entrepreneur' who was quoted by one of his associates as seeing Celtic 'almost as a proxy for Irish football in the European Cup'. Desmond himself insisted that the investment was justified on commercial terms alone, and was rewarded for his services by being appointed a non-executive director of the club in May 1995.

The success of the share issue was extraordinary. The target of £9.4 million was oversubscribed by £4.4 million and necessitated a supplementary share issue, making it the most successful venture of its kind in British football. It provided an eventual capital base of over £20 million, again unequalled by any other British club, and a reported global shareholding of 10,000 people, mostly individuals rather than institutions. Such a massive vote of confidence – or faith – in the club's future was reminiscent of the original feelings which had inspired Celtic to greatness in its early days more than a century earlier. Fergus McCann was delighted, and genuinely moved by the affection for the club which had prompted so many to reach for their cheque-books.

One astonished investment analyst, asked to comment on the stampede to buy shares, noted that Celtic supporters had done something deemed impossible in financial circles: 'To have an issue oversubscribed when the Stock Exchange is in a rough patch is good going. The Government can't even do it with Powergen when offering incentives.' One of those brand-new shareholders, speaking to *The Scotsman*, gave possibly the most basic of all reasons when explaining his emotional investment: '. . . social altruism, romantic fantasism and the pursuit of childish dreams apart, at £620 to stuff Rangers – it's cheap at the price!'

The whole club had been given a lift at a most difficult time. Before the start of the season, with hopes prematurely high, 18,500 Celtic supporters had purchased season-tickets; the figure was more than double the previous record. Now, although with a growing awareness of how far the club and team still had to go to revive a proud name in football, those same supporters had demonstrated a remarkable loyalty yet again.

On the field, things had to improve in order to justify the developments elsewhere, and Tommy Burns was only too aware that Celtic's chronic problems of the early 1990s still lingered at Parkhead: a defence which betrayed uncertainty at critical times; a midfield which rarely fired on all cylinders simultaneously; and forward permutations which tended towards over-elaboration, and whose cutting-edge was blunted by the absence of a top-class finisher.

The manager could derive some satisfaction from the moves he had made in an attempt to remedy the situation: in November 1994 he had imported Tom 'Tosh' McKinlay from Heart of Midlothian in the hope that this sound defender's overlapping and excellent crossing of the ball would compensate for Celtic's lack of 'wide' players, and in January 1995 he signed Pierre Van Hooijdonk, a proven goalscorer from the admittedly modest Dutch side NAC Breda, for £1.25 million. At 6 feet 5 inches tall, the newcomer was a figure who could add height and weight to Celtic's attack. Burns had also given an extended run in the first team to pint-sized Brian McLaughlin, a product of the Celtic Boys Club, and the youngster's innate ability was drawing hopeful comparisons with Jimmy Johnstone.

Similarly, the manager had taken a chance with young Brian O'Neil in a new role as central defender, a position in which the player, previously unsettled at Parkhead, started to make a niche for himself.

The giant Dutch striker made an immediate impression by scoring a spectacular goal on his début against Hearts at Hampden Park in a 1–1 draw; he controlled an awkward ball on the edge of the penalty area, and outwitted two Hearts defenders before driving the ball high into the net. Van Hooijdonk appeared to be the type of personality player that the Celtic supporters desperately craved, but shortly after his arrival in Glasgow he came face to face with the rancorous side of the Old Firm rivalry. His car stopped at traffic-lights and, while the Celtic player took the opportunity to make a call on his mobile phone, a total stranger walked off the pavement, came up to his car, and spat in his face . . .

With the championship well out of reach, everything depended on the club lifting the Scottish Cup. The possibility of another failure – on the lines of the Raith Rovers model – was raised often enough in the days prior to the final, because Airdrie, Celtic's opponents, were astute enough to play on such fears. Their manager, Alex MacDonald, was an ex-Ranger, and his highly experienced squad proved to be keen exponents of psychological warfare before the match: Celtic might be paralysed with the fear of failure; Airdrie had been a 'homeless' club since the bulldozing of Broomfield the previous summer; their crowds had dropped because of the distance involved in attending matches at their temporary home in Cumbernauld; their players had to take kit home to be washed, and they had to train in a public park, Strathclyde . . .

All the ingredients were there for an upset, and the question posed in virtually every pre-match analysis was a blunt one: 'Will Celtic bottle it again?' The fear was a genuine one as Airdrie, like Raith Rovers, played in the First Division and, indeed, had defeated Raith Rovers by 4-1 on their way to the final.

The answer came within the first ten minutes of the final watched by 36,915 at a Hampden Park sadly reduced in capacity due to reconstruction. Contrary to the general expectation that Airdrie, a well-organised and determined outfit, would harry Celtic from the start and strive to put extra pressure on the favourites by scoring first, it was the Lanarkshire side who appeared to freeze. In the early stages they surrendered the initiative and Celtic took immediate advantage of the signs of dishevelment in their opponents' defence. Tosh McKinlay threatened the Airdrie goal with well-delivered crosses: from one of them a relieved Airdrie defence was glad to concede a corner, and from McKinlay's kick young central defender Mark McNally should have done better with a free header. In the ninth minute, however, Celtic went ahead: the Airdrie defence cleared McLaughlin's cross only as far as the waiting McKinlay, who advanced some ten yards down the left before crossing a beautifully flighted ball into the penalty area for Van Hooijdonk to rise majestically and angle a powerful header downwards and beyond the outstretched hand of Martin.

The skilful Dutchman had been criticised for a tendency to drift out of things and, for such a tall man, a surprising weakness in the air, but here was a splendidly taken goal. The goalscorer had passed a fitness test for a hamstring injury only on the morning of the final, and he had to be substituted shortly before half-time. With his departure, much of the gloss went off Celtic's display but Airdrie, a team of honest journeymen, showed neither the flair nor the imagination to trouble Celtic's defence, which had been weakened by the absence of Mowbray through suspension and of O'Neil through a knee injury sustained in training.

With few shots on goal from either side, the rest of a nervy, scrappy final was forgettable – apart from the display of the frequently maligned Peter Grant. The midfielder had already been singled out by his manager as Celtic's most consistent player during the season, but his prospects of playing in the match had seemed remote when he was stretchered off at Tannadice two weeks earlier with a damaged knee ligament. Grant showed an extraordinary determination to get himself fit and, on a day when Alex MacDonald felt 'the Celtic jersey was bigger than the player', he was the most influential man on the pitch. The tenacious midfield grafter ran himself into near-exhaustion, effectively cutting off the service to Airdrie's strikers, while his more polished partners Paul McStay and John Collins struggled to impose some fluency on Celtic's play. His cajoling of team-mates and tackling of opponents was truly inspirational, and never more so than in the dying minutes when he raced back in pursuit of Lawrence to thwart the striker with a perfectly timed tackle as the Airdrie player bore down on Bonner's goal. Graham Spiers of *Scotland on Sunday* was suitably impressed: 'Take Peter Grant out of the Cup final and Celtic would have been impoverished. Erase his ferocious midfield interceptions and searing passes, and this win would have been more desperate for them.' (28 May 1995)

Those sentiments would have been endorsed by captain Paul McStay, whose relief at the final whistle was almost palpable, and Tommy Burns, equally relieved at casting aside Celtic's six-year-long stigma of failure. The triumph was the fulfilment of a prediction by the manager back in November when, in the wake of that numbing defeat by Raith Rovers, Burns had called the downcast members of his squad together and told them: 'Don't worry, you'll be at Hampden for the Scottish Cup final and this time you'll win!'

And so Celtic took the Scottish Cup home to Paradise and to a stadium now emerging as a phoenix-like symbol of the club's resurrection. Since the close season of 1994 massive reconstruction work had been under way. An impressive £17 million stand, with seating for 26,000, had been rising week by week on the north side of the ground on the site of the former Jungle. Just before the start of the 1995–96 season it was hanselled in a 1–1 friendly match with Newcastle United, another great club recently reborn. The new structure was only one part of a long-term plan to make Celtic Park the biggest all-seated club stadium in Britain, with an eventual capacity for 60,000.

Celtic had come back to life: back to Celtic Park and a brand-new stand; back as winners of the Scottish Cup (for a record 30th time); back to perform for their ever-faithful supporters, many of whom were now share-holders; back to play before huge and enthusiastic crowds at the club's spiritual home. In fact, back to their roots – and, with a fine regard for tradition, the first sod in the new pitch had been imported from Donegal, as had been the case when the present ground was opened in 1892. This time it had been ceremoniously cut in Mullaghduff and transferred to Larne for the overnight crossing to Scotland. During the journey, as the *Derry People and Donegal News* reported on 15 April 1995, the treasured turf had been kept well watered 'on the advice of a Celtic Park official . . . to ensure the shamrocks would grow when the sod was replanted on the field'.

Too often the return of the Scottish Cup has been a time for unrestrained jubilation for everybody at Celtic Park. In May 1995, however, only the most blinkered could fail to recognise that the latest triumph was only a stepping stone on the road to full recovery. Much work had still to be done . . . not least the mending of the relationship between the manager and the chairman.

Asked to comment on that relationship at his post-match press conference immediately after the final, Tommy Burns admitted that 'it was not what it should be'. Only two days later, ironically at the launch of the club's new range of champagne and spirits, he brought matters into the public spotlight by criticising Fergus McCann for diluting his managerial responsibilities and frustrating attempts to sign top-class players. In particular, the manager accused the chairman of treating the players like 'second-class citizens' by imposing budgetary restraints upon a training trip to Milan prior to the Scottish Cup final. As a consequence, Burns claimed, the players were deprived of the use of proper facilities and the customary perk of 'pocket money'. In addition, clearly exasperated when queried about future signings, Burns responded by jibing, 'We're in discussions – I just hope they have plenty of Ovaltine with them.'

Almost a week later, in the *Sunday Post*, Doug Baillie reported on the outcome of the manager's outburst: 'Burns was summoned to Celtic Park. He was shown press cuttings of his utterances and complaints since the Tennents Scottish Cup final. He was asked to read them, then tell the assembled gathering of the club's directors if he wished to continue as Celtic's manager. If the answer was yes, he would be granted his wish only if he made a public apology. Burns backed down and, at around 4 p.m. on Wednesday, Celtic's public relations manager Peter McLean read out a statement aimed at calming troubled waters. Fergus McCann, inevitably, had won the battle: the manager would do well to watch his Ps and Qs from now on – or else! (4 June 1995)

For his part, Fergus McCann still harboured some reservations about Burns, although he had described him in late 1994 as 'arguably the most talented young manager in the country'. His disquiet centred in part around the purchase of Phil O'Donnell from Motherwell for £1.75 million in September 1994, at a time when McCann was out of the country. Contrary to the usual practice of payment by instalment, the transfer fee was paid in a lump sum at Motherwell's request. McCann was annoyed to learn that the player was carrying an injury (perhaps unknown to Burns); an angry McCann actually wanted to re-negotiate the deal but, of course, it was too late.

There was also a lingering sense of displeasure with the manager in McCann's blunt assessment of Celtic's performance in 1994–95 as boring: 'We struggled and lost to some inferior teams . . . there was a lot of trepidation last season, and we were trapped into the Scottish style of defence . . . It's up to people here [Celtic Park] to get it right, to have a little bit of arrogance. That is something that has to be restored.' (*Evening Times*: 4 July 1995)

At the time it seemed that only a fragile truce had been negotiated: Burns claimed later that he had apologised for the consternation his comments had aroused among the supporters (and not for his sentiments); McCann admitted some time later to being peeved that the episode had seen him depicted as 'the baddie in a pantomime'.

Even before the Scottish Cup final there had been rumours of fall-outs and arguments between the two men; it was suggested that they were scarcely on speaking terms at times as a result of what Burns perceived as the chairman's preoccupation with profit-and-loss to the detriment of the manager's major concern, described by him as 'the supporters' hopes and dreams'.

In an interview with *The Independent* on 7 February 1996 Tommy Burns came close to suggesting that he had been emboldened to make his stand in the afterglow of having won a major trophy for the club when he hinted also that his position had been under threat in the wake of the previous season's Coca-Cola Cup final defeat: 'Quite a few people turned against me. Had we not beaten Airdrie to win the Scottish Cup, who knows what might have happened to me? I knew I was on shaky ground . . .'

Kevin McCarra, writing in *Scotland on Sunday*, summed up the affair succinctly, describing Celtic as 'the first club ever to mark a cup win with a week of despondency'.

There were to be more uneasy moments during the close season. Aware that the club had often been accused of resting on its laurels after an unexpected triumph, the supporters felt confident that, under the new régime, things would be different. Players would be purchased to bolster a squad widely recognised as lacking in depth and quality. Disappointment after disappointment, however, eroded the hopes of the supporters as several star players linked with a move to Parkhead failed to put pen to paper: David Ginola, the stylish winger of Paris St Germain, midfielder Marc Degryse of Anderlecht, Russian striker Dimitri Radchenko . . . The press, in general, blamed Fergus McCann's stubbornness for the breakdown in the contract talks, but this was manifestly unfair. Later, Ginola would admit he had used the talks with Celtic as a bargaining tool in order to facilitate his move to Barcelona (although he had to settle for Newcastle in the end), while Degryse claimed unconvincingly that he would be taking a salary cut of 50 per cent to come to Parkhead, and went instead to struggling Sheffield Wednesday.

Worse news was to come for the manager as he was preparing for the new season; on a continental tour, Celtic went down 2–0 to a part-time German side, Kickers Emden, and Burns learned that the transfer of Gordan Petric from Dundee United had suffered a glitch. In fact, the central defender was on his way to Ibrox. Rangers' delight in the success of their coup of one-upmanship was barely concealed. Tommy Burns' frustration was compounded by the fact that his promising centre-back Brian O'Neil was destined to be sidelined for a lengthy period following an operation to correct a cruciate ligament injury.

In addition, problems still had to be ironed out in the proposed move of Andreas Thom from Bayer Leverkusen to Celtic Park. Questioned by journalists at Glasgow Airport after the tour about the difficulties in signing star players, Burns snapped: 'You'd better ask the President [McCann] about that!'

After prolonged negotiations, highly suspenseful for Celtic supporters, the German international eventually signed for a transfer fee estimated at £2.2 million. The *Sunday Mail* claimed there was a touch of desperation about the capture of the player, suggesting that the deal had almost foundered at the last moment. After arriving in a rented Rolls-Royce, Thom was kept waiting for almost three hours at Celtic Park while McCann baulked at the player's personal terms. It was said that the chairman agreed only after being warned by advisers that the fans (and the manager) were at the end of their tether after having missed out on Ginola, Degryse, Radchenko and Petric. The newspaper quoted an insider: 'At one stage the deal looked dead. But he [McCann] was told the fans wouldn't accept being let down any more, and were liable to cause a riot if Thom didn't sign. Only then did he go ahead.' (6 August 1995) Whatever the difficulties, Celtic had acquired an intelligent, quick-footed player, a seasoned professional who, more of a goalmaker than a striker, could drag opponents out of position with unselfish play which enabled his colleagues to exploit the resultant gaps.

Burns continued to strengthen his squad: John Hughes, considered a journeyman stopper with Falkirk, was purchased in August 1995 for a fee set by tribunal at £380,000 and performed solidly in O'Neil's place throughout the season; Jackie McNamara, the son of a former Celtic player, was signed from Dunfermline Athletic in October 1995 for £600,000 and settled in immediately at right-back where his quickness, accurate passing and ability to join in attacks helped earn him the award of the Scottish Young Player of the Year; in December Morten Wieghorst, a Danish international, arrived from Dundee for £600,000 to add height and weight to the midfield and the attack; at the end of March 1996, unfortunately too late to affect the outcome of the championship, Jorge Cadete, a Portugese international striker formerly of Sporting Lisbon, belatedly joined Celtic in a complicated deal involving a reported sum of around £1 million. His clearance to play in Scotland took five weeks to resolve, a situation which an aggrieved Fergus McCann clearly attributed to some unhelpfulness on the part of the SFA.

Burns and McCann had had their difficulties and, at one time, it seemed that they were incompatible, but the air had been cleared between the two and the situation had stabilised. Both men had the interests of the club very much at heart, but approached matters from different perspectives. Burns was the football man, a young manager who wanted to put the best possible side on the field, while McCann had spent long hours poring over the accounts and felt the club had to put its financial house in order. Of course, the two concerns were interrelated, and often overlapping. Fortunately, the 'confrontations' between Burns and McCann in the close season had helped to clear up some of the confusion. McCann summed up their new rapport admirably: 'I think we have a good professional relationship. I don't always agree with him and, in turn, he doesn't always agree with me. The way I look at it, we are growing together in this business and at this club. What we do have in common is the prosperity of Celtic.' (*Evening Times*: 4 August 1995)

Burns' immediate concern was to re-establish Celtic as legitimate contenders for the championship, a competition in which they had not even attained the consolation of runners-up since last winning the title in 1988. An eighth successive league flag for Rangers was considered a foregone conclusion by most football pundits. It was an opinion that echoed the pre-season realism of Tommy Burns when he admitted that Celtic were still two or three players short of ending Rangers' domination of the championship. He knew only too well that Celtic remained prone to concede goals through uncertain defending, and at times were too elaborate in their attacking build-up, still lacking punch. At Ibrox, Rangers' ferocious determination to continue on top was articulated by David Murray, their chairman: 'Our fans talk about winning ten in a row and beating Celtic's record. *I* want us to retain the championship for ever.' As if to underline that ambition he had authorised the acquisition of Paul Gascoigne from Lazio for an estimated £4.3 million in the summer of 1995 despite question marks about the English midfielder's fitness and temperament.

Rangers would prove to be an insuperable barrier to Celtic in all three domestic competitions, with Celtic failing to record a victory in six encounters with their old rivals. In the first two matches, played at Parkhead within the space of 12 days, Rangers struck hammer blows to Celtic's hopes for the season – and Paul Gascoigne played a major part in their victories. In the Coca-Cola Cup quarter-final on 19 September 1995, McCoist headed the only goal of the match in the 75th minute after Gascoigne's tantalising cross from the right had eluded Gordon Marshall in Celtic's goal; in the first Old Firm league match of the season, Rangers again soaked up pressure from Celtic with Gascoigne netting the second goal in their 2–0 victory. With Celtic threatening to equalise, Gascoigne sealed Rangers' win by running 70 yards – from one penalty box to the other, and passing eight players on the way – to get on the end of McCoist's cross and slip the ball clinically past the exposed Marshall. It was the inspirational kind of goal that was to characterise the Englishman's eventful season. It also typified a level of consistent productivity that no Celtic midfielder would come close to matching.

The major difference between the sides was apparent at this early stage in the season: Rangers' defence could handle the threat from Celtic's strike force, and the Parkhead club did not have a midfield player with the genuine flair and forceful penetration of the likes of Gascoigne to compensate. Significantly, he scored as many goals as Celtic's recognised midfielders put together. However, at least one letter-writer to the *Celtic View* thought the Englishman was being afforded altogether too much respect: 'We have had players out there against Gascoigne who, by their actions on the field – lifting him up when he fell, patting his rear as he passed, and laughing and joking with him – looked as though they were being given an honour to play on the same pitch as him.' (15 May 1996)

At that stage of the season things had a depressingly familiar look for Celtic: knocked out of the Coca-Cola Cup, humiliated at home by Rangers in the league, and already falling well behind in the championship with points dropped in drawn games . . . and due to face the crack French side Paris St Germain in the Cup-Winners' Cup.

One of the problems seemed to be that of adjusting to the new Celtic Park, as nine points were dropped out of the eighteen available in the first six league fixtures there. Perhaps it would be more accurate to say that it was taking time for the new players to settle into their impressive surroundings while bedding down to the passing game advocated by their manager. Frustratingly, the promise was there and, even at the end of the season, Burns would insist that Celtic's best performance of the entire year had been against Hibernian at Parkhead on 14 October 1995, a game marked by silky, intricate passing and breathtaking movement from Celtic . . . but a match which ended with two points lost in a 2–2 draw.

After another draw at home in early November, 0–0 against an ultra-defensive Raith Rovers, Celtic's position looked hopeless: already six points behind Rangers, who had also stretched their goal-difference advantage to eleven.

However, there were encouraging signs that this Celtic squad had acquired some steel in its makeup. For one thing, it would be the season for comebacks: in the first fixture at Pittodrie, on 10 September, Celtic went two goals down early on before rallying for a highly impressive 3–2 win, despite playing without John Hughes for the last 20 minutes, ordered off for a second bookable offence; at Ibrox on 19 November in a thrilling encounter Pierre van Hooijdonk rose magnificently to head an equaliser from McKinlay's perfect cross after Rangers had taken a 3–2 lead; at Celtic Park on 2 December, Kilmarnock stole into a two-goal lead minutes before the interval, but another spirited fightback saw Celtic run out 4–2 winners; again at Pittodrie, on 14 January 1996, Celtic fought back after being a goal down at the interval to win through by 2–1 thanks to splendid goals from Collins and Van Hooijdonk; only three days later, at Tynecastle against a rejuvenated Hearts team, late goals by Van Hooijdonk and Andy Walker eked out another thrilling victory.

The supporters could see the return of the club's traditional fighting spirit and rejoiced at it; just as gratifying was a return to the playing standards long associated with the club; indeed, many neutral observers classed Celtic as the most entertaining and skilful side in the country, as the players buckled down to the challenge for the title.

Nobody showed greater effectiveness than Pierre van Hooijdonk. Previously noted for his deft touches and ability to involve others in the play, he had been criticised for his failure to capitalise on his physical advantages. Hugh Keevins, writing in *The Scotsman* on 6 November 1995, reported a rumour on the eve of Celtic's 2–0 win at Motherwell that 'the Dutchman was told in no uncertain terms' by the manager that 'it was time he started to earn his wages at Celtic Park'. After the discussion with Tommy Burns, the striker produced a rich vein of form and went on to finish the season as the top scorer in the Premier League with an impressive 26 goals. One indication of hard work on the practice ground was the Dutchman's significant improvement both in heading the ball and challenging for it in the air.

Early in the New Year, the supporters were beginning to speak with cautious optimism of the possibility of a league championship for Celtic. Three very tricky away hurdles – at Starks Park, Pittodrie and Tynecastle – were negotiated impressively within a period of nine days with victories over Raith Rovers (3–1), Aberdeen (2–1) and Hearts (2–1).

Crucially, however, they did not capitalise on their splendid form on the road by stumbling at Rugby Park with a 0–0 draw against Kilmarnock. Maddeningly, on the same day (20 January 1996), Rangers crashed by 3–0 to Hearts at Ibrox. A single goal for Celtic at Kilmarnock would have put Celtic one point clear at the top of the table – and would have created the intriguing situation of a Rangers side having to react to the uncommon sight in recent years of their greatest rivals heading a championship apparently destined for Ibrox before a ball had even been kicked in earnest.

On 10 February Celtic again ground to a halt, this time on a greasy playing surface at Brockville; the home side, desperate to avoid relegation, defended in depth from the opening whistle and thwarted all Celtic's efforts to break down their resistance. There was a report after the match of boot marks on the walls leading to the dressing-rooms, a 'testimony', apparently, to the anger and frustration of the visiting players. Rangers, meanwhile, had salvaged a late victory over Motherwell at Ibrox to stretch their lead to three points (and their advantage in goal-difference). With their greater experience in coping with the pressures of a title race, the Ibrox club looked well set as the last quarter of the championship got under way.

With no other clubs remotely in contention – a clear indication of just how much the financial muscle of Rangers and Celtic had reduced the Scottish championship to a two-horse race – the Old Firm fixture at Ibrox on 17 March 1996 was looming as the decider. Sadly the three-point gap remained the same after a tense clash; the 1–1 outcome favoured Rangers more although Celtic could derive consolation from a brave fightback after young Jackie McNamara was ordered off midway through the second half. John Hughes came up to meet Peter Grant's free-kick and head the ball powerfully into the net from eight yards out for a late equaliser – but it had been a contest Celtic simply had to win, and again had been found wanting.

Six days later the mood of the supporters was downcast – and angry – after another goalless draw, this time at Fir Park against a much-improved Motherwell side. The disappointment came with the dropping of two points; the rage came with the disallowing of a 'goal' by Van Hooijdonk late in the game by the referee, Mr Clyde (Bearsden), who ruled that the Dutchman was offside before he gathered a rebound from the crossbar of McStay's shot.

Leaving Fir Park, many fans could be heard fulminating against the standard of refereeing in Scotland, attributing this latest setback to yet another questionable – and costly – decision in a season which one supporter dubbed 'The Year of the Referees'. At Tynecastle on 23 September 1995 Peter Grant was ordered off after an off-the-ball flare-up with Robertson upon the say-so of a linesman stationed 60 yards away while the other linesman within a few yards, and presumably better-positioned, appeared to ignore the incident completely; at Rugby Park on 21 October 1995 John Collins was wrestled down inside the box by two Kilmarnock defenders as he attempted to break through, but no penalty was awarded; in another scoreless draw at Falkirk on 10 February Jackie McNamara was body-checked clumsily by ex-Celt Maurice Johnston on the edge of the box late in the game, but the referee ignored the frantic claims for a penalty . . .

This series of perceived injustices was made all the worse for those supporters by viewing the extraordinary leniency they considered to have been afforded Paul Gascoigne. Indeed, a John Grieve of Newton Stewart was still fuming after the league season had ended, as his letter to *The Herald*, printed on 13 May 1996, suggests: 'Gascoigne's undeniable talents have won matches, matches he should not have played in had officials not blatantly ignored his vicious assaults on opposing players – he should have been ordered from the field on several occasions. Many of Celtic's drawn matches would have resulted in victories had officials not intervened to deny Celtic. To summarise, Celtic were cheated out of the league championship by bigoted wee men masquerading as referees, an absolute disgrace . . .'

As if to underline the intensity of such emotions, a week after the fixture at Motherwell, the *Daily Mail* reported that 'a source close to Clyde [the referee]' was claiming that the official and his family had been subjected to a series of anonymous telephone calls from Celtic fans blaming him for 'destroying their championship dreams'. (29 March 1996)

After that draw at Fir Park, Burns continued to speak bravely of Celtic refusing to accept defeat in the title race which Rangers now led by five points; the body-language of his players as they trooped off the field told a different story. The cause indeed now looked hopeless, but Celtic roared back into contention with a dazzling 5–0 rout of Aberdeen on 1 April at Parkhead. Despite the attraction of watching the match live on TV, a crowd of 35,994 rolled up to witness Celtic in irresistible form, boosted by the belated appearance of Jorge Cadete. The Portuguese striker came off the bench in the second half to a rapturous welcome, and scored within three minutes, his delicate chip leaving Watt helpless.

Optimism had been revived, but only too briefly . . . for the moment of truth was only days away. And what a bitter reckoning it proved to be. Celtic, the holders of the Scottish Cup, went into the semi-final clash with Rangers at Hampden on 7 April 1996 with a feeling that their name might already be on the trophy again. After all, they had staged their own version of 'The Great Escape' against Dundee United at Parkhead in the previous round: United had been holding on stubbornly to a one-goal lead with only two minutes left when Van Hooijdonk towered above their defenders to head home the equaliser from McNamara's free-kick . . . and almost straight from the restart Thom latched on to a loose ball and raced 'like a scalded cat' clear of pursuers before slamming the ball past Maxwell to pull off an incredible victory.

Celtic, hoping to extend a 29-match unbeaten run in domestic competition, took far too long to settle and the confrontation soon took on a familiar pattern: Rangers were resolute and determined in defence, and dangerous on the break. At a critical moment in the contest, when Celtic were beginning to exert real pressure on Rangers' goal, the Ibrox men struck. Only minutes before the interval – a fatal time for Celtic in Old Firm clashes that season – Gordon Marshall could do little more than palm away a shot from Rangers full-back Robertson, and McCoist pounced on the ball to open the scoring. Rangers pressed home their advantage in the first ten minutes of the second half, and passed up two clear opportunities to add to their 1–0 lead.

Celtic had no sooner started to re-group when Laudrup raced free of the defenders in a well-constructed breakaway in the 66th minute to clip the ball over Marshall and settle the contest. Not quite . . . though, as Tommy Burns admitted later, 'We were two goals down before we showed the right attitude.' With nine minutes remaining, Van Hooijdonk glanced his header from McNamara's cross past a helpless Goram. Simon Donnelly then had two chances to bring a revitalised Celtic level: he was not quite tall enough to reach another cross from McNamara and his header went over the bar . . . but with only two minutes left, he should have scored when, after bursting through the middle to collect a header from McKinlay, he shot over the bar again with only Goram to beat. For the first time in two decades Celtic had failed to beat Rangers in the course of a season; once again, Rangers had proved mentally and physically tougher, the team for the big occasion . . .

There were clear signs that the after-effects still lingered a few days later, when Celtic could only draw with Kilmarnock at Parkhead, with Van Hooijdonk's spectacular scissors-kick earning a point in the very last minute. It was Celtic's 11th draw of the league season and another golden opportunity to exert pressure on Rangers had been passed up on a night when Hearts beat the Ibrox men 2–0 at Tynecastle.

In truth, the title chase was over, for all the defiant noises being uttered in public by certain players; inside Celtic Park the more realistic had privately conceded the inevitable conclusion which duly arrived on 28 April 1996 when Paul Gascoigne almost single-handedly routed Aberdeen at Ibrox.

It was a bitter pill to swallow for, in any other season, Celtic's performance would have been good enough to clinch the title. Consider the following. Two new Premier League records were established: only one defeat in the 36-game schedule, and the longest sequence of undefeated matches (31). In addition, Celtic were the only side unbeaten away from home in league football on either side of the border. A desperately sad case of so near and yet so far.

No consolation either from the club's 31st foray into European competition. Celtic's European Cup-Winners' Cup campaign was to be yet another graphic reminder of the standards required to restore the club to its eminence during the late 1960s and early '70s. Celtic managed to overcome the mediocre Dynamo Batumi on a 7–2 aggregate, an accomplishment which started with Celtic's first away victory in Europe in nine years when they edged the Georgians by 3–2 on 14 September.

In the next round Celtic were pitted against formidable opponents in the shape of Paris St Germain, semi-finalists in European competitions in the past three seasons. The French side may have been a team in transition after losing their star performers David Ginola and George Weah, but they were still considered to be an impressive outfit, one carrying too much firepower for Celtic. *L'Equipe*, the famous French sports daily, put Celtic's current status in true perspective by describing the Glasgow club as 'an illustrious name, but not a giant in European competitions'. (19 October 1995)

At the Parc des Princes, the Frenchmen carved out a narrow 1–0 win to take to Glasgow, and the same newspaper pointed out one particular longtime Celtic failing as having been a major factor: 'PSG were largely unimaginative, but Celtic could not take advantage because they posed no threat up front.' (20 October 1995) In fact, the only opportunity created by the Scots was missed by Van Hooijdonk when he headed a superb cross from O'Donnell wide of goal, the Dutchman claiming afterwards that he had been momentarily dazzled by the floodlights.

In the second leg, on 2 November, PSG swept aside any suggestions that they might be found vulnerable at a packed and noisy Celtic Park by producing a magnificent all-round performance. Celtic's worst-ever home defeat in European competition was on the cards from the moment Loko rushed in to net after Marshall had mishandled Fournier's shot in 36 minutes; only five minutes later the same player volleyed home a cross from the right after intricate passing had confused the Celtic defence. After absorbing Celtic's early pressure, the visitors had hit their opponents with a classic continental sucker punch. In the second half Celtic continued to surge forward gamely, while PSG waited patiently to exploit the resultant gaps in defence – and were duly rewarded with a third goal in 68 minutes.

To his credit, Tommy Burns acknowledged that the gulf in standards between Britain and the Continent had to be bridged as a matter of urgency. He immediately introduced extra daily training and coaching sessions for the entire first-team squad to develop and sharpen their skills; he arranged to visit Holland to view the workings of Ajax, the European champions, whose youth development programme is such that the club reportedly recruits a staggering 90 per cent of its players from the Amsterdam area; he continued to preach the need to introduce a coaching set-up at Celtic Park similar to what he had observed on the Continent; his vision, he told the press, incorporates a custom-built complex with training, catering and support facilities which would include a full-size indoor pitch to offset the Scottish climate in winter . . .

That night – 2 November – marked a turning-point in the season for the supporters as well as Tommy Burns. They watched Celtic go down to a resounding defeat, and they applauded the fine work of the visitors, standing at the end to cheer the French side off the pitch. The general feeling in the ground that night was that the Celtic support would be well pleased if the French side went on to win the trophy – a feat which they accomplished by beating Rapid Vienna in the final. One moment in the second half stood out in the memory: Gordon Marshall raced from his goal to intercept a pass, and thought momentarily about punting the ball far downfield but, instead, started another Celtic attack by throwing the ball to the feet of Vata. At that moment, the vast crowd broke into a chant of 'Tommy Burns, Tommy Burns, Tommy Burns'. The message was clear: the Celtic supporters wanted their side to keep playing football, to try to match the best on football terms . . . and they were prepared to encourage the players to play that type of football – even when facing defeat.

This latest season (1995–96) has been described as one in which Celtic gained 'compliments, not cups; tributes, not trophies'. One would, therefore, expect a feeling of bitter disappointment to permeate the club and its followers, but that is not the case . . . The last game of the league campaign, a meaningless fixture against Raith Rovers (arguably the least attractive drawing-card in the Premier Division) produced the largest attendance of the season at Celtic Park. The all-seated crowd of 37,423 saw a sparkling performance by Celtic in their 4–1 win, newcomer Jorge Cadete leading the way with two goals, and the atmosphere was a carnival one.

At the end of a season during which nothing was won, the mood was of exhilaration, appreciation and accomplishment. Yes, accomplishment – at least in terms of genuine progress on and off the field. Season-ticket sales had grown to the 30,000 mark, helping to swell the attendances at a stadium taking impressive shape in Glasgow's East End; it was the clearest proof yet that Celtic had won back their supporters. The developments were going hand-in-hand with team-building that was showing signs of reaping tangible rewards in the near future.

Both the ground-improvement and the team-building would gather pace as the close season loomed. Week after week the new stand behind the goal grew nearer to completion; day after day the newspapers speculated about new signings. Indeed, the season was scarcely over when the club paid out a record amount to capture the services of an English defender on a long-term commitment. The acquisition of the giant 24-year-old player was heralded in a significant way, the Press Association 'fl: shing' the news of the transfer as follows: '10.03 a.m. – Bolton central defender Alan Stubbs today joined Celtic for £5.5 million on a five-year contract, the Glasgow club announced on the Stock Market.' It was a sign of the times. Celtic had recently joined the Alternative Investment Market (AIM), and it is interesting to note that in the early summer of 1996 ordinary Celtic shares were trading there at three times the £75 purchase price at the start of the season. Fergus McCann, who has frequently expressed concern about the upward spiral of players' salaries, acknowledged the new reality by asserting that the Stubbs move was an indication that Celtic would not be outbid by any British club: 'We pay top dollar, and I hope that people will get the message that Celtic are very serious about competing with the highest order here and on the Continent . . . No one here is expected to play entirely for the jersey.' It was reported that the breakdown of the deal meant a transfer fee of £3.5 million to Bolton Wanderers and the rest to the player over the period of the contract – an estimated £1,000 per day.

The coup was overshadowed briefly by the news that John Collins would become the first Scottish-based player to benefit from the ruling in the test case involving Jean-Marc Bosman and UEFA. That player's victory in the European Court of Justice effectively ended the ramifications of the transfer system as practised for decades. Collins, at odds with the management for some months, is believed to be the first British player of note to join a continental club at the end of his contract without a transfer fee being involved. His move to Monaco reportedly pockets him £20,000 a week in a three-year deal – tax-free.

Shortly afterwards, Celtic further strengthened their squad by lining up Paolo di Canio, a winger from AC Milan, on a four-year contract in a £3 million deal. The Italian club, reportedly, received £1 million, with the remainder due to the player over the period of his contract. On the day of his transfer to Celtic, the club's shops reported more than four times the normal Saturday business – yet another indication of the sweeping changes at Parkhead, changes which make the takeover saga seem a part of ancient history.

And the story is not yet over. Next season (1996–97) Celtic will have players of eight different nationalities competing for first-team places.* A far cry from the side which brought the club its greatest moment at Lisbon in 1967, and yet another indication of the changes imminent in football. Celtic and Rangers have now become supra-national clubs as they increasingly submerge, or dilute, their identities as they continue their century-old tussle for supremacy in Scotland. That supremacy is now the passport for entry into European competition, and most notably into the European Champions League and the fortunes to be garnered there.

Celtic are now part of that corporate élite among football clubs. In May 1996 the sportswear giants Reebok were reported to be 'very interested' in replacing Umbro as the club's kit sponsors via a £20 million deal which would be the biggest of its kind in Scottish football history. The company's spokesman Gordon Fleet stated that Celtic's was 'a leading world brand name'. Fergus McCann is bullish about the future; when asked recently by the authors where Celtic would be in March 1999 (the fifth anniversary of the takeover) he replied: 'In the semi-final of the European Cup – aiming to participate in the final at Celtic Park!' The new

* As well as Scots, Celtic will have the following players in their squad: Bonner (Eire), Cadete (Portugal), di Canio (Italy), Stubbs (England), Thom (Germany), Van Hooijdonk (Holland), Wieghorst (Denmark)

stadium, as one observer put it, 'is not being built to play Raith Rovers or Dunfermline Athletic'.

McCann contends that Scottish football is badly in need of reform, assessing that roughly two-thirds of the gate-money taken in on an average Saturday by Scotland's 40 league clubs is generated by Old Firm supporters. 'Too many clubs,' he says, 'and not enough customers – and, just as clear, not enough quality players can be produced, or even attracted from elsewhere.' An interesting sidelight on that perceived subsidy of the rest by the Old Firm is his statement to the authors that he envisages Celtic as having their own cable station for transmission of their matches 'within three years'.

Fergus McCann's advocacy of a major league comprising no more than ten fully professional clubs with sufficient internal capital 'to make their operations self-sufficient and not dependent' is fiercely contested by at least one respected commentator. Bob Crampsey remains a champion of an extended 16-club top division, although he condemns the self-pity and defeatism of the management of such clubs as Hibernian, Hearts and Aberdeen. According to Crampsey, the present system, whereby 'a weak Premier Division in which the third side, Aberdeen, finished 32 points or almost 11 games behind the winners', is one which suits the Old Firm nicely as it affords an easy passage into Europe. The commentator does not see the unfettered involvement of business as a panacea for all its ills: 'I am not arguing that a business-like approach is out of place in modern football. It is essential, but what is certain is that not every football problem admits of a business solution, and this is because the bottom line in football is always sentiment. Men go to see teams not because of their stockmarket quotations, but because they are local, or a relative played for them, or a grandfather took them to see the club as a boy.' (*The Herald*: 8 June 1996)

Even Fergus McCann, a pragmatist above all, recognises the problem that an economy and a limited population such as Scotland's severely restricts the ambitions of the nation's biggest clubs, and he surely casts envious eyes southwards to the Premiership in England. There, a four-year television package worth nearly £750 million from BSkyB and the BBC can be drawn up. That is the sort of set-up to which Celtic and Rangers would love to aspire but, practical problems apart, how viable a prospect is it? As Eoin Jess, formerly of Aberdeen, recently revealed after a few months at modest Coventry, players in England have such a low opinion of the top Scottish division that they dub it 'a fish-and-chip league'. Celtic and Rangers, linked in that ambiguous term 'the Old Firm', may be viewed, therefore, as clubs with nowhere to go, or they may have to come to terms with a limited future.

And whither Fergus McCann? On record as being ready to quit in 1999, he listed for the authors the qualities that his successor as owner of the club might require: 'Business management ability . . . a strong interest in Celtic . . . and a thick skin.'

Controversy is never far away from Celtic, and McCann may well be bemused by the furore his 'Bhoys against bigotry' crusade aroused. This campaign, which commits the club to being 'a medium for healthy pleasure, entertainment and social integration', seemed to upset fans who fretted that they were being singled out for criticism. Matt McGlone, who came to some prominence during the takeover and is now a contributor to the *Celtic View*, was quoted as saying that he receives '. . . lots and lots of letters from people concerned that Celtic's Catholic identity is in danger. When you're singing these songs, you're not being threatening; you're singing about your identity.' (*Maclean's*: 29 April 1996) McCann, on the other hand, was quoted in the same Canadian publication as resenting the 'mindless' behaviour at Celtic Park which can create a bad atmosphere: 'It's bad for families, bad for corporate hospitality, and that is bad for business.' The owner of the club – and the man given the credit for saving it – could well shake his head at any possible adverse reaction to a programme aimed at eradicating bigotry. However, no criticism, veiled or otherwise, came from his awareness of the work of Celtic FC as a club founded for charity. In the past two years, there has been a welcome return to those traditional values: community work among the disadvantaged, visits by players and officials to hospitals, appeals for donations for worthy causes regardless of religious denomination; Fergus McCann, a member of the St Vincent de Paul Society and engaged in charity work when in Arizona, was following – consciously or otherwise – in the footsteps of those actively engaged in good works in Glasgow's East End throughout the 1880s.

Football, however, is primarily about football matches and the 1995–96 season came to an end for Celtic with exuberant scenes as the players took a prolonged bow before their multitude of fans at a sun-drenched, resplendent Celtic Park. A season to be savoured by the supporters, with memories of some marvellous flowing football; of wonderful goals and of glorious fightbacks against the odds – a testimony to the new-found vibrancy at Parkhead. Memories, too, of noise cascading from the vast new stands in celebration of sheer delightful football: at Paul McStay and John Collins displaying control and skill; of Pierre van Hooijdonk scoring spectacular goals, and the sheer intelligence in the play of Andreas Thom; of the quiet authority and maturity of Tom Boyd in the heart of defence; of the fulfilling of the potential in Simon Donnelly and Jackie McNamara; of the slim, flame-haired figure of Tommy Burns standing, always standing, beside the dugout. Dreams were coming true at the new Celtic Park for all Celtic supporters.

Encouragement was bellowed, praises were chanted mantra-like with fervour, and (of course) the songs, old and new, were sung: 'Pierre, Pierre – there's only one Pierre', delivered with a gruff tenderness by thousands of voices; 'The Fields of Athenry', an Irish ballad adopted by the Celtic support, and sung by the composer at Celtic Park, a man who worried a bit – entirely without cause – about being invited to sing unaccompanied before such a huge crowd; and, of course, the great swelling anthem of football, 'You'll Never Walk Alone', thundering and resounding around Celtic Park on the last day of one season, as the fans – reluctant to leave – were already anticipating the next with hope in their heart . . .

Celtic's Roll of Honour

Scottish League Championship		Scottish Cup		Scottish League Cup
1892–93	1937–38	1892	1951	1956–57
1893–94	1953–54	1899	1954	1957–58
1895–96	1965–66	1900	1965	1965–66
1897–98	1966–67	1904	1967	1966–67
1904–05	1967–68	1907	1969	1967–68
1905–06	1968–69	1908	1971	1968–69
1906–07	1969–70	1911	1972	1969–70
1907–08	1970–71	1912	1974	1974–75
1908–09	1971–72	1914	1975	1982–83
1909–10	1972–73	1923	1977	
1913–14	1973–74	1925	1980	*(League Cup*
1914–15	1976–77	1927	1985	*winners 9*
1915–16	1978–79	1931	1988	*times)*
1915–17	1980–81	1933	1989	
1918–19	1981–82	1937	1995	
1921–22	1985–86			
1925–26	1987–88	*(Scottish Cup*		
1935–36		*winners 30 times)*		

(League Champions 35 times)

European Champions Cup	1967
Glasgow Exhibition Trophy/Cup	1902
Empire Exhibition Trophy	1938
St Mungo Cup	1951
Coronation Cup	1953

This list does not include local competitions such
as the Glasgow Cup and the Charity Cup.

Memorable Celtic Line-ups

1892   *First Celtic team to win a national trophy by beating Queen's Park 5–1 in the Scottish Cup final at Ibrox on 9 April.*

Cullen, Reynolds, Doyle, W. Maley, Kelly, Gallagher, McCallum, Brady, Dowds, McMahon, Campbell

1907   *First Celtic (and Scottish) team to win the double of League Championship and Scottish Cup. The following line-up defeated Hearts 3–0 in the Cup final at Hampden Park on 20 April 1907:*

Adams, McLeod, Orr, Young, McNair, Hay, Bennett, McMenemy, Quinn, Somers, Templeton

By 1908, when Celtic beat St Mirren 5–1 in the Scottish Cup final, Templeton had been replaced by Hamilton. One of the club's most famous forward lines was being fielded.

1914   *Celtic won another double on the eve of the First World War with a squad described by one newspaper as 'the team of all the talents'. This line-up defeated Hibernian 4–1 in a replayed Scottish Cup final on 16 April at Ibrox Park:*

Shaw, McNair, Dodds, Young, Johnstone, McMaster, McAtee, Gallacher, McColl, McMenemy, Browning

1925   *Celtic's Scottish Cup final side against Dundee at Hampden Park on 11 April – a game always recalled as 'Patsy's final' because of Gallacher's spectacular equalising goal which paved the way for a 2–1 win:*

Shevlin, W. McStay, Hilley, Wilson, J. McStay, McFarlane, Connolly, Gallacher, McGrory, A. Thomson, McLean

1931 *The Scottish Cup final on 11 April at Hampden Park was famous for a dramatic Celtic fightback against Motherwell when Celtic came back from being 2–0 down with seven minutes left to earn a replay (which they won by 4–2). The same side was fielded in the replay, and also lined up against Rangers in the league match at Ibrox on 5 September 1931 in which John Thomson met with a fatal accident.*

J. Thomson, Cook, McGonagle, Wilson, J. McStay, Geatons, R. Thomson, A. Thomson, McGrory, Scarff, Napier

1937 *Celtic defeated Aberdeen by 2–1 in the Scottish Cup final at Hampden Park on 24 April. The match attracted a crowd of 146,433. This attendance – a record for a club match anywhere in Europe – is unlikely ever to be surpassed. Celtic's line-up was:*

Kennaway, Hogg, Morrison, Geatons, Lyon, Paterson, Delaney, Buchan, McGrory, Crum, Murphy

1938 *In the Empire Exhibition Cup, Celtic beat Everton 1–0 after extra-time with this side on 10 June 1938 at Ibrox Park:*

Kennaway, Hogg, Morrison, Geatons, Lyon, Paterson, Delaney, MacDonald, Crum, Divers, Murphy

1953 *For the Coronation Cup final at Hampden Park on 20 May against Hibernian, Celtic fielded this team in a 2–0 victory:*

Bonnar, Haughney, Rollo, Evans, Stein, J. McPhail, Collins, Walsh, Mochan, Peacock, Fernie

1954 *Celtic won the double again for the first time in 40 years. The team which won the Scottish Cup by beating Aberdeen 2–1 at Hampden Park on 24 April was as follows:*

Bonnar, Haughney, Meechan, Evans, Stein, Peacock, Higgins, Fernie, Fallon, Tully, Mochan

1957 *On 19 October 1957 Celtic defeated Rangers by 7–1 in the League Cup final at Hampden Park; this score represents the biggest margin of victory in a major British final.*

Beattie, Donnelly, Fallon, Fernie, Evans, Peacock, Tully, Collins, W. McPhail, Wilson, Mochan

1965 *The 3–2 victory over Dunfermline Athletic in the Scottish Cup final at Hampden Park on 24 April marked the first trophy won by Celtic under Jock Stein as manager:*

Fallon, Young, Gemmell, Murdoch, McNeill, Clark, Chalmers, Gallagher, Hughes, Lennox, Auld

1967 *Celtic became the first British side to win the European Cup when they defeated Internazionale (Milan) by 2–1 at Estadio Nacional in Lisbon on 25 May 1967. The*

same line-up had already won the Scottish Cup by beating Aberdeen 2–0 in the final on 29 April, and had clinched the league title with a 2–2 draw against Rangers at Ibrox on 6 May to secure Celtic's first domestic 'treble'.

Simpson, Craig, Gemmell, Murdoch, McNeill, Clark, Johnstone, Wallace, Chalmers, Auld, Lennox

1969   *Celtic won the domestic treble again in 1968–69 by lifting the League Cup, the Scottish Cup and League Championship. The side which gained the Scottish Cup by beating Rangers 4–0 at Hampden Park on 26 April 1969 was as follows:*

Fallon, Craig, Gemmell, Murdoch, McNeill, Brogan (Clark), Connelly, Chalmers, Wallace, Lennox, Auld

1972   *On 6 May Celtic lifted the Scottish Cup by beating Hibernian 6–1 at Hampden Park. The score created the largest margin of victory in a Scottish Cup final this century, and Dixie Deans scored a hat-trick (one of only three in the history of Scottish Cup finals).*

Williams, Craig, Brogan, Murdoch, McNeill, Connelly, Johnstone, Deans, Macari, Dalglish, Callaghan

1979   *Celtic won the league title at Parkhead on 21 May in dramatic fashion by beating Rangers 4–2 after trailing by 1–2 and having Johnny Doyle sent off in 55 minutes.*

Latchford, McGrain, Lynch, Aitken, McAdam, Edvaldsson, Provan, Conroy (Lennox), McCluskey, MacLeod, Doyle

1985   *In the 100th Scottish Cup final Celtic defeated Dundee United by 2–1 at Hampden Park on 18 May with goals from Provan and McGarvey.*

Bonner, W. McStay, McGrain, Aitken, McAdam, MacLeod, Provan, P. McStay (O'Leary), Johnston, Burns (McClair), McGarvey

1986   *Celtic went to Love Street on 3 May with only a faint chance of pipping Hearts for the League Championship, but won by 5–0 against St Mirren while Hearts lost 2–0 to Dundee. The Celtic side which won the championship on goal-difference was as follows:*

Bonner, McGrain (Grant), Whyte, Aitken, McGuigan, MacLeod, McClair, P. McStay, Johnston, Burns, Archdeacon

1988   *Celtic celebrated their centenary season (1987–88) by winning the double. The side which won the Scottish Cup by beating Dundee United 2–1 on 14 May through McAvennie's goals read as follows:*

McKnight, Morris, Rogan, Aitken, McCarthy, Whyte (Stark), Miller, P. McStay, McAvennie, Walker (McGhee), Burns

Index